When the Island Had Fish

The Remarkable Story of a Maine Fishing Community

Janna Malamud Smith

Camden, Maine

Down East Books

Published by Down East Books
An imprint of Globe Pequot
Trade division of The Rowman & Littlefield Publishing Group, Inc.
4501 Forbes Blvd., Ste. 200
Lanham, MD 20706
www.rowman.com
www.downeastbooks.com

Distributed by NATIONAL BOOK NETWORK

Library of Congress Cataloging-in-Publication Data

Names: Smith, Janna Malamud, author.
Title: When the island had fish / Janna Malamud Smith.
Description: Lanham, MD : Down East Books, [2023] | Includes
    bibliographical references.
Identifiers: LCCN 2022056492 (print) | LCCN 2022056493 (ebook) | ISBN
    9781684750788 (cloth) | ISBN 9781684750795 (ebook)
Subjects: LCSH: Fishing—Maine—Vinalhaven Island—History—19th century. |
    Fishing—Maine—Vinalhaven Island—History—20th century.
Classification: LCC SH503 .S635 2023 (print) | LCC SH503 (ebook) | DDC
    639.209741/53—dc23/eng/20230215
LC record available at https://lccn.loc.gov/2022056492
LC ebook record available at https://lccn.loc.gov/2022056493

♾️™ The paper used in this publication meets the minimum requirements of American National Standard for Information Sciences—Permanence of Paper for Printed Library Materials, ANSI/NISO Z39.48-1992.

For Deborah Judd, and in memory of
Molly Meijer (1930–2022) and Bodine Ames (1935–2019).

Contents

Preface

A Jar of Scallops

Should you linger under the covers, you *will* miss the ferry, a lesson learned quickly when you spend time on an island where ferries, rather like pendulums on clocks, or rising and falling tides, mark the passing of hours.

One April day some years ago, my husband and I jumped out of bed before dawn to beat out the traffic that chokes Boston, and sped north toward Vinalhaven, a small island off the coast of Maine where we had owned a house for thirty years. We needed to catch an early boat and meet with a carpenter.

Bo, the woman who watched over our old farmhouse in our absence, met us at the ferry landing. Sitting three abreast in her pick-up, we chatted as she drove us the seven miles to our property. At one point, apropos of little except perhaps time passing, I said, "I remember when the tidal pools were full of sea urchins." Sea urchins, brown-green and spiny, mostly vanished from Penobscot Bay during an eight-year harvesting spree. From 1987 to 1995 buyers for Japanese restaurants purchased as many as divers could gather, and for a long-time few shells have shown up on any beach.[1]

Bo, already well on her way to 80, was not impressed by my Johnny-come-lately memory. "I remember when I was a child," she mused, "I could go at low tide, wade in under the bridge near our house, and pick up enough scallops to make a chowder."

Her recollection grabbed me. I imagined a young Bo in rubber boots, wading, recognizing the shells, reaching her hand into the cold water, and one by one gathering up the elegant mollusks.

The fantasy evoked a past only lately disappeared and stirred up in me a flood of feeling—most particularly sadness. When we first visited the island in 1983, fishermen netted pollock and cod from spring through fall and layered long underwear and sweatshirts under foul weather gear in winter to fend off frostbite while fishing for shrimp and dragging for scallops. For millennia, island waters teemed with cod, mackerel, haddock, herring, swordfish, and halibut; shellfish like scallops, clams, mussels, periwinkles and sea urchins were bountiful. In truth "teemed with" and "bountiful" do little justice to a bay thick with all manner of creatures surfacing, dodging, mating with, chasing and consuming each other. The sight of waters roiling with life arrested the attention of observers across centuries.

Like many of us now wherever we live, I longed to rewind the centuries so I could survey a less beat-up and depleted natural world—in this case, the island waters when they were filled with fish.

Instead, I began writing this book, hoping, through interviews and research, to capture knowledge about what life is like now, but mostly what it used to be like on the island of Vinalhaven—for fishermen thousands of years ago and fishermen 50 years ago—as well as their families, and their communities. Also, for fish. I sought to set down as best I could the millennia of fishing history. In part I hoped to offer witness, in part to create a detailed portrait of a Maine island community that has had a commercial impact disproportionate to its modest acreage.

Along with gathering up fragments of its history, I have wanted to capture the ways fish were once everywhere in everyday island life. If you look at a world with wild fish and one without, what is obviously different? What is subtly so? Middens—shell piles left by earlier settlements reveal layers of fish skeletons—evidence of fish eaten for thousands of years by indigenous people long before Europeans arrived. Later records talk about bushels and quintals of fish caught and dried, archives offer lists of fishing vessels built and owned; all describe past enterprise. But when fish were plentiful, the sum of their presence was more than their market value. Writing in diaries, letters and newspapers, islanders continually mentioned them—watched them, studied them, thought about their ways and whereabouts, began and ended relationships because of them, bartered with them for other goods, gave them as gifts, cooked and ate them. They were a proxy for hope; they were dots scattered all over a multi-colored communal canvas. Islander Addie L. Roberts tersely noted in her diary on Mar. 7, 1918—*"Cut Max a suit, then went to a Fish Hash supper at church."*[2]

Across the twentieth century, as "industrial" fishing depleted oceans, fish and sea creatures' independent "right" to thrive on the planet has been negated, and their natural place in the daily lives of fishing communities and eco-systems has been largely erased. We think casually about a past when people lived on the edge of wildness. We often fail to observe the porousness created by proximity—the diverse, complex intimacies of relationships that are now simplistically reduced to "hunter and hunted" or "consumer and consumed." Every living creature and plant is connected to every other one. We once understood *that* reality—and accepted the accompanying mystery. But for a long time now, we have attempted to separate and privilege ourselves.

A subsistence or quasi "sustainable" way of living survived on Vinalhaven long after it disappeared in more urban parts of America. Since we live in a time of radical environmental crisis, it seems particularly urgent to capture—while it is held in living memory and retrievable—the intimate relationship between humans and the rest of the natural world as it played out in one robust coastal and ocean fishing environment.

It took me a long while to see what was before me. Even though I had visited the island every year for decades, walked and driven from end to end countless times, explored its land and water, gathered lupine and wild irises, chanterelles and ripe blackberries, gone swimming with our children in abandoned quarries, combed the shore for sea glass, kayaked coves while watching osprey, cormorants and gulls dive for fish, eaten wild mussels, periwinkles, halibut, shrimp, crab and lobsters, and even stuffed bait bags for lobstermen—and even though I had visited its Historical Society yearly—I had no understanding of the island's actual past. I genuinely missed the meaning—not to mention all the knowledge and artisanal skill. I was too caught up in the beauty and quiet to imagine it, but I had also been blinded by some premises of my urban life. As I looked more closely, I was repeatedly struck by the difference between the place I'd perceived while vacationing, and the island that gradually became visible through studied effort.

Only slowly did I learn its long history. How native people settled to live and fish on the island at least five thousand years ago; how successive indigenous groups continually occupied it and fished its waters until Europeans killed the majority of them and took over. How colonists began to arrive in 1757 and settled in more permanently after the American Revolution. How by 1850, when Maine caught half the nation's cod, Vinalhaven boasted the second highest value of cod, cod oil and mackerel landed in the state. Conditions across the nation changed after the Civil War, and lobstering increased. Vinalhaven became and remains one of the most active and successful lobster ports in the nation—and the world. Fishing continued on the island, too, and in the early 1900s, Vinalhaven hosted the largest fish processing plant in Maine. Local fishermen kept busy supplying national and international markets.

Fishing industrialized in many countries during the late nineteenth and early twentieth centuries, and across decades reached a frenzied production capacity. Gas and diesel engines, ever larger "factory ships," power winches and synthetic netting, refrigeration, radar and depth finders radically altered how many fish a boat could catch in a day. It became possible to fish down entire communities of species. Vinalhaven fishermen did what they could to master the new technology and scale. But by the late twentieth century inshore fisheries had collapsed, and island fishermen were closed out.

For the first time in many millennia, the ocean surrounding Vinalhaven is no longer alive with fish and men laboring to net or hook them. Whereas in the past, island fishermen harvested different species in different seasons, now (with a few exceptions) they fish for lobster. The effects of changes in fish populations, in ways of fishing, and in the ocean environment itself, have had a dramatic impact on island fishermen, enriching some as lobsters thrived, yet facing them all with the stress of their economic dependence on a single species.

Many of the men and women—the last ones who spent their lives catching cod, pollock, hake, and herring, or raising families while supporting the work—have died since I began interviewing. The stories they generously offered are vivid and particular. They allow us to glimpse how recent generations of people toiled on a rocky parcel of acres surrounded by ocean, and how changing fish stocks, ways of fishing, and markets continually altered their world.

For a long time, fishing communities had much in common with earlier hunter-gatherer cultures, where life was lived with family and neighbors and largely organized by season. They are transforming extremely rapidly today. And while uncertainty is and has always been the essence of fishermen's lives, this moment is more uncertain than any that have come before it. Lives in the past may have been more vulnerable to injury and disease, but most people imagined "their" natural world as consistently sturdy, perhaps even inviolate. Not so for many of us now. We know that our collective behaviors are causing extraordinary alterations in the planet. As we stumble forward into new circumstances, it seems crucial to contemplate not just the lost "ways" of the past, but how communities lived and labored when human power was weighted differently: when a cold winter day challenged one's ability to chop enough firewood, and a big halibut could snap a line and flee to freedom.

I use "fisherman" and "lobsterman" somewhat interchangeably in the text. As is customary on the island, women and men are both called lobstermen and sternmen. I recorded the interviews between 2008 and 2018. Some of the people I interviewed were happy to be named. Others requested anonymity and have been provided with pseudonyms (initially in quotation marks). I have slightly edited interviews for readability. Finally, Vinalhaven had different names and spellings in different eras: the South Island or South Fox Island, Vinal Haven and Vinalhaven. So too with Islesboro and Islesborough. I use the current name for both islands, but present quotations and historical documents as they were written.[3]

Introduction

Vinalhaven

The Gulf of Maine began to fill with water fifteen thousand years ago as the Ice Age waned and glaciers melted. Vinalhaven, fifteen miles from the State of Maine's mid-coast, is the largest island in Penobscot Bay. Measuring almost 8 miles long, it might claim five miles on the bias. Mostly much narrower, it's hard to stand on any bit that's more than a mile from shore. The total land area of 23.5 square miles doesn't do justice to the impressive circumference of its cove-filled, rocky shoreline, which, unfurled, would stretch to about 270 miles.[4]

The story of fishing on Vinalhaven likely starts sometime between 5000 and 8000 years ago when small groups of hunter-gatherers canoed (or crossed winter ice) from the mainland to the island. We know about them because they left tiny mementoes of their existence—bones and shells, in ancient shell heaps called middens. Some of these middens can still be seen on the island, though, since the Gulf is higher today than it was then, the oldest ones are underwater, making the first habitations hardest to trace.

The idea that people would settle on an island when the whole American continent was available at first seemed odd to me. However, hunter-gatherers have long located themselves on coastal ecotones, where land and water meet. In his book, *The Human Shore*, the historian and Maine island summer resident John Gillis points to recent underwater archeological studies confirming that, from very early on, homo sapiens have been "semiaquatic, foraging not just in freshwater but also . . . at the edge of the sea."[5]

To understand the migrations of hunter-gatherers—and the lives of settlers since that time—it helps to remember that, although Vinalhaven might seem "remote" today, that term did not always apply. Because paddling, rowing and sailing boats was easier until recently than hacking and hauling through

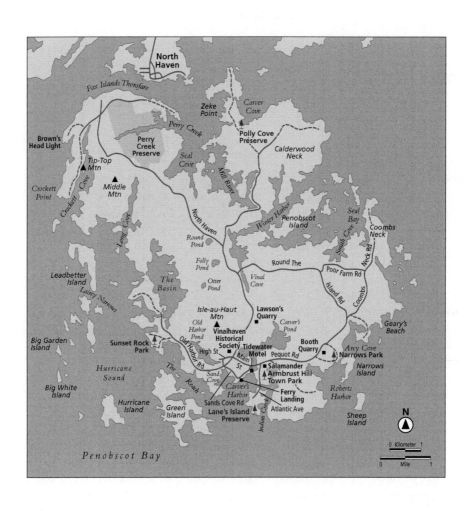

North
Haven

Fox Islands Thorofare

Zeke
Point

Carver
Cove

Perry Creek

Polly Cove
Preserve

Brown's
Head Light

Perry
Creek
Preserve

Calderwood
Neck

Tip-Top
Mtn

Seal
Cove

Middle
Mtn

Mill River

Crockett
Point

Penobscot
Island

Seal
Bay

Coombs
Neck

Long Cove

North Haven

Winter Harbor

South Cove

Neck Rd

Leadbetter
Island

Crockett Cove

Round
Pond

Round The

Poor Farm Rd

Lairey Narrows

Folly
Pond

Vinal
Cove

Island Rd

Coombs

The
Basin

Otter
Pond

Big Garden
Island

Isle-au-Haut
Mtn

Lawson's
Quarry

Carver's
Pond

Geary's
Beach

Sunset Rock
Park

Old
Harbor
Pond

Vinalhaven
Historical
Society

Tidewater
Motel

Booth
Quarry

Arey Cove
Narrows Park

Hurricane
Sound

High St

Pequot Rd

Narrows
Island

Old Harbor Rd

Main
St

Salamander
Armbrust Hill
Town Park

Big White
Island

The
Reach

Sand
Cove

Ferry
Landing

Roberts
Harbor

Hurricane
Island

Green
Island

Carver's
Harbor

Sands Cove Rd

Atlantic Ave

Sheep
Island

Lane's Island
Preserve

Indian Creek

N

Penobscot Bay

0 Kilometer 1

0   Mile   1

rugged terrain, for much of human existence islands were often less remote than inland places.

The earliest hunter-gatherers, who lived on the islands about 5000 years ago, are referred to as members of the "Small Stemmed Point tradition." Next to nothing is known about them. Their name is taken from the miniscule remnants of their lives that have been found: small-stemmed arrow points chipped from white quartz.[6]

The first group of people we know about in any detail settled on Vinalhaven around 4,300 years ago. In 1913 the archaeologist Warren K. Moorehead named them "The Red Paint People" because they possessed the distinctive practice of dusting their dead with red ochre before burial. Archeologist Bruce Bourque and his colleagues have devoted decades to studying them. Bourque has more lately written about them as the "Swordfish hunters."[7]

The group left many middens, including at the "Candage site" on Vinalhaven and, more famously, at Turner's Farm—the extensively examined site on North Haven (across the half mile wide "Thoroughfare"). According to Bourque, the two were part of one habitation.[8]

The Swordfish Hunters lived lives recognizable to us in their essentials: they navigated Penobscot Bay—coming and going regularly from the mainland in dugout canoes. They raised children, cooked, sewed clothing, kept pet dogs, hunted deer, buried their dead, and repeatedly took to the coastal waters in their dugout canoes. They knew how to get around, and they knew how to catch fish—including swordfish, which they pursued in those same canoes.

Careful work deconstructing layers of middens revealed that food for the early Turner's Farm inhabitants was plentiful. Archaeologists found bones from cod, swordfish, winter flounder, smooth flounder, sculpin, pollock, herring, dogfish, haddock and sturgeon—and they found turtle shells. They also identified bones from Canada geese, cormorants, loons, great auks, varieties of ducks, and other seabirds. While soft-shelled clams seem to have been the most heavily harvested shellfish, there were also plenty of blue mussels, sea urchin and whelk shells. Remains from smaller mammals included beaver, sea mink and red fox. Deer were the most common large mammal, but moose and bear bones appear as well.[9]

The Swordfish Hunters were one of the earliest cultures in the Northeast to carve rudimentary art—small "zoomorphic" figurines of seals, cormorants and porpoises, as well as land mammals—and they also made elegant stone tools.[10] Yuval Noah Harari asserts in *Sapiens* that hunter gatherers were "the most knowledgeable and skillful people in history"—each person had to possess an encyclopedic understanding of all the trees, plants, animals, water conditions, weather, climate and stars simply to survive.[11]

We can get hints of The Swordfish Hunters' knowledge through objects of theirs that have endured. A small plummet lies on its side in a Vinalhaven Historical Society display case. The stone is about four and a half inches long, not quite two and a half inches wide at its widest point, and shaped rather like a squat, rounded amphora, tapering slightly from the shoulder to the bottom. Its surface is rough, a rusty, dark orangish-brown, with flecks of black; its neck is stubby. Plummets were often found in middens and sometimes in graves. To contemporary eyes, the stone suggests skill and purpose.[12] Archaeologists believe that some plummets were used to weigh down fishnets or hooks and line for catching cod and other fish. In the late nineteenth and early twentieth century, digging for "relics" was a frequent leisure pursuit for islanders. The many objects turned

Vinalhaven Historical Society collection. A plummet—a tool likely carved four or five thousand years ago by member or members of an indigenous band then living on island that is now called Vinalhaven; possibly used for weighting fishing nets.

up testify to just how widely tools of daily life had been scattered by earlier dwellers. They also testify to the continual presence of "Maine" tribal families and communities living and fishing on the island for thousands of years.

As we look at the arc of island fishing, one more bit of knowledge about fish and the fishing habits of the Swordfish Hunters jumps out across time: Because of the rich plankton bloom at the base of the food web, the fish that filled the water around Turner's Farm four thousand years ago ate well and grew big. Excavators retrieved cod vertebrae the size of half dollars from the older levels of the dig. Bourque noted their surprise:

> *The bones of cod were abundant, but we didn't immediately recognize them as cod because they were so large. As a teenager, I had caught what I considered to be good-sized, 20-inch cod off the Fox Islands, but many of these 4,000-year-old cod were simply huge, 5.5 to 6 feet long and likely in the 100 to 130-pound range.*[13]

Measuring the remains of the giant fish eventually led to a startling finding about the ancient impact of local fishing, which the Turner's Farm archaeologists discovered because they worked systematically. At first, the Swordfish Hunters caught numerous very large cod close to shore. As centuries passed, however, they caught fewer, smaller cod and had to go farther out to sea to catch them. We know this because the vertebrae in the midden became smaller and scarcer, and isotopes in these bones showed that, while alive, those later cod had foraged offshore. At the same time, bones of flounder, sculpin, and dogfish became more numerous than cod. Since the changes in these later layers occurred in parallel, it seems that human fishing had put pressure on the local cod stock. In other words, these early dwellers had, in the words of Daniel Pauly, fished down the food web.[14]

The reach of human populations was modest enough that these depletions gradually repaired themselves. But they remind us that human impact on ecosystems is longstanding.

For several thousand years after they seemingly disappeared from the archaeological record, small groups of native peoples continued intermittently to settle on the islands. Across time, the area was populated with various Abenaki tribes, the Maliseet, Passamaquoddy, Micmac, Penobscot—now called the Wabanaki Confederacy. Archaeologists can say a bit about what people hunted and ate, contemporary Wabanaki can narrate their community history, but I have found nothing distinct about them as Fox Island dwellers. We do know that ancestors of contemporary Maine Wabanaki visited, lived and fished continually on the island.

The island now known as Vinalhaven was first mentioned in writing by Europeans in 1603. Martin Pring (twenty-three years old at the time) captained a voyage of two vessels and forty-three men that sailed from Bristol, England, across the North Atlantic to the unnamed Gulf of Maine, through Penobscot Bay, and down to Cape Cod. Pring came in search of sassafras, used then in Europe to treat syphilis and plague. As he learned, sassafras grew almost everywhere along the East Coast *except* in Maine; his crew eventually sent home so much from Cape Cod that they glutted the market.

The young captain wrote about seeing foxes on an island—and while his latitudes don't match up, many scholars since, recognizing Penobscot Bay from his description, have thought that he was referring to Vinalhaven, North Haven or Hurricane, all of which have since been grouped together as the "Fox Islands." Describing the "North Coast of Virginia"—as he called northern New England, Pring enthused about the abundance of cod around islands near Vinalhaven—"Heere we found an excellent fishing for Cods, which are better than those of Newfound-land, and withal we saw good and Rockie ground to drie them upon: also we see no reason to the contrary, but that Salt may bee made in these parts, a matter of no small importance."[15]

"Better than those of Newfound-land" was the right selling point to fishermen and investors back home. European explorers initially exulted in the New World's cod because it was a valuable commodity with a growing market. A good example is in Raimondo de Soncino's report to the Duke of Milan about John Cabot's 1497 voyage from Bristol to the New England coast. He writes, "And they say that it is a very good and temperate country . . . they affirm that the sea is covered with fishes which are caught not only with a net but with baskets, a stone being tied to them in order that the baskets may sink in the water."[16]

By 1600, Europeans had been fishing in eastern North America for about 100 years—one older French fisherman named Scavalet had made forty fishing voyages from France to Newfoundland by 1609. The enthusiastic descriptions of the New England fishery sent home by early observers extolled the promise of grounds hitherto unfished by Europeans and, understating hardships, conveyed a sense to would-be participants of a risk worth taking.[17]

Religious freedom notwithstanding, early New England settlers and sponsors sought to invest their money so as to accumulate more. If some sailed from the Old World with other ideas in the front of their minds, they reconsidered quickly once they saw the possibilities. Many labored hard and profited mightily from speculating in land, furs, white pine, oak, and cod.[18]

Within a century and a half, abundant resources (however wrongfully acquired) made these settlers wealthier, in aggregate, than they would have been had they stayed home. By the time of the American Revolution—Jeffrey Bolster tells us in his remarkable book about New England fishing and environmental history, *The Mortal Sea*—the thirteen colonies had the highest per capita gross domestic product of any country in the world.[19] Cod symbolized that plenitude. In 1776, when Adam Smith published *The Wealth of Nations*, he "singled out the New England cod fishery. . . . [as] an example of how quickly an economy could grow if given a free hand."[20]

Use of the Fox Islands for fishing and foraging by various Wabanaki groups declined during the eighteenth century. From 1675 to 1763, six wars between the British and the French and Indians, together with encroaching European-American fishermen, gradually killed many indigenous Americans and drove those who remained off these fishing grounds.

Although the 1763 Treaty of Paris ended these wars, and European-Americans, mostly from the Massachusetts Bay Province, began to settle the Fox Islands, peaceful opportunity to build lives there was short-lived. The American Revolution started just twelve years later, disrupting the handful of new settlers. A few enlisted; many left the island to avoid the English warships across Penobscot Bay at Castine. Some who stayed became prisoners of war. Only after the war ended did several hundred new Americans settle permanently on Vinalhaven. Incorporated in 1789, Vinalhaven, North Haven and Hurricane Island were initially one township, with North Haven separating itself in 1846, and Hurricane briefly becoming a separate township in 1878 before being re-annexed by Vinalhaven in 1937.

It took a few decades for the settlers to turn themselves into a full-fledged fishing community, but it did not take long for groups of islanders to pool their resources and begin to build or invest in small vessels. Fortuitously, Congress authorized a subsidy for the salt cod fishery in 1793 to stimulate boatbuilding as well as the fishery, and to train prospective sailors for naval service. A few years after the War of 1812 ended small vessels became eligible for the lucrative cod bounty—a development very helpful to Vinalhaven. Markets emerged, and fishing enterprises organized.

Today, a little over 1200 people make their homes on Vinalhaven year-round. A good number of these residents are descendants of the first European-American settlers. Others arrived across the nineteenth century from elsewhere in New England as well as Scandinavia and the British Isles to fish and work in the granite quarries. More recently, some young people, artists, craftsmen, and retirees have migrated to the island in search of natural beauty, quiet, and an active community life.[21]

During the summer the population doubles or triples thanks to seasonal residents, renters, motel and lodging guests, and day visitors. Builders and contractors labor to repair and expand homes; boatyards repair and maintain cabin cruisers as well as working boats. Though islanders complain about busy roads and the jammed grocery store in August, to someone from an urban area it seems quiet. Martha's Vineyard, off Cape Cod in Massachusetts with a land mass not quite 4 times bigger than Vinalhaven, swells from about 15,500 to as many as 200,000 people every summer.[22]

A visitor arriving to the island by ferry will glimpse (on a fog-free day) its shoreline of small harbors and inlets scattered with occasional houses, many with a moored lobster boat, a Whaler or rowboat, a dock, and a fishhouse. There are plenty of weathered shingles, and an attractive simplicity and utility in the houses. Much that is visible from the ferry seems either a semi-wild, rocky shore backed by a toothy "fence" of spruce trees or, when peopled, appears "working tidy"—functional, cared for, but not overly manicured.

When I first visited in 1983, I was struck by the casual ruggedness, and visible tools of fishermen's labor that marked the place—nets spread out for mending along the edge of a parking lot, piles of lobster traps waiting to go back into the bay. People had work to do.

By far, the largest source of employment on Vinalhaven today is lobstering. On Sundays, a legally imposed day of rest, the harbor is thick with tied up boats. The fisherman's daily labor of "steaming" to his or her lobster pots and hauling them is only part of a broader effort that demands a supporting cast onshore—from bait dealers and buyers to trap builders and diesel vendors. Although the variety of catch has lately narrowed and harvesting methods have changed, over more than two-hundred-and-fifty years post-settlement, fishing (hauling lobsters) is still at the heart of the island and its residents' livelihood.

Fishing success demands community. The "man alone against the sea" image of Maine fishermen does only partial justice to actual lives. It fails to convey how tight and interdependent fishing communities have had to be in order to finance fishing boats and equipment, and to bear the emotional struggle and risk of the work. It also obscures how men, women and children on the shore must labor as hard as the fishermen. And it ignores how, from colonial times, government policy has often—but not always— promoted the commerce of fishing.

Conversations with islanders offer a feel for the astounding recent decline of finfish. In the summer of 2015, I sat on the front porch of Marge and Herb Conway's house talking with them. Herb was born in 1926. The couple married in 1947. As we chatted, neighbors walking past on the sidewalk called out greetings, and others driving by gave a friendly wave and honk.

Herb, his father and his grandfather were fishermen. *"As far as fishing went,"* Herb observed, *"it's unbelievable how something could be so great and then be nil. Now, I never thought you would not be able to buy a fish on Vinalhaven, a fresh fish."* Indeed, the market's fresh fish section is lamentable. The haddock fillets, farmed salmon, and mussels, set out in Styrofoam under plastic wrap on the refrigerated shelf, ride the ferry over from a mainland supplier. Herb compared the present island to the one he knew just after the Second World War. After sardining with his dad for a year or two, he began going out on his own, *"and at that time it was great. There was plenty of fish and plenty of lobsters."*[23]

As Herb asked, how could something once so great now be nil? The question is as complex as it is existentially mystifying that it has to be asked. Fishing is but one reason for changes in fish populations. Fishermen have long understood that, whatever their own impact, the abundance of local species depends on many other shifting circumstances—water temperature, seasonal timing, variation in sunlight and plankton, the spread of disease, availability and quantity of forage, proliferation of predators, or excessive fishing by others elsewhere.

In recent centuries, population declines have been caused primarily by humans. Few "catch" records exist for Maine waters before 1870 to help scientists estimate fish abundance or learn the precise history of human impact, although some researchers are now applying novel analytical methods or conversing with fishermen to do so. Fishermen have spent their lives gathering an extensive understanding of their natural surroundings—the ways of ocean, water, weather, and fish. Because this knowledge has mostly been transmitted orally in families, or by working side by side, it isn't easily visible to outsiders. Older island fishermen with long memories like Herb's can tell you much about waxing and waning catches across the years. They know what each season brought or did not bring. They know what they found or did not find when they dropped their hooks or set their nets.

Speculating too much about what caused the bad years was often an unaffordable luxury. While they observed closely, fishermen's focus was on catching what they could eat or market at the time. If they couldn't find cod, they did their best to land pollock, hake or haddock instead. No one imagined that a day would come when they could not pursue and catch groundfish (bottom dwelling finfish). No one anticipated the impact of decades of Federal regulations (and somewhat better-attuned state regulations) and commercial trends that favored corporations and bigger boats. Slowly at first, but rapidly growing faster, expensive technology separated small-scale fishermen from their ability to fish for almost any species but lobster, leaving incredulity in their wake. Although some men and women feel bitter, most have been spared from poverty and some made wealthy by the extraordinary resurgence of lobster and its remarkable market prices. Ironically, lobsters have lately flourished in an emptier ocean rather the way wild blueberries sprout up bountifully after a forest fire bares the land.

Still, older fishermen feel acutely the loss of variety and the seasonal life that went with it. The happiest memories many relayed were conveyed in stories about times when fish were everywhere and biting hard; times when their boats were so deep in hake, cod, or herring, that their only care was getting home without sinking.

Ivan Olson (1926–2013) recalled a memorable day, around 1980, when he motored out alone to two of the best fishing places near Vinalhaven, Wooden Ball and Seal Island, to long-line for cod. At first it seemed hopeless; but then his luck changed.

> "*About noontime I guess I figured this was going to be what we called 'a broker.' I wasn't going to make any money, only coffee money today.*
>
> *But there was one other place I knew that I might try on the way home and it's a real shallow place. Generally, you don't get a lot on the shallow.*"
>
> He tossed a line in anyway, and after a bit, grabbed it up, "*just for the hell of it; and there was a pair of codfish probably 3 or 4 feet long.*
>
> *And I sat right there and part of the line never touch bottom. And I was out there 3 or 4 hours.*"

When Ivan got back to the harbor, his sons were home from school. Seeing him in the boat gutting the heap of cod, they jumped in their outboard and raced out to help him.

He reflected with satisfaction, *"That day I was all alone and I caught 2300 pounds all alone."*[24]

This abundance of fish resonates with two different but related human pleasures: First, the excitement of having something to trade for something else you want, or to sell at a profit. Second, the primal-adrenalin-rush of catching *a lot* of something. As Ivan noted, abundance grants the exhilaration of the chase itself, of finding and catching, hunting and gathering, and then it grants the sense of well-being that comes from feeling, thanks to your own efforts, you will have enough.

The codfish Ivan caught were—for now at least—among the last of what had once been a bounty of nature that made it possible for people to live on Vinalhaven, and for the community to prosper. Needless to say, lucrative harvesting and marketing have by no means been the majority experience. Fishing often brought meager returns to island fishermen. At times it brought overwhelming hardship and required extreme fortitude and resilience. You never knew what the nets would gather. Yet, hope flashed in that uncertainty. An outstanding day that might earn enough money for the season could just be dawning.

Today, the Vinalhaven community thrives because there are many lobsters, and catching them is often profitable. For a few who fish the most days and go into deeper water, it can be very profitable. A 2021 newspaper story reposts, "The top 20 lobstermen on the island had landings worth an average $579,000 apiece in 2019, placing them among the state's wealthiest residents, even with their staggering bait and fuel bills and hefty shares paid to sternmen."

But for how long? After thirty years of "ever-increasing landings," the Maine lobster catch fell 23 percent between 2016 and 2019. A likely culprit? Warmer water due to climate change. The effect of the warming has been complex—and almost ironic. The rising water temperature may initially have contributed to the abundance of lobsters, until it crossed a threshold and now could be becoming too warm for them to thrive.[25] The future is always opaque; it seems particularly so now.

I

FOUNDATIONS

1

Whose Island?

Thousands of years after the Swordfish Hunters inhabited Vinalhaven, Europeans settled in New England. The Pilgrims who founded Plymouth in 1620 knew so little about catching fish that, at first, they often went hungry. But it didn't take the settlers long to learn. By the late seventeenth century salt cod was sold in colonial markets for local consumption, but most went to Southern Europe or to the Caribbean. By 1700, some Massachusetts' cod fishermen were venturing far beyond local waters, fishing on the banks off Nova Scotia or even to the Grand Banks.

The importance of fishing to the New England economy grew during the eighteenth century. On the advent of the American Revolution, it "represented 35 percent of the region's total export revenue," which made it "the single most valuable export for this section of the British North American colonies at this time." Massachusetts ports like Boston, Marblehead, and Ipswich, together with Portsmouth, New Hampshire, were at the heart of the trade. Local fishermen found employment and fish merchants grew wealthy.[26]

Some fishermen followed the coast to the northeast and began to fish in Penobscot Bay and the waters immediately around Vinalhaven, or "South Fox Island." But it could be dangerous since the French claimed the eastern side of Penobscot Bay. Tribal people who had foraged or lived for centuries on Penobscot Bay islands, harvesting fish, birds and birds' eggs, felt threatened by the interlopers. They became hostile as English intruders proliferated, claimed land, attacked them, and seemed to be taking over. Northern New England became embroiled in turmoil that lasted from the 1670s to the end of the American Revolution.

Indigenous peoples paid the highest price of this prolonged conflict, but the price could be high as well for seventeenth- and eighteenth-century colonial merchants and for the fishermen who manned their vessels. In 1697, toward the end of intermittent strife now called King William's War (1688–1699), John Higginson of Salem wrote his brother that he had lost so many ships he was financially ruined. He was not alone: "of sixty-odd fishing ketches of this town but six are left" (his count did not include smaller boats).[27]

Destroying fishing vessels was part of war. Fishermen and their vessels were sometimes recruited into battles or made their status ambiguous by becoming privateers. Sometimes native men stole vessels for their own use. Members of coastal tribes were remarkable canoe builders, but they lacked the tools and materials for building and outfitting sailing vessels.[28]

Several murderous conflicts convey the struggle over the Fox Islands' resources and present a granular picture of how the Maine coast and its fish came to belong to the settlers.

Most famous in its day was the bloody brawl and unlikely victory of the Tilton brothers in 1722, a tale recounted in a contemporary ballad, and later in a history of Ipswich. The eighteenth-century ballad offers, through colonists' eyes, a glimpse of their interactions with the native people on and around Vinalhaven and helps us understand both the role the growing cod economy played in the 18th century history of Vinalhaven, and the human cost of the fishery.

> *Down at an Eastward harbor called Fox Bay,*
> *They in a schooner at an anchor lay,*
> *It was about the fourteenth day of June,*
> *Six stout great Indians in the afternoon*
> *In two canoes on board said schooner came . . .*[29]

According to the ballad, Jacob and Daniel Tilton, along with a "boy," sailed northeast from Ipswich, Massachusetts, in a "small vessel" to fish. On a mid-June day in 1722 they anchored "at Fox Island, in Penobscot" and tossed their lines into the water. Fishing trips from Ipswich to the Bay were common, but as this ballad signals, the fishermen feared more than fog. A conflict called "Governor Dummer's War" (1722–1725) was erupting as the French and their native allies battled the British to settle the boundary between their territorial claims. The Bay was a No Man's Land.[30]

That afternoon one of the brothers looked up from his work to see two canoes of Indians paddling toward them.[31] The men, led by "Captain Sam" and "Penobscot Governor," boarded the fishing vessel and started conversing with the fishermen in broken English. (These men were Penobscots, a band often allied with the English.) In the ballad, the Tilton brothers make a point of their own Englishness, claiming that they are on the same side. But the Penobscot men express anger about mistreatment by the English government, though the grievance is not recorded. Fragile allegiances could shift quickly.

Treaties were constantly being broken and atrocities frequently perpetrated, particularly by bounty hunting Colonists paid for native scalps. Hoping to avoid conflict, the Tiltons swore they hadn't fished in the Bay for a while and knew nothing of the troubles.

"The Penobscot Nation [is] part of the Wabanaki Confederacy, along with the Abenaki, Passamaquoddy, Maliseet, and Mi'kmaq nations ... The beginning of the 17th century ... there were probably about 10,000 Penobscots (a number which fell to below 500 in the early 19th century)... From about 1800 onward, the Penobscots lived on reservations."[32]

Suddenly, the Penobscot men jumped the Tiltons and tied them up. "Two principal Indians and four more, came off to them, pretending to be peaceful. But half of them, after a hard struggle, succeeded to tie the hands and feet of Jacob, and the other half did the same to Daniel." (The boy was not mentioned again until the end of the account.)[33]

"Two of the Indians went ashore to tell the result of their enterprise ..." Things looked grim for the brothers. The remaining attackers started plundering the vessel. Before long, Daniel persuaded one "to lose him that he might get something which they would like." They untied his legs, but not his hands.[34]

While the four native men continued searching the boat, Daniel slowly edged toward a knife. He grabbed it, cut his arms loose, and freed Jacob. "The Indians saw this and rushed toward them." According to the ballad, the struggle was fierce. The Tiltons, "with their knives, and what other instruments they could furnish themselves with, dispatched the Indians."[35]

One of the four Penobscot men dove off the schooner and swam to shore. The brothers, who were either uncommonly strong or exaggerated their prowess, tore into the three others still on board and threw them overboard. One feebly swam a few strokes before drowning.

Alive but injured, the other two crawled into a canoe they had tied to the side of the Tiltons' schooner. Daniel spotted them, picked up a gun, took aim and pulled the trigger. The gun misfired. He then grabbed "a stout great setting pole" (used to move a vessel through shallow water) and drove it down repeatedly, crushing their heads, until the canoe tipped, and they drowned.[36]

Now bleeding and weakened, the Ipswich fishermen saw other canoes approaching. Fortunately for them, a sturdy breeze was blowing, "On seeing three canoes on their way toward them, they cut the cable and hoisted the sails, and escaped, though badly wounded." Too injured to sail far, they steered toward Matinicus Island, where Massachusetts Bay Colony fishermen sometimes camped in summer. There they found men who bandaged and fed them until they could travel. The boy sailed the boat. "The lad, by his activity, was very useful to them. In a few days they reached home."[37]

The story, though recorded as history, reads like a tall tale—with the brothers overpowering twice their number and escaping thanks to a timely breeze. Even if truth was embellished, the tale offers a vivid glimpse of the endless conflict and "frontier" violence that was a part of fishing around the Fox Islands in the 1700s. Colonists willingly took great risks to earn a living. And native people desperately fought back.

In spite of the danger, men like the Tiltons regularly sailed from Ipswich, Salem and other Massachusetts towns to fish around the Fox Islands. The inshore fishery in Penobscot Bay was more robust and offered less competition than nearer to home.[38] In April 1724, two years after the Tilton affair and with Governor Dummer's War ongoing, Penobscot men again attacked fishermen near the Fox Islands.

This time, native fighters had "'a fleet' of fifty canoes" and had apparently been harassing the Colonists for a while on occasions when the latter went onshore to gather wood and water, or to seek shelter from storms. The Indians planned to head for Monhegan Island to attack the English fishing in its waters, "but going through the Fox Islands, and discovering many vessels at anchor, [they] surprised eight with little or no opposition in which were forty men, of whom they killed twenty."[39]

On August 24 the same year, another small boat fishing near the Southern Fox Island ran into trouble. A group of Indians surprised the fishermen, took them hostage, and held them for ransom, demanding to be paid in gunpowder and shot. Taking hostages to trade for arms was common around the Bay during wartime.

The native men sent two fishermen back to the mainland to procure the gunpowder, warning that the rest of the crew would be killed if more than two people returned with the "ransom." The captives and their guards waited through the long, warm August day for the emissaries' return.

A boat sailed into view. There were more than two people on deck. Thinking they had been betrayed, the nervous captors hastily murdered their hostages and fled. "The approaching boat," Vinalhaven historian Sidney Winslow recounts, sailed by, "its occupants blissfully unconscious of the horrible scene . . . in which they were playing such a tragic but innocent part."[40]

Coastal tribes steadily lost ground. Even by 1720, the historian Horace P. Beck estimates that the eastern tribes were only about "500 men strong," hardly the threat one might fantasize from the stories. In fact, Beck asserts, their numbers were so diminished by 1726 when the war ended, that the few remaining men offered little further resistance.[41]

Starting around 1724, some native families, their kin dead, their tribes decimated, took to the sea in makeshift houseboats, attempting to save their lives. They sailed or rowed, hid in coves, and moved continually around Penobscot Bay. Beck explains, "With the English marching up and down in the land, burning villages and killing every red man, woman and child they could lay hand on . . . [the native population] was faced with either death by starvation or death by the sword. Many of them, as a last, desperate measure, stole ships—not for battle or ransom, but as a new home. They could live aboard and survive by sealing and fishing. The men were near their families and could defend them." In this way they tried to hang on and await better times.[42]

After 1726, when Governor Dummer's Wabanaki-English war ended, the tiny surviving bands of Penobscot families that continued to fish around the Fox Islands had no way to protect themselves; they tried to persuade the colonial government to uphold treaties, with little success.

Several decades later, a long struggle between several Penobscot men and a colonist on nearby Matinicus offers a picture of early island life in the mid-eighteenth century amid ongoing tensions. The English settlers involved were not just random folks, but the ancestors of many people fishing on Vinalhaven today. Their story illustrates the rough and tumble of how land changed hands, and what it could mean to "settle" on an island.

> *"Matinicus Island, about 2 miles long and of varying width, has an area of 720 acres. It is 18 miles out from Rockland and appears to have a greater variety of vegetation than any of the other islands that far from the mainland. The shores are mostly rock bound, but there are three sand beaches extensive enough to furnish favorable habitat for sand-loving plants. . . . The plants that fix the character of the landscape on Matinicus are the abundant spruces, the low grasses. . . . Shrubs . . . are blueberry, huckleberry, and bunchberry, and outside, bayberry and juniper."[43]*

In 1751, Ebenezer Hall, with his second wife, Mary, and their five children, settled on Matinicus—the first year-round residents in some decades. Since the early seventeenth century, European and Colonial fishermen had camped there seasonally; and periodically, before hostilities with the French heated up, there had been semi-permanent fishing settlements. When Hall and his family arrived, they had the place to themselves.[44]

Ebenezer Hall was tough and seemingly fearless. He built a cabin, farmed and fished. The thin soil made it hard to feed his cows. To grow hay, he burnt over a nearby island called Green Island.[45] According to Colonial law in those years, unsettled islands were reserved for tribal use. Green Island rightfully belonged to Penobscot bands that paddled there to collect birds' eggs, hunt seals and birds, and fish in the surrounding water. Hall's activities infuriated them.

Familiar with the terms of the treaty, several Penobscot men warned Hall not to burn the island again. He ignored them and harassed any Penobscot who hunted or fished nearby. Some months later the native men initiated a meeting with colonial officials to complain.

A transcription from August 15, 1751, quotes a native spokesman named Loron, who expressed the group's palpable frustration: "There is a house upon an Island in Penobscot Bay that spoils our hunting. The Island is our Livelihood. The people there scare the Seals and Fowl. Govr Dumr's treaty says we shan't loose a foot of ground."[46]

Nothing improved. On April 25, 1753, four Penobscot men wrote a letter to Governor Spencer Phips of Massachusetts, complaining that all the harassment was going one way, and bidding the Governor to intervene and support their rights—so they would not have to take matters into their own hands. The letter captures their frustration and helplessness. Although they threaten to remove Hall themselves, they would prefer not to.

To the Governour

Brother, you did not harken to us about the Englishman on the Island, he hurts us in our seiling & fowling . . . we don't hinder him from fishing, if you don't Remove him in two Months, we shall be obliged to do it ourselves. We have writ to you before and have had no answer, if you don't answer to this we shan't write again. . . . I salute you and all the Council Present in behalf of the Penobscot Tribe. [signed] Cosemes, Modobt, Chebnood, Mugdumbawit.[47]

On June 13, 1753, Governor Phips directed Captain Jabez Bradbury to remove Hall who, he noted, did not own the property he occupied on Matinicus. "Sir—Whereas one Ebenr Hall has settled himself on the Island of Montinicus, at which the Penobscot Indians have taken much umbrage alleging that by his means they are much disturbed in their Fowling at said place, and it not appearing that the said Hall has any property in the said Island . . ." Phips directed Bradbury to gather as many men as he needed, and to remove Hall—if possible without using violence. He rationalized his order by suggesting that otherwise the Indians would show "their resentment against him."[48] Nothing happened, and Hall remained on Matinicus.

Besides serving as Massachusetts Lieutenant Governor, and twice as its acting Governor, Phips, from 1719 on, also developed land on Maine's mid-coast by attempting to attract settlers to the newly incorporated towns of Warren and Thomaston. This seemingly put him in the position of profiting by selling land that belonged to the native people he was charged with pro-tecting. Members of local bands were most unhappy about this contradiction. In fact, tensions over these land sales helped start Dummer's War.[49]

The Green Island struggle remained unresolved, and another round of fighting started in 1754. After a colonial Militiaman named James Cargill led a surprise raid at Owl's Head, killing and scalping a dozen Penobscots, the tribe decided they might do better to side with the French. In November 1755, in retaliation for their switching sides, Phips put a high bounty on their scalps. This conflict, part of what was called the "French and Indian War," came to be fought on a global scale.

Two years later, in this new political context, a Penobscot group laid siege to Hall's house on Matinicus. Hall and Mary lived there with two of her children by her first marriage (to a soldier who died battling the French) and the three children they had together. According to one story, Hall and his son, also named Ebenezer, were out fishing when the attackers appeared. On his return, Hall Sr. was immediately jumped and murdered by the Penobscots.[50]

According to Mary's written testimony, there was a longer siege before Hall's murder. The family hid in the house. Hall, who had battled the French in Nova Scotia, held off his assailants for ten days before they finally killed him. In her account, the attackers then scalped him, burned his house, and captured the family. Joseph Green, Mary's twelve-year-old son by her first marriage, hid to avoid capture. When he dared leave, he set out across the bay in a canoe, and was rescued by a schooner that took him back to Matinicus to help him bury his father. Afterward, the crew took him to Camden.[51]

The Penobscot attackers sailed away with Mary and four children aboard Hall's schooner. Eventually, Mary was taken to a prison in Quebec and separated from her children. She never saw any but Joseph again, though she searched for the others once she returned to the British Colonies.

Getting home was not simple. By all accounts, Mary was attractive and resourceful. While a prisoner in Quebec she caught the eye of a fellow cap-tive—a Captain Andrew Watkins, whom she later described as "a New Eng-land gentleman." Watkins borrowed money to pay her ransom and purchase her a place on a boat to London. From England, she managed to gain passage back to New York, and made her way north to Falmouth, Maine. In 1765 she married again to a man named Chipman Cobb. The Cobbs eventually settled in Gorham, Maine, where the remarkable Mary lived to 89 or 90.

Captain Watkins died of smallpox in a French prison. His widow, Jane, unhappy with his spending *her* inheritance on Mary, asked her to pay it back. Mary was penniless, so Jane petitioned the courts and was repaid from public funds.

In 1763 the British decisively won the "French and Indian War." Some French settlers and the few remaining native people settled in around Old Town. New England colonists streamed into the opened territory and onto the islands. Between 1763 and 1790 the population of Massachusetts' District of Maine almost quadrupled. Much of this growth occurred along the coast. Vinalhaven's numbers grew even more dramatically. In 1763 there were maybe a half dozen settlers. By 1790, together with Matinicus, the island claimed a population of 564 people.[52]

It was also in 1763 that Ebenezer Hall's grown son, Ebenezer Jr., married and settled back on Matinicus to continue the island fishing and farming life he had known when young. Ebenezer Jr. lived to at least 80. He and his wife had 15 children, all of whom grew up and married; they and their descendants have continued to populate the Fox Islands.

Indeed, many families living on Vinalhaven today carry Ebenezer Sr.'s DNA. Moreover, there is something archetypal about his and his wife's grit, his resistance to mainland authority, and her pragmatism and resilience. Island life has never been for the faint of heart. Two styles of living have co-existed (sometimes in the same individual) since the first European Americans settled the land: Many of the first island settlers came from families that had sailed to Massachusetts during the seventeenth century; they possessed a deep sense of community and family investment, and a strong civic sense. Side by side with this civic mindedness has always co-existed for these Massachusetts settlers and for their Maine descendants what islanders call a "pirate" perspective. You might call it lawless, violent, or antisocial; but you could also say it is a sense of individual prerogative, a willingness to trade hard labor for personal liberty, a resistance to outside authorities, and a belief that not all mainland laws are relevant for people living on islands.[53]

Other than in eighteenth century stories, there is little written record of Maine Indians on Vinalhaven. A few people living on the island early in the twentieth century mention summer and autumn visits from members of Penobscot bands and recall native women harvesting "sweet grass" to make baskets, which they used and also sold to tourists on the mainland: In 1923, Addie Roberts noted in her diary, "Aug. 17 *Elbra went up to see the Indians, but they had gone away.*"[54]

In, *Vinalhaven Reminiscences (1978)*, Bruce Grindle (1899–1992) describes (in the context of a longer story) how native people camped on the island in summer and hunted porpoises for oil. Porpoise oil, like whale oil, was used for lamps. The Penobscot Indians *"came down from Old Town each Spring to get porpoise oil and sweet grass at Roberts' Harbor. They came down to Captain Watson Y. Hopkins* [1800–1885] *farm, camped there all summer long, and generally left around the last week in September."* Grindle describes a friendly warmth between Indians and islanders, *"Every Spring when they would arrive, the kids from the house would rush down to the encampment on the beach to see if there were any new papooses or new dogs or to find out what else the Indians had brought with them."*[55]

2

Settling In

The early settlers spread out across both Fox Islands. Initially the North Island grew faster because its soil was better for farming. Being closer to the mainland and possessing sheltered harbors may also have helped. Gradually, as fishing became more important, the South Island came into its own. By 1850, four years after their official separation into two towns, Vinalhaven had 1252 residents, North Haven, 806. Although I focus on the South Island, it is important to remember that for five decades they were two parts of one township, and that kin, land and boat ownership, business dealings, and political matters overlapped on many fronts.

How did the families who initially settled the South Island go about settling in? Like their counterparts on the mainland frontier, most began by girdling, burning and cutting trees. Year by year, using axes, oxen and sledges, they cleared the land, and simultaneously plowed and planted fields they'd opened. Trading labor with kin and neighbors, they built rudimentary dwellings first, then sturdier ones along with sheds, barns, and docks. They cut undergrowth into paths and then roads. Often people rowed or sailed to do business and visit. Because of the thin, rocky soil, South Island farms mostly grew grain and vegetables for home use or local barter. Farmers raised cows, pigs, and sheep; some produced extra meat, milk, butter, and cheese to barter and sell. The early island economy worked largely through barter, with labor and goods traded among folks, and accounts sometimes settled out in cash.[56]

The spruce woods particularly drew settlers. It was no accident that the earliest known business on the South Island was a sawmill set up by Frances Cogswell in 1760. By 1798 William Vinal was running three mills on the islands. Coastal Massachusetts had exhausted much of its timber, and there was a market in Boston for wood and wood products of all sorts.

Trees were fundamental to the success of New England's fishing industry. Vessels were made of wood; and wood was also necessary for producing the flakes, boxes and barrels that allowed fish to be dried, smoked, packed, and transported. Starting in the 1760s, the earliest settlers on Vinalhaven began providing spruce "spars" (masts and yards) for vessels of all sizes. "Coasters" on both islands delivered cut spars and lumber to mainland markets where they were sold or traded for other goods.

Commercial fishing began in earnest only after the end of the War of 1812, but South Islanders started catching and trading small quantities of herring and cod soon after they arrived. Gradually some families saved enough money from lumber to diversify by investing in boats, vessels, and fishing gear.

Although the settlers eagerly traded in fish, consuming them too often could be a cause of complaint. Indeed, in the earliest days of the settlement you could be scorned or pitied for *having* to eat fish. In an eighteenth-century island petition to the Massachusetts government, "*Clambs & other Fish*" are portrayed as a food of last resort in hard times, which you were "*obliged*" to eat when you couldn't get anything better.[57]

In a 1772 plea, petitioners portrayed their lives as difficult and impoverished. Fox Islanders were petitioning for title to their land (a necessary part of establishing ownership and legally creating a township), and their self-description suggests hardship and struggle. They had, they claimed:

> But a Bare Subsistance being Exposed to Hunger and Nakedness for many years past and are to this day scarcely able to Raise Corn [wheat] for Bread to Live on more than Six Months in a Year and Many of us raise but a few Bushels of Grain have been and are still obliged to Live on Clambs & other Fish with Roots which serve us for Bread, and having never had a grant of said Island are threatened to be turned off our possessions.[58]

Because of the tightening British financial grip on the colonies, the pre-Revolutionary War years were hard for New Englanders whose incomes had been restricted along with their freedom to trade. The ensuing deprivations may have been emphasized in the petition to draw a more sympathetic response.

Shortly after the American Revolution ended and settlers returned to the islands, they resumed petitioning the General Court of Massachusetts to allow them to incorporate. At that time, they emphasized how much they had sacrificed during the war: how their loyalty to the patriot cause earned them the right to become a township. This round of petitioning succeeded, and in 1789 North and South Fox Island were incorporated into a single town called Vinalhaven.[59]

Incorporation came with its own demands. The Commonwealth of Massachusetts required that, to acquire autonomy as a township, towns put aside land for a school and a church and choose Selectmen to set up a government. Islanders immediately started building roads, paying men and oxen to clear the way and make them eighteen feet wide. In reading contemporary accounts, one sees a proprietary enthusiasm emerging as people created their own local government with its annual town meeting. In 1790 Vinalhaven hired two school masters; in 1791 the town voted to hire a minister for four months of the year. In 1793, North Island set aside money for a burial ground. By 1794 Vinalhaven was paying a tax collector, and by 1795 they had hired someone to plan out the town. The population grew quickly, and many seem to have prospered. Yet not everyone did well: in 1798 the town meeting voted to set aside forty-eight pounds to support the poor.[60]

The 1805 town meeting report captures how the islands were joined in their early years, but still remained separate: "This year it was voted not to have any school on the North Island and the article to raise money for preaching was passed over. Voted to have schools on the South Island and $230 was raised for that purpose."

A settler's life reveals more about the island's early trade and fisheries. Thaddeus Carver was born in 1751 in Marshfield, Massachusetts. His great-great uncle, John Carver, was the first governor of Plymouth Plantation. Thaddeus's genealogy is significant because it makes clear that he was from an established family that valued civic service, political office, and social power. Once rooted on the island, several family members continued in a similar civic mold.

In 1766, the not quite fifteen-year-old Thaddeus moved to South Fox Island with his brother Amos and his father, Reuben. The other two left, but Thaddeus stayed and worked for several years for Thomas Waterman on the North Island. In 1776 he married Hannah Hall, a grandchild of Ebenezer Hall of Matinicus. The Carvers had ten children, nine of whom grew up and married. Thaddeus lived to 80, and Hannah died just short of her 89th birthday.

Many early settlers lived long lives, and most children survived early childhood. The absence of crowding could be one reason for such longevity and relatively little infant or child mortality in these first generations. The cold climate probably helped, sparing people from diseases like yellow fever that arrived with cargo in port cities farther south. Fatal accidents were not uncommon. It appears, though, that daily dangers were well balanced with vitality.

As long as neighbors got on adequately with neighbors, they seemed to exercise control over their own realms. Certainly, laws and community restraints existed, and some people would always be richer and more powerful than others, but initially there was enough space to be let alone, plenty of resources to harvest and market, and, in peacetime, few outside forces impeding them.

In 1776 when the twenty-five-year-old Thaddeus married Hannah, he paid 260£ to purchase Francis Cogswell's "double" sawmill together with 700 acres of land. Thaddeus had worked for Cogswell, who likely had a good market. Boards, barrels, masts, and spars were already being exported from larger coastal ports in the eighteenth century, and vessels frequently carried wood products south to the Caribbean islands—especially in the autumn after the fishing season ended. Cogswell could have sold milled island trees to these merchants.

We don't know if Vinalhaven lumber went that far afield since island vessels generally did business with Boston. Much island soil is too thin to grow red oak or high-quality white pine, the most valued trade lumber; but a visitor in the 1820s reported that even then, more than half a century after it had begun, the trade in spruce spars was ongoing.[61] Island mills like Carver's and Vinal's likely sawed the trees their neighbors cut for use on their own farms. They also traded locally and on the mainland.

According to Thaddeus's son, Reuben, his father's mill was "carried away by a freshet," (a sudden flood) only six years after Thaddeus had purchased it. Reuben's memories were recounted much later in an 1885 newspaper story, and some of his dates vary a bit from other records. He remembers his father buying the mill in 1774, and the flood occurring in 1780. Since those years span the Revolution when few people were on the island, Thaddeus may have lost money on his purchase. After he came of age, Reuben rebuilt the mill and ran it for thirty-five years, likely turning a profit.[62]

Like most islanders, Thaddeus also farmed, and that work helped sustain his family during the year. The inventory done after his death lists oxen, steers, a bull and twenty-four sheep, and plenty of farm equipment. He owned half of a hog house, likely raising or buying hogs for trade or export.

The Vinalhaven Historical Society is in possession of the fragile, yellowed ledger from Thaddeus's first general store—another business effort that shows how buying and selling fish tied into the early island economy. By later island measures, his trade was tiny. An early entry, August 19, 1775, records that Thaddeus purchased 28 pounds of "cookfish" from Job Philbrook(s).[63]

Job's own life illustrates the perils faced by early island settlers, as well as the way fishing was one of many types of work they did to survive. Born in Greenland, New Hampshire, by one account and baptized in 1729, Job during his youth had much in common with his Biblical namesake. At fifteen, while plowing a field some distance from the family house, he was kidnapped and carried to Canada by a band of Indians. Later, he was ransomed and returned.[64]

As an adult he lived on Vinalhaven, in Castine, on 700 Acre Island by Isles-boro, on Islesboro itself, and then back on Vinalhaven where he died in his early seventies around 1802. He married three times. While on Vinalhaven, he captained a boat that freighted lumber for William Vinal. He also worked as a *"farmer, carpenter, shipbuilder and lumberman. He was also a scrivener, writing deeds, bonds and other legal papers for the settlers in the neighborhood."*[65]

Twenty-eight pounds is not much fish. Cod quantities were usually measured in quintals after the fish had been split, salted, and dried—with a quintal equaling 112 pounds. Pickled mackerel, herring or alewives were sold in barrels, with a full barrel weighing 200 lbs. The Midcoast Maine fishing "industry" was barely getting started in the 1770s, and the Revolutionary War depressed all colonial fisheries. After the war ended, it would take the Midcoast communities several more decades to create an adequate infrastructure and to accumulate enough cash to support a robust industry. The Maine fishing historian Wayne O'Leary, perhaps referring more to the deep water than the inshore fisheries, repeats an interesting observation from the historian John B. Brebner: It took about forty years for a community to gain the necessary skills to support the work, and create a group of mariners. He observes that such an "acculturation was taking place along the eastern shores of Maine after 1790."

In his reading of Carver's journal, island historian Ken Reiss points out that as early as 1771, Thaddeus began sharpening his trading skills by doing arithmetic exercises that helped him master British, Spanish and Portuguese currency exchanges, and learn various units of measure for cloth, liquids, dry goods, etc.[66] This underscores the broader observation about the time it took generally to master the mercantile skillset. And while we cannot know exactly what the "Navigational school" was that James Roberts "kept" for nine days in 1850, for which, an account book entry notes, he earned $2.50, it could indicate an ongoing island commitment to teaching seafaring skills.[67]

Likely, Vinalhaven was attractive to people, like the Carvers, who had lived in coastal towns like Marshfield, or on Cape Cod, or near other shores, because they already knew about fishing, boats, and how one could make a life from fishing and farming even on poor soil. Success was made more likely when settlers had an ample supply of timber, fertilizer from low-tide muck, and salt marsh hay for the cattle. Under these conditions, they would "acculturate" quickly.

We can assume that Thaddeus used his practiced skills when he captained a coastal trading vessel in 1810, the 85-ton sloop *Turkish Rover* carrying goods, like lumber; dried, smoked, and pickled fish, and other commodities to markets in larger ports farther away.[68]

Some island fish and other commodities directly or indirectly made their way to the Caribbean. European markets had higher standards; but markets in the Caribbean and the American south, even after slavery ended in different places but left very poor populations, purchased smoked or salted fish that was of a lower quality.[69]

Several ledger entries record occasional fish-related business with Job Philbrook and his sons Joel and Jeremiah. On September 1, 1775, Jeremiah sold Thaddeus Carver fourteen pounds of fish. On November 14, 1775, Jeremiah bought six "macrael" (mackerel). On July 11, 1785, Joel was in debt for a half "quentel" of codfish.

Apart from similar small quantities of fish traded with other islanders, the ledger offers a picture of what early settlers needed and wanted. Islanders traded in used clothes and shoes in an era before either was mass produced (apparently Thaddeus made shoes, too). One day "Mis Stinsom" came into his store and bought an "old shirt." The following summer she purchases a pair of "old shoes." Mis Stinsom may have been a sister of the early settler, James Stinsom (b. 1738). Over two years, she bought a little beef and pork, a bit of coffee, and some "meal"—which could be ground corn, wheat or rye. Mostly, she bought molasses.[70] Did Mis Stinsom use the thick sweet syrup for cooking and baking? Most likely. But molasses was a favorite substitute for barley in colonial beer brewing, so perhaps that was another use.

Coffee and molasses were items Maine vessels carried back from the West Indies or other Caribbean islands, including Hispaniola (today's Haiti and Dominican Republic) and Cuba after selling their cargoes. Perhaps Thomas Ginn, who was born in Liverpool in 1762 and active in Vinalhaven in 1785, brought them to Vinalhaven on the coasting schooner he ran to Boston.[71] Or perhaps Job Philbrook traded for these staples in Camden or Belfast on the mainland.

During the years he kept the ledger, Thaddeus additionally traded in hay, pepper, hog fat, oxen, sheep wool, shoes, salt, indigo, a silk handkerchief, rails, boards, rum, sugar, tobacco, "a dog puppie," butter, "foots of boards," a calf, and tallow. Many items came from far away, and risk was always involved in ventures upon the water, his last entry in 1789 reminds us: "Richard Combs [Coombs] and John Marshel was drowned this day."

With each passing year, Thaddeus invested more in trade. At the time of his death in 1831, he owned a general store and a fish market, as well as a third of a fish shed, and a third of a wharf. The wharf and fish shed both nod to his wholesale fish and shipping business(es), and his need for a place to store dried, smoked, and pickled fish for shipping.

Partial ownership was a way for family members, neighbors, friends, or business associates to invest in ventures too big or too risky to be owned by one person. In place of putting up cash, often not available, islanders interested in owning a partial share in a vessel might supply labor or raw materials like lumber, or make other material contributions. Such arrangements were based on mutual knowledge of character and trust, which were crucial to the development of Maine's fishing industry.[72]

Although Thaddeus apparently neither fished nor built boats, his two sons, John and Reuben, and later their sons, followed the changing economy and did both very successfully, likely helped by their inheritance. In his will of February 18, 1820, Carver bequeathed them *"all the lands (illegible) houses barns shops stores and other building situated in the town of Vinalhaven or elsewhere together with all my other freehold Estate"* Their seven sisters, in lieu of property, were each given forty dollars, (except for Lydia who was to receive thirty dollars and the feather bed, bedstead and bedding!) and another forty dollars two years later.

Thaddeus Carver made precise provision for his wife:

I do bequeath unto my beloved wife Hannah Carver one Cow and all the furniture that is in said House . . . excepting one bed—to her sole use forever and I will that my Executor furnish [her] with wood for one fire in the said Western room During her Natural Life.[73]

The cow provided milk, butter, cheese, and manure to fertilize the kitchen garden, but stipulating a fire was essential. It's easy to forget today the challenge of surviving a winter when your only heat came from a single fireplace, and you had to keep the fire burning. While women knew how to split logs and lay fires, even the hardiest usually couldn't cut or haul big logs alone. Indeed, when she was in her seventies and her husband was jailed for debt, Hallowell midwife Martha Ballard suffered mightily when forced to scrounge her own wood: *"I broke old logs with an old hough and brot in the pieces in a basket and O how fatigued I was."*[74]

Like Martha Ballard, Hannah also worked as a midwife for part of her life.

"Hannah lived in her old age in what was my grandmother's kitchen and her granddaughters took turns of two weeks each, taking care of her. She died July 15, 1848, at the age of 89 years. She was a first cousin to Henry W. Longfellow," wrote her great-great granddaughter in an undated letter.

"My grandmother always spoke of [Hannah] as a very strong, capable woman. Once two fishermen came over to Vinalhaven in a small sailing vessel to get her to go to Matinicus to attend a woman in childbirth. On the way over, the fishermen got drunk and she bound them with ropes, locked them in the hold of the boat and took the boat across by herself. My grandmother also remembered seeing her, many times, go outside our house and shoot a wild duck on the wing."[75]

How did islanders shift their emphasis from farming and lumbering to fishing over a generation? The trajectory of a second family, the Areys, helps fill out our understanding of the town of Vinalhaven's beginnings, and how it transformed in the early decades of the nineteenth century into a success- ful fishing community. In 1769, Isaac Arey, age twenty-five, his wife, Mary, twenty three, their two-year-old son, Isaac, and his baby brother, Ebenezer, set sail from Cape Cod for Mt. Desert Isle. Isaac was born in Yarmouth, Mas- sachusetts, in 1745, and his father's family had lived on Cape Cod or Mar- tha's Vineyard for generations. Isaac's great-great-grandfather on his father's side, Richard Isaac, born in 1624, had been one of the earliest settlers in Plymouth Colony. Mary Crosby Arey was born in 1747 in Harwich, Massa- chusetts—also on Cape Cod. One branch of her mother's family had arrived on the *Mayflower* in 1620. All of Isaac and Mary's earliest Massachusetts ancestors had settled around Cape Cod Bay by the 1650s.[76]

Stopping on the South Fox Island, the young couple settled there instead of Mt. Desert. A document records that, in January 1769, Isaac paid thirty pounds to Benjamin A. Carr of North Fox Island for a large tract of land on South Fox Island near "Isle Holt Bay." Arey's ability to buy land suggests either that, like Thaddeus Carver, he had family backing or had accumulated a little wealth on his own before he set out. The Areys built their first house at the head of what has since been called Arey's Harbor. They later built a house on one of the harbor islands.[77]

Like the Carvers and Areys, most of the earliest Fox Island settlers whose places of birth are known came from what is now Massachusetts. On one list of original Vinalhaven settlers, twelve of nineteen people were from Mas- sachusetts—often from Cape Cod, Martha's Vineyard, or the South Shore (Marshfield, Duxbury, Plymouth). One person had lived in Rhode Island, three moved from other parts of what we now call Maine, two were born in Liverpool, England, and one in Ireland. In this era, childhood was often short. James Roberts, born in 1770 in Liverpool, ran away from home at nine, and "shipped as a cabin boy" on a boat bound for the West Indies. At nineteen, he met a Vinalhaven sea captain—Isachar Lane—sailed north with him and settled for good on the island. James eventually married Sarah Hall of Matinicus—a granddaughter of Ebenezer Hall.[78]

A story survives about Isaac Arey's ready muscle. On his way home from felling trees in an island wood, Arey, "on a narrow footpath" surprised a "large Bear," who "refused to turn out of the path. . ." Rather than fleeing and perhaps invite a mauling, Isaac "[m]arched up in close quarters." The bear "reared up on his hind feet to receive him." Arey took aim with his axe, lifted it high and—with his woodcutter's might—struck "with such force and exactness that he split open the head of the Bear, and dispatched him immediately."[79]

However fearless the Areys were, we don't know if they stayed put during the Revolutionary War, which started only six years after they arrived. Most settlers fled the unprotected islands. By 1779, British soldiers at the fort in Castine (then called Bagaduce) and Loyalists who'd fled northeast seeking British protection were making life unpleasant for islanders by marauding and commandeering farm animals, firewood, and food, depriving them of adequate stores for winter.

The English seized island men and forced them to labor in the fort. John Smith, one Vinalhaven settler who was captured and "compelled by the British to work upon the fortifications at Castine" used to claim—with the wry humor so typical of Downeasters—that the English captors "got very little benefit from his labor, as he would pound his axe on a rock at every opportunity, so that it took him about all the time to grind it." The war ended in 1783 and by the spring of 1784 island residents were returning.[80]

Isaac Arey's will and inventory suggest that the family prospered. As they labored, clearing the land and farming, Mary gave birth to ten more children, for a total of seven boys and five girls. Four died before age twenty-one, including twins, an eighteen-year-old daughter, and their fourth son, Lewis, who at fourteen died at sea. Eight lived. With land to work, lumber to harvest, and many daily chores, the necessity of child labor made big families a plus.[81]

It's unclear exactly what allowed the Arey family to do so well. Isaac likely accumulated his wealth selling lumber and trading. His wife, Mary, a "skilled midwife," earned, too. Thanks to Laurel Thatcher Ulrich's extraordinary book *A Midwife's Tale*, an examination of midwife Martha Ballard's diary from 1785–1812 in Hallowell, Maine, we know something about Mary's livelihood. The women were almost exact contemporaries, living and working only sixty miles apart.

Midwives were crucial to their communities. They knew everyone, since they worked closely with each birthing mother, her kin and friends; and they earned payments or goods for delivering babies and tending the sick. It was a demanding profession. A midwife could be summoned day or night, and often left home for several days, sometimes even weeks, at a time—no matter the weather or the needs of her own household. An island midwife had to contend with every imaginable birth and post-birth complication with few medicines or colleagues to back her up. While we cannot know, we might imagine that Mary, like Martha Ballard, became more active in her work once her girls were old enough to assist with the household labors—among them childcare, spinning, weaving, sewing, knitting, wool-shearing, cooking, candle and soap making, washing, herb gathering, weeding and gardening.[82]

The 1790 census tells us that island families tended to be large. Of 106 families on the South Island, thirty-two had eight or more children at home.

There were 155 boys under sixteen, and likely about the same number of girls, who weren't counted in this census. The fecundity continued: By 1810, according to Reiss, 400 children under ten lived on the two islands together. Apart from Hannah Carver, we don't know how many other midwives were on the Fox Islands, but Mary was likely a busy woman who earned well.

Little else is recorded about the Areys, except for Isaac's death by drowning around 1800 when he was in his early sixties, and the property and possessions he left behind.[83] No death record exists. We know only that one day, late in winter, Mary went to assist a pregnant woman who was due to give birth on Isle au Haut, about eight miles across Penobscot Bay from the Areys' home. Fifty families lived there.[84]

Several days later Isaac drowned as he rowed across the bay to bring Mary home. It's hard to know what happened. He could have met with a snow squall or a wind that came up out of nowhere. Or he could have overestimated his stamina or underestimated the waves. He'd lived by his strength for such a long time, he might have felt it would never fail. No boat is listed in the inventory taken several months later, so it may have been lost with him.

Was Mary watching for him? Notions of time, of arrivals and departures, expectations of knowing someone's whereabouts were utterly different from today. People took for granted not hearing from loved ones for months or years at a time. Many mariners went to sea with only a vague notion of their destination, as it depended on finding markets for the ship's cargo or finding fish to catch. More than a few women and men I interviewed about a later era remember their mothers pacing when their fathers were fishing. We don't know what Mary experienced, but waiting in fear is a state of mind that has been a part of many island days.

Lacking letters or diaries for most early islanders, the probate inventories that sometimes-accompanied wills are one way to document a family's life and work. Most early colonial-era settlers on the Fox Islands didn't possess enough wealth to bother about wills or inventories. Often informality ruled and kin handled the dying and the dividing so that no list of possessions entered the public record. But occasionally, when an estate held more value, an inventory was made. In such cases, shortly after a death, someone trusted by the family and the community walked through the house and out-buildings carefully noting all the deceased person owned—livestock, tools, furniture, utensils, clothing, bedding. Early inventories also mention debts that must be paid as part of probate. There were no banks, and islanders often lent money to each other, or provided goods on credit. Thus, debt can be a sign of growing trade.

At the time he drowned, Isaac, a "yeoman" (farmer), possessed an estate valued at $2,835.93. The most valuable single asset was the tract of 843 acres, worth $2,529. His house was worth $50, his barn $50 more. When inventoried on April 28, 1801, his "personal estate" added up to another $206.93. His possessions show us how the family lived—the household goods, farm animals, tools they accumulated during their thirty-one years of habitation. I include the whole list so readers might form a picture of a life of relative prosperity on Vinalhaven in 1800.[85]

1 Pair of Oxen	$60.00
2 Cows	$36.00
2 Calves	$13.00
1 Sheep	$13.00
1 Horse	$20.00
1 Hog	$05.50
1 Feather Bed	$10.00
1 Bedsted	$01.00
3 Bed Quilts	$09.00
6 Blankets	$06.25
3 Pillowcases	$01.00
1 Mug	$00.20
4 Cups and Saucers	$00.12
1 Canister	$00.33
1 Tea Pot	$00.10
3 Knives 3 Forks	$00.25
4 Plates	$00.12
1 Decanter	$00.25
2 Bottles	$00.12
2 Tin Pans	$00.50
2 Milk Pans	$00.16
1 Candle Stand	$00.75
1 Table	$00.50
1 Pair of Sleeve buttons	$00.33
2 Chests	$02.84
2 Gimblets	$00.12
1 Trammel	$08.00 ($7.00?)
1 Long Coat	$03.00
1 Vest	$00.75
1 Grindstone	$00.75

2 Sleds	$02.00
Clevis and pin	$00.75
1 Axe	$00.66
Old iron	$00.62
1 Handsaw	$00.16
1 Hayfork	$00.16
2 Scythes	$01.42
1 set of nibirons	$00.16
1 Crowbar	$01.00
1 Hettle Barl	$00.75
1 Wine Sieve	$00.33
1 Looking Glass	$01.50
1 Canteen	$00.25
1 Pot	$01.25
1 Skillet	$00.25
5 Boxes	$01.50
2 Kegs	$00.67
2 Pails	$00.33
1 Firkin	$00.33
1 Basket	$00.12
1 Chest of Draws	$00.33
1 Earthen Pot	$00.12
1 Flatiron	$00.33
1 Broken Chain	$00.50
2 Hoes	$00.75
1 Ox Yoke, Staple & Bows	$01.25
1 Saddle & Bridle	$02.50

The list is explicit but raises more questions than it answers. Only three knives and three forks? The relative value of possessions seems quite different from today: The two oxen ($60.00) are worth more than the house. The feather bed ($10.00) is worth one-fifth the price of the house. Three quilts ($9.00) are valued at almost as much as the bed. The long coat ($3.00) is also valuable. Together, the value of the textiles equals the value of one ox. On the other hand, anything built of wood (Table: $.50) is worth relatively little.

Such items may have been made by Isaac, another islander, or a "joiner" (a finish carpenter) on the island or the mainland.

The Areys owned a looking glass; they also owned a flatiron: a clothes iron heated on the hearth. They owned a "Hettle Barl"—likely a heddle bar, the crucial part of a loom. If so, Mary and/or her daughters probably wove some of the cloth for the family clothes, as well as blankets, and perhaps sheets and pillowcases. Was their single sheep kept for wool? They also likely bought or bartered for imported textiles. Their wine sieve suggests they might have done the same for wine. The Areys owned the first horse on the island, perhaps for Mary's midwife work. Ulrich notes that Martha Ballard "fretted when a missing horse delayed her response to a call."[86]

But what about fish and fishing? Neither hook nor line is listed in Isaac's inventory. By comparison, an 1811 inventory of the estate of Uriah Norton lists a "Flounder spear . . . $.12" and "1 Eel Spear . . . $.75." But Isaac owned a trammel, a valuable possession at $7.00 or $8.00. In colonial era inventories, a trammel typically refers to a double ended, S-shaped iron piece hanging on a rod in the fireplace to hold a cooking pot. However, a trammel can also be a three-layer net—an old-style gill net. The Areys lived by the shore on a cove, and later on an island, so it seems reasonable that they owned a fish net, likely to catch herring for their own use.

Isaac mostly lumbered and farmed. William Vinal's three sawmills, built with Boston investment capital, seemingly confirm that lumber was where the earliest settlers made their money. However, Arey fathered a family of seafaring men, and in this family transition we can see the larger story of the birth and growth of island fishing. All six Arey sons who lived to adulthood (Isaac Jr., Ebenezer, John, James, Crosby and Thomas) owned parts of vessels at various times. Three were ship captains.

Surviving account books of the Vinalhaven merchant John Carver (1793–1877) show how fish caught by island men, including the Areys, increasingly played a role in the domestic barter economy.[87] In entries from January, 1820, the second generation of Arey men bought household necessities on credit, paying their debt later in the year, mostly with fish:

Jan 7 James Arey buys molasses, rum and tea and John Arey buys 2 oz of indigo.

Jan 12 Joseph Arey buys Sugar and Crosby Arey buys 1 q. rum.

Once the spring comes and the brothers are fishing, they deliver fish frequently to Carver. Two April days include:

April 15 John Arey delivers 2 cwt (224 lbs) "gross fish" worth $1.50; Crosby Arey delivers 4 cwt (448 lbs) of "fish" for $3.50.

April 17 James Arey delivers 2 cwt's of "fish" and (something illegible) for $1.62, and Ebenezer Arey delivers some combination of fish worth $1.62.

In the course of the spring and summer, the fish Carver purchased or accepted in barter from Vinalhaven fishermen included cod, hake, herring, pollock, and miscellaneous unspecified others.

Between the Revolution and the Civil War, investing in coastal schooners and shipping processed fish could be a good way to increase wealth. The population of the United States was growing. Entrepreneurs were building factories, cities were expanding, settlers were moving westward, the population of immigrants and enslaved people was increasing, and there were markets for cheap protein.

After 1792, the new Federal government also provided a significant source of added wealth for some island fishermen, offering a subsidy for cod fishing in the form of a bounty. This subsidy had little immediate impact. It was aimed at boats (defined by carrying capacity as under 20 tons burthen) and vessels (defined as over 20 tons burthen) in the cod fishery measuring over 5 tons burthen; tiered rates of payment favored the largest vessels and, therefore, ports with mature distant water fleets rather than Vinalhaven. But it may have encouraged families like the Areys to turn to seafaring for a living, and it did prove critical to building the fishing industry in Maine during the first half of the nineteenth century. As Congress intended, it also thanked coastal fishermen who had fought the British and suffered the loss of their vessels and ensured a future supply of sailors competent to aid their country in times of war.[88]

Like many coastal Mainers in the nineteenth century, the Areys changed their livelihood when the sea began to offer better prospects than the land. Even before the War of 1812, Arey men began buying and selling vessels. Many of Isaac and Mary's grandsons and great grandsons owned or captained trading and fishing schooners: The 1850 US Census lists eighteen direct Arey descendants who called themselves fishermen.

We can imagine that island men grew up familiar with rowboats and small sail boats from a young age, but our imagination likely falters in appreciating how much they hopped from house to house, or farm to town in boats to do chores or socialize. Still, going to sea even for short periods meant learning much more about living and working aboard a ship—the weather, the ocean, the stars, the currents, fish, and the ways of men who passed their days in close quarters.

Ship captains like the Areys men cared for their crews and vessels. They had to master trade, navigation, and fishing skills; moreover, they took on their shoulders the responsibility for the success and safety of the ship. Although, as Webster and Noah write, duties varied for coasters, deepwater merchant vessels and fishing schooners, they generally included hiring, overseeing, disciplining, and replacing crew members; repairing and maintaining vessels; keeping cargo safe and secure, trading it to advantage and replacing it with valuable cargo at each port of entry, and dealing with customs. For fishing vessels, it meant knowing how to find fish and catch, clean, and preserve them until they could be offloaded and sold. "The captain also acquired fresh provisions for the crew and saw to their medical needs."[89]

Below, I list the Arey children's, grandchildren's, and great grandchildren's vessel ownership to show how quickly the second and third generation moved into fishing and coastal trading, and the energy with which the men bought and sold boat shares.[90] This remarkable list is doubtless incomplete.

1811 Second son, Ebenezer Arey, co owns with Josiah Phillips the 9-ton *Hurtle*; fourth son, James Arey, co-owns with Joseph Rider the 8-ton *Industry*.

1818 Ebenezer Arey skippers and co-owns, with Levi Dana of Boston, the 43-ton *Marvel*.

1821 Ebenezer Arey co-owns the 8-ton *Humbird*.

1820-23 Third son John Arey skippers and co-owns with John Carver the 20-ton *Olive Branch*.

1822-24 Ebenezer and John Arey co-own the 43-ton *Marvel*.

1824 John Arey skippers and co-owns with John Vinal the 20-ton *Olive Branch*.

1824 First, John Arey is sole owner, then co-owns with Thomas Arey II the 21-ton *Herring*.

1824-1827, Fifth son, Crosby Arey, skippers and co-owns with William Witherle of Castine the-20 ton, *Betsy*.

1824 Ebenezer Arey is one of six co-owners of the 23-ton *Volant*.

1827 First son, Isaac Jr, co-owns with John Vinal and John Arey Jr., the 22-ton *Dolphin*, which John Arey Jr. skippers.

1830 to 1840 John Arey Jr skippers the 26-ton *Rainbow*, which he co-owns with Thomas Arey II (1830); with Isaac Burgess (1832), another Arey grandson; and with John H. Jarvis and William Witherle of Castine (1840).

1830 Thomas Arey II and Abra[ham] T. Jacobs co-own the 30-ton *Siro*.

1830 Thomas Arey II and Thomas Arey III are among 4 co-owners of the 10-ton *Chebago*. Thomas Arey II skippered this vessel in 1829.

1830 Sixth son Thomas Arey owned a share of the 21-ton *Two Brothers*.

1831 Ebenezer Arey and John Arey co-own the 21-ton *Herring*, with and John Arey II as skipper.

1831 Lewis Arey and Reuben Carver co-own the 36-ton *Constitution*.

1831 John Arey co-owns with Joseph Lane the 44-ton *Calypso*.

1831 Philip Arey co-owns the 20 ton *Rainbow*.

1832 John Arey owns a share of the 21-ton *Two Brothers*.

1832 Lewis Arey skippers and co-owns with Reuben Carver the 36-ton *Otis*.

1833 Lewis Arey and Silas M. Arey co-own the 23-ton *Horatio Nelson*.

1833 Rufus Arey and James Arey in Thomaston own 1/7th share of the 83-ton *Mirror.*

1836 Reuben Carver owns the 38-ton *Volant*, with James Arey skipper.

1837 Thomas Arey and James Fernald co-own the 33-ton *Trumpet*.

1838 Thomas Arey, Reuben Carter and John Smith own the 50-ton *Three Sisters* (skippered in 1836 by Thomas Arey Jr.).

1840 Thomas Arey co-owns with Joseph W. Sylvester the 35-ton *Martha Ann*.

1844 Mark Arey is skipper and co-owns with Joseph Lane, William Clater and Josiah Coombs the 33-ton *Rushlight*.

1845 Mark Arey co-owns with Joseph Lane the 30-ton *Banner*. (Note: Mary Arey is said to be Master. It is likely, but not certain that Mark is Master.)

1849 An "Arey" skippers the 199-ton *Manitou*.

To follow other branches of this extended family, we turn to Isaac and Mary's daughter Deborah, who married Uriah Luce. They had six children by one account, two daughters by another. Uriah's brother, Malatiah, fished and coasted. Mary and Isaac's daughter, Hannah Arey, married Jonathan Burgess. They had fourteen children, including eight sons. Jonathan, his brother, and their sons also owned shares in vessels and went to sea, as shown below.

1811-12 and **1815-16** Jonathan and Ezekiel Burgess co-own the 11-ton *Swallow*, with Jonathan as Master.

1831 Ezekiel Burgess (son?) co-owns the 20-ton *Eliza*.

1844 Henry Burgess co-owns and skippers the 27-ton *Aurora*.

1844 William M. Burgess co-owns with Benjamin D. Gay of Castine the 35-ton *Gay*. William is its skipper.

1844 William M. Burgess is one of four co-owners of the 35-ton *Oriole*.

1845 William M. Burgess and John Lindsay co-own the 44-ton *Torpedo*.

Evidence of the Arey family's transformation into fishermen and business-men can also be seen in a significant 1833 petition written by Fox Island vessel owners. Thomas, Mark, Rufus and Freeman Arey, together with William, Henry and Ezekiel Burgess were among the signatories. The vessel owners were angered by the high cost of marine insurance—and the high risk of not carrying insurance. Even when shared among several investors, they considered investing in vessels to be unsustainable without more affordable insurance coverage. As remedy, they proposed founding a Mutual Marine Insurance company for Vinalhaven to cover sea losses up to 75 percent of vessel worth at least $25,000. Wayne O'Leary notes that this effort may have led to the first mutual insurance company in the United States devoted to cov-ering fishing risks. It's unclear whether it endured more than briefly. How-ever, it signifies that islanders had amassed the capital to go beyond small, home-built vessels and invested in and operated large schooners capable of engaging in offshore fisheries.[91]

The Arey family's move from lumbering and farming to the sea ventures illustrates how a family, working together, were able to take advantage of new opportunity. Isaac's descendants transitioned to fishing and trading as soon as they could. But the family's early roots, their relative affluence, and the money available to the second and third generation suggest that—as with the Carvers—an established, supportive family was virtually a prerequisite for pursuing significant new business ventures. With each passing genera-tion, islanders intermarried and became entwined by kinship. Familiarity and knowledge of someone's character from long experience built firsthand trust or distrust, and this extended beyond the local community to other ports. The large web of personal connections contributed to the success of busi-ness ventures. We may no longer be able to easily imagine how personal it once was.

Meanwhile, the fishermen delivered barrels and baskets of fish to John Carver's store to pay for indigo, molasses, coffee, and rum. What a common sight dried, smoked, fresh fish must have been all over town before the Civil War.

Timothy Dyer's Halibut

Vinalhaven in the Early-Nineteenth Century

In 1893, a ninety-year-old Vinalhaven fisherman climbed into his dory and rowed out onto the bay alone. He dropped his fishing line into the water, and, after some time passed, hooked a 332-pound halibut. A very old person and a huge fish. By all rights, the halibut should have snapped the line, or wearied the aged man, or tipped the boat.

Instead, Timothy Dyer, hauled it in, killed it, and rowed six or seven miles home towing it in the water behind him. The feat was remarkable enough to warrant a newspaper story in the *Rockland Courier Gazette*.[92] Although Dyer caught the halibut at century's end, his family's story offers a different glimpse of fishing on Vinalhaven in the early nineteenth century.

Timothy Dyer was born in December 1803 in Provincetown, Massachusetts. He moved as a child with his family to Vinalhaven in 1814. Unlike Isaac Arey or Thaddeus Carver and born half a century later than either of them, Joshua Dyer, Timothy's father, was a fisherman with little wealth when he and his family arrived. Times were hard. The lead up to the War of 1812, and the war itself, had brought embargoes and troubles that made it difficult to sell fish.

At the beginning of the nineteenth century, a fisherman's life on Vinalhaven was modest. O'Leary observed about the typical Maine fisherman of the era, "His business, if he was an entrepreneur, was in most cases small."[93] As the reporter wrote about Timothy's childhood, "*Mr. Dyer says that in those early troublesome times, the battle for subsistence was a hard one and that his family suffered many hardships and privations. He avers that he himself had never worn a shoe of any kind until he was 18 years old.*"[94]

Timothy's childhood years were tough ones for many in Maine, and particularly for fishermen. In 1805, the first Vinalhaven vessel sailed for Labrador to handline for cod. Because Labrador possessed protected harbors, crews could sail small island boats into them, set anchors, and fish right off the decks sheltered from the trials of more open seas. Vinalhaven's Labrador fishery peaked in the 1840s but disappeared a decade later because of changing market demands.[95]

In 1807, seven years before the Dyers arrived, the state's economy took a turn for the worse when President Jefferson imposed a trade embargo to counter Great Britain's refusal to acknowledge American rights at sea. Loss of trade with Canada and the West Indies—the two favored trading destinations for Maine vessels—was disastrous.

Coastal Maine was impoverished and the War of 1812 made the economy worse. "*In Portland, seeing ragged and half-starved children roaming the streets, ships rotting on the wharves, and unemployed men became common. The people of Portland endured watered rum, sanded sugar, and short weighted flour and crackers.*"[96]

We know little about what the early Vinalhaven fishermen experienced during Jefferson's Embargo. Penobscot islanders may not have suffered as much as some people. Robust smuggling mitigated its impact. Historian Harvey Strum writes, "The inhabitants of the Penobscot Bay area so flagrantly violated the law that President Jefferson issued a statement condemning the residents of the Penobscot for their disrespect . . . In January 1809 alone ten vessels escaped from the Penobscot and evaded capture."[97]

An 1808 story about nearby Isle au Haut shows how wild times could get, and reminds us just how weak state and federal authorities were when island citizens disagreed with their decrees. The story goes that a Maine coastal vessel was smuggling food supplies when they were boarded by customs agents and their cargo taken. The "collector of customs" at Castine "deposited some captured flour and rice" on Isle au Haut "and sent five men to stand guard." Five men were too few. "The schooner *Peggy* with a crew of fourteen men from Eastport and Buckstown landed on the island. After killing one of the guards, the smugglers escaped—for the moment—with 150 barrels of flour and rice."

A "posse of volunteers" gave chase: After "a ten-mile race, the revenue cutter caught the *Peggy* and captured the fourteen smugglers," likely unemployed fishermen and sailors. "Eight of the smugglers were indicted for murder . . ." It looked like the jig was up. "[B]ut in mid-November a band of fifteen armed and disguised men broke into the Castine jail and released the eight men, who successfully made their escape."[98]

We would know little else about Timothy Dyer's youth except for the serendipitous survival of a separate 1884 newspaper story about his father, Joshua Sr.[99] In it, Joshua recounts his version of the family's early days on White Island, right off Vinalhaven, and about how he began trading fish:

"In the fall of 1814, I, with my wife and family, consisting of four children, . . . left Cape Cod, and arrived here all right; leaving my family for a few days, I went to the White Island, and built a camp out of such material as I could find there. After days of hard labor in getting ready, I moved my family there, taking for provisions two bushels of meal, [a] half bushel of potatoes and a few dry fish, also a scanty supply of bedding and a few cooking utensils."

This was a daring thing to do in the last year of the War of 1812. By the end of 1814, the British had taken control of northeast Maine, and once again occupied Castine. Local settlers skirmished with the enemy as heartily as they had with their own customs agents. In 1813, a famous story has it that Vinalhaven fishermen showed their stuff after the British privateer *Fly* captured the 90-ton American schooner *Oliver* sailing out of Rockland on its way to Boston.

The British privateer herded *Oliver,* and two other vessels they had snatched, across the bay to a harbor on the south side of Vinalhaven. The *Fly* intended to use the shelter of the island to transfer goods from the other two boats to the *Oliver* and make off with it and the looted provisions. *"In this secluded spot, in anticipation of uninterrupted security . . . the privateer commenced putting on board the Oliver the goods taken from the other two prizes."*[100]

Vinalhaven fishermen watched the vessels tying up in their harbor. Grabbing their guns, a group quietly gathered nearby out of sight. When the time was right, they challenged the *Fly* and, with two well-aimed bullets, killed its captain. The shock of having their leader suddenly felled panicked the British sailors. All 75 fled the deck. The *"brave and hearty fishermen"* ordered the boat to land and almost captured it. But the British rallied, cut the line, and drifted away out of reach.[101]

Under these treacherous conditions, did Joshua Sr. purchase or simply grab his acres on White Island? He doesn't say. He does say the first winter was rough. Newly arrived, the family had no time to clear land or harvest and store provisions before winter froze them in.

Joshua Sr. dug clams.

"The winter was a very severe one, and as my principal article of food was clams, I had hard work at times to procure enough to keep my family from going hungry; being very often obliged to cut through ice to get the necessary supply."

The family was saved from hunger by an amazing feat, *"Having some powder shot, and an old Queen's arm flint-lock gun, I managed one day to bring down 48 birds in two shots. This may seem extraordinary, but it was so. I was a good shot, and as the flock was very large and were trying to alight in a hole that had not been frozen over, and as the hole was already full of birds that appeared very reluctant to leave, is all the explanation I can give. I salted the birds, (dippers and whistlers) and managed to get through the winter."*

The story is told like a parable, and Joshua may have remembered it decades later both because of the extraordinary number of birds, and how close to starvation his family had been.

Fortunately, the spring of 1815 brought the end of the war and liberated Penobscot Bay from British occupation. Joshua's account ends in two favorable episodes of trading and selling fish.

"One day in spring I went with my oldest boy [Timothy] in a small boat, fishing, and had the good luck to get a few. On my return, I found a sloop of war at anchor. On going alongside the commander invited me aboard, telling me at the same time that peace had been declared, the first news I had heard since the fall before." (No news in half a year!)

Joshua Sr. quickly proposed to trade their fresh caught fish. *"The people on board were glad to exchange pork and hardbread for my fish."* His success encouraged him, *"Feeling pleased with my trip, I went out again and got a good fare, carried them to Castine, and exchanged for provisions, amounting in all to about forty dollars. I returned home, feeling happy in the thought that I had some good food for my family."*

We can feel Joshua's relief when the British occupation ended. He could move freely on the water again, deliver fish to Castine, bring cash and food home, and mitigate his family's privation. If he indeed received $40 worth of provisions, we might imagine that the people he sold to in Castine were as hungry as he had been.[102]

After 1819, as described in the last chapter, the fishing trade began to come into its own on Vinalhaven and generally in Penobscot Bay. Although he possessed little wealth, by 1819 Joshua Dyer co-owned, with Charles R. Tilden of Castine, and captained a small 7-ton vessel named *Jane*. In 1824 Timothy and Joshua were listed as co-owning the 14-ton, *Ursamia,* with Timothy as captain. Both were built on Vinalhaven, perhaps by the Dyer men. We do not know. However, it seems that Joshua Sr. and Timothy had begun seriously fishing for cod, and perhaps also for herring. In 1850, the US Census lists Timothy, forty-seven, Joshua, age sixty-nine, Timothy's brother, Joshua, age forty, and Joshua's seventeen-year-old son, Reuben B., all as active fishermen, but none of them appears to own shares in a vessel.[103]

Fishing grew and finances improved not only because trade had been restored, but because, as noted, in 1819 the cod bounty was extended to the smaller schooners often found on Maine islands. O'Leary writes "These vessels were crucial to the development of the state's fisheries. They were small and inexpensive (about forty feet registered length) and carried only four or five crewmen."[104]

These smaller boats were big enough to sail east and fish offshore for weeks at a time. They could be built locally, and owning one meant that entrepreneurs without much capital or experience had a "starter boat." Bounty money could be used for repairs or to outfit them for a season without taking on too much debt. And because of the New England tradition of "fishing for shares," where a predetermined formula decided each fisherman's share of the vessel's total earnings from fishing, five-eighths of the bounty went to the crew.[105]

One consequence of the burgeoning fishing and trade was the exposure to more illness. An 1820 island gravestone reads—"Mary wife of Samuel Calderwood Died Nov. 5, 1820—beside her repose her 10 children." Sidney Winslow wrote, "At the right of the headstone are ten little white marble headstones that mark the graves of her children. Several of these children died in infancy but the others and including the mother, died with a disease which was then known as ship fever [typhus] and which they contracted from the crew of a vessel who were suffering from the disease.

"The vessel with several sick men on board anchored in a cove near the Calderwood home and several of the men were taken to the house so that they might get better care. Mrs. Calderwood was the first to contract the disease to which she soon succumbed."[106]

When Timothy Dyer was coming of age, Vinalhaven was growing. The 1790 census listed 578 inhabitants. By 1810, the census counted 1411. Ten difficult years later the island had added 264 more residents. As Maine was achieving official statehood in 1820, two men wrote descriptions of the Fox Islands. In 1819, Benjamin Beverage visited the Fox Islands and concluded that "the town has many good harbors, and considerable fisheries are carryed [*sic*] on both in the Cod and Herring fisheries."[107] Surveying both Vinalhaven and North Haven—since they were still technically one town—Beverage wrote, "There are three Stores, about seven hundred tons of Vessels from 10 to 100 tons burthen mostly fishing Vessels, three Sawmills two Grist mills." He noted the growing of wheat, potatoes, corn and hay. "No part of the State produces better Beef parts, mutton, butter, and Cheese." There were, he observed, "ten paupers supported by the town."

In 1821, William Waterman described the South Island (Vinalhaven) as "Mountainous and barren" but added that "nature has in part compensated for this by reason of fine harbors: the great number of fish and mill privileges. The herring fishery is carried on here to great advantage."[108] Apparently, in spite of years of lumbering, Waterman found a healthy and harvestable spruce forest: "The growth of this Island being principally Spruce, affords plenty of spars which are often shipped to the Southern States for a market." Waterman counted "Ten Vessels of 50 tons and upwards." And a "large number of small Fishing Vessels, 5 tons and upwards."

A later estimate of the Vinalhaven fishing fleet during these years appears in George Brown Goode's 1887 report. "According to Mr. James Roberts [who worked caulking and sometimes partially provisioning island boats mid-century], Vinal Haven had twelve to fifteen sail of Chebacco boats ranging from 15 to 30 tons, engaged in the fisheries as early as 1817, the smaller ones fishing along the shore while the larger ones went to the Seal Island grounds and Brown's Bank. The fleet was gradually increased by purchase from Cape Ann and elsewhere and before 1830 a larger and better class of vessels had been brought to the town." Chebacco boats, built in the Chebacco district of Ipswich, Massachusetts, became popular after the American Revolution when fishermen needed to replace vessels destroyed during the war with inexpensive, quickly built craft that were typically between 24 and 48 feet long. "These were small, double-masted craft under 30 tons." Their decks were "ringed by cockpits, where fishermen stood and threw lines of baited hooks and hauled up fish. Below deck, there was a hold to store the catch."[109]

At about twenty-one (in 1828), Timothy Dyer married Susan Getchell (1808–1898). Timothy later claimed to have had but one serious illness in his whole life. *"About two years after his marriage Mr. Dyer . . . went through a surgical operation which was performed at Rockland."* Susan was apparently as hearty as her husband and lived to 90.[110] They were married for 66 years, until he died in 1894.

The Dyers raised seven children, two of whom became fishermen. Freeman C. Dyer (b. 1845) died at fifteen. The other six all married: Hannah Jane at the startling age of twelve, Susannah at fifteen, and the others before age twenty-one. They were a fertile brood and produced at least thirty-five children.

Still, five out of six Dyer siblings had lives several decades shorter than their parents, and none of them lived to eighty. Studies of nineteenth century US white mortality suggest that the Dyers were not unusual: By mid-century people died younger than earlier generations, and life expectancy improved only slowly after that.[111]

Daniel (b. 1829 - married at age 20) had ten children and worked as a fisherman; he died in 1886 at age 57.
Eliza (b. 1831 - married at age 18). Apparently, she had no children. She died in 1896 at 65.

Susannah *(b. 1833 - married at age 15) had eight children and died in 1888 at 55.*

Hannah Jane *(b. 1837 - married at age 12) had eight children and died in 1894 at age 57.*

Melzer T. *(b. 1844 - married three times, first at age 18) had nine children, and died in 1897 at age 53. At the time of death, he was listed as a stone cutter. Melzer enlisted in the Union army in 1862 and survived two tours of duty during the Civil War. This contributed to his ill health. A scrap of a record suggests he filed for benefits as a war invalid.*

Thomas A. *(b. 1848 - married at age 17) had three children and died in 1925, at age 77. He also served in the Civil War, but only for six months. The 1920 census notes that at age 72, he was working as a small boat fisherman.*[112]

Timothy fished his whole life. "[His] *vocation has always been that of a fisherman, which he follows to this day,*" the 1893 *Gazette* article continues, "*One day the past Summer 'Uncle Tim,' as he is familiarly called, astonished the people of Vinalhaven by bringing in a monster halibut that weighed 332 pounds, which he captured alone and in an open dory.*"

Dyer's catch was newsworthy not simply because of the fisherman's age and strength and skill. Bigelow and Schroeder write in *Fishes of the Gulf of Maine* (1953), "It seems that halibut heavier than 300 pounds always were rarities anywhere in the North Atlantic." And, as if confirming "Uncle Tim's" prowess, they note, "Halibut caught in shallow water are very active, usually starting off at great speed when they are hauled up from the bottom, and often spinning the dory around in their attempts to escape."[113]

Atlantic Halibut

Members of the flounder family, Atlantic Halibut are very big, thick, flat, chocolate-olive colored groundfish with eyes close together on the top of their heads. They are larger than any fish but tuna, swordfish and sharks; and one documented Gulf of Maine catch weighed almost 700 pounds. Halibut have huge appetites and need a fish-filled sea to thrive.[114]

Halibut were overfished in the 19th and 20th centuries, and their numbers declined radically. To this day, little is known about them or about their breeding habits. Since 2005, NOAA (National Oceanic and Atmospheric

Administration) has listed them as "*a species of concern*," noting that an average of 1,500,000 pounds a year of Atlantic halibut were harvested from 1893 to 1940, whereas less than 200,000 pounds a year on average were harvested from 1977 to 2000—a decline of 87%. In 2018, catch rose to almost 345,000 pounds. 52, 000 of those pounds were harvested in Maine. [115]

In 2007 and 2008, several Maine fishermen, including Steve Rosen on Vinalhaven, worked with the Maine Department of Marine Resources, fishing for halibut to weigh, measure and tag in an attempt to learn about them. The researchers set up 51 "stations" from which the fishermen fished – using bait, line, and 300 hooks per station, on longlines set out for between 5 and 24 hours.

The results were meager. A total of 15,300 hooks baited with herring or mackerel caught (tagged and released) a total of 47 halibut (as opposed to 1125 spiny dogfish sharks). They were tiny beside Timothy's. The average weight was just short of 29 pounds.[116]

4

The Heyday

Vinalhaven Fishing in the Mid-Nineteenth Century

Vinalhaven fishermen were at the heart of the mid-nineteenth century American fisheries. Initially, I imagined the island population as small-time farmers who fished, or fishermen who mostly fished inshore waters in Penobscot Bay. Many islanders fit that profile. But by the mid-1800s there were others who primarily fished for a living, sailing offshore far from home to make their catch.

Between 1840 and 1850 the United States population grew by almost 36%—and many immigrants settled in New England, ensuring a market for fish. Equally important to the ongoing growth of Maine's fisheries were the country's westward expansion, the sale of poor grade salt fish to cotton plantations in the American South, and the developing interest in luxury seafood like oysters and lobsters.

To accommodate this burgeoning trade, fishing schooners and wet-well smacks sailed in and out of Vinalhaven harbors. Herring smokehouses dotted its shores, and racks spread drying cod under the sun. Yards were active with men building and repairing schooners and boats, sails and nets, and constructing smaller crucial wooden items like boxes and barrels for smoked or pickled fish. On the docks, men landed the catch, and loaded full barrels onto vessels that would carry the cod, mackerel or herring all over the world, but first to Boston. [117]

In 1850, Vinalhaven boats landed $54,592 worth of cod, and produced an additional $4,400 of revenues from the manufacture of cod oil. The numbers are meaningful. First, because between the 1840s and mid-1860s, Maine caught half the nation's cod. And second, because Castine was the only port in Maine that, in 1850, registered higher revenue ($59,000) from cod than Vinalhaven. [118] In other words, at mid-century, the very small island of Vinalhaven was one of the most important cod fishing ports in the United States.

The fisheries, according to Goode, "continued to increase from year to year from the first settlement of the island to the middle of the present century (the 1800s). They were most prosperous between 1845 and 1858, when from ninety to one hundred sail were owned at Vinal Haven, and thirty-five or forty belonged at North Haven. Probably four-fifths of these were under 50 tons, carpenter's measurement."[119] He adds, "These vessels usually fitted at Castine, but cured their fish at home, and sold them to the Boston dealers."

Records show that some Vinalhaven fishermen took part in the Grand Banks cod fishery, the Gulf of St. Lawrence cod fishery, the Labrador cod fishery, the Western (Sable Island Bank) cod fishery, the Quereau Bank (Banquereau) cod fishery, the Cape Sable and "Cape Shore" cod fishery, and the Bay of Fundy cod fishery. They also took part in the Gulf of St. Lawrence mackerel fishery, and the Northern (New England Shore) mackerel fishery. And they always fished for lobster and herring.[120]

LOBSTERS

Lobsters were large and abundant when the early European explorers arrived. In 1605, James Rosier of Weymouth's expedition noted a wealth of them: "Towards night we drew with a small net of twenty fathoms very nigh the shore; we got about thirty very good and great lobsters . . . [which] sheweth how great a profit fishing would be. . . ." Rosier's enthusiasm was premature; it would take over two centuries before anyone became seriously interested in buying them.[121]

Lobsters are delicate and their meat spoils quickly. They need to be cooked while alive. The critical piece of equipment, invented as the nineteenth century began, was the "lobster smack," a small sailing vessel with an open "well" drilled full of holes. Cold seawater ran through the openings in the well and kept the creatures alive en route to market. By the 1840s Vinalhaven fishermen were selling lobsters to traders with smacks. Elisha Oakes ran a smack for a while in that decade, regularly buying about 40,000 lobsters from five or six lobstermen on the islands during each four-month season and selling them in Boston to the firm Johnson and Young.[122]

The fresh market supplied by the smacks made little dent in the lobster population, but that changed thanks to the development of the tin can. Around 1810, inspired by their mutual animosity, both the English and the French figured out the basics of canning food: the two countries were at war and each desperately needed a reliable food supply to feed men battling at sea or on land.

The new technology quickly crossed the Atlantic, and by 1840 the Maine coast was dotted with small canneries. The first one on Vinalhaven opened in 1847, but it lasted only briefly. In 1866, a second lobster cannery opened and lasted twenty-one years under three different owners. Lobster canneries encouraged a fishery targeting small lobsters that fit neatly into cans. This led in turn to minimum size regulations to enable lobsters to grow to maturity. These early Maine lobster conservation efforts were not well enforced; nevertheless, they contributed to most lobster factories closing by the early 1890s.

HERRING

Although cod quickly became the most important commercial fish for Vinalhaven, the herring fishery started first and continued steadily after markets for salt cod began to decline.

Some of the earliest settlers built weirs to catch herring, and the practice continued until inshore herring disappeared in the 1950s. In 1880, the US census listed 221 weirs in Penobscot Bay alone. Building them by hand was arduous work. A 1900 report offers a picture applicable to earlier times. "The weir is made of brush and poles. Stakes to form the body of the weir are driven about three feet apart." These stakes could be eighteen to thirty-five feet long, depending on the water depth, and six or seven inches in diameter. To be sturdy enough to last the summer, each one had to be pounded six feet into the mud, a challenging task. "Brush is then woven in and out between the stakes alternately. There is a wing extending from the body of the weir towards the shore."[123]

Typically starting sometime between early April and late May, men felled young trees and dragged them out of the woods and down to the water; they worked while the tide was out, sometimes over weeks or months. Laws governing weirs required that they be dismantled by a certain date in the autumn; thus, they were rebuilt each year, though some materials could be recycled.

The wing of the weir created a barrier between the shore and the trap. Fish swimming near the shore were stopped and "conducted into the weir, which is circular—and slightly mazelike." Once in, they couldn't leave: "the entrapped fish will swim round and round without discovering the entrance."[124] At low tide, when shallow water concentrated the fish into a smaller space, fishermen would gather or "pocket" them, and dip or haul them out.

Weirs are always ready to catch fish, but they lie empty until a school wanders in. "The location of a weir . . . is one of the purest gambles in the whole aleatory fishing industry. Fishermen never tire of telling about worthless weirs which have been located within a few rods of the best weirs on the coast." A weir man might earn as much in two or three good days one year as he earned in several less successful years. "The production of even the best weirs is sporadic. . . ."[125]

Waiting for herring to swim into your weir was tolerable when you didn't own a vessel, but not so good if you needed a reliable source of fish for bait or trade. Still, when inshore herring were abundant, weirs could trap them with little risk or cost.

By the mid-1820s, Vinalhaven fishermen also pursued herring in Penobscot Bay and further north. Vessels from the Fox Islands were regularly sailing six or seven hundred miles to the Magdalen Islands in the Gulf of Saint Lawrence. The height of the Vinalhaven herring fishery was between 1840 and 1850, when eight or nine island boats sailed north each spring. The fishermen both caught and purchased herring. "The crews often purchased their fish from the natives, though this practice was not universal, and many of them 'went on shore,' catching, salting and smoking their fish, and carrying them to Boston to be marketed."[126]

Why take the risk of traveling to the Magdalen Islands? Because the northerly specimens were more abundant in early spring—and larger. Once smoked, 30 filled a box, as opposed to 40 or 50 of those caught closer to home. (There was some local fishing as well as the weirs.) Additionally, when the long winter was finally ending, many islanders needed income. They couldn't afford to wait for the fish to come to them. Fortunately, O'Leary points out, the Magdalen fishery was well-suited for small boats like the ones from Vinalhaven. The Gulf of the Saint Lawrence was a relatively sheltered place to fish and could be reached by sailing near the coast. Trips began in April and were over by May, so fishermen didn't have to stay out too long; they were home in time to plant spring crops.[127]

An unconsidered aspect of herring fishing was the pleasure watching it gave spectators. Herring, Lorenzo Sabine noted in his 1853 report, were mostly fished in Maine bays using "lighted torches, made of the outer bark of the white birch." Torchlight drew the school in pursuit of the boat. "A boat requires four men; one to dip, two to row, and one to steer," Sabine wrote. "While in pursuit, the boat moves with great velocity, that the fish may be induced to follow the light, and that they may be kept within reach of the man with the net, who stands in the bow."[128]

Often, many boats worked at once in a small area; their undulating lights and shifting reflections drew people out of their homes to the shore. Watching the "movements of the 'herring-drivers,' has been a recreation there, for some, for years . . . The spectator sees a spacious harbor, and the coves and indentations in its neighborhood, mostly beautifully lighted up, as with hundreds of lamps, and each light heaving and falling with the motion of the sea. Far in the offing the torches, no larger to the eye than a candle's flame, move and dance, approach and cross each other, and then vanish away. . . ."[129]

We are lucky for Sabine's account. What records we have from the mid-nineteenth century Penobscot Bay fishing most often pertain to business transactions, catch numbers, bits of family news, stories of shipwrecks—but not occasions of bystander delight. In such moments, pursuing herring became a different type of communal pleasure. Fishermen's kin and neighbors gathered and watched, enchanted by the glimmer of distant torches.

When the island fishermen landed herring from the Magdalens, they sometimes sold directly to Boston fish merchants, other times to traders on Vinalhaven. "The herring were landed on the island, where the bulk of them were smoked. Some crews contracted their catch in advance to the Vinal Haven dealers, agreeing to land their cargoes at a stipulated price."[130]

Captain David Vinal (1811–1886) was an important trader in the island fishing business who did very well marketing both herring and cod. We know little about the daily workings of his business, but several letters offer a single glimpse. One written to Vinal concerns a sales transaction: on December 30, 1841, James R. Jewett—apparently a dealer who sold herring in Boston—wrote to Vinal about money Jewett owed him. The letter's tone is defensive, awkward and apologetic.

The letter offers an idea of the expenses of herring fishing, the informality of selling arrangements, and the small profit this time for Vinal, whose herring made up one part of a larger sale in Boston. As was standard practice, Jewett collected herring from a number of fishermen and traders to gather enough to transport. His letter is vague and suggestive of loose arrangements.

"The reason that I have not written you before is that I expected to see you in Boston. I told Father to settle with you. I had forgotten your given name but I should have sent you this week if I had heard from you."

Jewett offers details of the sale—or at least his effort to recreate it. *"We had 3100 boxes in all we allow 6 boxes to the barrel. According to our calculation we had 520 barrells. I suppose we had about 450 barrells out of other seines and nets. We sold our Herrings for $40 on an average. We shared $72.00. We had 6 ½ hogshead of salt . . . amounting to $14.30. Leaving you $8.30. I am sorry that I did not see you and caused you some trouble."*[131] Vinal may have had to pursue Jewett to get paid.

Two expenses are illuminating about the larger herring fishery. The first, "we shared $72.00" refers to the money paid to the crew of a fishing vessel under the share system. Shares, as opposed to wages, were a common feature of nineteenth century New England fisheries (mandated by law in the cod fishery). Under this system, crew members were not paid by the hour or the trip. They worked as independent contractors. They arrived on board with their own gear, and collectively paid a percentage—often five-eighths—of the cost of outfitting the schooner for the voyage. Once vessel expenses (supplies like salt) provided by the owners and other costs were subtracted, the crew received five-eighths of the profit made selling the fish. Percentages varied by time, place and fishery.[132] The share system could be harsh when a voyage yielded little or nothing at all; but generally, it felt fair to fishermen and kept everyone on board invested in the success of the endeavor. It still is the norm in the island lobster fishery.[133]

Jewett's deduction of the cost of the hogsheads of salt reminds us how critical salt was to nineteenth-century fisheries. Thousands of years ago Egyptians figured out that they could preserve fish with salt, which removed moisture and killed bacteria. With almost no fat in its flesh, cod preserved particularly well with salt—better than herring. "Fat resists salt and slows the rate which salt impregnates fish," Mark Kurlansky explains. "This is why oily fish, after salting, must be pressed tightly in barrels to be preserved, whereas cod can be simply laid in salt. Also, fatty fish cannot be exposed to air in curing because the fat will become rancid. Cod, along with its relatives—including haddock and whiting, can be air-dried before salting. . . ."[134]

Efforts were made by early settlers to establish salt works (through boiling sea water) at Indian Creek, Calderwood's Neck, the Basin and other places on the island, but "it was a slow and tedious process, as it required about four hundred gallons of water to make a bushel of salt."

Slaughtered or hunted animals and birds also had to be salted, and it may be that domestic needs used up the small amounts initially available on Vinalhaven. The best quality salt came from Spain and Portugal. After the War of 1812, mainland traders— those in Castine in particular—imported enough salt to establish an adequate, high quality and reliable supply. By 1860, the wealthiest island traders may have been importing their own supplies.[135]

"Starting in the 1820s," Richard M. Ames writes, "Castine-based merchants developed their own version of the triangle trade to satisfy demand for massive quantities of salt required to cure fish caught by the Penobscot Region fishing fleet." On the first leg to southern ports, including New Orleans, Charleston, and Savannah, Castine vessels carried "fish, timber and farm produce," some of which likely originated on Vinalhaven. For the second leg, the boats carried cotton to Liverpool, England, or Le Havre, France. Then, either in Liverpool or Cadiz, Spain, they loaded salt to carry back to Castine.[136]

A second formal and likely official letter—a request by William Vinal (1817–1891) to his older brother, David, to appoint him an "Inspector of Fish," gives us a glimpse of two island brothers helping each other out, another example of the kin assistance at the heart of island entrepreneurial success. William had been smoking herring for a Captain Turner and promised Turner that David would transport the fish on his vessel, the *Oregon*. William apparently wanted to inspect and certify the cargo himself. In 1840 and 1845 David had served as Vinalhaven's Representative in the State Legislature. He was likely well connected in the state capital, and in a position to help William.[137]

The Inspector of Fish made sure that herring shipped to foreign ports was of good—or good enough—quality, which was not always the case. If fish were not salted promptly, handled too harshly, or poorly smoked, they spoiled or became inedible. "I have," noted Lorenzo Sabine, a man never short of opinions, "seen whole cargoes that, unfit for human food, were entirely worthless, except as dressing for grass lands."[138]

David Vinal prospered. By 1860 (the first census to record individual "worth") he was the fourth wealthiest man on the island with a total worth of $10,800. William apparently abandoned fish trading. In 1860 he was working as a joiner, and his real estate and personal estate were valued at $1,300.[139]

Because of its role as bait in the burgeoning cod fishery, herring fishing also contributed to mid-century strife between Vinalhaven fishermen and the Provincial Canadian authorities who patrolled waters near their rich fishing banks. Such struggles were nothing new, having occurred in colonial times.[140] The Convention of 1818, following the US victory in the War of 1812, mostly restored New England fishermen's access to fish in the waters around Nova Scotia, Labrador, the Gulf of St. Lawrence, and Newfoundland. However, it stipulated that American schooners fishing Provincial waters had to stay three miles from shore, except to make repairs or collect wood and water. Canadian fishermen did not want their American neighbors to deplete nearshore stocks. Great Britain sought to protect its fisheries by keeping foreign vessels away. But American fishing schooners couldn't carry enough water, wood, or bait for an entire voyage; and repairing storm damage sometimes required port facilities—so the exception was written in. It was in part to compensate for this three-mile restriction that the US Congress raised the cod bounty— which, together with the opening of post-war markets, ushered in "the golden age of the Maine fisheries."[141]

What created the strife? Although cod fishermen baited hooks with salted clams or "pickled" herring when they had to, cod preferred fresh herring, and herring was freshest when caught near the fishing banks. Herring schools often swam into coves at night and were easily netted in relatively shallow and protected shore waters—precisely those that the treaty designated off-limits. Not surprisingly, political boundaries drawn against their interests felt arbitrary and punitive to the fishermen. If herring crossed an invisible three-mile line, were fishermen supposed to stop in their tracks? And exactly how did the Provincial authorities measure that line, anyway?

Consequently, Vinalhaven captains and crews played frequent games of cat-and-mouse with Nova Scotian and other Provincial authorities. US schooners often surreptitiously sailed into inshore waters, caught the herring they needed, and slipped out again. Their boats were fast, and they didn't mind risking a chase.

These jaunts did not always go smoothly. In 1839, Vinalhaven Captain John Lindsey (1811–1858) master of the 37-ton *Magnolia*, assumed he could catch the herring he needed for cod bait, and easily outrun the slower Provincial cutters. He was mistaken.[142]

Trespassing boats faced the infamous Captain Darby, whose unenviable job it was to enforce the law. Darby's "cruising ground extended from the head of the Bay of Fundy to Halifax." In spite of the threat of arrest, "it was not uncommon for some of the Yankee fleet to dodge into the Tuskets." They would fish for bait on these little islands off the southern tip of Nova Scotia, intent on leaving before Captain Darby found them. "[O]nce they got the start twas 'farewell, Capt. Darby,' for his cutter was not a fast craft and the Yankee pinky would leave him far astern." A "pinky" [or "Pinkey"] was a small, fast, double-ended fishing schooner with pointed bow and stern. In 1839 it was the most commonly owned craft on Vinalhaven. Often they were built locally by crews of neighbors, including experienced boat-builders, who typically contributed their labor in return for a share in the ownership.[143]

One morning Captain Lindsey slipped in close to shore, caught bait, and got becalmed. No breeze; no escape. "Capt. Darby, who happened to be lying at anchor a short distance from the pinky, seeing the situation, manned his boat, and armed and equipped, boarded Capt. Lindsey and made a prize of the good pinky 'Magnolia' and some two or three other fishing vessels and took them up to Yarmouth." Darby meant business, "To prevent the retaking of them some dark night, he caused them to be stripped and the rudder unshipped."[144]

Seven years later (1846) in a letter filling David Vinal in on island news, John Carver writes about the departure of the fishing schooner, *Rival*, "Mr. Lindsey was carried on board drunk when they sailed after living a tea-totaler one year. How the mighty have fallen. Do all you can for the suppression of ardent spirits . . ." (He adds, "David Arey had his child scalded to death a short time ago.")[145]

The Lindsey family's fortune was not good. Possibly the "Mr. Lindsey" carried on board drunk was John's older brother Ephraim, also a fisherman, lost at sea in 1852. Ephraim's twenty-two-year-old son, Lewis, was lost with him. Another of Ephraim's sons, Joseph, had already died in 1849 at age twenty-one. Captain John Lindsey died in 1858, at the age of 47. In 1865, Ephraim's seventeen-year-old son, also named John Lindsey, (b.1848), died at sea when the fishing schooner *Northern Chief* got trapped in bad weather. The prime fishing areas on the offshore banks were often athwart the main steamer routes, but the seasick crew were too ill and exhausted to set a night watch. The steamer *Bosphorus* struck them mid-ship. Lindsey and four other Vinalhaven men drowned.[146]

Ship life was tough. An island captain's mix of piety and violence displays itself in an 1857 letter Captain David Lane Carver (1822–1902) sent home to his parents after hearing of his grandmother's death. David wrote from New Orleans, where he was loading goods aboard the Sch. *Eddystone* to deliver in Liverpool, England.[147] David at first rather stiltedly recalls happy memories from his island childhood. Then he reports on disciplining his crew, matter-of-factly creating order by instilling terror. The violence Carver describes might disabuse us of any remaining urges to sentimentalize nineteenth-century seafaring.

Dear Parents i received your letter last Sabbath . . .

It is a pleasant thing for a family to meet after a long absence from home. It remins us of the days of our childhood when we used to play Blind Mans Buff, hide and find, and all those old familiar plays that we was pleasd with and i think that Father and Mother was pleased to see us enjoy our selves and on. Grand Mother i fancy i can see her all most split her side with laughing at our jollity. But those days are gon never to return. Thare will be one missing. . . .

He continues,

My health is quite good much better than I fear it would be. You may think i have not much to do but your are mistacon. i never worked harder than aboard this ship. Twenty men to look after and keep strait and you know how discipline on shipboard is needful the first thing. i have to do it to get them afeard of me and then all is well but i have had no dificulty onely one morning they refused to turntoo (after I got in the river) when i shot one of them and threatened the rest and finely they thought it better to go work (which they did very quiet).[148]

From at least the 1830s to the early 1890s when steam power and iron or steel hulls became the norm, Maine was one of the leading shipbuilding states in the United States. Maine-built vessels supported a robust sea trade, which brought wealth to coastal towns. Vinalhaven followed the larger coastal pattern both in trade and boat building. Although many mid-century island fishing boats were built in Essex, Massachusetts, and the north island initially had more shipbuilders, from the eighteenth century to the present, the

South Island has been home to wooden boat builders and merchant traders. Examples include the *Barbara*, a 94-ton schooner built in 1804, *Agenoria* 54-tons, built in 1820, and the 97-ton *Cherokee* built by Reuben Carver and his carpenters in 1847.

Investors from the islands and the mainland[149] put up money to build fishing vessels because in 1850 the Gulf of Maine had plenty of fish and a robust market. "Dried salt cod was exported to the West Indies, pickled mackerel to the West Indies and urban markets along the eastern seaboard," writes Maine historian Stephen J. Hornsby. Some vessels (like D. L. Carver's) sailed to southern US ports or the Caribbean, especially during winter months when the Penobscot Bay Maine harbors were often frozen, most fishing was suspended, and the Southern yellow fever and hurricane seasons could be avoided.[150]

Islanders who stayed home also had more foods and goods available to them thanks to local vessels involved in distant trade. Knowing that David Carver had just been in Havana, and that he would visit other ports, his brother, Reuben, wrote him in February 1848, "I want you to fetch me some molasses and sugar if you can as well as not and a few Bbls of flour if you gow [*sic*] to any port where it can be purchased cheap and a lot of the oranges you spoke of." A bit later he added family news, "Mother . . . has failed more in one month than she has for five years I think."[151]

Hornsby's mention of the West Indian markets and Ames's of the triangle trade out of Castine remind us that, as was broadly true throughout New England, Vinalhaven's fish wealth mid-nineteenth century rested in part in Caribbean and Southern American slavery, as had some of the wealth from lumbering when the island was initially settled. Yes, most island merchants sold their lumber and fish to merchants in Boston; but we know that since the 17th century. Boston merchants had been deeply enriched by selling goods to southern colonies and Caribbean plantations. While much is unknown and maybe unknowable about the cargo and markets of vessels voyaging internationally from the island, we know just from the Carver letters that some island vessels traveled to sell fish in Southern ports or the Caribbean and brought molasses, sugar, and likely rum back to Vinalhaven. Furthermore, Carver's reference to loading in New Orleans for Liverpool suggests that he likely delivered cotton produced by enslaved people to English cotton mills as well. From Liverpool, though we do not know, he could have brought salt back to Castine.

COD

What did it mean that mid-century Vinalhaven had 75 to 100 fishing schooners that pursued cod? If you sail eastward from Vinalhaven you will encounter the fishing banks off Sable Island—which include Banquereau and, sailing past Cape Breton and southeast of Newfoundland, the Grand Banks themselves. Both banks fall within what is called the North Atlantic archway. When Europeans first arrived and for a long time after, Cod—*Gadus morhua*—was one of the most abundant fish they found, and potentially the most profitable.

Because of different water depths and different temperatures of currents in this part of the North Atlantic, the vast archway has historically been a remarkably productive fishing ground, as well as a place of turbulent water and weather. Naturalist and writer William Warner explains, "[T]he archway is a transitional zone between contrasting climates, where colliding weather systems create fog, storm, and occasionally, the freezing condensations so dangerous to all ships." He notes that the currents under the water are a "similar zone of conflict, in which shifting masses of water of markedly different temperatures shear against each other, producing turbulence and vertical mixing."[152]

Boats that sailed into the archway before the twentieth century always faced significant risk. Spring and summer were generally calmer than late autumn, but crews never knew what they'd encounter. As islanders gained enough wealth and market incentive to build slightly bigger vessels, and as they gained familiarity with the waters, some sailed eastward.

Around the time the Penobscot Bay fishing industry was taking off, an 1830 record from one island vessel shows the pace and intensity of a summer's fishing. *Two Brothers*, owned and captained by Matt Calderwood, made four round trip "cruises"—destination unspecified, but likely not too far since they made four voyages in one season and the crew was small. The first voyage left the harbor on April 15 and returned on June 26 with 84 quintals of cod. The second sailed June 28 and returned July 20 with 100 quintals. The third departed two days later, on July 22 and returned August 15 with 101 quintals. The final outing of the season sailed away on September 6 and returned September 25 with 25 quintals. The total from the four voyages was 310 quintals or 65,720 pounds of salted, dried cod, cured using 25 hogsheads of salt. The vessel was at sea for 163 days with only 26 days in port.[153]

Though not listed in the 1830 census, Matt Calderwood was born on Vinalhaven in 1802 and, at some point, served as a local fish inspector. John Calderwood, "the header," and David Calderwood "the throater " were islanders counted in 1830. "The salter," Ezekiel Brown, unmentioned in the count, was island born in 1804. Typically, the four men would fish all day, and then work into the night cleaning and salting down the fish. After the end of the season, when the fish were sold, the costs tallied, and the bounty collected, they would collect their shares. The wait for payment often outlasted family savings or their ability to barter for supplies, and, as we've seen in ledgers, island or shore businesses typically advanced credit.

Twenty-two years later, thanks to another log, we learn about two cod voyages made in one season. From 1852 until the cod subsidies ended in 1866, Federal laws required captains of fishing boats to keep logs of their daily catch and submit them to the local Collector of Customs in order to receive their bounty payments. This practice existed to prevent "bounty catchers" from claiming the subsidy without fishing hard enough: indeed, Midcoast Maine was well-known for "bounty catching."[154] A number of logbooks were saved, including one that records "Captain Carver's" 1852 trip to Banquereau, a fishing bank at the northernmost end of the Scotian Shelf fishing banks between Sable Island and Nova Scotia, in the schooner *Flying Arrow*. The logbook itself does not contain the captain's name; it was found serendipitously.

Captain Carver and his crew sailed from Carver's Harbor on **April 25, 1852**. Their voyage lasted two months. Carver's log is terse. He daily notes latitude, longitude, wind, and weather. When they meet up with other boats and exchange information, he may mention a detail or two. The captain carefully records each day's catch, rounding his numbers to the nearest 100.

The fishermen begin looking for cod on their fifth day out, "*no fish of any account*", but their first six days of effort yield them nothing. It is only on the eleventh day, **Wednesday, May 5**, that they finally hook some. "*This day light winds from the westward and clear weather caught 200 fish.*"[155]

In 1852, New England cod fishermen were still hand-lining from the decks of their schooners. In their study of the logs of voyages like Carver's, Jeff Bolster, Karen Alexander, and Bill Leavenworth describe how the boats sailed east "until they found the edge of the banks by sounding with a lead line. They tried for fish at intervals as they sailed or drifted across the banks until they found a place where fish were plentiful." They scanned the horizon for a "'sign of fish,' that is, flocks of piscivorous seabirds and/or many marine mammals, feeding."[156]

Once anchored, "each man fished with two or four hooks over the rail until the fish became scarce." The best fishermen were good indeed. "[A] skilled hand-liner adept at catching substantial numbers of large fish was an artisan with status by virtue of expertise."[157] Each fisherman had a separate "kid" which held his catch. Whenever he landed a fish, he'd call out to the captain who kept running tallies for all his men; the ultimate, individual, sub-division of "share" profit was based on each fisherman's total count.[158]

In order to qualify for the cod subsidy, a boat had to fish for 120 days a year. Whereas coastal fishing vessels accumulated their time in as many as seven short trips, called fares, vessels fishing distant water usually made two trips, the first in spring, the second in late summer and fall. The captain and crew sought to fill their hold and return home as quickly as possible, and they often fished in bad weather: **Tuesday, May 25**, "*This day first part light winds latter part strong gales from the Southard foggy on the [bank] caught 300 fish.*"[159]

We don't know how long they worked when fish were plentiful, but Goode describes a typical 24-hour day—referred to as fishing "watch and watch . . . The day and night were divided into watches of four hours each, half the crew being thus constantly occupied in fishing. While one watch was fishing the other watch was employed in dressing the fish and then in sleeping until they were called."[160]

The means of dressing the cod varied on different boats. This vivid passage gives us a sense of what it was like: "The 'throater' cut the throat across and tore out the tongue, ripped open the belly and cut in on each side of the head. The 'header' removed the liver, which was saved for the oil, drew out the entrails, and, breaking off the head, shoved the body along to the skipper. He was always the 'splitter.' With a wide-bladed knife he undercut and stripped out the backbone and then dropped the dressed fish into the hold. A fourth man, called the 'idler,' handed the whole fish to the throater, took away the tongues and livers, and when the cook was busy, took his place tending "the salter." Since salting the fish correctly was essential to preserving them well, good salters were esteemed.[161]

Cod guts and other waste, called "gurry," were tossed over the side. In enough bulk, gurry could scare off the fish. Writing home from the Grand Banks in 1857 to his family in Castine, nineteen-year-old fisherman Solon Hanson describes how gurrying from other vessels limited the week's catch, "We finished the week with 22,000 we might have had ten more if the vessels to the Southward of us had not gurried up our shoal."[162]

On **May 29**, Captain Carver's schooner arrived at Banquereau, and their catch numbers immediately improved with days of 1000 fish becoming typical. June 14 is so good that even the laconic captain is moved to metaphor: "**June 14**, *this day fine calm and pleasant and plenty of fish and big as horse caught 1800.*" Big cod were sought and preferred; fishermen used larger hooks to catch bigger fish.

Two days later, on **June 16**, they caught a final 800 fish. They've "made the trip" and their hold is full. They are "home ward bound," and "clearing up." **June 17**, "*At 7 AM got under way on Banquereau home ward bound all hands employed in clearing up—light winds from the south and foggy.*"

On **June 22**, they encounter the schooner *Maine* of Vinalhaven and note that it is carrying 250 "quintels" of fish (28,000 lbs.). Schooners crossed paths often and made a point of stopping to exchange news about fish, fishermen, current events, and other boats.

June 23 brings "*heavy showers of rain, with heavy thunder, and sharp lightening.*" Fortunately, they are close to home.

June 24, their last day. "*These 24 hours light breezes from the SW and clear weather at 4 AM came in to Carvers harbor Vinalhaven alongside the wharf. So end the 24 hours.*"

Even when safely back to port, their labors did not end. The pressing task was to unload the fish, wash them and re-salt them for drying or pickling. They needed prompt attention to guard their quality. The fish would be spread on "flakes" and dried on the island before getting packed and sold.

Sat., June 26, "*As yesterday as is today all hands employed taking out fish.*"

Sun., June 27, "*These 24 hours light winds and warm—all went to church.*"[163]

The vessel was at sea for sixty-one days and caught 24,600 fish. It was a very good haul, quickly "made." For comparison, the average schooner out of Beverly, Massachusetts, which went to Banquereau in 1852, stayed out for 78 days and brought back 26,000 fish.[164]

After spending two more days unloading, on **June 30** the Captain and crew sailed to Camden to fit out the schooner. The crew spent all of the gray, drizzly day of **July 1** filling their hold with salt and provisions. By 6 a.m. Saturday, **July 3**, they were back on Vinalhaven, and preparing to go to sea that night. "*At 6 PM all ready for sea.*" The winds did not oblige, so they waited—and enjoyed the holiday: "**July 5**—*this 24 hours light winds all round the compass all employed in celebrating the great day of independence.*"

They departed **July 7**, but this second trip was as unlucky as the first had been bountiful. Once on the water, they encountered the schooner *Superior* out of Beverly, Massachusetts. It had just come from Banquereau and reported that fish were "*scarce.*" Over the next few days, they spoke with other vessels and heard the same news. By **July 18**, they had only 500 fish to show for 11 days at sea.[165]

Things get worse. One foggy night they were "*standing*" on the bank, when the schooner *Petrel* out of Beverly struck them starboard. The impact broke the *Petrel's* mainmast into four pieces and damaged its bow. No one was reported injured, but all were likely shaken up.[166]

Monday **July 22**, they worked in the rain to repair their vessel, though the account reveals little. "*All hands employed in repairing Mainsail and bent it, on the foremast—killed A porpoise and had A time.*"

The journal ends abruptly on **July 26**, on Browns Bank, still with only 500 fish. They apparently abandoned the second trip, so neither the crew, the captain, nor the owners earned back their costs. Perhaps the log sat a century and a half in an island house because, lacking the 120 days at sea required for the bounty, there was no reason to turn it in.[167]

From the mid-1850s on, catch numbers fell steadily, and the cod caught were smaller. Some boats moved off Banquereau to the other banks, others started carrying more fishermen so they could fish more lines, and eventually many turned to the more dangerous dories and tub-trawls (long lines strung between buoys, holding hundreds or thousands of baited hooks.)[168]

Rosenberg et. al. looked at over 1700 schooner logs like Carvers to calculate the cod biomass on the Scotian Shelf in 1852, which they estimate to have been 1,260,000 metric tons. To put that number into perspective, they note that in 2002 the cod biomass was 4 percent of what it had been 150 years earlier. We also know that cod today are less than a third the size of those caught in the sixteenth century.[169]

Cod catch continued to fall. "[C]od landings from the Gulf of Maine decreased steadily, from about 70,000 metric tons in 1861, to 54,000 in 1880, to about 20,000 in 1900."[170]

What did the heyday of cod fishing mean to everyday life and work on Vinalhaven at mid-century? It touched everyone on the whole coast, really—those who went to sea and those who worked onshore. Thanks to a ledger kept by the island caulker and provisioner, James Roberts, from 1842 into the 1850s, we can get a more textured feel for harborside labors. Good examples are several of his transactions with the Schooner *Acteon* in 1853. On April 22 of that year, Roberts wrote a bill of sale in his ledger. It came to $21.85 and included half a day he'd spent caulking the boat. (He sometimes charged for caulking by the number of "tides" the job required.) The bill mixes together supplies he'd used making his repairs, and provisions he sold to the *Acteon*: ½ a qtl (quintal) of codfish plus a bbl (barrel) of bait for codfishing; ½ a lb of Ocum (oakum, tarred rope fiber for filling seams between the strakes, the horizontal planking on the hull); 75 lbs of lead (for ballast), 1 gallon of oil, 5 lbs of verdergreece (verdigris, used to color paint), 8 ft of "bords"(boards), 120 fathoms of line, 27 yards of net, (fishing) licenses, and the "youse" (use) of other nets, a fork (perhaps a two-pronged pitch fork for pitching cod out of the hold), and cork rope (which floated). The balance was paid in cash to him almost a year later on March 6, 1854.[171]

A Rockland newspaper from the mid-1840s expands on Roberts' ledger and tells us more about the diverse labors that went into getting ready for voyages. The article about outfitting in Castine describes the myriad of activity that serviced schooners like the *Flying Arrow*, and acknowledges that the vessels fitted out there were "principally owned by people living upon islands in the Penobscot Bay."

In the spring of 1845 about 300 sail of vessels were fitted at this place, for the bank and shore fisheries. These vessels were manned by crews, amounting to nearly 200 men and boys who are supplied with all, or nearly all their necessaries for a fishing voyage, such as glazed hats, oil clothes, fishing boots and clothing, nearly all of which are made in this town, thus giving employment to many poor women, as also to mechanics. An immense quantity of goods of various descriptions, are consumed by them, and more than 2000 tons of salt, which is imported direct from Liverpool and Cadiz, by ships owned there.[172]

Wherever schooners provisioned, it took a community to support a season of fishing trips. In 1850, 1252 people lived on Vinalhaven: 608 females and 644 males. There were several small villages scattered across the island, but, according to one later visitor who reflected back to the decade's beginning, little prosperity was yet visible, "Carver's Harbor, the largest village, had but a half dozen unpainted houses and an old school-house, and the roads were but little better than sheep paths. . ."[173]

The 1850 Federal census was the first that asked for the occupations of men 16 years old and older, a group I calculate to include 366 males, 198 of whom were listed as fishermen. Another 28 were listed as mariners. At least 226 men—or almost two-thirds of the adult male population—were catching fish or delivering them to buyers. However, boys often started fishing and working on boats well before they reached 16—some during the months they weren't in school, others full time. Records suggest that 274 boys under 16 lived on the island in 1850. Of these, 63 between 10 and 16 years old were sons of fishermen. Most fishing family youngsters fished, along with many of the sons of laborers, farmers and residents with other occupations. The total number of island males participating directly in fishing was likely at least 300.[174]

In "supporting roles" the census lists two lighthouse keepers; two coopers who built barrels to transport fish; 1 caulker; and ten carpenters, many of whom likely spent a portion of their time either building boats or repairing them. Five men in the 1850 census called themselves merchants, and some, if not all of them traded in fish. There were two shoemakers and one tailor, who may have supplied clothing for seagoing men. The island's fifty-one farmers likely sold provisions to ships, or to women feeding families while their husbands were at sea. I imagine the single "millman" ground grain to be eaten and/or milled lumber to be turned into herring boxes or other necessary items. Beyond his sermons, the island's Methodist clergyman likely comforted seamen in port, and families whose men were at sea.

Fishermen farmed and farmers fished, so the single word listed beside each man's name in the census tells only part of the story. For example, in the 1850 census, Reuben Carver called himself a farmer, but we know he built boats, inspected fish, and traded. In 1850, thirty-six Vinalhaven men called themselves laborers, a broad category which included several men who owned hundreds of acres of property, as well as much poorer men. No doubt some laborers fished, unloaded fishing boats, or worked at other fish-related tasks.

As far as records reveal, no women or girls fished on schooners. On the other hand, Maine captains of distant water vessels, who could be absent from home for six months to several years, sometimes took their wives and families with them. David Lane Carver, whom we last met in New Orleans, took his wife, Jane (Ginn), with him in 1874 on a voyage to an island off the coast of Peru called "Leobos de Terre" (Lobos de Tierra) to get guano—sea bird excrement, deposited so deep on some South American islands that it could be mined, then packed in the vessel's hold and brought back to be used for saltpeter or fertilizer.

Living in Bucksport in 1857, Jane—like so many island women—had to bear her worries when David was very far away.Writing to parents on Vinalhaven she tells them, "Since I wrote to you I have had 3 letters from India one dated August 21st stating David had been sick with ship fever for the last fortnight but had so fare recovered that he was able to attend to his duty. . . ." An anonymous note in the Historical Society offers a glimpse of Jane: "Capt. David's wife, Jane, often accompanied him on his voyages. At one time, when there was mutiny on board, Mrs. Carver helped the captain place a man in irons. Another time, when Capt. David was ill, Mrs. Carver was placed in temporary command of the ship and took her into port."[175]

The absence of evidence about the direct involvement Vinalhaven women in fisheries could reflect our lack of records as much as their degree of participation. Applebee's notation that "Mary" Arey was briefly Master of the *Banner* is likely a typo for "Mark." On Vinalhaven, Emma L. Berry is listed as co-owner of the 76-ton schooner *Harvester* in 1884, and Annie Pulk is listed as sole owner of *The Breeze*, an 11-ton sloop in 1910. Other Maine mainland records are suggestive. [176] We know, for example, that Plina (Paulina) Grant of Surry was listed as owner of the *Rozella*, a schooner captained by her husband, Thomas Grant, in 1853. And on Blue Hill Bay, a woman played an important role in the cod fishery. M. J. Berry, listed as shoreman for the *Water Witch*, a small schooner out of Trenton, was Mary Berry, the wife of the captain, Albert Berry, listed in the 1860 Census as a caulker.[177] As shoreman, Mary was directly responsible for the quality of the cod the *Water Witch* sold that season, and she got the shoreman's share of the profits.

On land, then as now, island women were crucial to fishing success. Not until 1860 did census-takers ask about women's work, so to glimpse the situation in 1850 we have to extrapolate from the later document. In 1860 on

Vinalhaven, 33 females over 16 described themselves as "seine makers" who made fishing nets used for catching herring, mackerel or other smaller fish. Some may have been at work in the 1850s. We know that by 1859 Thaddeus Carver was agent for the "Net and Twine Manufacturing Company of Boston." Thaddeus ran a local net factory that employed "eight to fourteen girls weaving" in their homes. Also in business by 1851 was a small lobster cannery run by J. B. Hamlin from Boston, which by 1860 employed seven females.[178]

Women in fishing families worked growing vegetables, milking cows, caring for farm animals, churning butter, baking, splitting wood for stoves, spinning wool for clothing, weaving, sewing, knitting nets, supervising and teaching young children, attending church and community gatherings, scrubbing clothes, tending the ill and aged, caring for paying boarders, shoveling winter snow, hauling water from wells, and attending to a multitude of seasonal tasks. Older children and kin often helped. All of these labors made it possible for the men to go to sea.

Excerpts from a letter by Charlotte Ginn Carver (McDonald) (1828–1916) to her father, John Carver, give a nice feel for domestic life, and also show how families sent news and kept in touch during separations. Charlotte seems to want her father to know she's doing her best to take care of his mother.

> *Vinalhaven Feb. 27ᵗʰ 1848*
> *School has been keeping four weeks and has three more to keepe our master is a first rate one. He boards to our house and Granmother fails very fast. She takes very little notice of anything. We have hade a very plesent winter indeed. . . . Business has been very lively here this winter. Everyone seems to have enough to do. We make plenty of buttere . . . and have sold $15 worth of buttere . . .*
> *I have just took up my pene to commence writing again after being in to help wash grandmother. She is very feeble. She knows no one hardly that come in . . . we will try to take as good care of her as if you were here with us. . .*
> *The rest of the family, have all gone to the temperance meeting this evening but me. Temperance is as lively as it was when you left.* [179]

That the others have "all gone" reminds us that homes often included many people; even if most of the men were away, the women were not alone.

Another indicator of the island's vitality is that between 1820 and 1870, Vinalhaven and North Haven together supported "thirteen curing yards." The yards received cod from the schooners, dried it outside on wooden racks, and shipped it. *"Four freighters were kept busy carrying the salted products to Boston."* It's not clear how many of these yards were on Vinalhaven or which islands each freighter serviced.[180]

We do know that by 1860, Timothy Lane (1805–1871) was the most successful fish merchant and curing yard owner living on the island. Like so many of his neighbors, his family had arrived in Massachusetts in the seventeenth century.[181] The Lane family tree is a challenge to untangle because the same names are shared by cousins and appear in multiple generations. Elizabeth Bunker of the Historical Society sorted it out and observed, *"This isn't a family tree anymore . . . it's a wreath!"*[182]

The image of a family "wreath" again underscores why, when 19th century islanders invested in businesses or schooners, they so often invested with brothers, sons, cousins or in-laws. When they fished, the person at the next station was likely related by blood or marriage. It's hard to overstate the extent to which individual endeavors built upon family ties. Just as the financial well-being of the cod fishermen rested partly on the federal subsidy, many other successful enterprises got their start from inherited wealth or land, and/or family investors.

Timothy's father, Benjamin Lane, Sr., was born in Gloucester and settled on Vinalhaven in the 1780s. He and his brother Issachar, (who came with him, but left soon after) each married one of Ebenezer Hall's granddaughters. In 1823, Benjamin Sr. was listed as co-owner of the 26-ton *Dolphin* with another brother, James, who lived in Gloucester. Benjamin was patriarch of an island family that has remained involved in the business of fishing until the present day. Emily Lane, who married into the family, ran a fish plant on the island and consults on lobster marketing in Portland.[183]

When Timothy's older brother, Joseph, grew up, he started a fish-curing business on Vinalhaven. In 1834, he was said to be the first person on the island to outfit fishing vessels. It's unclear how closely and long Joseph and Timothy worked together. By 1860, Timothy was the wealthiest man on the island according to the census. Timothy owned 10,000 acres of land and had a "Personal Estate" of $15,000, making a total estate of $25,000. Joseph listed himself as a farmer. He owned 2000 acres, a sizeable holding on the island, but claimed only $500 of personal estate.[184]

In 1859, the anonymous newspaperman for the *Democrat & Free Press* used Timothy's story to illustrate the island's success. Timothy, he explained, had "gone to sea in the coasting trade" at twenty-one (perhaps in the family schooner, *Dolphin*). He quit the sea in 1833. "In 1835 he commenced in the fishing business with a part of a small schooner. Soon after he began to trade. His first attempt was so small that the only counter he had was a wide board placed upon two barrels."

His business grew, "To-day however, he is the principal owner in twelve or fifteen vessels, which he fits from his own store, and the trade at his present counter, this year, will amount to $20,000. During the past season he has cured and carried to market more than four thousand quintals of fish. A few of these were not his own, but belonged to others who pay him one sixteenth part for curing and marketing." After noting Timothy's trade in fish oil, mackerel, halibut and pickled fish, the article concludes, "[T]he net amount of his fishing business this year has been $22,120—a very pretty business to be done on a little island across which a man might almost sling a stone, and in a place where people in general suppose nothing is to be found but peace and poverty."[185]

Generally speaking, while fishermen risked their lives at sea, traders made the real money. The 1860 census lists both the worth of a person's real estate, and the worth of his personal estate. (Family wealth is listed as the husband's unless a woman has been widowed.) In 1860, the island population was 1667 people, including children, living in 312 households (more than one family could live in a household).

> The four wealthiest men on the island after Timothy (age 55) were also traders:
> James Fernald age 65 - with a total estate of $17,000.
> Reuben Leadbetter age 66 - with $12,500.
> David Vinal age 49 - with $10,800.
> Reuben Carver age 62 – with $9,800.

I counted 266 master fishermen and fishermen listed as such in the Census, including a few as young as fourteen or fifteen. Of these fishermen, 163 possessed either real estate or personal estates, or both. Another 103, often but not always younger, had no real estate or personal wealth at all. Some lived with family so their earnings were pooled with the others. ($100 was the lowest amount listed.)

For fishermen with wealth, the average total wealth was $654. If you included all 266 fishermen, the average total was $400. Though their earnings were modest, their worth was considered respectable. By comparison, the traders were very wealthy indeed.[186]

However distributed, by the end of the 1850s a new prosperity had come to the island. The visiting observer noted, "Now Carver's Harbor is a trim looking village as one could wish to see, has five stores in and around it, a spacious school-house of the latest style, a fine packet to connect it with the rest of the world twice a week, and the hum of well-paid industry all about it."[187]

The Civil War started on April 12, 1861, and 180 men from Vinalhaven would serve in the Army and Navy before war's end. In a letter home from Liverpool dated September 6, 1863, Capt. David Carver tried to comfort his parents at the loss of one of his younger brothers, their son, Thaddeus.

Likely, everyone's grief was complicated by their shared memory: a decade earlier, in December 1853, David and his older brother Ebenezer both set out from Bucksport, Maine, one captaining a vessel that carried a load of coal, the other a vessel filled with lumber. They encountered a terrible gale that wrecked both of their vessels. David survived but Eben did not.

David writes,

> *Eben & Thaddeus are gone, taken away, both at nearly the same age leaving the same family and in the full bloom of health, but they are in Heaven where we all hope one day to meet them.*
>
> *Jane writes that brother Thaddeus was killed instantly; he did not suffer on the battlefield by wounds, neither is his bones bleaching [in the] hot sun but that he was buried.*[188]

Jane, apparently, had been told these details because her own brother, Horatio, was killed in the same battle at Port Hudson, Louisiana. (One cannot help but wonder how often family members were told that their kin did not suffer when it was not true.) The losses were not over, David's younger brother, Lafayette Carver, would die in June 1864 from wounds received in the Battle of Cold Harbor.[189]

In August 1862, David Vinal's son Woster Smith Vinal joined the 19th Maine Regiment and was present for duty at Fredericksburg, Chancellorsville, Gettysburg, and other battles. Along with two island friends, Alden Dyer and Joseph Norton, Woster was captured and imprisoned in June, 1864. Woster survived Andersonville Prison Camp in Georgia and returned to Vinalhaven, where he lived to 93. In 1870, still only 26 years old, Woster is listed as living in his father's home and working as a blacksmith. Years later, he wrote, "No one can know what our boys suffered, except the knowledge be had through bitter experience. It all comes back to me like an awful nightmare after all the years that have passed since the long months of hunger, sickness, and brutality."[190]

5

The Merchant Letters

One Fishing Family at Mid-Century

A small collection of letters written from 1851 to 1862 between a man and woman on Vinalhaven, first courting and then married, reveal the ups and downs and ongoing struggles of a mid-century island fishing family. They capture the weight on lives—and marriages—of physical distance and financial uncertainty.

Sarah Garrett Barton (1832–1905) one of seven children of Edward and Henrietta Barton, was born on Vinalhaven in 1832. Her father was a fisherman, as was her grandfather, Freeman Garrett. Freeman (b.1772) had made his way from North Carolina to Vinalhaven, possibly via Massachusetts, the birthplace of his wife Abigail. Around 1851, at age nineteen, Sarah and twenty-one-year-old Andrew W. Merchant (or Marchant) (1829–1912) began courting.

The 1850 Census lists Andrew as a fisherman living on the island in the home of his mother, sixty-year-old Nancy A. Shaw. Andrew was born in 1828 on Vinalhaven, the last of eight siblings. His mother, then Nancy Brown, was an islander; his father, John Merchant was from Deer Isle, though both his parents' families had lived on Cape Cod. John died young, at forty-six, when Andrew was only two years old. His mother remarried Otis Shaw a year later, in 1831.

Sarah and Andrew married in 1852 and had four children born across seventeen years—from 1857 to 1874, an unusual pattern that may speak of frequent and lengthy separations. They remained married for fifty-three years until Sarah died at seventy-three.[191]

Seven letters survive, four from Andrew and three from Sarah. Both mention others they exchanged. These letters bring us a little closer to an island "fishing" couple—courting, then earning a living, but mostly struggling to get by. The letters suggest how hard it could be to accumulate money if you stayed with fishing and had no family connections to wealth. In 1860, Sarah's fisherman father Edward's combined real estate and personal property comes to $200; Andrew's that year is $400, a tiny fraction of Timothy Lane's wealth. The premature death of Andrew's father may have contributed to his difficulties.

LETTER 1, TO SARAH FROM ANDREW, ON A FISHING VOYAGE, NOVEMBER 20, 1851

"Dear Sarah"—Andrew begins this correspondence telling Sarah that the fishing season has ended, and he is returning home. Letting your kin—or girlfriend—know that you are safe and about to return was one of the most important messages sent by fishermen who'd been away. Andrew had survived another season. Nothing terrible happened to him. And he expects to be back soon, though he's uncertain just when.

Writing and inquiring about health is a convention, but it comes through sincerely in their letters. "*I take these few moments to inform you that I am well and I hope those few lines will finde you enjoying the same great blessing. i expect to go to Boston in two or three days. We have quit fishing for this fall.*"

He wants to hear from Sarah before he returns. Perhaps he's asked her to marry him, and she has not yet answered. "*I don't know as I shall come home quite yet. I should like to hear from you firstate. I 'hant ben in Hingham this month. I am in hopes to hear from you when I get thare.*"

The letter is teasing, eager and playful; Andrew seems to want to remind her of how they enjoy each other. He wants to hug Sarah and be with her and refers to something that they laughed about together. "*I 'hant forgot the good times we use to have I laff to myself when I think of the mackerel story that we laft about when I cam away.*" Both men and women must have wondered how tender relationships would hold up during long separations. Did out of sight mean out of heart?

Andrew is apologetic about writing often, and attributes it to having nothing to do—the slack time of fishing was often tedious. "*Your must excuse my riting so often for I have nothing to amuse myswelf about. I hope you won't forget to take care of youself and not drive on to hard and keep your shoes tied up if you don't I will pull your ears.*"

He describes Cape Cod as a "*hole,*" a general term for small places, but the "*last one.*" They are likely on their way home. He seems to suggest that stories of the places he's seen are something he can offer to a potential island-bound partner. And he feels affection: "*when I can't teach you of all the holes that ever I was in Cape Cod is the last one. . . If I was with you tonight I would hug you up as snug as one mice."*

But Andrew doesn't want Sarah to think that he is closer to returning than he is: *"I should like to see you for company. Take for the company that I have here. I don't like very well I assure you. I am in hopes to be where you be in corse of a month or so you must not look for me until I com."*

He reassures her that the weather and danger on the fishing boat haven't been too bad. *"There has ben considerable many rucks up here this fall but we have escaped all the blows."* Rucks are folds or pleats in cloth, slang for a roughed-up ocean, which are preferable to major storms, or blows. *"Yet we haven't had to reef but once this fall . . .,"* that is, the wind wasn't strong enough to require reefing, or shortening the mainsail by bunching its foot up along the boom and tying the bunched sail with the reef points,[192] *"and then we coul carry it all but we thought we would reef in time. . ."*

The letter hints particularly of longing for her company, but also at loneliness and boredom amidst an uncongenial crew. Signing off, he again expresses his fondness for her, and his desire to hold her. He reminds her that he is holding her in his mind—even when he is away: *"When this you see think that I remember the[e] and still are in my mind. And I do hope before one month I to be hugged in your arms*

I hope those lines will finde you as smart aged rosted cricket. you must excuse my nonsense for I can't think nothing to rite so I shall have to bid you good evening by saying that I will call some other night yours and nobodies else. Andrew W. Marchant."

Andrew's location on Cape Cod and his reference to mackerel suggest that he could have been fishing in the mackerel fleet. Together with cod and herring, mackerel made up the triumvirate of mid-century Vinalhaven fisheries.

Mackerel fishing started early on Vinalhaven. Thaddeus Carver's 1775 journal note that Jeremiah Philbrook owed him for labor and provisions, including "6 macrael" is the earliest evidence I found of mackerel in island trade. In 1807, another first settler, Anthony Coombs Sr. (1751 or 1754 to 1843), provided David Vinal with several sheep, lamb, pigs and mutton and "a couple of half barrels of mackerel."[193] That year Anthony and James Coombs co-owned the 20-ton *Fox*, built on Vinalhaven in 1794, so it is likely that the Coombs family and other islanders already fished or traded locally for seasonal mackerel.[194]

By the 1850s, however, fleets of big mackerel schooners were cruising off the coast from Maine to Maryland or venturing up to Canada following enormous schools of the migrating fish. Mackerel was big business and Castine was the center of the mackerel fishery around the Penobscot Bay region.

Most of the area's bigger schooners outfitted there before heading north to Canadian waters or south along the mid-Atlantic coast.[195]

Unlike inshore fisheries where fishing was organized around trusted family members, friends and neighbors, most offshore cod and mackerel schooners were solely business ventures. Captains and mates were professionals hired to run the operation efficiently, although some invested in vessel shares to become part owners. Fishermen were employees hired for the season. Writing home to his family in Castine in 1853, Captain John Hanson (b. 1811), skipper of a mackerel schooner, tells them, "The crew are all first-rate fellows ever one of them it is the first crew that ever I was with whare part of them was not drunk. . . ." Uncongenial, unruly crews were an occupational hazard in the offshore fleets.[196]

Pursuing the schools of migrating fish could be frustrating for fishermen like Andrew. Migrations were unpredictable. There were years when crews signed on and went out, but the mackerel simply didn't appear. In good years, at least by the mid-nineteenth century, competition within the fleet could be stiff. Men took turns on the mastheads scanning the water for signs of fish: a characteristic rippling of surface water dimpled by the backs of millions of mackerel, flocks of gannets and seabirds or dolphins and whales gorging on them, even sudden course changes by other fishing boats, suggested the presence of fish. Once a school was spotted, the schooner raced to beat out others that might have spotted it too.[197]

By 1850, Goode writes, purse seines were already in use in Massachusetts waters, and Andrew may have fished with one. The large purse seine nets revolutionized the mackerel fishery. Schooners used two smaller "seine" boats—sometimes stored on deck, often towed behind the vessel until needed. When close on the mackerel, the crew jumped into the boats and encircled the school of fish, letting out a long curtain of net with a cord on the bottom. Once they closed the circle, they pulled the cord tight to close the bottom—forming a "purse" that trapped whole schools of mackerel at once. Staggeringly more efficient than "jigging" with hook and line, purse seining was almost universally employed after the early 1860s. *The Belfast Republican Journal* of August 1, 1839, mentioned purse seines being newly invented for the mackerel fishery on Cape Cod.[198]

More likely, Andrew jigged—as, according to a Sabine informant writing in 1851, the year of Andrew's letter to Sarah—many mackerel fishermen still did so.[199] In that case, his schooner likely sailed along with a "trail line" out, looking for a school. If mackerel bit the line, the vessel hove to. The bait man—working from a big box of bait (often menhaden) he'd chopped up—started tossing bits of fish into the water. When mackerel were "tolled," or came to the surface to eat the bait, the fishermen rushed to their stations and prepared to jig two fishing lines at once. The foresail was "taken in, and the mainsail hauled out with a boom-tackle" to create deck space and allow the boat to drift near the school.[200]

Wonderfully observant of fish and fishing, Sabine writes: "While the school remains alongside and will take the hook the excitement of the men and the rushing noise of the fish in their beautiful and manifold evolutions in the water, arrest the attention of the most careless observer." A fisherman couldn't leave "the rail" even briefly while the fish were biting. Men worked fast, sometimes catching sixty fish a minute. It was tricky work. Fishermen had to haul their lines "through the left hand with the right, and not hand-over hand as you do for cod . . ." Otherwise, they would "lose [the] fish after it breaks water." To intercept the fish before it hit the vessel's side, they leaned over the rail and quickly—with the right hand alone—grabbed the line close to the fish, unhooked the mackerel, tossed it into a barrel, and tossed the jig back out. A slow pace or awkward movements could mess up everyone. "You must be quick in case a mackerel takes your other line and entangles your comrades."

"Oftentimes the fishing ceases in a moment, and as if put an end to by magic: the fish, according to the fishermen's conceit, panic-stricken by the dreadful havoc among them, suddenly disappear from sight." Yet the work onboard continued. Fishermen couldn't rest until all the mackerel were gutted, washed, and salted. "You must take care to dress your mackerel quickly, as they are a fish that is easily tainted. When you stop fishing, the captain or mate counts the fish, and notes down in the fish-book what each man has caught . . . Then the crew goes to "dressing and splitting," a job that, Sabine notes elsewhere, "covers the persons of the crew, the deck, the tubs, and everything near, with blood and garbage; and . . . is often performed in darkness and weariness, and under the reaction of overtasked nerves . . ." About thirty-five years later, Goode writes that a good splitter could split 45 to 60 mackerel a minute.[201]

Once gutted, the fish were soaked, washed and salted. "The salter sprinkles a handful of salt in the bottom of the barrel, then takes the fish in his right hand, rolls them in salt, and places them skin down in the barrel until he comes to the top layer, which he lays skin up, covering the top well with salt."

Sabine notes that 1851 was a successful year for vessels pursuing mackerel. Maine fishermen, he writes, exported 18,240 barrels of mackerel.[202] Of those, 461,130 lbs, 2305.5 barrels—or a little over one-sixth of the state total—were from Vinalhaven. From the Maine Fish Inspectors Reports (25 between 1834–1891), Karen Alexander and William B. Leavenworth were able to aggregate numbers for mackerel export on Vinalhaven: 1851 is the peak year.[203]

LETTER 2, FROM SARAH, ON VINALHAVEN, TO
ANDREW, NOVEMBER 28, 1854

Three years later, and two years after their wedding, Sarah writes to Andrew. *"My dearest and ever affectionate husband I now take this oppertunity to right you a few lines . . . I have receved two letters from you."*
Health and Andrew's absence are both on her mind. The letter makes vivid the stress of separation, its wear and tear. She is struggling with the news, learned second hand, that he has found work that might keep him away for a year. She had believed he'd be home in the spring and seems to want to know if what she's heard is true. She is glad he's working onshore, but she is worried and lonesome.

> *I was glad to hear from you that your health was good and you arrived safe . . . I wont to see you now and I don't know what I shall do before you get home for sense you went away I have heard that you and Freeman was going to stay till next fall year from now. I tell them I about believed that for you thought you should come home in the spring. I'm very glad that you have got a chance to work ashore. you say that you shall right to me prety often that is right for im lonesome for I miss your company.*

She reflects back his distress—perhaps a bit defensively—that she forgot to pack a portrait of her he wanted to carry. *"You say thare is one thing that you miss in your trunk and that is my miniature. I fogot to put it in your trunk and im sorry, but it can't be help."*
Families missing absent men is a large psychological piece of 19th century Maine maritime life. Sarah speaks of the way self-consciousness about her poor writing skills interferes with her self-expression. And the truth of her observation hits home when we look at excerpts from this extraordinarily expressive letter written eight years earlier by an eight-year-old boy in Castine, Solon Hanson, to his father, John Hanson, a sea Captain:

Nov. 13, 1846

> *My Dear Father I want to See you very much its not quite a week and it Seems a year since you left home mother is getteng [sic] Supper . . . I wish I knew where you was a going this winter Sometimes I fear you will never get back again and I had rather bee with you fore what could a little boy like me without a father do I couldant do nothing a tall you don't know how we miss you evenings I want to see you so I am almost dead I wish you would write me a good long Letter when you arrive at Boston . . . From your Dutifull Son Solon Hanson.*[204]

Solon went to sea at age twelve in 1850, and died in London of cholera at age nineteen, outlived by the father he had missed so much.[205]

LETTER 3, FROM SARAH, ON VINALHAVEN, TO ANDREW, FEBRUARY 11, 1855

"My Dearest Husband," writing three months later, Sarah notes that they have both been ill but are now better, *"I was sorry to hear that you had been sick."* She addresses his worry. *"My cough has got most well you must not worry about me so much for it will make you feel unhappy."*

Sarah attributes her delay writing back to the frozen harbor, which prevented the packet boat from crossing the bay with the mail. *"The harbor is frose over so she can't git out."* She is embarrassed about her difficulty writing. *"You know I can't spell nor wright very well. if I know how t wright letters as well as you I wood rite oftener."* She tells Andrew that his mother is "okay."

Alluding to the ever-present dangers of fishing, Sarah reassures Andrew that Rufus Arey didn't drown at sea as everyone had feared. Arey finally returned *"after so long time,"* he *"got blowed off* [course and badly delayed] *a-coming home from Boston."* Perhaps to lure her husband home, she tells him that her father has taken a fishing boat, and Andrew can join the crew. *"Farther has took the Almond to go in this summer and he says that if you want to go fishing this summer you can go with him. he says that you can go and find yourself and have all you can git."*

She seems to be suggesting that Andrew won't have to share his catch profits with his father-in-law but can keep all he earns for himself.

LETTER 4, FROM ANDREW IN STONINGTON, TO SARAH, DECEMBER 15, 1855

"Dear Sarah"—just before Christmas Andrew writes her from Stonington (likely Maine), having just returned there from Virginia, and tells her he will soon be in Rockland. *"Tis with great pleasure to think I have this opportunity to rite you a few lines . . ."* He reassures her that he's on a sturdy boat, *"She don't fear the storms."* He's eager for news, and asks her to send a letter to Rockland for him, even as he professes that he will be home soon: *"I wood rite more but I soon shall be thare so good nite."*

He is concerned that she lacks basic necessities: *"Rite all the news be sure to rite how yu get along for wood and gruel."* His request suggests the worry fishermen must sometimes have felt—especially in winter, the hardest season for finding extra food. His sense of helplessness—about not only what he doesn't know, but what he can't remedy—comes through.

The letter also suggests how Andrew follows the news from afar: *"Rite how Tom and his wife get along."* It must have been challenging to resume your place in a family that has worked to get along without you, as well as in a community of kin and neighbors, in which much may have happened in your absence.

LETTER 5, FROM ANDREW, IN MENEKAUNE, TO SARAH, SEPTEMBER 2, 1857

"My dearest and ever affectionate wife"—two years later Andrew has traveled halfway across the country and writes to Sarah from a lumber camp on the Wisconsin frontier where he has found work. He would like her to join him.

> *I spoke about leaving the other day and they had me reckoned into a company to go into the woods this winter to cut logs. I can take twenty six dollars per month now but I tell them no I must go home first. They ask me why I don't bring you out here to live.*

He seems to anticipate that she won't want to leave Vinalhaven. Still, he describes all the amenities that will soon be in place, including a house lot in the town, a school, *"Miss Page is teaching school here now,"* and a new tavern *"three stories high"*; there are Sunday meetings, and Sunday school, too.

He wants her to understand that if he could stay working in Menekaune, he could make good money without having to go to sea. At the same time, his boat knowledge would help his employment.

> *I can have one of the scows to run if I want next summer. They pay thirty-five and board them to board themselves forty-seven per month for bossing them I mean right to ten men per scow that is better than I can do at home. Sarah and not exposed to the seas so mutch neather.*

In reality, lumbering was also grueling work—even if they have told him they'll make him a boss. But he's excited, and he wishes she could see the sawmill, *"Sarah I wish you was here to see the mill when it is all going,"* and the abundance of work available. *"If I was a dozen men I could get work for them all but still I never shall ask anyone to come. They can do as they like any man that wants to work can get a nuff to do."*

He'd never ask anyone to come? Does he mean Sarah? Why was Sarah unwilling to join him? Did she not want to leave her family and island community to live on the frontier? Did she distrust his staying power with a job? The letter made me wonder if she no longer believed he was someone she could fully count on.

LETTER 6, FROM SARAH, IN VINALHAVEN, TO ANDREW, MARCH 23, 1862

"Dearest Husband"—five years later, in 1862, times are tough. Sarah is thirty, Andrew thiry-three. The country is at war. The letter begins with a confusing paragraph of recrimination. Andrew seems to have suggested that he isn't writing more for fear of wearying her patience. She is distressed by the thought and emphasizes how she writes as often as he, and how lonesome she gets when she doesn't hear from him.

> *This makes four letters that I have sent you and I have got five from you so I don't think you have much to brag of. you know i love you and I luv to hear from you to if you know how pleased im to get a letter from you. You would rite instead of saying that you don't know as you shall rite again.*

Sarah refers to his leg problem. When he registered for the draft after the Civil War started, a note beside his name references a disability. Perhaps he injured the leg at the sawmill? *"You did not tell me how your leg was getting along."*

He has told her he'll be home in May, and she allows how *"tired"* she is. She refers to the war and her hope that it will end soon. *"The war hangs on yet the North is whiping them fast."* She lets him know that they are struggling to get by and fear hunger. *"Father went down to the harbor the other day after some things and they would not let him have any thing we are about out of everything and he says he don't know but we shall starve all in a heap."*

She asks Andrew to send a little money if he has any, but doubts he does. *"Do yif it is so that you can send me a little mouny but I don't expect you have got it to send."*

LETTER 7, FROM ANDREW, IN ROCKLAND, TO SARAH, AUGUST 10, 1862

"Dear Sarah I take this opportunity to rite you a few lines to let you know where I am." Andrew is back in Rockland, temporarily working as a stevedore on the wharf.

I am at work in Rockland on a wharf rite below whare Uncle Silas use to live to the southward of it I board in the same house where you and I lived and sleep in the same room upstairs. I suppose thare is a months work or more. I pay two dollars and a half per week.

He seems to have no intention of coming out to the island even though he's very close. (Unless, of course, it is not Rockland, Maine.) The letter seems quite distanced. However, he does still want to hear from her. "*I will send you three dollars now and some more soon that is if I work here. If I go to New York, ile send some as soon as I can Rite when you get this direct your letter to rockland.*"

The letters make a reader feel that Andrew is almost always away, but we possess too few to say. In 1870 and 1880 Andrew is apparently back living on the island. The census has him listed again as a fisherman, perhaps pursuing the last of the mackerel. Although it was the most valuable fishery in the country during its heyday, it had been a boom-and-bust fishery starting in the 1840s when purse seines were introduced. Its collapse in the 1880s was related to the collapse of the menhaden fishery less than a decade earlier. Like whale oil, oil extracted from menhaden was widely used industrially, and the fish oil was processed in large New England factories. The fishing pressure from the steam-powered vessels was relentless. New England's menhaden fish stocks collapsed some time after 1878. When they did, many of the steam powered menhaden seiners, some of the largest fishing vessels in their day, were converted for mackerel fishing. Those fish stocks collapsed soon after, in about 1884.[206]

We know that Andrew and Sarah's last child is born in 1874. In 1900 Andrew is seventy years old and working as a "day laborer." Their marriage lasted fifty-three years until Sarah died in 1905. Andrew survived her by seven years. In 1910, he is eighty and boarding in someone's home. When he dies in 1912, his death certificate states he had been living at the island poor farm.[207]

6

Vinalhaven at Century's End

1870-1900

Of the 502 men on the island who were sixteen or older in 1860, one hundred and eighty Vinalhaven men served in the Civil War, a remarkable number that, among all it altered, left fewer men and boys at home to fish. At the same time, the need to feed Union soldiers expanded the islanders' market, so those who remained fished harder. When they went to trade what they'd caught, the war sometimes came close. Fear of Confederate commerce raiders intermittently disrupted fishing and sea trade, including fish exports.

Even after the Confederacy finally surrendered, the massive disruption from the conflict waned slowly. A recession in the war's wake contracted markets. In 1873, the national economy fell into the six-year Long Depression. It pressed hard in many places, including on the lives of some islanders. Three newspaper stories from 1876 suggest the local troubles that broader financial hardship could bring.

In 1876, Capt. Lyman Leadbetter absconded with the season's fishing pay. Deemed a *"young man who has heretofore sustained a good reputation,"* he

left for parts unknown; taking with him the entire proceeds of the season's catch and leaving his crew to whistle for their pay. He made off with, *about $6,000. He left his vessel in Portland, where he went to sell his fish.*[208]

Two other stories told of suicides by Vinalhaven men. In 1876

Mr. Warren Norton, of this town, committed suicide last Monday, by hanging from a beam in his barn. . . . He was about 45 years age, and weighed about 225. He leaves a family of 8 children in destitute circumstances.[209]

In 1877

Mr. J.P. Stinson, who keep [sic] a boarding house at this place, left home Wednesday forenoon, with a small coil of rope in his hand and proceeded to Lane's Island. . . . Mr. Stinson . . . was a faithful soldier through the war, and was esteemed a good citizen by the people of Carver's Harbor. He leaves a wife and several children. Financial embarrassment is supposed to be the cause.[210]

Maine faced new hardships during the post-war decades. The natural resources that, starting in colonial times, had created commercial activity and wealth were less valuable by the late nineteenth century. "The lumber, leather, granite, ice, slate, fish, and lime industries still supported more than 40 percent of Maine's working population at the end of the century, but these industries were technologically stagnant and plagued with seasonal layoffs and declining markets. The net value of Maine's products was falling when compared to that of other states."[211]

With less to carry, Maine's shipping industry diminished and many of its smaller ports stagnated. In *Country of the Pointed Firs (1896)*—a nostalgic evocation of the era—Sarah Orne Jewett describes the sadness and increased provincialism that seemed to seep into villages as trade fell. A retired sea captain explains, "In the old days, a good part o' the best men here knew a hundred ports and something of the way folks lived in them. They saw the world for themselves, and like's not their wives and children saw it with them."[212]

Although the island population expanded because of the burgeoning granite industry, Vinalhaven offshore fisheries quieted after their mid-century peak. Maine's cod fishery went into a sharp decline. The Federal cod bounty ended and small operators lost the extra money that had made the fishery viable. Meanwhile, expenses climbed radically. Civil War inflation lingered, and the price of outfitting a fishing schooner doubled.[213] Additionally, the need to purchase equipment like dories or purse seines, together with a sharp cost increase from needing to use so much more bait when trawling with dories, made it hard for small-scale, independent fishermen to compete with the fleets of bigger vessels owned by wealthy merchant conglomerates.[214] Post-Civil War, insurance policies became more grudging with fewer repairs covered; and the constant damage wooden vessels incurred decreased profitability.[215]

A number of fishermen seem to have left the island before the war. Of the first ten fishermen listed in the 1850 Vinalhaven census, four were still fishing there in 1860, one had gone to work in the quarries, and five had left without a trace. Of the four remaining fishermen, one was still active in 1870, the second had disappeared or died—his wife is listed as head of household. The third was killed in the Civil War, and the fourth had become a farmer.[216] The transition to farmer was common for older Maine fishermen who had built wealth over the years, and in 1880 the last of the 1850 fishermen listed himself as a farmer.

This tiny sample is likely misleading. A man who farmed, fished for a few months, worked in a factory and lobstered might list different occupations in different decades. And people moved on and off the island all the time as they followed available work or signed onto vessels from other ports. In 1870, the population of 1851 included 150 stonecutters, 120 quarrymen, 149 fishermen, 82 farmers and farm hands, 20 lobster factory employees, and 4 net factory employees. A good number of these men set a few traps or nets whatever occupation they listed for themselves. Overall, Census figures between 1860 and 1950 (the last year for which a breakdown by occupation has been released) suggest that, depending on the decade, somewhere between a quarter and half of adult male islanders listed themselves as fishermen.

Year	Total Vinalhaven Population	Total Self-Declared Fishermen
1860	1667	241
1870	1851	149
1880	2855	160
1890	2617	(no data)
1900	2358	179
1910	2334	219 (148 lobstermen, 60 fishermen, 5 herring weir tenders, 2 men on trawlers, 3 seiners and 1 "sailor on a fishing vessel")
1920	1965	157 (33 lobstermen and 10 weir tenders)
1930	1843	124 (2 seiners, 4 hand liners, 35 trawlers, and 83 lobstermen)
1940	1629	138 (110 lobstermen. 12 clam fishermen, 8 draggers, 2 seiners, 4 fish on trawlers and 1 each "fishermen" and "ground fisherman")
1950	1358	202 (158 lobstering and fishing, 16 fishing, 24 clamming, 4 weirs). Additionally, 22 women and 16 men worked in the fish factory, 6 women and 1 man made netting.

The thirty-five years at the end of the nineteenth century were an up and down proposition for island fisheries, and fishermen adapted to it. Some islanders continued to bait hooks and catch finfish. Many others gradually drifted into the lobster fishery as they realized it was the best remaining way for them to make a living. Details are hard to know; only in the 1910 census were net/hook/trawl and weir fishermen distinguished from lobstermen.[217]

National trends affected islanders' ability to sell their catch. Competition emerged from new fishing regions—in Southern, Great Lakes, Pacific

Northwest, and Canadian waters that hadn't been fished as hard for as long. Perhaps the biggest change was the vast cross-country network of railroads with refrigerator cars (developed in the 1850s), which made it possible to transport fresh fish (and even more-sought-after Western beef). Once fresh fish was more available, it became more popular. Maine's traditional salt fish—Vinalhaven's strength—was demoted to something poor people ate when they could afford little else.[218]

The impact of market changes and the economic downturn is visible in the smaller number of fishing vessels on the island at the end of the 1870s. According to Goode's *Fisheries and Fishing Industries of United States* (1884 and 1887), a massive and ambitious report on the nation's fisheries for the 1880 Census, Vinalhaven was home to only twenty vessels in 1879.[219] With a combined capacity of 390 tons, most would have been small. Two delivered lobsters to canneries, another two sailed further afield for ground-fish, herring or mackerel. The remaining sixteen fished inshore, employing ninety-eight men. Eventually, the number ticked up; by 1910 at least twenty-six licensed vessels under twenty tons were owned by islanders (significantly, this number does not include small boats, like the "Friendship Sloops" that were increasingly used in the near-shore fisheries).[220]

THE QUARRIES

Fortuitously for Vinalhaven families, work in the granite quarries expanded after the war. Although Maine's population fell slightly from 1870 to 1880, the island's population grew by a thousand during the decade, reaching an all-time high of 2,855 in the 1880 census. The increase occurred largely because of the active quarries. Small granite companies had started mining on Vinalhaven as early as 1826, but it wasn't until mid-century that the industry came into its own, thanks in large measure to government contracts for public buildings. The Bodwell Granite Company, formed in 1871, was the island's dominant company and biggest employer until 1909.[221]

Because quarries, according to Goode, "furnish regular employment to the men at good wages . . . many have sold their vessels and remain at home."[222] How much better off a man was who went from gutting fish to cutting granite is hard to say, though having the choice was a plus. Coastal fishing has always been seasonal, but quarry work was also dictated both by the weather and by the availability of contracts to fill. An 1878 news story offers one snapshot of a season's activity, "*The Bodwell Granite Co. has a large force of stone cut-ters (400) preparing the stone for the 3rd story of the Cincinnati Post Office and the State, War and Navy buildings, Washington, D.C.*" But employment was not steady. The reporter added, *"How long the job will last for all hands, we cannot presume to say."*[223]

Not surprisingly for an effort dependent upon dynamiting and hauling heavy stone, quarry work was frequently loud, always dangerous, and sometimes deadly. The risks, different from those encountered fishing, were as omnipresent. Breathing granite dust eroded the health of many workers, causing diseases like chronic bronchitis, emphysema, chronic silicosis and chronic obstructive pulmonary disease.[224]

There were constant accidents:

John S. Hopkins, the granite contractor, was very badly jammed between two heavy stones at his quarry, on Tuesday of last week. No bones were broken, but his hips and legs were very badly wrenched and lacerated. He narrowly escaped being instantly killed. A terse 1914 entry in Addie Roberts's diary: *"Apr. 20 Herbert Young killed up to Wharff's (quarry) by stone falling on him."*[225]

For a while granite was in great demand. Many buildings in the United States were built at least partially from Vinalhaven granite—perhaps most famously the columns of the Cathedral of St. John the Divine in New York City.[226] Yet, wages in the quarries were erratic and often low, so that in the late 1870s, Vinalhaven men organized the Granite Cutters Union. They struck repeatedly in the hopes of improving pay, hours, and working conditions.

When conditions became intolerable some men returned to fishing. An 1892 note about the "Vinalhaven branch of the Quarrymen's Union," reports, *"The quarrymen of this branch took a decided stand against the January settlement. Most of them being accustomed to going upon the water engaged in fishing, and thus were enabled to keep the 'wolf from the door.'"* These struggles also taught local fishermen about unionizing. A generation later, Vinalhaven lobstermen, who as children surely heard about or witnessed union activity, would organize not just the island, but much of the coast.[227]

The island's granite industry lasted barely a century. The growing popularity of steel and reinforced concrete caused Bodwell to shut its doors in 1919. While several small island quarries lingered almost until the Second World War, they mostly produced paving stones.[228] All the same, the notion that quarry work might offer a better life—or a steadier wage—reminds us just how challenging nineteenth century fishing could be.

Island families survived the decades at century's end by being flexible, switching among inshore fishing, quarrying and farming depending upon the market, season and available work. But this flexibility didn't extend to the Banks fisheries. According to Goode, "but one vessel from Vinal Haven [*Black Swan* active in 1861–1862] has fished on Grand Banks, and this for but one or two years only."[229]

Even when there were cod or haddock to catch, once out of the Banks fisheries it was hard for local fishermen to reenter. Expenses for larger schooners, equipment and provisions had skyrocketed, and after incurring such debt, few small-time entrepreneurs could afford to ride out any bad years they encountered. In 1885, in a letter published under the heading, *"Our Fishing Fleet,"* one disaffected islander warned others about the risks.

> *Some three years ago, a number of our stonecutters, formerly fishermen undertook to try the fishing business again, but they found they were behind times and had to give it up as a failure, so returned to their hammers, and still remain to them. Two years ago, I invested in a few pieces of fishing vessels, in hope to make a fortune, but the result was I was money out.*

After losing over a thousand dollars his second season, the writer realized that it was the *"parties who own the controlling parts of these small vessels,"* who *"profit by them."* Small timers *"will be lucky if they come out even, but generally they find they are in debt."* He counseled not to invest. *"The surest property is government bonds. D."*[230]

FISH PROCESSING

Vinalhaven merchants continued for a while to find markets for salted, smoked, pickled, or occasionally canned fish. Thanks to the Lane & Libby plant, and to several local dealers trading in fresh herring, lobsters and sometimes groundfish, the island gradually found a toehold in Maine's fresh fish market. Generally, as America industrialized, so did fish "processing." Though drying racks for salt fish and smokehouses for herring had dotted the shore since the 1700s and the racks lingered on the island well into the twentieth century, industrial preservation by canning, refrigerating and eventually freezing gradually sidelined earlier methods of preserving fish.[231]

The most significant fish processing plant, considered a boon for the island since it bought the catch of local fishermen and employed islanders, was Lane & Libby, incorporated on Vinalhaven in 1878. A reporter in the *Courier Gazette,* announcing the plant's establishment the year before, sounded the familiar theme of fishing as "freedom," a liberating alternative for

> *the many who are sick and tired of the granite business, and who wish to return to their old vocation of "following the sea" and enjoying the liberty which is as free as the air we breathe, and which their forefathers cherished as their most sacred birthright.*[232]

In truth, the fish plant's beginning could hardly have been more modest. On "the 3rd day of May, 1878, Lane & Libby bought the first lot of fish, which consisted of 379 small cod, for which they paid $2.87 to Edwin Arey. . . ."[233] In its first year the firm purchased 751,201 "green" (fresh) fish in quantities so small they could apparently count every last one. A decade later, a local observer proudly told a newspaper, "784,000 fishhooks are spread upon the fishing grounds weekly by the fishermen of Vinalhaven."[234]

Lane & Libby initially made the bulk of its sales in dried fish—often still via Boston to the West Indies market. Merging the north and south islands, Goode notes, *"In 1879 there were nine curing stands on the two islands, employing an average of two men each. 18,400 quintals [3,680,000 lbs] were dried and the greater part sold in Boston."* Fish curing continued to contribute to the Fox Island economy, as the company's sales made up about 20 perecent of the combined island total.[235] Lane & Libby also processed and sold cod liver oil and hake "sounds," used to make isinglass (a gelatin like substance used as glue and for clarifying ale.)

The processing plant helped island fishermen and others nearby. Eight of the vessels supplying Lane & Libby were from Vinalhaven. Twenty-two came from ports off island. And while boats (under five tons) aren't broken down by port, we know that 65 of them also sold fish from local waters to the plant that first year, and that some of those were undoubtedly also from Vinalhaven.

By 1883, the company was likely shipping some fresh fish, as it had installed an icehouse that could hold 300 tons of ice. William Warner wrote about ice and fish in a later era, "Sixteen days, as it happens, is the generally accepted maximum-preservation period for iced fish, beyond which it is judged putrid or inedible. Even six to twelve-day-old fish are considered by food technicians as 'spoilage affected' in both firmness of flesh and flavor."[236] Probably a fair portion of what the nineteenth century merchants and inspectors deemed saleable, whether salted or fresh, would not make it to a table today.

Although small groups of islanders could no longer finance big vessels, companies could. This shift, too, is part of the industrializing of fishing. Eventually, Lane & Libby owned several 70-80-ton vessels that made trips to Georges and the Newfoundland banks. In its heyday in the early twentieth century, the organization was the largest wholesale fish dealer in Maine, and one of the largest in the United States.[237]

For fishermen who continued to sail far from the island, life was no easier than it had ever been. On July 25, 1884, an anonymous Vinalhaven fisherman aboard the *Sch. Charles Haskill* begins his letter home from Tigmish, Prince Edward Island, near the Magdalene Islands fishing grounds, *"Dear Wife"*—and in a handful of sentences lets her know, *"i am as usual and i hope these few lines will find you and the children the same.*" He explains that he had been out of touch because, after going through the Canso Straits and then traveling north, he was unable to find "harbours" from which to mail a letter. His note is terse and lets us picture the vicissitudes of offshore fishing in mid-summer: "*it has ben raining and blowing ever sence we got here with the wind to the eastward.*" Sodden clothes, swells and spray, slippery decks, torn sails and other wet miseries easily come to mind. His plaintive ending reveals how much he is thinking of home: "*now be shure and write when you get this for i am aufull lonesome don here evry day seams a week you had better sell the cow if you can for i don't think that we can get eny thing to feed her on this winter.*"[238]

A few Vinalhaven fishermen joined other Mainers who moved to Gloucester, Massachusetts, where large fish processing and marketing facilities, such as the Gorton and Pew fish companies, and a well-financed offshore fleet adapted better to new times. Its Banks fishery was also more active, and fishermen were paid better. A news story from the mid-1890s gives us a glimpse of how perilous the work could be, especially as winter approached. The *Schooner Lawrence Murdoch*, captained by Reuben S. Hopkins of Vinalhaven, left Gloucester November 18. Fishing on the Banks, the vessel was struck by a gale on December 18, "*which carried everything before, and lost both anchors with 70 fathoms of cable and a dory.*" They sailed into Halifax, repaired the damage and returned to the Banks, but "*found the gales frequent and fishing poor and finally started for home.*" Another gale struck, covering the vessel and men in a layer of ice. It took eight weeks to limp home—fishless. They had struggled at sea for three months with nothing to show for it but their lives.[239]

Inshore fishermen and lobstermen had the advantage of staying close to their families. Yet, even inshore in fair weather, disaster could strike. In mid-May 1888, the crew of the *Grace Lee*, a schooner owned by *Lane & Libby*, were fishing 21 miles southeast of Matinicus Rock. It was a calm, late-spring day. "*The crew of the vessel was away in dories running trawls . . .*" When they returned to it, their schooner was sinking—without visible cause. "*The crew lost largely as they have just fitted out for the trip. Their fishing gear that was out is all that was saved by them . . .*"[240]

Whaling

While never significant in the island fishery, a brief period of shore whaling, which started on the island in the 1880s, merits mention. Reeves et. al. write, "A whaling station was established on Greene Island near Vinalhaven, Maine, in 1885 and another at Carver's Harbor, also on Vinalhaven, sometime after

1900, apparently at about the time of World War I (Calderwood, 1972; Webb, 2001). Nothing is known about catches at these sites, but a contemporary photographic postcard depicts a humpback whale, dead and bloated, at the Carver's Harbor station (Webb, personal observ.). That station employed Portuguese flensers, and its catcher vessel was the *Palm*, a 51-ft gas-powered yacht (Calderwood, 1972; Webb, 2001)."[241] Whales coming close to shore were pursued by the catcher vessel and dispatched. The carcass was towed back to the whaling station where the blubber was removed by the flencers and boiled down. In 1885, several clippings from the *Vinalhaven Messenger* mention going to see "the whale." One added that "This whale is said to be about as large as the last one. Another smaller one arrived on Monday."[242]

THE INSHORE FISHERY

In assessing their character, Goode, like other commentators in the era who sought to privilege the (non-immigrant) New England virtues, noted admiringly that Maine's inshore fishermen were "wholly of American birth" and "brought up from their boyhood to a life on the water." The experience of being "frequently compelled to spend the night in their open boats waiting for the turn of the tide or a favorable wind" made them hardy, but still not, he opined, as stoic as their Banks counterparts. Inshore fishermen were "chronic grumblers," although their complaints may have been justified by "the miserable prices they sometimes obtain[ed] for their fish." If a fisherman "goes contrary to the advice of his patron he has a very poor chance of receiving from him any sum for his fish which will compensate the loss of time and labor."[243]

Turning from men to fish, Goode listed "a very large number of rocky or gravelling patches" around Penobscot Bay that were "the favorite resorts for cod, haddock, and pollock, while in the muddy bottoms between hake [were] generally found." In multiple places "among the numerous islands," the "different species of the cod family can be taken. . . . Herring and mackerel [were] also very abundant" during summer "along the entire coast."[244]

Five island vessels still pursued mackerel in 1880, none exclusively, and all were still hand-lining with jigs instead of purse seining. Nor did they make the long treks to southern waters, routinely made by the bigger mackerel vessels. There is mention of an island "mackerel and clam canning factory, Vinalhaven Packing Co.," run by Lyford & Ginn at some point during the 1880s, eventually purchased by Lane & Libby.[245]

Herring was one fishery that improved for local fishermen in this era. Vinalhaven had two small vessels in the herring fleet in 1880 totaling almost

39 tons and employing seven men. Taking advantage of the post-Civil War sardine market, more islanders built and maintained herring weirs. Fishermen erected weirs *"at Crockett's Point, Pleasant River, Wreck Ledge, Calderwood's Neck, Green's Island, Lane's Island, and others."* Frequent notices in the 1880s newspapers confirm ongoing weir construction. *"Messrs. Roberts & Arey are making rapid progress on their weir at Crane Island. They have built a new little hut, and have driven all their piles down, ready for the netting."*[246]

Weir owners could sell herring to canning factories that were appearing down east, starting with Eastport in 1875, and spreading southwest along the coast. Fishermen who targeted groundfish (cod, hake, pollock, cusk and haddock) and mackerel jiggers also bought herring for bait.

In time, lobstermen began using herring as bait for the lobster fishery. Originally, lobsters could be picked off the bottom in shallow tide pools or gaffed in deeper water. But as the crustaceans grew scarcer near shore, traps baited with herring were employed, which could fish on their own. Frank Rogers (1870–1965), an islander who fished for sixty-seven years, claimed that as a sixteen-year-old in 1886 or 1887, he was the first person to use salt herring for lobster bait on Vinalhaven. First, he attached the bait to the trap using skewers, but that didn't go well. His informant on Matinicus hadn't told him to use knitted bags to hold the rotting fish.[247]

News stories mention other fish caught inshore—including menhaden ("pogies") and smelt. Sometimes islanders caught halibut. In 1884, *"Charles Horr and son caught five halibut last Friday, that brought when sold $54.16. A big day's work for small boat fishermen."*[248]

You can get a snapshot of the island fishery mid-1880s by looking at a single week's sales to merchants in high season. Standing on the island docks during a July week in 1884, an observer would have seen two schooners and an unstated number of small boats (including some from other villages) deliver just under 20,000 pounds of *"mixed fish"* (usually unidentified groundfish) to *Lane & Libby*. The same week, a second island wholesale firm, *"Lane Sanborn & Walls,"* bought a total of 16,400 pounds of cod, 12,200 of hake, 1,800 of pollock, and 4,000 pounds of *"mixed fish."* *F.M. Brown*, a smaller buyer, acquired about 600 pounds of cod, 2,428 of hake and 3,404 of mixed fish. *Lyford & Ginn* bought 221 barrels of mackerel. The week's numbers totaled 60,832 pounds and 221 barrels, or approximately 44,200 total pounds of mackerel, making 100,000 pounds for a single week. In comparison, by 2018, groundfish catch for all of Maine was a little less than 3 million pounds, none of it by Vinalhaven fishermen.[249]

Although fresh fish spoiled quickly, they increasingly became the market standard as railroads and steamships carried shipments on ice to distant places, and wet-well smacks carried live fish and lobsters to markets in Portland, Boston, and New York. To the degree that they lived in a cash economy with little investment capital, Maine inshore fishermen were often among the less powerful members of their communities. Their fresh fish market was largely limited to what they could sell or deliver locally. Only when the market was strong and buyers competed did they gain leverage. Their autonomy came from what they provided for themselves and their families, or what they could gain from barter. "A fair average return per annum to the fisherman, since 1875, when bait began to be scarce and the price of fish to diminish, is estimated at $175; in 1879, however, the majority did not realize $100 apiece." To offer perspective, a laborer in Maine in 1875 who worked a seventy-two-hour week (full time) averaged $1.67 a day—nearly $500 a year.[250]

LOBSTERING ON VINALHAVEN

Goode waxed enthusiastic about the singular abundance of Maine lobsters and noted that the value of lobstering greatly exceeded that "of all the other States combined." Concerning Vinalhaven, his investigators found, "Lobsters occur all about the island . . . and during the summer and fall are found in all the coves, creeks, and inlets . . . The fishermen are rarely obliged to go more than a mile offshore at any season."[251]

Lobstering began to attract commercial interest on Vinalhaven in the 1840s when wet-well "smacks" made it possible to deliver the creatures alive to markets in Boston and New York. Although smacks appeared as early as 1820 along the Maine coast, they seem not to have reached Vinalhaven until two decades later.

Elisha Oakes, who ran a smack in the 1840s and bought from the island, described the essentials of the early island effort, "[The traps] were constructed of round oak sticks, and with four hoops or bows to support the upper framework. A string of bait, consisting mainly of flounders and sculpins, was tied into each trap. About fifty traps were used by each fisherman, and they were hauled once a day."[252]

Men made their traps and buoys. By the 1870s and 80s the traps were "semi-cylindrical" or rectangular "Lath Pots" that were about four feet long. The shape and size would stay basically the same for a century (the placement of openings moved). Fishermen constructed them from thin strips of wood, or lathes, and knit the netting from twine. "The door is hinged on by means of small leather strips and is fastened by a single wooden button in the center, or by two buttons, one at each end." Buoys cut from cedar or spruce were tapered into wedge or spindle shapes about 18 inches long, sometimes painted in "distinctive colors" but mostly simply boiled in "coal tar to prevent their becoming waterlogged."[253] You could haul several traps on a line, but Vinalhaven lobstermen tended to haul one trap on one line. Hauling by hand, one was heavy enough.

Island fishermen also built or repaired their own boats during the off-season. A Vinalhaven man wrote to the US Fish Commission, "A peculiar style of row-boat, called a 'peapod' or 'double-ender,' is used quite extensively in this fishery hereabouts." With two tapered ends (think of a fresh peapod split open with its peas removed), peapods are elegantly spare, graceful boats, on average "15 ½ feet long, 4 ½ feet broad and 1½ feet deep," well-adapted to fishing and hauling traps, and able to carry "quite a load." They could be rowed with ease in either direction as the labor required, and they dipped nicely as men hauled. (Islanders often rowed standing up.) "Occasionally their owners added a sail and center-board to catch the breeze."[254]

Sails on peapods and on large schooners had to continually be repaired and replaced, and Vinalhaven had a sail loft during these decades—and later. First Reinhold Boman, his son, Claes Boman, and eventually a grandson, Charles, sewed canvas into sails of all sizes and purposes. Claes was already a young man when the family immigrated from Sweden to Vinalhaven. At first, he worked cutting stone in the quarries, but later joined his father making and mending sails. He stayed at it until he was eighty-five years old and died in 1936 at eighty-eight.[255]

A single 1871 receipt from Boman's Loft surviving in the Historical Society, lets us see the kind of work they did, and the constant need for it. The bill, with multiple entries—January through September—is for the *Grey Hound,* a 50-ton schooner-rigged packet built on Vinalhaven that ran between the island and Rockland. The total due and paid by season's end is $64.45. Included in the labors performed are repairing at various times a "jib" sail, a fore sail, and a main sail, and making a stay sail, a labor requiring 67 yards of Ravin Duck—a canvas long used by sailmakers.[256]

Sail lofts gradually disappeared in the early decades of the twentieth century as motors proliferated. We don't know how Boman's loft looked inside, but clearly the space had to have been large enough to spread out and cut sizeable pieces of canvas. Writing in the 1930s about an abandoned Maine loft, George S. Wasson conveys their feel. "Near the center of the loft hangs the usual, large, cylindrical stove, suspended by rods a foot above the fully worn floor, to allow the spreading of canvas . . ." There were "low, time-darkened sailmakers' benches with their array of queer-looking tools . . . A small room partitioned off from the loft and capable of being heated with a stove, shows where the sailmakers could limber up a bit on the frequent below-zero days . . ."[257]

Perhaps the later arrival of wet-well smacks on Vinalhaven contributed to its healthier lobster population. The mainland was getting depleted. In an 1884 lecture, *"Notes on the Decrease of Lobster,"* Richard Rathbun, one of Goode's investigators, pointed out that the big lobsters (literally three and four feet long) had disappeared from Maine waters. Not only were lobsters smaller than before, men had to fish harder to catch the same weight. Using a fishing ground near Rockland as his example, Rathbun explained that, although the catch of three men could fill a smack in 1864, "In 1879 the same smack was obliged to buy the entire catch of fifteen men in order to obtain full fares, and at times required to visit other localities to complete the load . . . "[258] Likely culprits were the numerous lobster canning factories on the coast. Canned lobster extended the market and, until regulations stopped it, led to overfishing, particularly of juvenile lobsters.

By the early 1870s the Maine legislature started to place restrictions on the lobster fishery. Taking egg-bearing female lobsters was prohibited in 1872. By 1874 fishermen couldn't keep "short" lobsters under 10 ½ inches. By the 1880s, rules governed the length of the season. Initially not universally obeyed, the laws gained support as they proved to be effective, and local lobster gangs used social pressure (and violence) to enforce compliance. Although the canneries closed in the early 1890s, lobster did not disappear as Rathbun had feared.[259]

When the supply _was_ good, it could quickly become too good. Fishermen remained at the mercy of buyers, who provided an essential service but dictated the price. They would only buy what they thought they could sell—as this gloomy 1888 news report illustrates.

> *Johnson & Young of Boston who have the big lobster pound here have closed buying lobsters this fall . . . the only sale for lobsters now is through our commission merchant, R.T. Carver, who is shipping as usual, but says that he is snowed under . . . Unless some change takes place some lobster fishermen will be obliged to take up their traps and give up the business.*[260]

The invention of the lobster pound contributed to market success since it allowed marketers to hold lobsters until they could get a better price—for example, by shipping to cities for holidays. Higher seasonal profit may have benefited the pound owners more than the fishermen, but it was good for both parties. Managing pounds had its own challenges. Keeping the lobsters alive and healthy could be difficult. They had to be fed, or they ate each other. A bad storm, a contagious infection, a hole in the enclosure, predators like raccoons, or human thieves, and a season's profit could slip away.[261]

According to the 1889 report of the *Maine Commissioner of Sea and Shore Fisheries,* Vinalhaven had seventy-five lobstermen in 1887 and 1888 and eighty in 1889. Part-time fishermen likely accounted for the 121 boats in the fishery in 1888 and 1889 and 127 in 1889, which set 5300 traps in 1887 and 1888, and 5775 in 1889. Few Maine communities had more fishermen during these years.[262]

Lobstering didn't make islanders wealthy in the late 1800s. The average Vinalhaven fishermen made 85 dollars in 1880 for "the full season"—two and a half months of work. Goode's report confirmed, "The earnings of the lobster fishermen upon our coast afford, at the most, but a meager living, and according to all accounts, they have been gradually falling off during the past fifteen to twenty years . . . At Vinal Haven most of the regular lobster fishermen do little else out of the lobster season than prepare their gear and boats for the spring fishery. Some cultivate small gardens and raise some stock; others engage in other kinds of fishing to a slight extent or work in the quarries."[263]

Goode's "do little" would have grated on many a nerve had island fishermen read the report. He may have failed to imagine all the work demanded in daily living. Loosely translating, we might say that many islanders still lived partly outside of the cash economy. They grew as much of their own food as they could, raised a pig or cow, a few chickens, fished and hunted, traded goods and services, and bartered.

And some worked longer seasons. Newspaper notes suggest that at least a few island men lobstered in winter. *"The Claytor Bros. are catching lobsters at the rate of 200 per day,"* The Echo noted in mid-January 1888. Other times the weather and water curtailed activity when men wanted to fish, as this March story recounts. *"No lobster traps have been hauled for three weeks on account of disagreeable weather and hubbly water."*[264]

Even on land, lobstering work carried risk: One April day in 1885 on Vinalhaven, "Mr. Fred Hall" had hitched up his "valuable" colt to transport his lobsters to the *Pioneer* to be shipped to Boston. Hall was "unloading the lobsters at the boat" when a loud ship whistle suddenly sounded, spooking his colt, who broke its leg, and had to be shot on the spot.[265]

Daily Life

1892, Maria Webster diary

Wed. Oct 5. This a terable windy day . . . my cold is bad to day have not feelt like anything al day trying a new medicine oil and turpentine mixt together for Lungs this Evening couldn't go to meeting and prepaird me for bed.[266]

In the decades after the Civil War, whatever the economic ups and downs, Vinalhaven was a lively place. People socialized constantly. They held parties like the "hulled corn and milk party" hosted by F.M. Lane where *"Demuth and Meservey furnished music."* They attended concerts like the one *"given by the 'Old Folks' and the Vinalhaven Band, last Friday evening . . . 'Grandfather's Old Arm Chair,' sung by Mrs. J. P. Hunt, and the duet 'Wandering Hope,' by Mrs. Hunt and Mrs. Whitney, received hearty applause . . ."* They bought tickets to shows, *"Burton & Burke's minstrel troupe are billed to appear at the Rink Saturday evening of this week."*[267] And they formed or enrolled in all manner of civic and secret societies: *"A special meeting of Island Home Encampment, I.O.O.F. (Independent Order of Odd Fellow), is called for Friday evening, Dec. 23."*[268]

One weekend in October 1878, Mrs. Margaret W. Campbell, *"a lady of considerable talent, with an easy flow of language,"* traveled to Vinalhaven and delivered two lectures. The first on "Woman Suffrage," drew an audience of 300, *"who paid good attention and carefully noted the speaker's argument."*[269]

Perhaps because of Mrs. Campbell's own passion for both issues, perhaps because two topics earned twice the fees, the next day she offered up an even more successful talk.

> *Mrs. Campbell also delivered a lecture on Temperance on Sunday evening . . . She handled the subject with skill and convinced her hearers. . . . It was considered that there were seven hundred present at her Temperance lecture, who paid all attention to her remarks . . .*[270]

Seven hundred is 38 percent of the island population in 1870—a noteworthy turnout even for a place where citizens enjoyed social outings of all sorts—marching bands, horse races, dances and balls, secret societies.

Mrs. Campbell's crowd suggests that having a prohibition law on the books had done little to curb excessive drinking. In 1851, Maine became the first state in the nation to go "dry." Although there were violent protests in Portland and a brief repeal in the mid-1850s, prohibition remained the law of the land until 1933; Vinalhaven technically stayed "dry" much longer—until 1986.

Whatever the realities of local imbibing, calls for temperance were an ongoing crowd-pleaser. Other speakers followed in Mrs. Campbell's footsteps: *"W. H. Littlefield delivered a temperance lecture at Union church Sunday evening to a large audience,"* the *Vinalhaven Echo* noted in December 1887.[271]

Alcohol was (and is) a staple of many fishermen's lives, and it's hard to imagine them giving ground easily. To what extent Prohibition, the several local Temperance societies active on the island in those decades, or the visiting proselytizers, actually altered drinking habits is unclear. A news story from 1875 captures the community's ambivalence. Under the headline *"Auction Sale of Liquors"* a reporter recounts how the new year began on Vinalhaven with a much-anticipated auction of confiscated alcohol (the public auction of an ostensibly illegal substance is puzzling in itself). Twenty or thirty gallons of "smuggled liquors of various kinds," that had been "Seized by the Deputy Collector," were to be sold at auction. Eager men and boys began to gather "long before the sale commenced." Those who bid successfully and secured bottles, went off in small groups "to 'have a jolly time.'"[272]

An undated story from mid to late nineteenth century suggests the sentiments of some women, and the familial tensions alcohol consumption created: Rosanna Coombs Arey, (1812–1897), hearing that a local merchant had decided to begin selling rum, organized a group of women in a "Hatchet Brigade" to change his mind. Armed and angry, they greeted a keg-carrying coaster as it docked at the wharf and raised a ruckus that dissuaded the merchant from making his delivery. Married at sixteen in 1828 and having given birth to twelve children, Rosanna seemingly possessed the stamina to execute her intentions.[273] "Hatchet Brigades" were not uncommon in fishing towns. In 1856, 200 women "with hatchets hidden under their shawls" (and a few men) in Rockport, Massachusetts, swarmed into the downtown and smashed every bottle and barrel of alcohol they could find. "Rockport was mostly a fishing town then, and the women were frustrated [by] male members of their families spending money on booze."[274]

The jailing, in 1876, of a hard-drinking Vinalhaven saloonkeeper referred to only as "Coombs" may have been deemed newsworthy not only because he abandoned his wife and fled to Boston with "a woman of doubtful reputation." As well as selling illegal rum, Mr. Coombs enjoyed provoking local law enforcers. Once, knowing his tavern was under surveillance, he arranged to have two men walk toward it from opposite directions, each with a tin-sealed "ten-gallon keg" on his shoulder. When the officers pounced and opened the kegs, they found that both had been carefully filled with saltwater. A good laugh was had at their expense.[275]

Despite the laws, alcohol was everywhere. In *Sailing Days on the Penobscot*, George Wasson tells how the nineteenth century lobster smacks traveling from island to island buying lobsters didn't just purchase crustaceans and deliver news from the mainland. In *"special facilities"* on board, they carried *"stone jugs"* with *"contents of far more cheery nature, to patrons ordering such in advance."* Wasson claimed that rum was such an important part of their cargo that any skipper who wouldn't deliver it was closed out of sales, *"No rum brought, no lobsters sold."*[276]

Similarly, Italian barks that delivered salt to the Lane & Libby fish plant (officially incorporated in 1895 as the Vinalhaven Fish Co.) in the early twentieth century sold alcohol—but only if you knew whom and how to ask. Captain Salvatori G. Trapani, in a 1906 letter, written in Italian, to the unnamed Captain of "*Italiano Janni*," introduced the holder of the letter as,

> *a certain Philip B. Johnson*" and explained that "*Knowing he was coming to Vinalhaven, he asked me if I could give him a presentation letter to you, in order to ask you if you had some bottle[s] of liquor you could sell to him.*[277]

All the stories remind us how Vinalhaven was active in the contentious issues of its day. Whether debating suffrage and Prohibition, re-integrating veterans who'd suffered in the Civil War, or organizing unions and fighting for fair wages, the island was both separate and closely linked with the mainland.

Adding to this conversation were the summer visitors who in the 1870s and 1880s began to arrive and stay in the Lane's Island House (later the Rockaway Inn) or The Granite Hotel before it burned in 1886.

It was also in 1886 that Murray Howe and Tucker Daland made the first "landfall" by "Rusticators" (wealthy summer people who wanted "rustic cottages rather than Newport-style mansions) on Vinalhaven when they bought an 1845 farmhouse built by Ephraim Mills. They altered it extensively, adding porches and dormers, and turned it 180 degrees to face north instead of south so it looked out onto the water of the Thoroughfare. It's easy to imagine their labors causing some talk about the different habits of people from "away"; for example, the notion that summer people used their waterfront for leisure not labor.

North Haven's summer colony developed earlier, but by 1909 a report suggests that Vinalhaven had caught up. That year a survey found that North Haven had twenty-five summer cottages and one hotel, while Vinalhaven had twenty-six summer cottages and three hotels just for summer guests.[278]

Initially, the summer colony made little difference to the island except to add a few jobs. Young women sometimes found work cleaning rooms and waitressing in the hotels. A handful of men took on seasonal work as builders, caretakers, and boatmen for the Rusticators whose large cottages soon dominated the shore of the Thoroughfare on the northern end of the island. During hard times, farmers and fishermen gradually offered up their shorefront acres to Bostonians or New Yorkers with ready cash.[279]

In the late 1880s, just as Daland and Howe were altering their farmhouse, people who knew the water well were noticing declines in fish stocks, though not everywhere right away. Indeed, in early October 1887, the *Echo* reported,

"Lane & Libby's daily average of fish landed at their docks amount to about twelve thousand pounds. The total amount for the season will be about two million pounds."

The numbers made the reporter exuberant, *"This town is in the most prosperous condition it has been for a long time. . . . The industries of this place are furnishing employment to a large force, placing it among the liveliest places in Maine, and its future prospects are predicted to be brighter still."*[280]

The reporter's hopeful vision belies an emerging reality. An 1888 report by the *Commissioner of Sea and Shore Fisheries* is discouraging: "mackerel were scarce, alewife catch was falling off each year," and, apart from a brief uptick, so was menhaden.[281]

According to fishermen interviewed by the *Maine Labor Bureau*, fish were disappearing in the 1880s, and earning a living from fishing had become more difficult. These first-person accounts from late in the decade, offered anonymously by men and women who worked in the fishing industry in Maine (some perhaps from Vinalhaven), convey what the fishermen were noticing and experiencing—how sensitive they were to the environment, and how aware they were that the "new" technologies of seines and trawl were damaging their fisheries.

A "granite cutter and fisherman" reported that he'd worked at both professions for the past forty-five years, dividing his year with them. He was aware that the new technologies of tub trawling and purse seining, and the scale of their usage, were killing too many fish. He had to travel much further from shore to find fish than he had in the past. He added, *"The fish business [has been] monopolized to the injury of the fishermen, as the buyers are about all members of fish bureaus that control prices and sales."* And it was harder to live. *"At best there is but a bare living and a life of hardship for those who catch the fish."*[282]

The complaints and concerns continued. A "vessel captain" turned lobsterman who fished for six months of the year, rued that he *"can't make a living . . ."*[283]

A "fish buyer" who had spent his life in the business warned, *"Fish are growing scarcer every year."* He used to easily catch all the fish he wanted on a hand line. *"Now he had to 'go from five to ten miles from home, and fish with trawls having 500 to 1,500 hooks, in order to get any fish at all.'"* His expenses had become too high, and he recognized that tub trawling and purse seining were terrible for the fish and

disastrous to the fishing industry, for the reason that there are so many more fish killed than are [being] marketed; they die on the trawls and are eaten by sharks, dog-fish, &c., before the trawls are hauled. The same is [true in] the case [of] *seining mackerel; large schools and small ones are [all] taken [at once] and virtually destroyed.*[284]

A thirteen-year-old female "fish curer" described her labors: *"I get two months' work at drying fish and earn $1.80 per week. I put the fish on flakes and get five cents a dozen flakes of 120 to 150 fish to a flake."* It took her nine or ten hours to do her daily allotment of six-dozen flakes, except *"in hot days when the fish are soft it takes longer. I get very tired and the odor often makes me sick."*[285]

In the years after the Civil War many island fishermen lost ground both because they could not raise enough money to buy bigger boats or travel to the Banks and because they had less leverage in a more particular market that increasingly wanted fresh fish. Selling to Lane & Libby and other smaller factories that came and went was a lifesaver, and Lane & Libby continued to salt some fish. Lobstering became the island fallback, but it, too, was up and down because lobsters were vulnerable to overfishing, and because when caught they had to stay alive until they were sold. So the local lobstermen were dependent on fluctuating prices and markets, and the fairness of the buyers. Little wonder they sometimes sold their best acres to "Rusticators." Island fishermen managed because they could grow or raise a lot of their food, because there was some onshore work from granite and because the community made its own entertainment. Whether dancing, singing, boating, acting, playing in the band, or participating in different clubs . . . there was ready fun to be had.

Into the Twentieth Century

Letter fromHanson W. Calderwood (b.1855) to Herbert Calderwood (1869-
1964). At the time of this letter, Hanson is out West, working as a carpenter on
a boat running between Seattle, Washington, and Nome, Alaska. Herbert is on
Vinalhaven.

Dec. 1900
Dear Brother Herbert,
Dear Sir I will admit that I never was so neglectful in my life in writing as I have ben
in the last year. I made 5 trips to Cape Nome . . . Nellie's husband got killed on
July 4th again up in a balloon or otherwise he went up a hanging on by his teeth
with a leather strap with a glad in each hand and the strap broke when he was up
about 500 fet. Nellie was not with him at that time. Sence on Aug 5 she had a
girl baby. Thay live at home. . . .[286]

Diary of Evelyn W. Arey (Hall), Age 14-15.
Tues. June 29, 1909. Went down on the Point this afternoon with the Kirkpatrick
girls, Hazel, Dorthy, and Eliza. Had a fine time. Went in a wading and the girls
went home and I got some tripped fish, pickles, crackers and cookies. It wasn't
very much but didn't it taste good.

Mon. July 11, 1910. A very warm day. When I went to get the milk this morning
there was a little coal black kitten eaten some of Nanny's fish. Nanny got after her
and gave her a dig which made the blood come. I took the kitten up in my arms,
wiped the blood off and gave it some milk. I then tried to find out whose it was but
couldn't so I left it out on Pleasant St.[287]

On December 10, 1898, a young schoolteacher named Alice Paine left her home in New Hampshire to travel to Vinalhaven, where she'd been engaged to teach "a winter school." Later she wrote several paragraphs offering a view of her sojourn and island life at the turn of the twentieth century.

Paine's journey from Dover, New Hampshire, about 150 miles door to door, took two nights and included two train rides, a steamer trip, and a long morning in an ox- or horse-drawn wagon. Her description offers a feel for the expanse of the tiny island and the relatively isolated communities within its perimeter. Your neighborhood was your world.

Arriving at the dock in Rockland to board the ferry, Alice met three other young women who'd also been hired to teach for the winter. They departed for Vinalhaven on a steamer. Paine's first ocean trip featured very rough seas. *"[T]ruly the wind blew fearfully,"* she wrote. On the open deck, even the crew clutched the railings. Yet, Paine showed her mettle, *"Many of the passengers were sea sick and some well frightened, but stranger to say I thoroughly enjoyed the trip."*

She was assigned to a "rural school" eight miles from the village and given board on a farm owned by one of the Calderwood families. Trying to alert her to local ways, her new boss, Mr. Coombs, immediately warned her of neighborhood jealousies, and admonished her to be careful what she said about the children. She must not praise *"the right child to the wrong people."* Maybe he was being crotchety, but I imagine he sought to convey how much care it required to get along in close quarters in an island community. Life went more smoothly when people bit their tongues. Coombs also told Paine that families in her school district kept clocks *"from one half to three quarters of an hour faster than standard time."* He suggested she would save herself trouble by following suit.

The next morning, Paine set out promptly for the farm. *"The roads were very muddy and progress necessarily slow. After riding a long time I asked the driver if we were nearly there. He gave me a look of mingled surprise and disgust and said, 'No we haint come morin three miles, and tis eight miles to Mr. Calderwoods, you know.'"* The following morning Alice walked the half-mile to her schoolhouse and met *"eighteen scholars."* As she got to know them, she found that *"they had been well taught and were well disposed."*

Looking back later, she concluded, *"on the whole I remember those months with much pleasure."* We don't know what discomforts were glossed over, but clearly she enjoyed island sociability. *"In the Dogfish district [#11 of 13 elementary school districts on the island in that era] there were quite a number of young people and parties were much in favor. I attended these gatherings . . . Sometimes we walked, sometimes we went in the dory, and once or twice we went in the sleigh as there was snow enough for hauling. Never did we fail to have a good time. The evenings were passed in games and dancing. These parties usually broke up about midnight.*"[288]

A decade later we get a glimpse of a student choosing courses that will prepare her for college. On Tuesday September 13, 1909, fourteen-year-old Evelyn W. Arey wrote in her diary, *"Yesterday school began. I entered High School and didn't tremble nearly as much as I thought I would. . . . I am going to take the college courses, Latin, algebra, Greek, History and Rhetoric."* A year later, on Sunday, November 6, 1910, she notes that her friend May *"is translating Virgil while I'm just scribbling."* Nevertheless, Evelyn scored a 96 on her Latin exam.[289]

Interviewed in the 1970s about her childhood on the island, Elsie Calderwood (1890–1982) described how basic material existence had been during her childhood, *"When I was a child, most of the money I earned went for shoes and stockings. Sometimes we picked blueberries to earn money. Blueberries sold for five cents a quart. We usually carried them to North Haven and sold them. We picked other kinds of berries, too."* She recalled her pleasure in nature, *"When we lived at Crockett's River, someone would often row across the river just before sunrise and then climb up to Tiptoe Mountain, where they would watch the sun rise. I did that many times, even after I was married."*[290]

Paine's and Calderwood's accounts evoke an island at the turn of the twentieth century where life felt quiet and people got together to make their own fun. Two anonymous 1906 entries in a diary later kept by Addie Roberts capture the community tradition of easing effort by sharing tasks: *"Feb. 13. Sewing Bee here—15 women. . . . Feb. 20. Big chopping bee. 38 men to saw and split—dance in eve."*[291]

It may have looked quiet, yet new technologies were quickly altering older island ways: A telephone company started up in Vinalhaven in 1895, though the cable connecting to the mainland in Rockland was not laid for three more years. By 1903 Main St. had gas lights, and Will Merrithew brought the first automobile to the island in 1906. A "Carnegie" library was completed in 1907, and the next year, Melvin and Herbert Hunt opened the first moving picture theater. In 1910 the Vinalhaven Water Company was organized, and the Electric Light and Power Company came online in 1914.[292] Addie L. Roberts observed the ups and downs of the early days of the "new" world in her diary: *Dec. 16, 1908, Patience came over and we went to the "Moving Pictures." Feb. 11, 1909. Tree fell across telephone wires and we could not talk. May 3, 1915, electric lights to-night.*[293]

Engines revolutionized fishing. Mariners began using steam winches, called donkey engines, on vessels in the nineteenth century to move heavy loads.

As diesel and gasoline engines became smaller, mariners put them on smaller vessels and boats, first to augment, then to replace oars and sails. This transition marked the largest technological shift in fishing since humans took to boats. Motors enabled fishermen in relatively small vessels to cover wider areas in pursuit of their prey, and to operate heavier equipment. They freed them from being at the mercy of the wind, and saved many holds filled with fish from rotting when vessels became becalmed.

One way to understand twentieth-century fishing is as the story of ever-more powerful engines in larger vessels towing ever-larger nets and longer lines. As the scale of fishing grew exponentially, the danger and brutal physical toil for fishermen slowly diminished. At the same time, the ability for fish to hide from fishermen, reproduce, and for species to survive, diminished.

It took time for fishermen to embrace the new technology. Island historian Sidney Winslow observed that "When these engines first came into vogue the fishermen were somewhat wary of installing them in their boats as they had great fear of gasoline and with good reason for many of them were severely burned before they learned how to handle it and the crude engines of that era." Initially, fishermen minimized the importance of motors and resisted their growing dependence, boasting to each other that they would use them only when there was no wind. But the pleasure of the speed proved irresistible. Before long, they were "going to and from their work, even when there was a good stiff breeze, with all sail set and engine running wide open." Two cycle engines ranging from four to ten horsepower were in general use among local fishermen in the year 1910, but many of the larger boats had much more power. Still, most fishermen kept their sails for years, "[e]ven after gas engines had been installed in nearly all of the fish boats. . . ."[294]

Early, when in inexperienced hands, often unreliable motors brought their own dangers. A 1908 newspaper story tells how islander Joseph W. Gerrish, a twenty-three-year-old newlywed, died, and his family barely survived the explosion of a gas engine on his sloop: "*In the vicinity of Pole Island the engine acted badly and Mr. Davis proceeded to make an examination with match or lantern, it is not known which. There was an explosion which set fire to the boat.*" When help arrived, "*Mrs. Gerrish and her brother Maynard, though greatly exhausted, were still clinging to floating timbers.*"[295] It's unclear if more lives were lost in gasoline explosions during the era than rowing in dories. This sampling of island drownings conveys the omnipresence of boats in daily life and the ongoing peril:

In 1904—Herbert A. McNicol drowned when his "*boat capsized 30 feet from the shore of Green's Island . . . McNicol tried to swim and handicapped as he was by oiled clothes and rubber boots soon sank.*"

In 1910—Howard Wooster left Rockland for Vinalhaven in "*a 16 foot dory Tuesday night*" and never made it back to the island. He'd ridden over for a dentist appointment, missed the steamer back, and decided to row . . ."*Mr. Wooster is 32 years of age, is an employee of the Vinalhaven Fish Co. and is married.*"

April 1915—"*David W. Lawry and Sidney E. Lawry, who left this port on a trawling expedition one week ago Saturday in a 15-foot dory . . . A heavy northeast storm overtook them and probably blew the frail craft to sea . . .*" David, 46, left a wife and three children. Sidney was 37 and single. Later they were found locked in each other's arms in the dory having starved to death. A third brother, James, had died at sea eleven years earlier.[296]

The first decade of the twentieth century was a pinnacle moment for the "industrial island" with granite mining and fish processing both going strong. Thanks to a 1908 Knox County tax ledger we can take a quick tour of businesses and tradesmen and glimpse the town. Although past its late-century heyday, the Bodwell Granite Company remained active—with Cutting Sheds, a Polishing Mill, a Blacksmith Shop, and a Machine Stonecutting Shed among its buildings. Its employees and other islanders enjoyed an array of shops and services: a dental office, a doctor's office, a few general stores, a barbershop, a pool room, a "*Cigars and Pool Room,*" a "*Tobacco and Candy*" store, several restaurants, liveries, blacksmiths, a "*Lock-up,*" a Masonic Lodge, and a millinery supplying hats to island women. There was a drug store, an undertaker, an icehouse, grocery stores, bakeries, and a fruit store. There were cobblers, a Christian Science Hall, the Advent Church, the Union Church, a clubroom, a bowling alley, a bicycle repair shop, lodging houses, the Central Hotel, a steamship office, an engine house, a "*Band Room and Town Hall*" (as mentioned, marching bands were big on the island and many people learned to play instruments), a "*Country Store,*" two photography studios, a wheelwright, a "*Hardware and Tin shop,*" a jeweler, a paint shop, "*Clothing and Men's furnishings,*" a Post Office, a store selling "*Stoves and Tinware,*" another offering "*Dry Goods, Furnishings, Boots and Shoes,*" and, one that claimed to be selling "*Groceries and Junk.*" It's hard to imagine goods you might need that you could not get—or at least order from your shopkeeper.[297]

There were fish related businesses on the island as well. C. E. Boman continued to manage his sail loft and ship chandlery (boat supplies). Reuben T. Carver owned a "Boat Shop" as well as a "*Grocery and Fish store,*" and also a "*Smoke House and Fish Packing Company*"; and Reuben and G. S. Carver operated a Cooper Shop (for making barrels). George Ginn ran a machine shop. E. H. Smith was the proprietor of a "Boat Builder's shop," and, nodding to the new century, also had a boat shop for boats that use "gasolene" power. The census additionally lists three boat builders, two lobster dealers, and a lobster buyer.[298]

Electricity and motors transformed fish processing. By 1903 the Vinalhaven Fish Co. (Lane-Libby Fisheries Co. starting in 1908) was the biggest fish processing firm in Maine. The company constructed a large cold storage plant on the harbor in 1909. *"The capacity of the cold storage plant is about 1,250,000 pounds. Here the fish are taken in fresh from the water—such as herring, shad, blue-backs and mackerel—and frozen in the best possible condition, being frozen the same day they are caught, supplying bait to the fishermen, also, fish food in the winter season which is marketed mostly in the large cities."*[299] In 1910 the population of Vinalhaven was 2,334.

Motors also made it possible for the first time for fishermen in the area to drag for scallops. We don't know exactly when Vinalhaven fishermen started in the scallop fishery, but a state fisheries report suggests that Knox County fishermen were regularly harvesting Atlantic scallops by 1908 and had temporarily depleted them by 1919.[300] This 1906 entry in Addie Roberts's diary confirms that islanders were eating scallops: *"Jan. 10 Fair and cold at zero. A mess of scallops from Susie Filbrook."* Susie and her husband Ed Philbrook were Addie's neighbors. Ed sold his fish in town: *"Feb. 10, 1906: Philbrook & Tolman hauled their fish to the harbor—13 loads."* He also fed his neighbors, *"Feb. 26, Edw. Phibrook brought us a mess of cod heads."*[301]

What was it like to be a "trawler" on a vessel with a motor? Richard Young (1889–1984) moved from Matinicus to Vinalhaven when he was twenty-three. He worked as a tub trawler, fishing in a dory off the schooner *Gladys Simmons* (registered to Ralph Bickford in 1913 as a forty-foot schooner with a gas engine—said to be part of the island "cod fisheries"). Thinking back in the mid-1970s, Young vividly remembered fishing during the famously cold winter of 1918, describing tub trawling at its hardest: *"That was an awful winter!"*

Vinalhaven's harbors were all frozen solid, so the *Gladys Simmons* sailed out to Isle au Haut to fish, where the deeper ocean kept its small harbor from freezing. Overnight, ice came *"down from the eastern bay, hit the point, and sheered around it,"* closing in. The next morning, they found enough open water to set their trawl *"just inside in what they call the Old Bull."* Frigid temperatures made the work miserable.

Vapor was so thick that morning when we set the trawl, we couldn't see anything, couldn't see from one dory to another; just as thick as any fog you ever saw. . . . When we were hauling the trawls, we used to holler back and forth so we could tell how far apart we were; couldn't see a thing in the vapor, you know. All at once we couldn't hear Dal. We figured there must be something wrong. We kept on hollering.

They couldn't search for Dal until they'd stowed the gear and catch aboard the schooner. Then they were able to follow the trawl line to him. *"As luck would have it, we did find him. It's a wonder we ever did. He was just lying there in the dory. We took him back and got him aboard. I never saw anyone frozen before. I thought you turned white; but being frozen turns you blue. His hands up to his wrists were blue, just like ink."*

They tried to return to Vinalhaven to get Dal to a doctor, but the ice closed in. They turned back toward Isle au Haut. *"We were stuck there in a snow squall, and didn't it blow! We never got back into Head Harbor until after dark."* The next afternoon they sailed home. *"Later, Dr. Brown said that if [Dal's] hands had frozen a little deeper, he would have lost every one of his fingers."*

The experience made Young want to give up fishing. *"I told Ralph* [probably the vessel owner and captain], *'I don't believe I'll go any more. This is a little too much for what I'm getting out of it.'"* More experienced, Ralph counseled Young, *"You wait a month or two, and we'll strike out again. You'll feel a little better about it."* The men waited until April, and *"then we went pollocking. I went with Ralph almost two years. Sometimes we went haddocking."* Young added, *"Sometimes the boys complain to me about going on the water. I say to them, 'you ought to go out trawling in a dory. You don't have a thing to protect you, not a thing. You have to stand there and take it.' Now they have those boats with beautiful gear, automatic haulers, nice and warm cabins—they do all the work for you anyway."*[302]

Although the future had looked bad for lobsters at the end of the 1880s, they did not disappear—though a good living was still hard to come by. On February 22, 1905, Vinalhaven men formed the first union of lobster fishermen in Maine. The problem of markets made collective bargaining attractive to fishermen: If "they" don't buy, you can't sell, and if they pay poorly, you suffer.

Lobster had a shorter shelf life than salted, smoked or frozen fish. Thus, lobstermen were vulnerable negotiating prices. There was little competition among buyers in the largely local system of supply and demand. Rumor had spread among lobstermen that an unnamed group of businessmen were going to promote a "trust" to corner the lobster market and reduce competition further. Their interests threatened, some island lobstermen unionized to protect their freedom to sell to diverse buyers.

According to a contemporary account, the union promised not just to fight for better prices, but to help fishermen become more "fraternal"—and thus increase mutual aid in tough times. A lone man might take on the natural world; but he needed allies when the industrial world pitted him against speculators.[303]

Although motors had increased the distance the fishermen could travel between traps, and thus the total number of traps they could haul, a year's earnings were still often modest at best. Winter conditions were harsh and motors meant higher equipment costs, and more annual expenses—like gasoline. The few pennies a pound lost to speculators would have made lobstering untenable.[304]

Labor historian Charles A. Scontras quotes a union granite cutter from Vinalhaven who summarized the shift underlying the new willingness to cooperate: *"These fishermen never realized the necessity of their organizing, because the buyers were generally in competition and the highest bidder got the catch."* . . . But when it began *"to look as if the fishermen were 'up against it,'"* they realized that *"the remedy was in their own hands. Organize! was the slogan."*[305]

Learning that seventy (soon to be more than 100) Vinalhaven men had joined together, an American Federation of Labor (AFL) organizer, Stuart Reid, encouraged them to join the larger union, and worked with them to organize other communities along the Maine coast. A.W. Roberts of Vinalhaven became Reid's deputy. AFL president Samuel Gompers (1850–1924) visited Vinalhaven in 1905, that same summer. Born in England, Gompers immigrated with his family to New York City as a thirteen-year-old and worked in his father's cigar factory. He later started the AFL and grew it "from a marginal association of 50,000 in 1886 to an established organization of nearly 3 million in 1924."[306] Everyone on the island turned out to meet him, *"crowds at the wharf greeted him with three cheers, and the Vinalhaven band played a 'patriotic air.'"* After feasting on lobsters, Gompers spoke, stirring the crowd and complimenting the men on their success.[307]

The fishermen flexed their new muscle. In 1907 the union demanded twenty cents a pound for their lobsters, up five cents from what they had been paid. The compromise deal of 18 cents benefitted not only them, but all organized fishermen on the coast.[308] However, their victory was short-lived. The nation's economy plummeted in 1907, and the union movement quickly stalled. Unemployment increased, wages and prices fell, the lobster market faltered, and the men hunkered down. By 1909 Vinalhaven was one of only four communities that still had an active union, but it also faded.

This experience, though brief, helped pave the way for cooperative efforts throughout the twentieth century, including the Vinalhaven Credit Union (c. 1941), the Vinalhaven Handicraft Cooperative (1940s), the Lobstermen's Association (1954–the present); the Maine Lobstering Union started on Vinalhaven in 2012 after a lobster glut forced prices down. The Vinalhaven Fisherman's Cooperative was established in 1974 and is ongoing. Many lobstermen and women on the island sell to the Co-op, which works as a distributor. It also buys fuel and bait in bulk for fishermen. When profits exceed expenses, each member gets a rebate.[309]

The apparent vitality of Lane-Libby Fisheries Co. indicated an ongoing market for fishermen's catch. Although by 1910 herring, shad, blue-backs and mackerel were being frozen, the plant still salted cod as well as fillets from a variety of groundfish species, including haddock, cusk, pollock and hake, a diversity which no doubt helped maintain their supply.

Several bookkeeping pages that year offer a glimpse of the weekly work of fish-skinners. (If you've ever skinned a single fish, these numbers impress.) During the week of July 18, 1910, a nineteen-year-old "laborer" named Frank Small (1890–1965) skinned 410 lbs. of "Extra-Large Cod", 934 lbs. of "Medium cod," 201 lbs. of "Small cod," 1,243 lbs. of Cusk, 108 of Haddock, and 340 of Hake. In all, 2826 lbs. of fish, for which he earned $10.20. Fishing continued into winter. The week of December 26, 1910, Frank skinned 81 lbs of "large cod," 1,772 of "Medium cod'" 126 of "Small cod," 78 of Haddock, and 158 of Hake—2215 lbs. of fish, for which he earned $6.87.[310]

In 1910, approximately thirty fishing vessels under 20 tons were registered to Vinalhaven owners.[311] Sixty-two islanders worked for the "Fish company". Twenty were women, the majority of whom worked as "packers." Several were trimmers, and boners. Almeda O. Smith (1848–1928) was a manager. Male job titles include "salter," "splitter," "weigher," "trimmer," and "dresser." Only five men were listed as skinners. But Frank Small is called a "laborer," so his designation doesn't fit with his work.[312]

A Maine state report on Lane-Libby published in 1910 suggests total production numbers much bigger than the random "skinning" pay sheets predict, though not all fish were skinned. "Yearly output varies from 6,000,000 to 8,000,000 pounds of groundfish, consisting of cod, cusk, haddock, hake and pollock; from 1,000 to 1,500 barrels of glue; 300 to 400 tons of fish fertilizer; 200 to 300 barrels of oil and 50,000 to 100,000 pounds of sounds."[313] The company sold throughout the western hemisphere. "They pack boneless fish in all sizes of packages, etc.; also, many different grades of fish which are marketed mostly in the New England States, New York, Philadelphia, Baltimore and the West. Also, large quantities of hard dried fish of different kinds are shipped to the West Indies and South America."[314]

Lane-Libby bought from fishermen and dealers: "Their supply of fish is secured from boats and vessels which land at their factory at Vinalhaven. They also buy largely of the smaller fish dealers at different ports along the coast of Maine and in Nova Scotia." The report bursts with enthusiasm. "They are the largest wholesale dealers in Maine and it is the only plant in the country combining a cold storage building to furnish bait for the fishermen, a fish factory to take care of their catch, and a glue and oil factory to take care of all the by-products." The company continued to import salt "from the Mediterranean ports and supply to a great extent the other fish concerns along the coast. . . . They can salt in their buildings at one time 3,000,000 pounds of fish."[315] Sidney Winslow, who wrote in the 1940s when that era's fishermen could give him first-hand accounts, reported that during the factory's heyday it bought almost everything that the local fishermen could catch. By 1913 the company ledgers mentioned that they purchased lobsters, too.[316]

A good number of island families partly supported themselves by laboring in the factory or selling to it. "The Company employ at their Vinalhaven factory from 75 to 100 men and women. They also operate a glue factory at Eastport . . . also a great many fishermen in boats and vessels which go after the supply of fish, varying from 100 to 200 men at different seasons of the year."[317]

But an outside audit in 1915 suggests that Lane-Libby's claims were inflated. The company's bookkeeping was inexact. Profit margins during the years the auditor examined were thinner than claimed, and their inventories smaller. Why they struggled for profit is unclear—though as the century progressed similar situations repeated in other local fish processing plants, usually as market prices varied or fish stocks fell. After changing hands several times, the company was purchased by General Foods Corporation, and then shuttered in 1940.[318]

What was the working harbor like in the early years of the twentieth century? Wendell Smith (1901–1984) described hanging out on the fish wharfs as a boy. During school vacations he earned ten cents an hour working in a fish factory—likely Lane-Libby.

His task was cleaning cod "napes and sounds." Napes are "the thin flaps covering the gut of the fish." Sometimes they were saved for chowder or fishcakes. Sounds were used for glue and to clarify beer.[319] While Wendell worked downstairs, a group of fish skinners—perhaps Frank Small among them—labored in the loft above him stripping the fish. Wendell's memories of going up to pester them hint at the rough and tumble side of the wharves. Playful, but with an edge:

> *We kids used to go up there and raise the devil. After a while they'd get tired of it and grab one of us, put us in a barrel, and shove the barrel under the bench. There wasn't much more than two inches from the top of the barrel to the bench. We'd kick and thrash around, trying to get out. When they finally did let us out, we'd put the fish to them!*[320]

Years later, Isabel Barbara Fraser Calderwood (1900–1996) described how her friend armed herself with hatpins when they went into town:

Vinalhaven was a busy town when I was growing up. . . . Many boats came here to sell fish to Lane Libby Fish Wharf. Some of the men from these boats were rather rough looking beings, which gave rise to the story that they would cut off a girl's braids of hair. So my life long girl friend, Ruth Billings, used to carry hat pins when we went down town—just in case![321]

All was not scary. Recalling the lively harbor of her childhood, Vera Johnson (1895–1995) added a more lyrical detail to the scene. "*I remember the big boats that brought salt. The boats would be anchored out in the harbor. In the evening you could hear the sailors singing and violins playing.*"[322]

As the Teens became the Twenties, and World War I ended (around 90 islanders had served in the war), island fishing continued, though the island population (numbering 1965—down 16 percent from 1910) and the total number of fishermen and lobstermen (down by 51, almost 25 percent) diminished. The 1920 Census counted 157 fishermen: 33 specified that they fished for lobsters, and 10 managed or attended weirs. Only 23 islanders listed employment as fish factory workers, confirming the downturn at Lane-Libby.[323]

The 1920s and 1930s marked the end of the transition from sail and oar power to motor powered vessels. Islanders continued to lobster, dig clams, and catch groundfish, mackerel and herring. Markets and buyers changed continually. Alton "Sunny" Oakes recalled that for many years local processing plants used the railroads to ship fresh mackerel south.

Then they used to ship a lot of mackerel down there too on ice. Of course, on ice it would last two or three days and they would ship them by train. The train would run out of Rockland . . . We used to ship them in those kegs with water and ice. That was probably through the 20s, 30s and 40s even.[324]

Large racks of drying salt fish still covered open ground around the harbor. Lane-Libby evolved briefly into the Libby-Burchell factory. The Sawyer sardine factory kept on into the mid-1920s before closing. From 1921 to 1947, C. F. Grimes ran a fresh and cured fish business. Burnham-Morrill opened a plant on the island in the 1940s that canned mackerel, herring and clams as well as fish cakes; and Clyde Bickford opened C. L. Bickford Fisheries in the early 1940s. When fishing improved or new species became marketable, new processing plants appeared to replace the old, shuttered ones.[325]

In the 1930 census, Vinalhaven's population had fallen to 1843, thanks to the closing of most of the quarries. There were also fewer fishermen. Of the 124 listed, 83 men lobstered, 2 seined, 4 still fished with handlines, and another 35 were trawling. Unlike tub trawling, where hooks were strung at intervals along a line that could be 1000 ft long, these fishermen were likely otter trawling, using a motorized vessel to pull a large net through the water close to the bottom, the mouth of which was held open by two pieces of wood called otter boards. Seven men worked as lobster buyers. And 29 worked in local sardine, clam or glue factories.

By 1940 the population had fallen to 1629. The Depression hit the island hard, and many islanders left to find jobs on the mainland. The Works Progress Administration (WPA) employed a large number of those who stayed. Mary E. Arnold, an organizer who came to the island to help fisherman start credit unions, summed the bleak island prospects as the 1940s began. Note that her population figure is lower. Perhaps by 1941 several hundred more people had left:

> Vinalhaven needed rebuilding. Population 1,276. 455 men. 107 men between the ages of eighteen and forty. Quarries closed. Most of the young people leaving Vinalhaven. Paving block industry folded up. Net factory closed. Fish wharf shut down. Wharf rotting. Only lobstering left as a means of getting a living, lobstering and some sixteen dying stores. 176 lobster fishermen, most of them older men. One third of the population registered for surplus commodities.[326]

Woodrow Bunker later recalled the era's hardship,

> *I graduated high school in 1936 and my first year out of school I got a job at Bay State Fish cutting fillets. We were paid thirty cents an hour and the women got twenty-five cents an hour for packing the fish. One week I made $30.00 but I did not enjoy the hundred hours it took to earn that much! That winter was the worst I ever put in as there was no work of any kind, credit was cut off at the stores . . . There was not much work to be had in 1939, winter was coming and I had a new family to support. I was lucky and got a job with the WPA—$11.00 a week. We managed to get by on that. The WPA was a Godsend to the town and kept it from closing down altogether. All able-bodied men who wanted to work could get a job even though it didn't pay much.*[327]

Perhaps due to the absence of other work, perhaps because there were fish and lobsters to catch, the number for fishermen ticked up slightly to 138 in the 1940 census. One hundred and ten men called themselves lobster fishermen, twelve clam fishermen, eight were draggers, two seiners, four fished on otter trawlers. One called himself a "ground fishermen," and one was just a plain "fisherman."

Two hundred and sixty-five islanders served in World War II, upholding once again the island's long tradition of service. Even the town's beloved doctor, Ralph P. Earle, took a leave of absence to offer his medical skills to the war effort.[328] But the island needed a doctor. Serendipitously, a British woman named Ana Balfour, fleeing the bombing in England with her two children,

Amelia and Elliot, and staying with friends in North Carolina, learned of the opening. War restrictions prevented her husband, also a doctor, from sending money abroad, so she badly needed work. She applied for the island job and got it.

At some point Balfour wrote a short manuscript for her children—she refers to herself as "Mummy"—that gives a charming view of Vinalhaven during their stay (1942–1945). The simple, quiet, bucolic island she describes—the island that summer people would seek out in years to come—seems to have reemerged from the failed industries, the Depression, and the War.

We pick up Balfour's tale as the family sets out:

Mummy borrowed money to buy railway tickets to Maine, which was a long journey—two nights and two days on the train. They reached Rockland . . . early one morning. It was a rough, windy, little port. . . . Before the war there had been two proper paddle steamers to take passengers to and fro, but these had both been requisitioned by the government. All that was left was a little fishing boat with Captain Philbrook—"Charlie" . . . in charge. The boat was called the "Ruth M." . . . [S]he was loaded with goods and luggage—Mummy sat on a sack of corn and Amelia and Elliot perched on a trunk. . . .

The journey over took nearly three hours. . . . When Charlie put his boat in at the big wharf there was a crowd of people waiting—more even than usually waited, since the villagers heard that the new doctor was arriving. The undertaker had been asked to meet Mummy, and he drove them away in his car.

They stayed in a pleasant white house with Elva Teel (1888–1964) for a few days, and she gave them lovely things to eat—clam chowder and lobsters and lovely apple pies. . . . There was a patient waiting at Elva Teel's when Mummy arrived. Mummy had to get all the former doctor's medical things out of storage, and she had to buy a car which she promised to pay for as soon as she made some money. . . .

The first winter there was a great deal of snow and ice. Amelia and Elliot loved it. Mummy bought them sleds and they had great fun sliding down hills with the other children. The snow made Mummie's work very hard, as the roads were often blocked. More than once she had to ask the road men to drive their snow plough along a road to a patient's house so she could follow with her car. It was very cold—often 20 degrees below zero . . . Once the harbour froze over mail nor food could be brought in for nearly a week. Mummie at these times was very worried, because she knew she would never get a patient to the hospital on the mainland if she had urgent ones. . . .

The summer was lovely beside the sea. Amelia and Elliot were awakened early each morning by the sounds of the fishermen rowing out in the dinghies to their boats. Then, all day, while they were away fishing out at sea, their dinghies bobbed at their buoys. In the setting sun the little fishing boats came in again, and the men shouted to each other across the water to discuss the day's catch. . . .

In the summer the children

watched the fishermen drying and mending their nets, making new lobster pots and painting their buoys.

*   The house they lived in had belonged to a boat builder and the fishermen were accustomed to haul up their boats in the late winter, in order to repair them and scrape them, and paint them for the spring. They asked Mummie if she minded if they still did this, so the house was surrounded by boats, and Amelia and Elliot helped the fishermen with their work. It was very exciting when the spring came and the boats were finished and all the neighbours came to help launch them.*

As soon as the war ended, the Balfours headed home to England. After a "long and trying" voyage, they reached the port of Liverpool on Christmas Eve 1945.[329]

CODA: RELICS AND SKELETONS: VINALHAVEN, 1939

On May 21, 1939, a cloudy Sunday, John Gordon went out Indian "relic" hunting on Lane's Island, a part of Vinalhaven, Maine, connected to the larger island by a short causeway. Gordon, already in his late sixties, was an itinerant "tramp" printer, born in Scotland and raised in Canada, who had drifted to the island three years earlier and set up a small printing shop.

We don't know why John Gordon went out digging in a "shell heap" that particular Sunday morning—except that it was one way some islanders spent leisure hours. We do know that, unlike many such efforts when shoveling yielded little, this one unearthed an ancient grave. Gordon's labor began a chain of events that included the uncovering of three fragile skeletons, a self-appointed watchman falling to his death into the grave and crushing one of them; and local "vandals" attempting to steal them all. Some days later, the remains would be declared those of "Red Paint People"—believed at the time to be a "mysterious" band that had settled on the Fox Islands a thousand years earlier, and then inexplicably disappeared. After a few weeks, they would be donated and delivered to the Peabody Museum of Archaeology and Ethnology at Harvard University by a Rockland Medical Examiner named H. J. Weissman (or Weisman), ending the island saga.

In 1939, digging for "relics" was still a fairly recent societal phenomenon. A handful of eighteenth and early-nineteenth century Americans had shown interest in earlier peoples, their artifacts and ancient sites. Thomas Jefferson partially excavated a Native American mound in Virginia in the 1780s. In the 1840s Henry David Thoreau closely observed how much of New England bore traces of its pre-European inhabitants; he wrote about hunting arrowheads—including in Maine. But the two men's interests were hardly mainstream. Historians point to the 1876 Centennial Exposition in Philadelphia and later the 1893 World's Columbian Exposition in Chicago—where crafts *and living native people* were displayed—as popular events that awakened broader interest in "Indians," as well as excitement over the possessions they left behind.[330]

Other late nineteenth century cultural shifts helped the enthusiasm for "relics" coalesce. In the decades after the Civil War, archaeology in the United States was just beginning to become professionalized. Acquiring artifacts for newly created museums soon became one focus of the young field. The American Museum of Natural History opened in 1869 in New York City. The Field Museum in Chicago opened in 1894, and the National Museum of Natural History in Washington, DC, opened its doors in 1910. The final conquest of the Plains Indians occurred within these same decades at the Battle of Wounded Knee in South Dakota in 1890. The end of fighting may have transformed "enemies" into objects of popular and academic interest, as well as artifacts to be collected.

A good number of citizens likely felt more comfortable thinking of the defeated people as inanimate "relics" than as fellow countrymen. The word "relic" describes an object preserved from the past. It often has a religious connotation—the once living bone slivers of saints, or the religious tokens they carried. Whatever tangled mix of ideas and feelings the word expressed for contemporaries who heard and repeated it—romance, religious fervor, triumphalism, exoticism, remorse, treasure, guilt, curiosity—the pursuit of relics gradually gained momentum.[331]

Abundant artifacts had been left on Maine islands by native bands. In Sarah Orne Jewett's classic Maine novel *Country of the Pointed Firs* (1896) someone mentions "Shell-Heap Island" and adds, *"'Twas 'counted a great place in Old Indian times; you can pick up their stone tools 'most any time if you hunt about.'"* On Vinalhaven, a man named Ulmer Smith (1875–1946) is said to have assembled an extensive collection of arrowheads that disappeared after he died.[332]

John Gordon and other islanders may have spent Sundays "relic hunting" because it was something free and sociable to fill empty hours, or because they simply enjoyed the chase. It's likely that at least some of the under-employed men who searched the rocky beach dreamed of unearthing valuable treasure. A decade into the Great Depression, islanders were as squeezed as Americans everywhere. Later the same May week Gordon went digging, island chronicler Sidney Winslow noted in his diary, *"It is quite apparent that this is going to be the hardest summer in the history of Vinalhaven as there is but little prospect of being any work at the quarries. . . . There is no work at the fish wharf and the report is that there will be none for an indefinite period."*[333]

At least one local relic-hunter had had contact with an off-island archaeologist, which suggests that some islanders were aware of outside interest, and perhaps of a market. In a diary entry on August 19, 1935, Sidney Winslow wrote,

> *Les Dyer recently unearthed a pipe made of soapstone out of one of the shell heaps at Dyer's Island. Prof. Moorehead, a famous archaeologist says it is a relic of the mysterious Red Paint People and is probably 700 or 1000 years old—perhaps older than that.*[334]

Warren K. Moorehead (1866–1939), archaeologist and excavator of Maine sites, was among the first American academics intent both on protecting the country's remaining native inhabitants, and on preserving their culture. Starting in the 1880s, he explored and documented sites in the Midwest.

In 1901, the year it opened, Moorehead was made head of the Robert S. Peabody Institute of Archaeology in Andover, Massachusetts. While there he became interested in long ago maritime inhabitants that he and some contemporaries called the Red Paint People, a group that could be studied because they had left middens along what is now the Maine coast. Middens are ancient, multi-layered piles of shells and debris left all along the Atlantic seaboard by long ago hunter-gathers. While originally seen as garbage heaps, some contemporary scholars suggest that some middens may have been intentionally constructed to create monuments. Middens are sometimes small, sometimes huge (like the Whaleback midden on the Damariscotta River in Maine, over a thousand feet long, and equally wide until much of it was dredged up, hauled away and ground up for chicken feed in the late 19th century). As noted earlier, because of millennia of rising seas, many of the oldest middens are underwater and inaccessible.[335]

The miracle of middens from the perspective of later Maine excavators is that the calcium carbonate in the mollusk shells, together with Maine's acid soil, prevented the thousands-of-years-old organic matter—mammal bones, fish vertebrae, plant fibers—from breaking down the way it would have in other soil conditions.

Some middens also contain pottery shards, and stone or bone tools; and the newly minted archaeologists quickly came to view "shell heaps" as hoards awaiting their shovels. In his 1922 book, *The Archaeology of Maine*, Moorehead offers a snapshot of how he and his teams worked.

> *During several years of exploration in the state of Maine, we dug in some thirty-five or forty shell heaps. In those heaps in which very little pottery or few bone or stone implements occurred, we stopped work after opening four or five pits. A large crew was taken along and therefore it was possible in one day, with an average of ten men and boys, to excavate an area 8 [meters] in length, 6 [meters] in width, and 1 [meter] deep. Therefore, if a day's work in a shell heap resulted in finding less than fifty or sixty objects, the heap was abandoned and we got aboard our boat and moved to another site.*[336]

From our vantage point today, Moorehead's high muscle-power, high-speed approach seems reckless, even disastrous. Only gradually did the new field realize that the site mattered as much as, or more than, the objects taken from it; and only reluctantly did the awareness dawn that one person's museum-filling mission was another's sacrilege. Not surprisingly, surviving members of Indian bands often experienced the digging as an outrageous plundering of their past, particularly when human remains were unearthed and carried away. Twentieth century Federal laws have finally acknowledged this point, and bit by bit offered increased protection as well as repatriation of some museum holdings.

It is also true that middens were unprotected. Many had long since been disrupted, and Moorehead's crew may have felt that they were working against time to "save" what they could. Beside his list of potential "Red Paint" graves in Maine, Moorehead annotates, "*destroyed by roadbuilders,*" "*destroyed by railroad,*" "*destroyed*" next to many.[337]

The "Red Paint" people dusted their dead with rust-colored ochre before they buried them, and this ritual was the source of the name. Twenty-first century Wabanaki archeologists and some members of the Wabanaki Nations in Maine object to the "Red Paint" appellation because of the disrespect implicit in it: Moorehead and others described this band as a "mysterious" one that appeared out of nowhere and then disappeared—a narrative apparently offered because the band's sophistication, careful devotion to burying its dead (including domestic dogs), and obvious skills belied contemporary assumptions about "primitive" peoples. The Wabanaki believe that the Archaic era dwellers were not enigmatic outliers who appeared and disappeared, nor a band that possessed unusual skills, but simply the ancestors of populations that continued to inhabit the coast until conquered by Europeans millennia later.[338]

On that May Sunday morning in 1939, John Gordon dug in the Lane's Island shell heap for a while until he hit stone and gave up, moving on to an easier spot. A young man named Kenneth Snowdeal (1921–1981), one of several people nearby, took Gordon's place, lifting the big stones or pushing them aside. (The eighteen-year-old had previously collected arrowheads and a fragment of a flint knife blade from the same area.)[339]

Snowdeal lifted a rock to toss it. Much to his and several bystanders' astonishment, his effort opened up an intact grave later described as "*clam-shell lined*" and "*about 40 feet above high-water mark.*" As he peered into it and moved other stones, he saw three intact, mottled brown skeletons—apparently two adults and a child. "*The news spread quickly and then, of course, there was a grand rush to the spot,*" Sidney Winslow recounted a few days later in his newsletter, *The Vinalhaven Neighbor.*[340]

Winslow noted in his diary, "*Ada Creed called at my house today with her car and wanted me to go to Lane's Island and see the Indian skeletons they had unearthed there . . . It was surely a sight worth seeing when we consider the mystery that surrounded it.*"

The events that followed were calamitous. "*While I was there Gust Carlson, a Swede, who had been one of the relic hunters, seemed to be looking after one of the skeletons to see that it was not disturbed.*" A short time later, the fifty-eight-year-old Carlson collapsed, fell into the grave and died.

His body *"shattered the best-preserved skeleton as it plunged into the pit. The other two skeletons,"* Winslow continues, *"had crumbled as they were removed shortly after their discovery by Snowdeal . . ."*[341]

The 1930 census lists Gust Carlson as a "paving cutter," seemingly without kin on the island, who lived in a boarding house. A May 23, 1939, front page story in *The Courier Gazette* in Rockland headlined *"Dies in Indian Grave: Gust Carlson a victim while delving among skeleton remains"* reflected onlookers' shock about the death, *"Nobody could recall that the man had ever complained about his physical condition, and his sudden demise was entirely unexpected."* Trying to offer some explanation, they added that a postmortem examination found Carlson to have heart disease.[342]

After nightfall on Sunday, the broken bits of the third skeleton disappeared from the Lane's Island site. According to *The Courier Gazette*, V. H. Shields (1890–1973), the island doctor and *"an amateur archaeologist,"* had wanted all three left in the grave overnight so he could study them there. *"When yesterday morning [Monday] came, it was discovered that vandals had not waited for examination and a quick investigation resulted in the finding of one skeleton in a Vinalhaven home, and a bag containing the bones of two other skeletons in another home. The grim relics were promptly surrendered . . ."* [343]

Writing in his newsletter the following week, Winslow fumed *"how deplorable it was"* that the skeletons were taken from the site by amateurs. When V. H. Shields did get to examine them, the doctor speculated that one had been a man, one a child of maybe seven years, and one either a woman or a young man. He noticed a dent in the left side of the man's skull that made him wonder if it had been "crushed by a weapon."

News of the discovery spread. A week later, Frederick Johnson, a curator from the Peabody Institute in Andover, traveled to the island apparently hoping to find other artifacts. He *"spent a few days in town last week and gave a considerable amount of time in digging in the shell deposit at Lane's Island near where the ancient skeletons were recently found."*[344]

In August 2012, I interviewed Phil Dyer (1927–2018) an eighty-five-year-old boat builder whose great-great-great-great grandfather, Joshua Dyer, arrived on the island in 1814. Phil was a son of Leslie Dyer who found the soapstone pipe. I spoke with him about his lifetime of fishing and boatbuilding. I hadn't yet learned about relic hunting or of the pipe's existence and didn't know to inquire.

Yet, when I asked about his childhood, Phil spontaneously recalled the day and the sudden death:

[T]here were Indians on this island, it was loaded and everybody went to hunt Indian relics. But one year they opened a grave and the man that owned the land stopped them from digging. That was a weird experience. I was only about 10

years old. . . . I stood alongside the man who fell face first right into the grave.
. . . He opened the grave of some Indians and he fell into the grave.

I asked Phil why Carlson had collapsed, and I appreciated his succinct response, *"Because there's a curse opening graves. "*[345]

An ancient, skeleton-filled grave, sudden death, newspaper stories, and visiting archaeologists. My own interest aroused by Phil's memory; I poked around in the Vinalhaven Historical Society hoping to learn what had happened to the skeletons. A 1939 newspaper story reiterated that they had been shipped to the Peabody Museum at Harvard University. Nothing more recent was on file.

Why, I wondered, had the skeletons gone to Cambridge, Massachusetts? And, with all that museums were scooping up in those decades, would they even have catalogued and kept them?

In the autumn of 2014, I emailed the Peabody at Harvard. This museum is a generation older than the Peabody in Andover, having been founded in 1866. Perhaps it was also better endowed and more able to make acquisitions during the Great Depression.

Silence. Two weeks later, I wrote again. The next day I received a positive reply. Yes, they did have "human skeletal remains" collected on Vinalhaven in 1939. I found the news rather too exciting, as though I had wandered into the buzzing crowd at Lane's Island. In retrospect, I think I was simply moved to learn that someone, in spite of the bungled and dubious acquisition, had preserved the bits of bone. Someone had taken care.

I wrote back and asked if I might visit and see the skeletons for myself. The careful response, a qualified yes, quickly showed me how far archaeology, museums and Federal Law have moved since the 1930s. Caught between the lawlessness of the past, and the anger and legislation it created, museums at some point learned to behave more respectfully—perhaps even to tiptoe.

The Wabanaki Confederacy claims all Maine excavated Native "skeletal elements"—and the individuals they once were—as ancestors. I was told that *if* I wrote a research proposal that justified my interest, and if I agreed to their regulation—restrictions calculated to support "ethical curation and respectful learning," and intended to protect the very fragile material and to prevent further emotional violation or controversy—they would arrange a visit.[346]

The research purpose on my application described my desire to fill in and bring full circle the story of the Vinalhaven skeletons. A second one, unwritten, was to continue amending my own partial collusion in a travesty. When I was in grade school Indians were portrayed either as savages to be righteously killed, or as subordinate allies, like Tonto on *The Lone Ranger*, one-dimensional representations best described as insulting cartoons. Though I had read history and fiction about Native American lives, it wasn't until I read Charles C. Mann's 2005 book, *1491: New Revelations of the Americas before Columbus*, that I more fully grasped the distortion of our societal lens and the skew of my own miseducation.

Mann explores the multiple cultures within the Americas before 1491, all in possession of skills and complex knowledge, and decimated by smallpox and other illnesses (mostly transmitted by late 15th and 16th century European fishermen, trappers and explorers) ahead of any attempts to colonize the land. So many Native Americans died of illness—numbers, Kevin Baker summarizes in a 2005 review, as "about one-fifth of the world's population at the time, a level of destruction unequaled before or since." The damage to their societies was devastating. He observes, "European misreadings of America should not be attributed wholly to ethnic arrogance. The 'savages' most of the colonists saw, without ever realizing it, were usually the traumatized, destitute survivors of ancient and intricate civilizations that had collapsed almost overnight . . ."[347]

Mann writes, "Having grown separately for millennia, the Americas were a boundless sea of novel ideas, dreams, stories, philosophies, religions, moralities, discoveries and all the other products of the mind. . . ." The illness together with colonists' belief in their own world view, and their wish to control and profit from the land, combined to foreclose the cultural exchanges that could have been enriching to people on both continents. Baker observes, "In the end, the loss to us all was incalculable."[348]

Some days later, I spent an hour with Olivia Herschensohn, the Collections Steward who carefully unwrapped the bones and taught me how to look at them. The normal visitor to this locked-off part of the Peabody is an academic osteologist (a person who studies skeletons and bones) often from another university, sometimes another country—someone who spends a few weeks carefully testing, measuring, and comparing features of remains from sites all over the world, in order to contribute knowledge to the field.

The bones that Olivia, hands in latex gloves, set out for me to contemplate, had a slightly mottled, tan to mahogany brown surface. Some were whole, and impressive in their apparent sturdiness, others were crumbled into bits and pieces. I could easily recognize parts of jaws with teeth, and long tibias; but many shapes were as unfamiliar to me as they were obvious to my guide. Nothing about them revealed the century when they entered the ground or anything much about the humans to whom they gave stature. The museum record states that that they are somewhere between 500 and 2700 years old. It would now be possible to know their age and provenance more precisely, but my amateur interest offered no justification for such testing.

Olivia assured me they were indeed the three individuals I sought. She commented that they were unusually well preserved for coastal Maine "skeletal remains"—since the sea and the air often deteriorate them. I took their relative intactness as a reflection on how effectively sealed away they had been. Someone had built the stone and shell grave very deliberately.

Two of the skeletons are more complete, a young child and a middle-aged adult male. I learned that the nuchal crest where neck muscles attach to the cranium is one of many features used to infer the individual's sex. There was no evidence of traumatic injury. Olivia quickly put to rest my thought that perhaps a family had met their end together, explaining that the presence of three skeletons in the same grave did not necessarily mean that the dead had been related. Such an idea is an overstep unless supported by additional information. I appreciated her care. (A Peabody Museum curator who reviewed this essay before granting me permission to publish it revised this paragraph and parts of several others in accordance with their dictates of "ethical curation").[349]

The impact of Gust Carlson's body meant that the museum had received only a few bits of shoulder and foot bone from what the third skeleton had once been. The museum's record states that the skeletons arrived by way of the Rockland Maine medical examiner, Dr. H. J. Weismann, but there is no fuller story of their journey.

Sometime after the Native American Graves Reparation Act was passed in 1990, members of the Wabanaki council traveled to the museum and spent time alone with the Maine remains. They left small offerings (that I may not describe) with each of the skeletons, including those from Vinalhaven. As we were looking at the bones, I glimpsed the tiny gifts and felt moved to tears. The visitors paid tribute, and re-hallowed their ancestors' remains. Their ritual also offered a simple, elegant response to the notion of "Red Paint People," rendering it a kind of graffiti, a wish to have difference mean "less than," a misleading "tag," sprayed over other people's inevitably mysterious lives.

The visit, the careful instruction and unexpected intimacy of the encounter shifted the remains from bones to unreachable strangers. I wished for a time keyhole so I might watch the man, woman, and child each go about their day. Who were they? Family? Victims of illness? One year's winter deaths? What knowledge did they carry? What were their words for *starlight, canoe,* or *rough waves*? How were the child's feet kept warm during the long winters? The evidence was too thin for story making, and I banged hard into the opaque Plexiglas that walls the past.

After maybe half an hour more, I thanked Olivia and left. I walked down the staircase distracted, a little dreamy, mulling the brevity of living flesh, and the fraught quest to preserve what bits remain.[350]

Dick Matthews Photo. c. 1955 Seining in Arey's Harbor. In the dory, Bruce Johnson, Wallace Smith, and Lyford "Dike" Conary haul in the net to collect the fish. Dick Matthews. Vinalhaven Historical Society

c. 1955 Unidentified man uses a pitchfork to transfer fish into barrels (as seen here) or nets, which were then hoisted from the boat Dick Mathews. Vinalhaven Historical Society

c.1955 Seining in Arey's Harbor. Men in the dory are "seining the pocket" after closing off Arey's Harbor. Dick Mathews. Vinalhaven Historical Society

35mm film c. 1936–39. Nelsons Fish House in Sands Cove, Vinalhaven, Vinalhaven Historical Society

35mm film c. 1936–39. Cod skins are laid out to dry and cure on racks called fish flakes at C. F. Grimes fish company on the west side of Carvers Harbor, Vinalhaven. Vinalhaven Historical Society

35mm film c. 1936–39. Fish house near C. F. Grimes fish company

The Ruth-Mary loaded with herring and barrels of fish scales. c. 1960 Isabelle Osgood. Vinalhaven Historical Society.

Seine net repair on the Christina M. operated by Robert "Bobby" Warren. Chandler Blackington. Vinalhaven Historical Society

Traps and buoys on the dock at Carver's Harbor. Penobscot Marine Museum and Elin Elisofon, 1967

Elsie Wooster Calderwood netting at home, c. 1970 Milton Ackoff. Vinalhaven Historical Society

One of the earliest photographs of Carvers Harbor, taken in the 1860s. The original Union church steeple can be seen in the center of the image between the masts of the schooner. Vinalhaven Historical Society

William Merrithew glass plate negative, c. 1900. Barker's boat shop on Old Harbor Road with several boats in production. The area of what is now Pond Street can be seen in the distance on the left. Vinalhaven Historical Society

Eastern Illustrating postcard image of the Ingerson and Dyer fish houses. Capt. Frank Rogers seated outside.c. 1945 Vinalhaven Historical Society

Roberts Brothers Net Factory workers c. 1890. Pictured standing: L. Julian, F. Shirley, M. Crandall, L. Smith, B. Mullen, J. Sanborn, and C. Hopkins; middle: C. Smith, E. Roberts, and E. Shirley; front: E. Shirley, H. Smith, H. Creed, and F. Nightingale. Employees at the factory-made nets to fit over horses to keep off the biting flies. Vinalhaven Historical Society

Family snapshot courtesy of Elsie Holmquist Dunham. Rosa D. Anderson Holmquist working at her net stand, late-1940s. Vinalhaven Historical Society

Benjamin Coombs and his son Lyford plowing their field on Coombs Neck, c. 1905. Vinalhaven Historical Society

Photo by William Merrithew, c. 1893. Timothy Dyer, 90, caught this 332lb. halibut by himself in an open dory, reeling it in by hand. Vinalhaven Historical Society

Eastern Illustrating postcard image of the inside of a lobsterman's fish house, with rope, buoys, and traps. Early 1940s. Vinalhaven Historical Society.

Vinalhaven Historical Society, Lyle Griffin glass plate negative collection. c.1910 Fish to be processed at Lane & Libby Fisheries on Carvers Harbor, Vinalhaven. In 1887, it was estimated that Lane & Libby processed nearly two million pounds of fish.

Lyle Griffin glass plate negative collection. c. 1910 Women here are working on salt fish, which they trimmed and packed in wooden boxes for retail sales in the Boston market. Vinalhaven Historical Society

Lyle Griffin glass plate negative collection. c. 1910 Drying racks outside of Lane & Libby Fisheries on the east side of Carvers Harbor looking towards West Main Street. Vinalhaven Historical Society

Lyle Griffin glass plate negative collection. c.1910 A successful hunting trip in Maine. Vinalhaven Historical Society

Lyle Griffin glass plate negative collection. c.1910 Unindentified men with large cod. Vinalhaven Historical Society

Undated. 1940s? Unidentified woman with two flounder outside Bridgeside Inn, Vinalhaven. Vinalhaven Historical Society

Vinalhaven Fisherman's Co-op buying station Janna M. Smith

Victor Ames off Matinicus, 1952. Courtesy of Lorraine Walker

II

WITHIN LIVING MEMORY

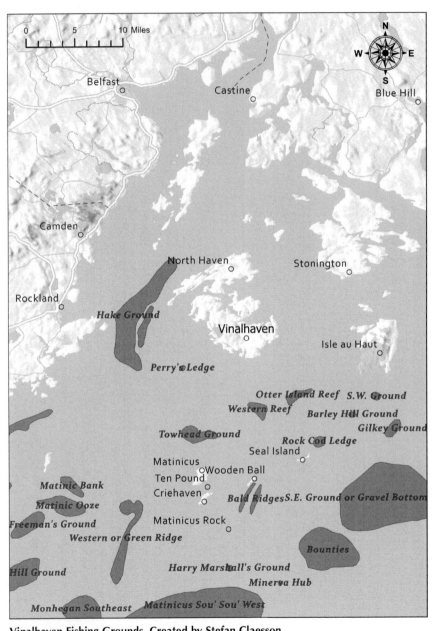

Vinalhaven Fishing Grounds. Created by Stefan Claesson.

8

Seasick

LOBSTERING TODAY

At dawn one summer morning in 2007 I joined Ronnie Walker, an island friend and lobsterman, on his boat as he and his sternman (in this case a woman) set out to haul traps. Forewarned that we'd be out all day, I'd packed a sandwich. The August weather was perfect, sunny and cool, the bay calm. I was happy for my sweatshirt and felt exhilarated just sitting on the dew-wet deck.

Today, lobstering is the one kind of fishing that remains vibrant and profitable on Vinalhaven. In Carver's Harbor, Sands Cove, and Indian Creek many other boats were untying lines and departing docks or moorings and beginning their day's work. Some, like ours, were big, powerful and expensive. Others were on their 4th or 5th owner and 2nd or 3rd engine. To an outsider, the bright glint of white hulls catches the eye. But fishermen (like lobstermen and sternmen—a term used for both genders) see the familiar faces and well-known boats of kin and neighbors—"Mr. D.," "Bounty," "Sea Spray," "Independence," "Illusion," "Night Moves"—painted neatly on the sterns. Some names recall actual people, others allude to the natural world, or to intangibles. They can be sincere or ironic, straightforward or tongue in cheek.

The best fishermen carry decades of knowledge about where to find lobsters and the nature of the bottom in each place they choose to set their trap. They know lobsters' habits and growth cycles, how water depth, tides, currents, seasons, temperatures, and other species affect them, and more. Ronnie started fishing as a boy, and few people know island waters as well as he does. Nor can most keep up with his pace, though many lobstermen share his satisfaction with the work.

In his 7th decade, Ronnie keeps in his head the exact location of all his 800 traps, even as he continually moves them around. Today's traps are lighter than the old wooden ones, and instead of being pulled up hand over hand, they are hoisted from the deep by a hydraulic winch. The work is still physically demanding. It requires constant lifting, bending, tossing, and moving about in a small space on a rocking boat. An island friend who fills in sometimes as sternman noted that, in middle age, he can't stay fit enough to do it if he only goes out once a week. It's like trying to run a race without training. Success takes knowledge, muscle, endurance, and ability.

The lobster traps Ronnie and his sternman handle are made of plastic-coated wire—simple but functional. In 2017, I visited *Island Lobster Supply*, a small trap-building factory on Vinalhaven run by Walden "Jo-Jo" Lazaro. There I learned that a fisherman can shape his trap any way he wants, but by law it cannot be bigger than 22,950 cubic inches. According to Kathy Young, who showed me around, most islanders want theirs 4 feet by 15 inches by 21 or 22½ inches.

Each trap is a rectangular mesh cage with a primary opening (called the entry head), and a smaller escape vent. Usually, bricks are secured in the traps to sink them and help stabilize them between hauls. Runners attached on their undersides raise them off the bottom just enough to spare crushing lobster claws that might protrude. The outside wire mesh comes in a number of different colors—yellow, lime green, black, blue. Local wisdom is that red doesn't work.

Basic traps at the Lobster Supply cost $75 in 2017 (and approximately $115 dollars in 2023), but buyers can add on special features, like a composite bottom runner, or a steel runner instead of the standard oak. Each fisherman has his preferences. Some people like steel runners for their weight, since bricks take up a trap's inside space. Those who do use bricks no longer employ bits of old houses or sidewalks. Contemporary trap bricks are manufactured in different shapes to fit the desires of different buyers.

An arrangement of metal rings and netting divides the trap into two parts, a "kitchen" where the bait hangs in a knit string or plastic bag, and a "parlor" where the lobsters are meant to linger. In recent years, "ghost panels" have been added. These pieces eventually disintegrate under water and free the catch when mishap separates trap from rope, or rope from buoy; they prevent "ghost fishing."[351]

The lobster caught in Maine, *Homarus americanus,* ranges between 8 and 24 inches long, and between 1 and 9 lbs. It can be legally sold in Maine if its length from the rear of the eye socket to the end of the body shell measures between 3¼ and 5 inches long; and if it's neither an egg-bearing nor a "v-notched" female. To preserve breeding stock, a fisherman catching an egg-bearing female puts a v-notch in her tail, designating her off limits until, after several years, the notch grows out.

Lobster traps are designed so that legal-sized lobsters, lured in by bait, can't leave, although undersized ones are free to exit. At least that's what people thought. Recently, researchers who made underwater videos learned that lobsters of all sizes go in and out of the traps freely. It's like Russian Roulette. Lobsters in the wrong trap at the wrong time get hauled up. Aside from the conservation regulations and the absence of traditional predators like cod, *Homarus americanus* is so plentiful because hundreds of thousands of bait bags have turned Penobscot Bay into a feed lot.[352]

Today, the Maine lobster "industry" is highly regulated. A Maine resident can set five traps but cannot sell lobsters. Harder to come by are commercial licenses: in 2018, the total number of licenses was capped statewide at 4800. One license must be relinquished before a new one is issued. Area C, where Vinalhaven is located had 945 in 2018. The Maine coast is divided into zones, and each lobsterman must set over 50% of his or her traps in his or her home zone. The lobsterman has the right to set the balance of traps in an adjacent zone. Each trap must be registered and possess a tag bought from the state that provides the owner's name and license number. Between June 1 and September 1 boats can only be on the water from half an hour before dawn to half an hour after dusk, and in summer they may not haul from after 4 o'clock on Saturday afternoon to before dawn on Monday. Regulations even dictate how the stripes are to be painted on fishermen's buoys.[353]

Conservation is a complex subject. It's not hard to imagine how these rules could sometimes rest like irritating burrs on the skin of people who have long assumed that some freedom from rules is a fair return for hunkering down on a granite rock in the cold sea. Still, for over a century, lobstermen have often worked with the state to protect lobsters. And in 1995, Maine explicitly split the authority for managing the fishery between the state and the industry. The resulting regulations and others like them have helped produce a booming lobster population that in 2021 generated $725,000,000 of sales for Maine. Most fishermen recognize some benefit from the rules though there is always controversy when new ones appear on the horizon, and many actively participate in the politics of the ever-changing regulations. In 2021, for example, some Vinalhaven fishermen strongly protested federal laws intending to prevent deadly entanglement of endangered Right Whales.[354]

One example of effective advocacy is an island-friendly section of Maine's license law: Maine waters are divided into 7 zones overseen by the Maine Department of Marine Resources. Each Zone has a governance/advisory group elected by fishermen in the Zone. In the area known as Zone C, which includes Vinalhaven, families who have fished for generations are now considered valuable contributors to the state's culture and heritage. Because this heritage warrants protection, island children are favored for licenses. If they complete an apprenticeship, they are eligible to get their licenses ahead of the long waitlists that frustrate everyone else.[355]

The aim of conservation may be good, and fishing restrictions often necessary, but the actual history of regulation *vis-à-vis* island fishing suggests ambiguous, even sometimes destructive results. Like most of us, fishermen prefer government that removes rather than creates impediments to their work; at the same time, some islanders' "pirate" sensibilities can lead to flouting regulations that support the common good. Although the stereotype may be of independent Maine fishermen speaking out against government's heavy hand, the truth is more nuanced.[356]

Lobsters have lately been staggeringly abundant in Penobscot Bay. A 2020 assessment notes, "The Maine lobster fishery is one of the world's most successful fisheries. Despite decades of increasingly heavy fishing pressure, lobster catches have grown to record high levels." There is little doubt that climate change is now driving lobsters toward Canada in search of cooler water and the future is uncertain, but everyone agrees that 2010 to 2021 were unrivaled years. Vinalhaven has been at the center of this plentiful catch; it is one of the "the busiest and most profitable" lobstering communities in Maine, and thus, one of the most successful in the world. In 2021, 199 islanders had commercial lobstering licenses. In 2017, according to Maine's Department of Marine Resources, Vinalhaven lobstermen set 144,505 traps.[357] In 2020, Vinalhaven fishermen hauled 7.04 million lbs that sold for $30.81 million. In 2020, 96.6 million lobsters hauled statewide sold for $406 million. Historical numbers offer perspective: from 1880, when state record keeping started, to 1980, the annual haul statewide rarely got above 20 million pounds. And it was often lower.[358]

What clouds the future? There are concerns today that fewer juvenile lobster are settling on the bottom—and thus surviving the early larval stage, the most vulnerable of their lives. The "American Lobster settlement index," which predicts lobster stock size in the future, is currently lower, but the meaning of the dip is unclear. For now, the stock is deemed healthy and its fishery "sustainable."[359]

Climate change is the big threat. Because it's relatively shallow, the Gulf of Maine is warming very quickly—two degrees centigrade between 2004 and 2013, "a rate faster than 99.9 percent of the global ocean." Lobsters don't like any water warmer than 18° Centigrade (64.4° Fahrenheit). The center of abundance is shifting to colder places "Down East." Hancock County recently nudged ahead of Knox County for highest harvest. And Canada looks like a destination. Some Vinalhaven fishermen are responding to these territory shifts by lobstering in winter in deeper, offshore water that requires a separate Federal permit.[360]

Speaking at a climate event in Augusta, Maine, in 2017, lobsterman Richard Nelson summarized some of the problems the Gulf of Maine is facing. Not only is the Gulf warming, he said, it's become more susceptible to acidification because of the "influx of nutrient-laden fresh water and atmospheric CO^2." He listed diverse troublesome phenomena currently being observed, including "an increase of severe weather events, harmful algal blooms, sea level rise—and . . . the decrease in shrimp and cod fish." Meanwhile, anomalous species like squid, black sea bass and red hake are inhabiting the warming water.[361]

The Gulf of Maine *is* suffering; but it is not dead. While most species (though not lobster) exist at levels radically below where they were when the first Europeans arrived, some stocks are more robust than others. Indeed, an ongoing battle between the remaining Gulf fishermen, and regulators from the National Oceanic and Atmospheric Administration (NOAA) concerns observed differences in fish stocks. A fisherman on the water each day on roughly the same grounds may see varieties and numbers of fish that he feels have been overlooked by the Feds; and the short version of the argument articulated by some fishermen is that you can't find fish if you don't know where to look. Meanwhile, the government assesses species using trawl surveys, during which an agency vessel of known dimensions and horsepower drags trawls of a specified gauge for thirty minutes at a randomly chosen place, depth, and substrate type within a management area. Scientists on board identify, count, and measure the fish taken from the haul and compare results statistically to earlier surveys done the same way. They argue that if you fish only where the fish are, you can't generalize what you see within the whole management area.

A crucial point of dispute is the best baseline from which to measure depletion or restoration. People argue about it because what is declared the baseline affects key decisions. When should fishing be restricted because stocks are too low? When have stocks recovered enough to support more fishing effort? In recent decades, many baselines used in management reflect less than 10 percent of historical levels of fish populations, which outrages conservationists. Yet, to fishermen threatened with losing their life's work, insisting on higher baselines feels controlling and punitive.

For Vinalhaven, the unexpected lobster bounty seems a miracle. No one could have predicted, amidst the turmoil of fish stock collapse in a rapidly changing Gulf, that lobsters would turn this huge reprieve into a glory-moment. But when I went out with Ronnie in 2007, this bull market was still hiding around a corner. Fuel costs were up, prices down; everyone on the water was a bit worried and grumpy. And the situation got worse before it got better. After the Icelandic banking system collapsed a year later, Canadian lobster plants could no longer borrow to buy Maine lobsters for processing. The recession also slowed coastal tourism for a few years, hurting the restaurant business. Paradoxically, the recession underscored again how Maine lobstermen's well being rides warily upon the ups and downs of international trade: it didn't matter how many crustaceans fishermen hauled from the deep if there was no market for them.[362]

The 2008 recession brought foreclosures and trouble to Vinalhaven. Younger lobstermen worked without much financial cushion—something their worried elders noted to me frequently when we talked. Then as now, lobstermen carrying home and boat mortgages need steady earnings, and sometimes overextend themselves. During good times, like the past dozen years starting in 2010, some buy big expensive boats to increase their comfort and allow them to go into deep water in winter, but also because it's exciting and they like to compete and showcase their high-earning status. (There is more money currently being made from lobstering on Vinalhaven now than ever in the past. A *Boston Globe* story in 2021 noted about Vinalhaven, "The top 20 lobstermen on the island had landings worth an average $579,000 apiece in 2019, placing them among the state's wealthiest residents, even with their staggering bait and fuel bills and hefty shares paid to sternmen.")[363]

To pay for the boats, they have to haul more lobsters . . . and around it goes. Contemporary costs for a boat, diesel fuel, bait, a sternman, and up to 800 traps to keep in repair far exceed what they were in the past. Bad seasons are inevitable, but there is always potential for profit in investing more. Older fishermen with less debt, more savings, and a better understanding of the ups and downs of catch across decades generally absorb the bad times better. And, of course, climate change is a wild card of a whole new order.

Some islanders feel mixed about the ways lobstering money has changed the island. "Hank," was not alone when, in 2015, he described his ambivalence about the shift in the community once serious money could be made. On the one hand, he was proud that his teenager could work hard and earn a year's college tuition in a summer "sterning." On the other, he felt wearied about the relentless pace of work and competition among fishermen that the boom had produced.

"*Now lobstering is a big business. Not a way of life, it's a business. . . . When I first started, people would have 400 traps, it was kind of friendly. Fun. But now, it's not fun. It's like a cut-throat business. Everybody's jealous of each other.*" In previous decades, the pace was slower, "*I mean if it was foggy people wouldn't go. Now everybody goes because everybody does.*" Everyone hauls all the time, because, if they don't, they're, "*afraid they're missing out and not getting their share. . . .*"[364]

Most Maine lobstermen's earnings are still fairly modest. A 2012 survey reported: "Seventy-three percent of active lobstermen are averaging $38,000 a year or less from the fishery and 97 percent are averaging $68,000 or less. Only three percent of the active license holders are earning an average of $125,000 or more."[365] As recently as 2019 the Maine median family income was $57, 918. But, as noted, the handful of island fishermen who fish hard all summer and then fish offshore in the winter can earn much more. *"[S]ome of those guys are making close to a million dollars . . . The offshore boats."* So, there's more pressure. Everything is scaled up. *"I mean you spend more now on bait than you even made back then."* Yet, some of the fun has gone out of daily life. [366]

It's hard now to remember the many years on the island when the take from lobstering was meager. Sadie Dyer (b. 1931), married for over six decades to Phil Dyer, recalled how difficult their lives were in the 1950s when Phil tried to make a living lobstering. It took endless work to build and repair their own wooden traps, and it was impossible to get ahead.

> *There wasn't any money in it. When Phil and I were first married he'd go out some days and I'd be out in the yard working in the garden. And I'd see him coming and he'd row in. We'd live from haul to haul. Some days he'd come in and say, "Gosh, I had a good day today. I made one hundred dollars." And other days, he'd come in and say, "I'm sorry, Sadie, I didn't make anything today, I went in the hole." You never knew; things were so uncertain. That was in the early 50s.*[367]

Wooden traps were fragile and tough to manage. Lois Day, who lobstered with her husband in the 1980s, recalled the exhausting labor of hauling by hand. *"The old wooden ones you had to fill with rocks on the bottom to sink them. Oh God were they heavy. It would take [both of us] to pull them over the railing."*[368]

On Ronnie's lobster boat in 2007, we were heading for the morning's first string of traps. Hauling traps is pretty straightforward—at least on a calm summer day when you are a guest. Having gone out before, I knew the basic drill: The captain drives the boat to the traps he wants to haul. A brightly painted buoy made from dense Styrofoam connects to the rope fastened to each pair of traps. It's not uncommon for Ronnie to haul almost half his traps in a day—and hauling 400 traps is very hard work. Other fishermen told me that hauling 250 is plenty.

The engine idling, Ronnie gaffs the buoy and sets the rope in the hauler. Watching a trap nose up to the surface—seawater pouring out of it, bits of seaweed dangling from the wires, lobsters flapping, squirming and everything else wriggling—feels like Christmas. A trap is filled with surprise. A little dopamine blip of primal pleasure reverberates in our old hunter-gatherer brains each time one reveals its bounty, its bit of treasure.

Once it's out of the water, the sternman pulls the trap onto the boat's "washboard," empties it out, and sorts the legal-size lobsters from those too "short" or too large to keep. Crabs are usually saved, and the occasional finfish by-catch, perhaps too injured to return to the water, might be quietly cut up for bait. (A good number of lobstermen see finfish, especially cod and haddock, as pests that consume larval lobsters. Fishery managers, seeking to restore finfish, feel differently.) Everything else gets tossed back.

What is everything else? In August 2015, I asked a young lobsterman to tell me what creatures he'd found in his traps around Vinalhaven. He thought for an instant, then listed: "*skate, baby eels, horn dogs, sea bass, cunner, saltwater catfish, baby pollock, wolf fish . . . bream, little baby bream, and redfish . . .*" I believed him; but he also seemed suspicious about my intent—as if I were a spy from a conservation group who had to be placated.[369]

Most islanders I spoke with thought the ocean was emptier than it used to be. Beba, who started lobstering as a ten-year-old, remembered in the 1970s, "*. . . when we'd haul up traps and they'd been full of starfish, we used to get the big starfish; they were full of sea urchins—whore's eggs we called them. You'd have to tip the trap up. But now I barely see a starfish.*"[370]

Once several traps are emptied and resting on the boat's washboard, the sternman sticks a full bait bag into each, and throws it back into the water. If the lobsters are migrating or catch has been poor, they may move the underperforming traps to other spots before tossing them back.

Eager to join the day's effort, I donned rubber gloves, and began grabbing handfuls of dead fish from a bucket and stuffing them into the bait bags. Gulf of Maine herring has been commonly used for more than one-hundred years, but the once ubiquitous fish is now so depleted that the catch is variously apportioned and not always available. The price of herring bait can go high. But they were on hand that morning.

By the time the herring have been salted, loaded into the bait bin on the dock, and shoveled into a bait box on the boat, they're in pieces, flecked with salt grains and scales, and decaying. Their smell is singular. It fills the nostrils and permeates clothing. It signals the sea and the work. Lobstermen's spouses, typically full partners on the home front—from late-night bookkeeping and filling big lunchboxes to washing work clothes at the end of the day—have their work cut out keeping ahead of that signature scent.

After mushing soft herring flesh for maybe five minutes, I began to feel seasick. I ignored it. The water was flat. I'd filled bait bags before. I decided my nausea was silly. Except that it was visceral and unstoppable. I took a break, but it was too late. The rotten fish, the breezeless day, the boat circling as we hauled, and the whiffs of diesel exhaust were more than I could handle. The next hours were not pretty. The crew worked around me, kindly dumping buckets now and again. Eventually emptied and exhausted, I crawled into the cabin and fell asleep on a pile of old rope.

After they finished hauling, they steamed home, scrubbed down the deck and hosed it off, weighed and sold their catch to their dealer, bought more bait, filled the tank with the next day's diesel, and helped me out of the hold so I could drive home. Ronnie's phlegmatic comment, reported to me days later, was simply put: "Well, Janna won't be coming out again for awhile."

At first I was embarrassed. I was just another summer person who couldn't tolerate a fair-weather outing. And while that version is true as far as it goes, I missed an interesting point. It turns out that seasickness is common among island boys starting to fish—almost a kind of initiation. I wasn't just sick; I had taken part in a very long tradition.

The "good" part of my memorably bad day lobstering was that it made me wonder how local fishermen got their sea legs. This led to a larger question: what was it like for children to grow up fishing on Vinalhaven, and how has fishing knowledge been passed from generation to generation?

Recalling his own early years, Ronnie told me, *"I would go hand-lining with my father when I was about 10 years old. I would get seasick just about every time I went, but I kept going and I finally got over being seasick."* The thrill of being a boy fishing with men, of being in the midst of the activity, helped him stay with the work. *"It was exciting because almost every time there would be these big sharks that would come around the boat. . . . They would be trying to get the fish we was catchin."*[371]

Lee Osgood, now in his sixties, had two older brothers who fished, but, *"I wasn't going to be a fisherman because I got seasick terrible. Wicked terrible seasick."* Like Ronnie, he persevered, and gradually improved enough to keep fishing. *"I [still] have days I don't feel good. I don't know . . . you just wallow through it. The worst for me is if it's a real thick a'fog day, and I can't see the horizon. And at night . . ."*[372]

When another fisherman in his early sixties offered a fuller account of his childhood experiences, I realized that getting sick and learning how to keep going was part of the way island men taught the boys how to fish and the work ethic it required—you might feel terrible, but you had to learn to put your feelings aside and keep working. At the age of ten, Jerry Doughty's task was to "dress" the fish the men pulled out of the water and take off the hooks: *"Cut the heads off and [take the] guts out."* After slicing a fish open, he'd stick his arm up into the big body, grab its innards and pull them out. *"That's when I would get seasick. The first hake, because hake blow up. The bellies blow up. . . . cod don't do that. But hake will blow up, so you stick the knife in it, the air lets go and the smell of it—that would get me every time."*

Yet, however bad he felt, he had work to do. If he didn't stay at it, his father and grandfather would have been disappointed. He would have let them down. *"The fish are coming in and that's your job to clean them, so you have to get over it. You just keep going. Throw up and start again."*

If the fish weren't gutted, they would spoil and couldn't be sold. Sometimes Jerry cut off 1000 fish heads in a day and cleaned that many fish.

We'd have to dress all day long. We'd have to dress sometimes 10,000 pounds. Each one probably weighed 10 pounds. So, a lot of them . . . You couldn't stop; you wouldn't get paid. A lot of times if we had too many, my grandfather would steer and my father would help me.[373]

I began to think of seasickness as an informal initiation ritual after "Hank" told me his experience. Since his father didn't live on the island, Hank went out as a sixteen-year-old with Louie Romer, an island fisherman. Romer's crew of three or four went haking overnight in summer.

"You go out at 11:00 or 12:00 at night. I was just the dresser so I could go to sleep." The men would set the trawl while Hank slept. He'd wake up ready to work when they started to haul in the fish. The work was tough.

So I went one summer and I was sick every day. Just the smell of them. It could be as flat as this table, but when the first hake . . . it could be 20 feet under water and I could smell the thing and I would start getting sick . . . There I was cutting the heads off and pulling the guts out, and throwing up. . . . After a while you didn't have nothing to throw up.

I asked him what the older guys did when he threw up: *"Laugh at you."* His tone suggested that the laughter wasn't mean. Instead, it implied that seasickness was not the end of the world. It also seems the men wanted to convey to the boys how much grit it took to stay with fishing. Hank tried to resume the next year. But when he smelled the bait, bad memories overwhelmed him. *"I said I can't put another summer in like that. I just can't."* So he started lobstering on his own, which he's mostly done since.[374]

At fourteen, Tim Dyer (1947–2020) started working summers in one of the island fish factories. His father's leg had been badly hurt during the Second World War, and eventually amputated. The family needed Tim's help:

So I would work in the fish plant on Harbor Wharf when I was 14. . . . I would work there some weeks 90 hours part time, and then go fishing during the day

*and then work in the fish plant at night. I'd start in the afternoon about 3:00 and
get done about 3:00 in the morning. So that was my work ethic.*

Tim slept from 3:00 a.m. to 5:00 a.m., then he'd get up and help his father
haul traps. *"I'd get up and we'd haul. Back then we only had probably 180
traps out."* He'd finish at 1:00 or 2:00 in the afternoon, relax for an hour at
one of the swimming quarries, then go back to work for Clyde Bickford down
at the fish plant. *"There were 2 factories in town. Burnham and Morrill had
a factory and Clyde Bickford had a factory. . . . And lots of nights [Clyde
would] have 100,000 pounds of hake piled up on the floor down there."*
Tim earned $1.30 an hour.

*Pitching fish, putting them in barrels, loading trucks whatever needed to be
done . . . I have pay slips from there. My mother saved some of them."* He elaborated, *"This was the 1960s. Like I say, the boats would come in and I mean a lot
of the boats, 10,000 or 15,000 pounds of hake aboard the boats, so before the
night was over there'd be . . . lots of nights . . . 100,000 pounds piled up on the
floor. We would load . . . the fish in 300-pound barrels and you'd tier them up
[onto the trucks] by hand. Three people tiered them up. Two people lifted and
one person shoved the barrel home. That's what you did. You iced the barrels
down and the hake went to Baltimore.*

When Tim started in the factory, the older men tested him.

*The first week I worked there, all I did was pull the guts. All the old guys, there
were a bunch of old guys there and they would look at me . . . Course they knew
who I was. I mean the people there lived here just like I did and they knew my
family, my grandfather and everybody. But they looked at me as a young kid and
they said, "He'll never make it. He won't last a week." So, they were cutting the
fish with a big knife and I was pulling guts.* He was determined to keep going.
Up to his elbows in fish guts, and trying to figure out the work, he drew some
guffaws. *"Course the first day I worked, I didn't know enough to wet my arms
down because the stuff didn't stick, of course they thought that was pretty funny."*

I asked if he thought he was being hazed a little. *"A little bit,"* he
allowed."But mostly he felt he was being tested. *"Anyone who started there
they didn't figure you'd last. Especially a fourteen-year-old kid."* But Tim
won them over, *"[A]fter I worked there a week, they were my best friends. . . .
I mean I could walk up to them twenty years after I worked there and it was
like I just left."*[375]
The older fishermen tasked the younger ones with "showing you have what
it takes." The tall tales islander Ivan Calderwood (1899–1998) wrote about
his fictional alter ego, "Uncle Dave," offer revelatory stories. Calderwood
fed the Rockland newspaper a steady diet of down east tales and humor, and

several books compiled his columns. He was a gifted salesman into his 80s. One afternoon soon after we bought our house, he came around in an ancient station wagon and knocked on our door. He easily charmed us into buying a book.

Ivan ignored dates and facts, but his tales convey the texture of life on the island. Some stories feel deeply true if not exactly factual—like this one about the initiation of Tim's grandfather, Les Dyer Sr. (1898–1980) into the fishing life. According to "Uncle Dave," when Les was thirteen he made his first trip with "Capt. Reuben" Hopkins (1854–1914). Dyer asked to go, and the Captain shipped him on as "*cook, splitter and gutter in his spare time.*"

One "*sticky, sultry day, the kind with no wind but a little fog . . . the kind that would make a greenhorn half sick to his tummy*" when he was already queasy from sticking his hand deep into the corn-beef barrel and pulling out a big greasy chunk of horsemeat to cook for the crew's supper, Les made the mistake of mentioning the meat's unpleasant greasiness to Captain Hopkins. Apparently seeing a "teachable" moment Hopkins grabbed a bucket of lard, dug his hand in and "*dropped a great handful into the kettle.*" He intended to get Les seasick and it worked. "*Les got all white and pale around the gills and hot-footed it for the rail.*" Uncle Dave's laconic rationale, "*Anyhow, that's what makes a good seaman,*" signaled general approval for the captain's action. Les was tested again by greasing one of the masts with pork fat. But "Uncle Dave" had already reached his conclusion: "*he was only thirteen years old, and he sure showed that he had what it takes to make an old salt.*"[376]

Traditional fishing included a lot of nasty, strenuous, exhausting, dangerous work. In a video interview in 2000, Les's son, Ed Dyer (b.1936), talked about his life as an engineer off island, and about how much he admired his father. Working "against the elements" beside his dad as a boy and watching Les sell the fish, they caught to earn a living, had filled him with respect. "He was my hero . . . I wanted to make him proud of me."[377]

Once a boy won over the older fishermen, they treated him generously. Thinking back on the island of his childhood, Roy Ames (1902–1983), in a 1970s interview, described how the men in town helped out an island teenager.

Braddy Bray (1892–1971) had to support the family after his father died. Braddy wasn't much more than a boy himself. He'd do anything possible to earn ten cents . . . Well, the men around town, the fishermen, admired what he was trying to do. He'd dig clams, make pot buoys—he'd do anything. He had a few traps and an old dory. Ernest Smith was a boat builder here then. The fishermen went to Ernest and told him what they wanted to do. He built a small

boat, an eighteen-footer, for $125. They paid for it and gave it to Braddy. Boy,
he was made then![378]

LEARNING TO FISH

Boys needed to acquire many skills, and they started young. Since the eighteenth century, the knowledge required for fishing, boat building, net making,
and much else involved with life on Vinalhaven, has been taught in an informal apprenticeship starting in childhood. Girls as well as boys often learned
net "knitting" and mending, trawl baiting, fish "pickling," boat painting and
other vital skills from local men and women.

Such continuity doesn't mean that island life has been static. Its fishing
industry has always responded to evolving conditions, and almost everything
about fisheries changed radically during the twentieth century. Families
changed, too. In recent decades, many teenage girls as well as boys have
started "sterning," with the support of their families (in 2016, 4 percent of
state lobster licenses belonged to women captains).[379] Still, the island holds
on to pieces of "older," more communal ways of living, including the personal, generational transmission of "work" knowledge—now missing from
so much of the post-industrial United States.

Many Vinalhaven fishermen began learning their work when they were
tiny. When I asked Walt Day (b. 1951) about his earliest memories about
fishing, he recalled going out in a boat with his father and brother when he
was three years old. His father worked as a sternman on another lobsterman's
boat, but also set 25 or 50 traps of his own that he'd row to and haul after
hours. *"Me and my brother would sit on the stern seat and play with crabs*
and periwinkles and whatever and just watched him for the lobstering part
of it."

I asked how he'd learned to fish, and he answered that the whole community taught him.

I followed my father around and different people in other fisheries. . . . A guy
who passed away, Larry [Marshal] Coombs—"Penny" . . . we used to bait eight
[tub] trawls for him . . . [H]e'd take us out at night once in a while when he'd
go set the trawls, so we saw the whole process. And most of the stuff you learned
just like that . . . just watching or going with somebody that did it.

During the 1960s, the tub trawl that Walt and other boys were baiting was
mostly being used to catch hake. Long lines with baited hooks at regular
intervals, trawls are set in the water and marked by buoys and sometimes lan-
terns on either end. The fishermen carried the baited trawl in half-barrels and

used a "heaving" stick to toss the lines from the barrel off the boat. The lines rested near the bottom, with a baited hook dangling from each of many short lines called "snoods" or "gangions." The spacing and the hook size depended on the fish fishermen hoped to catch.

In the afternoons, islanders of all ages, recruited by family members or in need of cash, would go down to sheds on the docks to bait the hooks. As they worked, they'd carefully wind the trawl back into the "tub" so it could be lifted onto the boat, and then set without tangling when it was let out.

Walt thought he was maybe nine, ten, or eleven years old when he started. *"We used to bait two tubs a day. 800 hooks on a tub . . . and when I first started, you could get $1.75 for baiting 800 hooks, and I remember one summer it went to $2.00 and we figured we was gonna be rich."* [380]

Boys also learned about fishing by haunting the fish wharves. I interviewed John Beckman (1919–2010) when he was ninety. His recollection of "prowling" with Burt "Junior" Dyer, offers a glimpse of the lively working waterfront where the boys could go more or less anywhere.

> *[I]n them days they was making cod liver oil. . . This was before the [Second World] War. Quite a while before the war. We was just kids . . . and we used to prowl around the waterfront. All the young fellas did then. There was a lot of action going on on the waterfront. . . . We found the girls down there. They was working on baiting trawls or painting, stuff like that. Of course, we was after the girls and they was after us.*

John's nickname, "Sneak" referred to his knack for "prowling" after members of the opposite sex. [381]

Boys ran in and out of the fish plants freely—and without much supervision. John Beckman recalled entering a warehouse and sampling the cod liver oil. John Morton (1929–2003) described using scrap wood they found to build hideaways and clubhouses in corners of the fish plant. The factory had a night watchman, but informality ruled. All the while the boys familiarized themselves with the fish business: knowledge about the work came with the casual proximity. [382]

Learning to fish, Ted Ames (1939–) observed, *"was just part of life"* for island boys. Fish were all around them. *"The millstream pollock was going; and we would fish for flounder. The pond was half full of them."* When I asked Ted at what age he started fishing, he thought he had been between five and seven. Elsewhere, he mentioned catching his first cod when he went out with his grandfather at seven. There was no particular beginning. [383] *"[W]e grew up with it,"* Ted reflected. *"So it's hard to say where it started. It's bits and pieces. It's like the typical kid growing up in Vinalhaven: You ask him when he learned to handle a little boat or a powerboat or whatever. You couldn't put your finger on it, it's just that you grew up in it and didn't think twice about it."* Whatever its obstacles or hardships, Ted remembered his childhood with delight, *"As a child's paradise,"* he observed. Then he qualified it, *"Or a boy's paradise."*

Seventy years later, Ames' detailed memory of setting his first tub-trawl—to catch eels in one of the quarries—offers a nice illustration of how he and his friends had the run of the island, how they learned their work day by day in a way inseparable from play, and how adults helped them out.

> *The trash man in town back then said he'd give us kids maybe . . . 15 or 25 cents for big eels. The quarries were full of them, so I went down to the shore and . . . Ruth Gray's husband had a shop . . . He tub-trawled, and he had a tub of old gear with the hooks still on it. . . . I asked him if I could have a line of it; that's 50 hooks . . . He said, "Sure, it's not good for anything, it's all rotted."*

Rotted was the important word, but it slipped by the boys' ears. Sands Quarry, near town, was one of many on the island that filled with fresh water after the granite industry wound down. Sunfish lived in it, and the boys spent the morning catching "sunnies" for bait.

"By noon time [we were] ready . . . to throw the trawl over. So we tied ballast rock on one end and slung it out as far as we could into the lower end [of the quarry] which is mostly just grout . . . and went off for lunch. Came back after lunch and sure enough, we got a lot of eels." But the hooked eels had hidden themselves. *"We couldn't see the hooks because [the eels had] crawled into the crevices amongst the grout. So, we started hauling them back. And, of course, the gear parted off."* The hooks pulled off the old "rotted" fishing line, and the eels were lost. *"We didn't get a single one. We had visions of dollars and we didn't get one. [The eels] all just locked themselves in their hiding places."*

No success that time. Still, Ted and his friends had spent the day on their own, working out their project without anyone second-guessing or directing them. They'd enjoyed the chase, and their play anticipated their work, teaching lessons about equipment, technique, and earnings. Some days you come home empty handed, other days with a pretty good catch. *"But fishing,"* Ames reflected, *"I always found it exciting, lots of fun, always a challenge. Same as everyone else who gets sucked up into it."*[384]

Much of the learning, as the men remembered it years later, came from watching and participating. When I asked "Hal," another successful island fisherman, about what his father taught him, he emphasized that his father *didn't* teach him, he just let him come along in the boat. Hal had known he wanted to fish since he was little. *"I hated school, hated school. Never, never went. I had traps out, lobster traps when I was 9 or 10."*

About the same time, his father started taking him out stop-seining for herring. He humorously described himself as *"being underfoot, thinking I'm helping my father."* He watched. When I asked if his father had let him try stuff, he quipped, *"Not willingly."* Eventually, having absorbed as much as he could, Hal explained the next step, *"You'd just go on your own and do your own thing."*[385]

Offering a father's perspective, Sonny Warren (1929–2022) an island fisherman, observed, *"[M]y son, he started with me, I don't know he was probably about four-years-old. I used to take him fishing."* He recalled how the boy loved to go with him. In good weather when the water was calm, he would take him out. Sometimes Sonny lifted him onto a lobster crate so he could reach the wheel and help steer.

Nowadays lobstermen put thick rubber bands around the lobster's claws to keep them closed, but back then they used wooden plugs. The little boy would

> *set the lobsters down on a crate . . . and he'd put the plugs in them—and you had to be careful not to get bit.* Learning wasn't always smooth: *one day he started screeching . . . I looked at him and I couldn't see nothing wrong with him . . . and he was screeching blue murder. He had put a lobster down, and he turned around and set down on the lobster. The lobster had him by the tail.*[386]

Other men told me their grandfathers had taught them more often than their fathers. George "Burt" Dyer, (1922–2011), whom I interviewed when he was in his late eighties, recalled his childhood education: *"I had lobster traps out when I was 8 years old and I had a license for $1.00, and I had an old pea-pod that I bought from Al Miller for $3.00 and my grandfather helped me put some new timbers in it, and I used to row and I had about 50 traps out."* Burt sold the lobsters for twelve cents a pound and saved some of his earning. At the age of twelve, he bought his first used outboard motor.

He recalled his "teacher" with enthusiasm. *"Oh Boy! My grandfather was a wizard of a man, my God and he taught us all how to go fishing when we was kids."* Burt's grandfather, Frank Rogers (1870–1960), was nine years old in 1880 when he and *his* father, Joseph (1843–1912), moved to Vinalhaven from the mainland. Both were weir fisherman. According to Burt, Frank *"had a weir in Lane's Island Cove and he was twelve years old. And his father had a weir over on Greens Island."*

Burt spoke with pride about a particular day during his grandfather's youth. He told the story often, so I imagine it was important to him. In the early 1880s, it seems that herring were scarce on the mainland coast. Some Gloucester vessels, needing bait for cod fishing on the Banks, sailed to Vinalhaven one summer day looking maybe to buy them, or maybe to take them. As Burt told it, the Gloucester captain saw Frank's weir and demanded of the boy, "*Where's the weir man?*" The twelve-year-old answered boldly, "*I am the weir man, and if you want herring, there's my weir, Lane's weir, and that is my herring and you're going to buy them from me.*"

"*You're nothing but a boy,*" challenged the captain. "*If you want any herring out of my weir, you're gonna pay for it,*" Frank retorted.

Burt continued, "*They latched 4 dories, and they helped my grandfather seine out, and they loaded 4 dories, $4.00 or $5.00 a piece. So that was pretty good money for my grandfather in them days.*" When the twelve-year-old went aboard to get his money, "*the captain said, 'You're going to make a fine captain someday and I'm gonna give you a $10 bonus.' . . . [H]e was tickled to death.*"[387]

The story suggests lessons for a boy: working industriously to build your own business is a good thing, but it's not enough. You have to learn to stand up for yourself. You have to be tough so other tough people won't get the better of you. The story also implies that you should try to live up to the deeds of your forefathers. Your pride and worth are partly based in who they were. They are your models. And you need to strive to equal or best them.

Several other men told of having been helped by neighbors or kin. One told me outright that it was because his own stepfather was abusive. A good-natured neighbor could offer comfort, skill, and alternative ways to make a living. Ivan Olson, (1926–2013), another fisherman of Burt's generation, fished for almost eighty of the eighty-seven years he lived on Vinalhaven. Ivan's father came to American from Norway and worked in the quarries. Olson recalled, "*He cut stone; it's all he ever done until the depression started in the 1930s. With the depression everything folded up. Boy it was tough when things folded up because they was living from day to day. Just like half the people do today.*"

Ivan turned to Herbie MacDonald (1906–1998) for help learning to fish.

I wasn't interested in cutting stone, I watched my father cut stone once in a while. . . . I was interested in the water more than anything. There was a fisherman that lived up the street, close to us. He kinda took me under his wing and I started going with him. . . . Yup, nice old guy. Everything I ever got, I think I learned from Herbie. He got me started anyway.

Olson described how the fishermen would gather and talk about fishing. He loved listening. His memory is so vivid you can almost taste the tobacco. "*There was an old store up here.*" From his workshop where we were talking, he pointed past his neighbors' lawn.

We used to get together at the store after supper. All the fishermen, they'd all come in to buy their chewing tobacco, gloves and everything—and stuff for the

*next day. I'd go over to listen to those guys talk about fishing. It was awful in-
teresting to me. How they did fishing and all that stuff like that.*

As a ten-year-old, Ivan was so eager to go out with MacDonald that he
would get himself up before dawn.

*[Herbie would] tell me when he was gonna go in the morning, you know 4:00 or
4:30 a.m., and I knew where he went from, and I'd walk over and everything and
I'd be there. . . . Most of the time I was asleep down there on the wharf waiting
for him. We'd go, and I'd help him if I could. I was just a little fella anyway.
Probably ten years old . . . We'd be hand-lining two hooks on a line and we'd
go catch codfish or pollock . . . If we caught 1,000 pounds that was a big day.
We was getting five or six cents a pound for them.*

Ivan fished summers with MacDonald until he enlisted to serve in World
War II. They resumed for a bit after the war, and also lobstered together,
using redfish "racks" for bait. Noting the dearth of redfish in recent years, he
reflected, *"We never see one now."*[388]
The two men sometimes lobstered in winter. Talking about hauling in winter made me think about the cold. *"You'd just bundle up,"* Sonny Warren had
explained to me when I wondered how they'd tolerated spending mid-winter
days in open boats. I flashed to a big hand-knit wool mitten on display in the
Historical Society. Sonny had described how they were made,

*We had wool mittens we used to use. They knit mittens about a foot longer than
your hand and you'd keep dipping them in water and of course they'd keep
shrinking up and by and by the mittens would get about three quarters of an inch
thick and your hands would never get cold in them. Of course, your hands were
wet, and your mittens would be covered with ice. You'd take your hands out of
the mittens, and your hands would be all steaming and warm.*[389]

Ivan described how the older men taught the younger ones where to find
fish. In the 1930s some islanders were still rowing out in the western bay—
between Vinalhaven and Rockland—to fish for cod. Because fish species
favor different water depths and different kinds of "bottom," knowing what
was below you was crucial to successful fishing. To find the bottom, Ivan
explained, you made a "sounding." You dropped a piece of line with lead at
the end and measured how far down it went. Lee Osgood elaborated, *"My
father always told about bringing the weight up and seeing if it was clay or
mud; or, if it was clean, it was hard bottom."*[390]
Once a fisherman found good bottom with good fishing, he wanted to
remember the location of the fishing ground. He would pick out two land-
marks on the shore and find the direction to these "marks" with his compass to

triangulate the spot. To return to that ground, he'd sight both marks visually and find the spot on the water where the compass readings for each mark matched his original readings. Only then was he where he wanted to be. Ivan explained, *"[The cod] were always up on the shallows places, and we'd know that, and the old guys would tell us the land marks. . . . Like one mark we used to use is the stand pipe on Vinalhaven."* Out in the bay, they'd line up a big block of stone at the Heron Light on Green's Island with the standpipe behind it. *"You'd used that standpipe over that steep bunch of rocks, and then there was another marker we used up the bay, I think it was Duck Trap Mine . . . I forget now."*[391]

Herb Conway, eighty-nine when we spoke, told how his grandfather had carefully written down everything he had_learned about where to find good bottom, perhaps 100 years ago. When he stopped fishing, he passed the book to Herb's uncle, who later passed it to him. I thought that book was a great gift. *"Well it was,"* Herb reflected, *"It was a great thing. It would save you a lot of hunting, I'll put it that way."*

Technology has now mostly made personal knowledge and generational instruction obsolete. For instance, Herb's son-in-law had recently told him about a piece of bottom where he was fishing. Herb thought he knew the fishing ground and asked its location by name. *"And I'd say, 'Would Candy Mountain be there . . .?'"* The question was meaningless to the younger man. With sophisticated equipment, fishermen today *"never look up,"* Herb allowed. *"They just look at the chart, and look at the GPS position of it, and go."*[392]

As Lee Osgood put it, *"It took me my whole lifetime to learn what they can learn in a month."* Unspoken is how old knowledge is no longer valued. There was a time when a lifetime of fishing and studying the water yielded singular knowledge of a particular patch of the ocean. As fishermen aged, they would share what they knew with younger men coming up—maybe kin, maybe neighbors. Electronic equipment has altered, even usurped this particular kind of conversation once an important function that defined fishing communities.[393]

One or two islanders spoke off the record about mistreatment as children, childhoods taken away by abusive adults, overwork or hardship. But most expressed pleasure in learning to meet challenges and winning respect from older fishermen. Charles Eliot, nineteenth century Harvard president and early Mt. Desert "rusticator," wrote a book about a Baker's Islander named John Gilley, who he thought epitomized the best sort of fisherman. Eliot believed that early struggles with ocean dangers made a boy grow up brave and self-reliant.[394]

Ronnie, whose lobster boat I visited, has both qualities. His description of surviving a hurricane shows just how dangerous a fishing education could sometimes be.

I was with my father and was trawl fishin', hake fishin', outside Matinicus Rock. It was probably back in the 50s, I was pretty young. Back then we didn't have long range forecasts and stuff. We was out there and there was a hurricane comin' and we didn't know it.

We had the boat completely loaded with fish. We had so many fish aboard that day. It started to get really, really rough and my father, back then, we didn't have any money so he didn't want to leave the trawls. He didn't want to lose his gear so we just yanked the trawls aboard as fast as we could.

We knew that something wasn't good and we threw the fish overboard. We weren't keeping the fish. We just wanted to get the trawls. It got really, really rough. Terrible. Like I said we didn't know it was a hurricane. We were pretty scared by the time we got home. . . There was three of us that time. All we had was just a compass. We didn't have no radars. . . Just using a compass.

It was a thick fog. We made the sunken ledge, which is just outside the light-house, and it was so rough. We come in around the ledges and . . . It was quite an intense moment and we got in by the ferry dock there and we were runnin' out of fuel. . . . Well, just a miracle that. . . If we'd run out of fuel out there we never would have made it.[395]

At home as well as on the water, children had to start contributing early, and more than a few had to provide their own clothes and extras. They learned to look after themselves.

Walt recalled,

I can still sew a button on today, iron a shirt so it's passable. Washed a lot of dishes. One night I'd wash my brother would wipe, the next night he'd wash, and I'd wipe. But everybody just contributed, and it was part of family life. . . . I was expected to buy half of my school clothes by the time I was 8 or 9 years old.[396]

Although all the adults in the community kept a close eye on them, the boys had a lot of independence and responsibility. Did autonomy balance hardship? It may have depended, as Ted Ames observed, on how much you loved to fish.

9

Fishing the Seasons

"All I had was a compass and a watch..."

Nothing is ever certain when you fish. As in Ronnie Walker's story, weather comes out of nowhere. In a flash you must choose what to sacrifice: the fish and the money you hope to make selling them, the trawl you can't afford to replace—or your own lives. So after hard hours catching the fish, you shovel them overboard and run for a safe harbor. If the weather is better the next day, you go back out. Each day is different. Maybe you can't find any fish or, if you make a good haul, there might not be a good market for them.

Vinalhaven's earliest settlers experienced much the same thing. In their own way, they, too, were caught in the obscure machinations of world markets. Like a giant invisible hand randomly reaching through the clouds, sometimes fortune dropped bounty in their nets; sometimes it ripped the nets apart and left them fishless. By the twentieth century, the giant hand flexed ever more rapidly due to nearly instantaneous communication among larger global commodities markets, scientists, conservation groups, warring politicians and "experts," revolutionized technology, and regulations from governments near and far. Individual resourcefulness is a great asset, but changing circumstances have powerful impacts no matter how resourceful you are.

In the twentieth century the ocean sometimes vied with outer space for the title of "last frontier." For thousands of years there were always new opportunities, new places and new species to catch. If one type of fish was no longer abundant, men did their best to catch and sell another, or counter overall depletion by sailing farther away to increase their access to new grounds. Starting in the mid-nineteenth century and accelerating through the twentieth, fleets kept expanding. Nets and longlines, vessels and engines kept getting bigger and better until fish were caught faster than they could reproduce.

Particularly after the Second World War, governments all over the world eagerly adopted overly enthusiastic scientific estimates of the abundance of fish and began to empty the world's oceans. Speculation carried the day in the interests of providing protein and economic growth to a world ravaged by war, and in the spirit of the unstated, yet widely shared assumption that ocean creatures, like all natural "resources," existed primarily for human use—and were inexhaustible. At the same time, submarine warfare during the Second World War had produced sonar, a new technology that completely changed the fishing equation. Fish could be located and captured in unimaginable numbers.

By the mid-twentieth century, Vinalhaven was one small place in a big world full of growing human populations and improved fishing technologies. International markets had gotten too big. There were too many fishing vessels. Ted Ames—a scientist as well as a fisherman—believed the worst depletion in the Gulf of Maine was caused by Russian factory ships that fished too close to shore. *"At the time I started, Seal Island was still very productive. . . . but after the Russians hit the area in the mid to late '60s there wasn't enough fish for [the factories] to hang around for, so they closed up."*[398]

William Warner, a Pulitzer Prize winning writer who summered on Vinalhaven for many years, spent time on the foreign factory ships, and wrote *Distant Waters*, a book about the huge, government sponsored fishing vessels and the havoc they wreaked. Warner recounts how there were so many boats catching so many fish that it was hard for anyone to grasp just how quickly fish were disappearing.

The year 1974 marked the turning point. In that year alone 1,076 Western European and Communist-bloc fishing vessels swarmed across the Atlantic to fish North American waters. Their catch of 2,176,000 tons was ten times the New England and triple the Canadian Atlantic catch. For anyone who cared to analyze this catch figure or compare it with previous years, moreover, a picture far more disturbing than sheer volume would emerge. Huge as the total catch might seem, the catch per vessel was down and the fish were running generally smaller than before, even though the foreign vessels fished longer hours with improved methods over a larger range for a greater part of the year.

He sums up,

A new generation of fish killers had come across the Atlantic. In twenty years in North American waters, they had by their own account taken over 72,333,000,000 pounds of fish. Very few among them could see that this was too much or that they had fished too well for their own future.[399]

Seventy-two billion pounds (36,166,500 tons). It's a hard number to grasp. The wild ocean frontiers were no more, and the future of fish stocks and ocean life fell into the hands of human managers.

Although it was clear that factory ships were destroying fish stocks, the Magnuson Stevens Fisheries Conservation Act in 1976 addressed the problem in a way that signaled the beginning of the end for island fishermen—even as it removed foreign vessels from American waters by establishing an Exclusive Economic Zone that extended US territorial waters out to 200 nautical miles from shore.

At that time, NOAA, the new Federal agency charged with fisheries management, received two conflicting mandates: to keep fish from going extinct, and to allow as much commercial fishing as possible. They had to try. Sometimes they were successful. Other times, not so much.

The monitoring and management system created over the next forty years increasingly favored the biggest "most-efficient" fishing vessels. Robin Alden, former Maine Commissioner of Marine Resources and founding Executive Director of the Maine Center for Coastal Fisheries, observed, "It was the sum of myriad small decisions by regulators and the industry who participated in the regulation. Fishermen had to adjust to each round of new regulations, and in many cases lost access slowly through this period. As each successive decision didn't "solve" the problem, the regime drifted toward privatization. Also, large conservation organizations, Environmental Defense Fund in particular, had participated and advocated for this approach, which had theoretical grounding in neo-liberal economics, during the entire forty years."[400]

From the point of view of markets and government regulators, a few big boats catching all the available fish made perfect sense. It was efficient and easier to control. What was to be gained from having hundreds of small home-built draggers fighting for towing space, each bringing in fish that might be stored or treated in unpredictable ways, each needing to find a market and make a deal with a buyer? From their viewpoint, small boats were wasteful and hard to monitor. Regulators decided that privatizing the fishery and turning it over to corporations would serve fish stocks and consumers well.

Their bottom line is concisely described by fisherman and writer Paul Molyneaux:

> *Regulators, struggling with the tough issue of how to control effort and limit access to finite resources, wanted to let the market do the allocation job. Privatization would enable the most economically efficient fishermen or anyone with deep pockets, to amass as property the harvest rights to the nation's wild fish.*[401]

No one acknowledged the extent to which "market forces," "privatization," and "progress" would strangle fishing communities by privileging big business over neighborhoods. Initially, some fishermen bought into the approach since legislation made borrowing money cheaper, offered subsidies, and encouraged them (and non-fishermen investors) to build bigger boats and buy new equipment.

But because of inaccurate fish stock estimates, the relentless drive toward consolidation that rewarded corporations proved deeply unfair to small-scale operators in small fishing communities, and Vinalhaven fishermen were gradually driven out of the game. Had lobster not become so profitable, it is likely island fishing would have entirely ended by now.

The fishermen in this chapter tell about how they fished and what they fished for. They also tell how the story ended for them.

The older fishermen on the island have lived through a remarkable moment in history. In a few decades, fishing transformed from work that involved the pursuit of diverse species season by season—as it had since people first lived on the island almost 5000 years ago—to hauling up a single species of crustacean. Today a few people drag or dive for scallops. In 2021 fourteen fishermen had herring licenses, another handful had Menhaden licenses, two had whelk licenses, 3 had periwinkle, and 40 had halibut licenses. (Halibut fishing in Maine is allowed for four weeks from mid-May to mid-June only.) Whether they actively used them, or just held them against a future time is unclear. Some island women pick crab. People enjoy the occasional mackerel or flounder for dinner. All the fisheries are monitored intensely and any catch is—by necessity—limited; some would argue that even so, it is not limited enough. Apart from lobstering, none of these efforts earn a living. The very seasonality that sustained both the fish and the fishermen no longer continues.[402]

The island fishermen coming to the end of their lifetimes may be the last to live by hunting wild fish. For almost 150 years, most Vinalhaven fishermen both lobstered and caught finfish near the island in small boats. At least through the first half of the 20th century, their navigation tools were rudimentary. On an undated scrap of paper from the Historical Society, one fisherman tells how to navigate with a watch as a compass: *"Holding it flat on your palm with the hour hand pointing toward the sun. Halfway between that hand and the figure XII by the shortest distance will be South."* In an effort to help me see a world now lost, many times I heard men say with quiet pride, "All I had was a compass and a watch."

To understand what fishing was like on Vinalhaven during the decades the oldest fishermen (interviewed by me between 2012 and 2017) can recall— back to the 1930s and further when we include stories their fathers and grandfathers told them—the single most important fact was the diversity of fish in the Gulf of Maine and other "harvestable" creatures. Within living memory, island fishermen have fished for cod, haddock, pollock, cusk, hake, redfish, flounder, mackerel, menhaden, herring, halibut, swordfish, eel, crab, clams, sea urchins, shrimp, scallops, the occasional tuna, and lobsters. Plenty of other fish, like sunfish, cunner, rock gunnel and dogfish—the bane of fishermen—also live in nearby waters. This plethora of species offered fishermen work year-round as different creatures migrated in and out of reach. There was always the chance to make up for a bad catch today with a better one tomorrow. If clams were hard to find one March, you might do pretty well hooking hake in July.

Just about every island fisherman lobstered for at least part of the year. How many fished for finfish each year is unknowable. Sometimes a handful of boats pursued a species, sometimes more.

[W]hen I was a young boy, Ted Ames explained, *during the war years and immediately thereafter—there was a whole fleet of draggers, and a number were based in Vinalhaven . . . you could go down to Seal Island and get your 10,000 pounds of haddock and cod and steam back home. You could start towing when you got outside Old Horse Ledge. There were fishing boats everywhere. It was much better then.*[403]

Burt Dyer thought there had been 12 or 14 island boats going for hake in the late 1940s. Sonny Warren remembered three or four Vinalhaven crews dragging for redfish in the late 1950s and selling in Rockland. Six or eight gangs of men went stop-seining for herring starting after the War. Stop-seining is a near shore way of trapping fish, usually herring, by stringing a net across a cove after a school comes into it.[404]

Herb Conway said that in the early 1950s maybe 30 island boats went handlining for cod and halibut, but the numbers dwindled by the 1960s, until only a few were left. Herb also remembered that, in the late 1960s and early 1970s, several island boats went gill netting. There was overlap among these crews.[405]

Rather than creating an encyclopedia of crews and vessels, what follows is an anecdotal history, told to me by islanders, that conveys the feel of island fishing when fish were more abundant, when daily life was to a large degree guided by tides and weather, and work varied by season.

WINTER

The snowdrifts, the frozen harbor, fireplaces and stoked coal stoves—winter on the island was cold indoors and out. Among descriptions of the season, one bit of writing from the 1892 diary entry of Maria Dollof Webster (1829–1914) conveys vividly how bad the cold could be. She lets us glimpse her daily life and her growing misery:

Dec. 22, 1892. This is a nice cold day the coldest day of the season I have been Boiling a dinner. Flora and children came in to eat with me this afternoon. There was a man called and I Bought a bottle of cleaning soap for clothes and carpets.

It is so cold I have moved my bed out into the kitchen . . . I have lost all of my plants

Dec. 23. O Dear it is so cold I cant do any thing but keep fire and read. This morning. . . . Mrs Calderwood called and I bought a chicken . . . I do believe I shall freeze.

Dec. 24. I cant keep warm when my back is at the fire my nose is cold and my nose is warm my back is cold. . . . o dear it is terable cold.[406]

During winter men worked close to their stoves in their workshops, repairing and readying their gear for the year to come. Here's Walt Day's memory of what winter was like for fishermen in the 1950s and 1960s when he was growing up. I asked him to describe the scene:

Well everybody's pretty much in their shops building new traps and patching their old wooden traps to get ready for the next season because most of the coves are full of ice and the clams flats are pretty much froze up so you can't get at the clams. Everybody's just doing their shop work, painting their buoys, fixing their traps.[407]

Workshops—whether part of a home or separate "fish houses"—are still at the heart of fishermen's shore lives. Visiting one, you might see big workbenches half-covered with tools, damaged traps or boat gear, shelves of paint cans, piles of buoys, oars, and all colors of coiled and tangled rope. On the walls often hang framed faded color photos of boats and crews; sometimes, holds overflowing with the catch of the day. One graying islander recalled his uncle's mid-twentieth century workshop—*"probably 12 × 18 feet long."* He pictured his uncle sitting on a work bench building or repairing different traps, some to catch lobster, some to trap minks for fur. Deer antlers hung on the wall.

In midseason, you might see my grandfather setting in his chair by the stove cleaning up his [lobster]traps. A whole lot of time . . . if nothing else was going on, he'd whittle out plugs for lobsters' claws. He'd be doing that . . . he never had new traps, he just got ones that [my uncle] didn't want anymore and he'd patch it up best he could.

Neighbors came in and out to visit, including six or seven children who, waiting for the school bus on cold mornings, enjoyed the heat of the fire.

"[I]f there was any work that needed to be done on his boat, he would be scraping and painting then." His uncle would cut spruce to make traps and

he'd steam the wooden lathes himself so he could bend them. *"[H]e had this thing on the shore where you built a fire under a little water tank and you then bowed [the spruce] from that. He also had a steamer in the shop that you could do it that way. A kerosene heater under it. . . . ."*

Built under the house on a hillside and close to the shore, the workshop was "a man's place."

> *My grandmother ruled upstairs and he ruled downstairs. And if she wanted something she would [open the door] stick [out] her head and hollar down. I never seen her come down there and he would stay down there, work on his gear and drink beer.*[408]

Steve Rosen remembered hanging out in his father's fishhouse when he was growing up, *"Fish houses were kind of the pubs and everything happens in pubs. All the politics and all the fish talk. Usually all men. A lot of the talk years ago was how to do things differently—How to improve fishing, how to improve fishing gear, fishing traps. How to be more efficient . . . Lot of drinking involved in hanging [out] in the workshops."* The tone changed as fishing changed, *"Lobstering is the only game in town now. It's talking about regulations more than actually how to do things better, it's how to get around something more than how to do something."*[409]

During winter, a handful of men continued to lobster. A few others "rigged" their lobster boats to drag Atlantic scallops and then northern shrimp, usually taking a family member or a friend as crew. If a processing plant was open and buying, more fishermen would go out or join crews and fish hard. Otherwise, they would catch what they could use, and freeze or sell the rest on the mainland to pay a few bills or to tide them over until spring.

Sea Scallops

Sonny Warren remembered good scalloping years on Vinalhaven from the 1950s into the 1970s. *"You could make a day's pay and then they kept going down and faded. A few years they might be back again."* His next comment captures the mystery of fishing, and how little fishermen often knew—or even know now, *"It's hard to tell what goes on on the bottom of the ocean."*[410]

Starting in 1950, annual statewide harvest numbers describe a mostly waning scallop fishery. Nineteen-eighty-one was the banner year for Maine harvest after mid-century, with 3,813,685 pounds of meat sold. In 2021, the total was 533,429 pounds of meat, up from a low in 2005 of 33,000, thanks to a rotational management system that allows areas to rest.[411]

Writing in the *Maine Coast Fisherman* in March 1956, Alice Lawry Gould (pseudonym, Larry Gould) offered this snapshot of Vinalhaven scalloping: "*Except for Wallace Young who drags for scallops out of Old Harbor, Henry Gross is the only boat-owner scalloping on a commercial scale from Vinalhaven this winter.*" Henry "*started scalloping with his grandfather and uncle (the 'Murch brothers') when he was only ten or 12.*" Mid-fifties island catches were modest. Gould reported that Gross and his partner, Ed Smith, often came home with "68 to 100" pounds of scallops which they sold to stores and "private customers." Describing the seasonal shifts, Gould sums up, "*When the scallop season closes, Henry changes to haking; when lobsters begin the crawl, well, he turns lobsterman: until as the earth turns, it is time for the cold job of winter scalloping again. An adaptable Yankee fisherman.*"[412]

On his first scalloping days in the 1970s, Tim Dyer enjoyed the fishing more for its own sake than the income, "*Well, I can't really say that we ever made a whole lot of money—made a living at it. I used to like to do it. It was kind of challenging . . .*" In the 1980s and 1990s, Tim and his son went out together and towed a ten-and-a-half-foot drag. To visualize the drag, think of a net like chainmail with an open rectangular or triangular mouth. A metal cutting bar at the lower mouth edge runs along the surface of the bottom and scrapes up and keeps everything it encounters. The two men would set out around five in the morning and spend an hour or two steaming to Matinicus or Seal Island—timing their arrival with the rising sun. They would drag in circles for about twenty minutes at a time. "*The boat when you're towing is probably only doing 5 or 6 mph. But you're fishing in anywhere from 15 to 30 to 35 fathom water. So you've got out probably 200 to 250 fathom* (1200 to 1500 ft) *wire. . . .*"

When the drag is full,

> *You bring it up, tip the drag upside down; it dumps onto the platform [on the deck]—and you've got a big rubber rug on the platform. So all the scallops are on the platform, you're picking through the stuff getting scallops out; [then] you pick the mat up with a boom, and dump the stuff overboard while the drag is still going around and around. So you've got a sequence you're doing all the time.*

Simultaneously with dragging and dumping, the men hastily sorted the scallops out from the mud, stones and rubble. "*You pick through it and get scallops out and you got about fifteen minutes and the drag is coming up again. It's hard work.*"[413] They cut the scallop meat out of the shell right away; otherwise it spoils. A really good day might yield 300 pounds of meat. On a bad day they could tow for hours and get 20 pounds.

Describing what dragging felt like, Bodine Ames remembered her discomfort:

The boat hangs way way way down. So it's close to the water level and it's all you can do to hang on. You're thinking, "Oh my God we're going, we're going." After the full drag is winched up and dumped on the deck, *"Then all of the sudden it rights itself up."* The pleasure in it for her came when the ocean bottom yielded unexpected treasures: *"We'd get everything from false teeth to chamber pots to old bottles which is something I loved to get."*[414]

Ivan Olson also enjoyed the bottles. *"I couldn't seem to get the hang of [scalloping] . . . I did drag up an awful lot of bottles and stuff. Old antique bottles I hung on to them."*[415]

When a fisherman found a good place to drag, others often found it too. Tim explained that a fisherman's catch frequently depended on how many other boats were fishing. And it could get nasty.

"It takes a while for you to find a place to tow. One day we towed at Seal Island there were 48 boats in a little place. They were all towing the same place. Sometimes the bigger boats didn't want the little boats there so they'd have one big boat and he would go around and pick up everybody's drag and then take back" to intentionally tangle with and cut the drag wires of the smaller boats. Two other big boats got into the act so that *"at the end of the day the 3 big boats . . . were the only ones in there. Just eliminated the rest of them."*[416]

As scallops were depleted, and the remaining shellfish were in places too rocky or too small to drag, divers became more common. Bobby Warren explained,

A lot of times a diver can get them when they are scarce like they are now . . . because there's places divers can go that draggers can't go. Close to the shore, up in the rocks and stuff. So, when the scallops get scarce as they are now a lot of times the divers can make a living. They can get a hundred pounds, you know, out of 5 or 6 [air] tanks.[417]

Northern Shrimp

At present in 2022, there is no shrimping season in Maine because northern shrimp are too depleted. In 1962, when tracking annual catch began, Maine fishermen caught 367,000 pounds of northern shrimp. In 1968 they caught over 24 million pounds. The stock soon crashed, later returned, and diminished steadily thereafter, in part due to warming water. In 2013, the last year of legal shrimping, fishermen caught about 560,000 pounds of shrimp.[418]

Starting in the 1960s and 1970s, some island fishermen dragged for shrimp in January and February. Sonny Warren described the cold.

I remember it was mighty cold in the wintertime. Out there you know with a boat, there was no heat in the boat. Sometimes it was thick with vapor, you know like a fog, I was out dragging shrimp when you couldn't see nothing. It would be ten below zero. My nephew and I were out years ago and it was—two differ-ent times—it was ten below zero. And of course, the only heat you had was the engine, and that was down forward so you couldn't be down there.[419]

"John" described a typical mid-winter outing.

"[We'd] leave early in the morning, and I kid you not, we'd paddle through the ice cakes to get to the boat. And we towed a 60-foot net. . . . Down off the western head of Isle au Haut . . ." For warmth they had *"an oil heated stove . . . You'd wear a monkey suit, whatever you could get on. You know long underwear, the whole works. Rubber gloves, insulated gloves, whatever you could get."*

The trick was to tow on soft bottom so you caught shrimp without ruining your net.

Of course we didn't have the electronics like they have today. I mean the sounding machine we had had a flash on it. . . . A flasher just goes round and round and beeps sound off the bottom and tells you hard bottom from soft bottom. So you'd stay on the soft bottom 'cause if you get on hard bottom you'd tear your net up.[420]

On a good trip they might not have to tow more than an hour; usually they towed two or two and a half to fill their nets.

"John" happily recalled a trip in 1969 or 1970, when they hit the jackpot. That day, the towing wires quickly came together from the weight of the net, and at first the men worried they had shifted onto hard bottom and picked up a rock. Hoping they could remove the rock before it ruined the net, they decided to hoist the net.

We kept hoisting . . . and she was full of shrimp. We split it—what they call split-ting the net. We heisted the net up and you cut it off, and opened the 'cod' end of it and let 'em go into the boat. We did it 5 times. [We got] around 5,500 in one tow. We came in that day with over 10,000 [pounds].They only paid us like 20, 15 or 20 [cents] per pound, back then. But money went further. We made $100 it was like $1000 today.[421]

Speaking about the complicated relationship of catching to selling and processing, which haunts all fishing, Bobby observed, *"We were shrimping through the 60's and 70's . . . There were a lot of shrimp back then. They had a lot of processors along [the coast] and they put up a lot of shrimp. They was even doing it on the island here."* Trouble was, the small processing plants the men relied on often couldn't survive a downturn: *"Then there was a few lean years where there wasn't many shrimp and of course the plants got tore down. The machines got taken out and then after the shrimp started to come back there was no place to process them."*[422]

In spite of the cold, and the obstacles, Walt Day enjoyed the relative ease of a single-species' fishery—one where you're not sorting and tossing back a lot of dead fish. *"Shrimping is a lot of fun. . . . When you got into shrimp it was quick, easy money. When you caught 'em your net would be full of mostly shrimp. . . . [I]t seemed like you wouldn't have to tow very long . . . The net would come up and it would be red with shrimp. So that was fun."*[423]

I asked if men exchanged information when shrimping was good? Actually, they did their best to stay mum. *"[If] you got into good shrimping usually you tried to keep it to yourself. There were a lot of boats shrimping back then. So every little haul had two or three boats on it."*[424]

One way that fishermen experience the invisible "giant hand" is when government managers suddenly close fisheries, cut quotas, or make regulations stricter. The impressions of fishermen and regulators have often been at odds. Trying to preserve the shrimp fishery in 2004, Maine instituted new rules for net size and seasonal timing so that the shrimp had time to drop their eggs. Nevertheless, in 2013, northern shrimp "collapsed." Because the Gulf is warming quickly, and "temperature seems to be the important predictive factor for overall stock health," the future of northern shrimp in Penobscot Bay is unclear. They seem to be moving north with the colder water.[425]

As "John" implies, whatever the species, the value of your catch depends on what the dealer or fish plant will pay for it that day. This, in turn, depends on who the buyer can sell to, the overhead on the transaction, the profit margin, and how many other fishermen sold their catches before you. Clyde Bickford was the steadiest and most successful lobster and fish buyer on the island from the 1940s until he sold his business to Bay State Lobster in 1970 (and continued to run it). One islander, in a casual conversation, said that Bickford single-handedly set the lobster price—*"and controlled everything. He'd say this week it's 45 cents a pound, and that's what it would be."* You only had leverage if there was more than one buyer, and their market was strong enough for them to compete for the fish. Meanwhile, an endless series of fish plants opened and closed during these decades. Burnham-Morrill, the Penobscot Bay Fish Co., Claw Island Foods are a few often mentioned.

Beginning with ice and refrigeration in the late nineteenth century and into the twentieth century, the fresh fish market grew rapidly. Vinalhaven fishermen became more dependent on processing plants located on the island, or on buyers in Vinalhaven or Rockland who could ship their product to markets often in Portland or Boston. Fishermen trapping herring in a weir or stop seining (closing off) a cove often waited a long while for the sardine carrier to come, purchase their catch and carry it to the mainland.

When the Maine State Ferry Service started running ferries to Vinalhaven in 1960, and especially in the early 1970s when the number of daily ferries increased, selling options improved. For one thing, the ferry was subsidized, so the price of transporting fish went down. But it was never simple. Once trains and trucks replaced boats as the fastest transport to an auction site, islanders could be disadvantaged by the extra time it took to get to the mainland highways and railroads.

Because fresh fish spoils quickly, fishermen were vulnerable if buyers wanted to strong-arm prices down. Men did their best to make and maintain good ongoing relationships with buyers they felt were fair, and who treated them well by advancing diesel and bait on credit when they needed it. But not all buyers were fair. One islander told of taking a truck full of fish to sell in New York City in an effort to find a better market. It was an era when the Fulton Fish Market was dominated by organized crime. The islander pulled into the unloading bay, and the moment he shut off his engine he felt the cold muzzle of a gun against his temple. If he wanted to unload and sell the fish, he needed to give the gunman all his grey sole—which were fetching a high price that day.

Market problems contribute to the pressure a captain feels about earning a living for his crew. Hank put it this way,

> *After I got out of school, I got a boat, a 36-foot boat and I rigged it up for scalloping and shrimping. But when you're running it it's up to you to catch them. People were depending on you. [So I was] always thinking about it. [When] you're in the stern, you can growl, 'How come there ain't nothing?' But when you're the one catching them it's all on you.*[426]

EARLY SPRING

Soft Shell Clams

"Then when it starts to warm up a bit in March and the ice starts to leave," Walt continued, *"and we start getting some good days, and everybody would have most of [their winter repairs] done and they would start out clamming, digging clams here and there. The price would be high when you first started—like maybe if you was lucky $10 or $12 a bushel . . . If you got two bushel a tide—I mean 12 bucks—you could buy enough groceries for the day and a few dollars-worth of gas for the truck to go, so you know you had enough gas to go the next day."*[427]

Clam digging has often been the island labor of last resort, what you did when you ran short and needed quick cash. You need almost no equipment.

Sonny Warren remembered, "*I got married. I had $4.00. I gave that to the minister. I had to go clamming the next day to get a loaf of bread to eat.*" For a while he earned money shucking the clams he dug, putting them in jars, and selling them to neighbors.[428]

"Hal," a generation younger, reflected, "*I did a lot of clamming. When we were just kids, maybe 14, 15, 16 years old. To get money you had to work. Our parents didn't have money to give us . . . So we went clamming for money . . . anywheres around the island.*" Mill River on Calderwood Neck was a favorite place.

> *[Y]ou didn't need a fork, you'd just see the holes and drive your hands down into the mud and do it that way. . . . You'd get in that soupy mud . . . You'd just stick your thumb in the hole and pull it out . . . Most always there was a bunch of us that went. There'd be 4 or 5 of us. Usually in the spring . . . If you did have a car that's how you'd put gas in it. I think it was getting $5.50 a bushel. My best day was 5½ bushels.*[429]

John Beckman was famous as a clam digger. He remembered (and others remembered about him) he could dig 8 or 10 bushels in a day, an astounding quantity. During our interview, Sonny Oakes (1925–2012) spontaneously confirmed Beckman's prowess, "*I've dug clams with him over on Narrows Island up on the east side here and he's dug as much as 12 or 13 bushels. In a day.*"

Beckman, as he turned 90, recalled it fondly: "*It was hard work but jeez it was good. I look back on them days and I like them days clamming.*"[430] Oakes had a different memory, "*They claim, but I didn't see him at the time, that he dug so hard that he'd crawl up on the bank and throw up. Of course, he had a big family, six or seven kids. So he had to.*"

Nor was digging the only hard toil. The bushel baskets were heavy, and the walk long. "*They used to have to lug them all the way up that road to that field just below one of the houses there before they would get down to the truck to pick them up.*" Oakes associated clamming with the worst of the Depression misery—times when they couldn't even wait for a spring thaw before they went out. He remembered with bitterness how the one buyer on the island exploited his upper hand.

> *I was a child going to school. It was poor times and all the men was clammin' in the wintertime so I went with my dad up on the "bar" on the other end of the island from here. There were about 25 men digging clams up there in the same spot. [The buyer] was getting forty-five cents a bushel and they was taking an extra peck for a bushel, to buy you know? [There are four pecks to a bushel, but*

*this dealer took five and paid for four.] They use to have an awful time. He still
was the only buyer . . .*

    *Two fellas—one had a model T truck—and they'd collect them up and then
get 'em to Rockland. I don't know if they took them over or put them on the
steamboat. But anyway, he got them to Rockland some way to sell them. I don't
know what they got. But, the clam diggers used to rave like the devil because
he'd take an extra peck for a bushel. . . .*

The harsh cold took its toll. "*I was just a small child. . . . I was so cold I
almost froze to death. My father couldn't take any more after that of the cold
weather.*"[431]

Soft-shell clam landings in Maine peaked in 1977 at nearly 40 million
pounds; the harvest average in 2020 was 6.5 million pounds. This decline
has been associated with climate change and the warming Maine waters in
which the green crab, an invasive species and an aggressive predator of soft
shell clams, thrives. Nitrogen from fertilizer run off has also been identified
as accelerating the decline, as has acidification of the water—caused by the
ocean absorbing CO_2 from the burning of fossil fuels. [432]

SPRING INTO SUMMER

In early April you could set your lobster traps and begin the more substantial
spring fishing. Roughly from the 1960s to the 1980s, fishermen would lobster
through the third week of June. Then, when "the spring crawl" was over and
the lobsters were shedding, those who had wooden boats would pull them out
for about two weeks—through July 4—to scrape and paint them.

Groundfish and Finfish

During the decades that the fishermen I spoke with went fishing, they sought
herring or hake most consistently and caught them most often. But the older men
had regularly fished for other groundfish—including cod, haddock, and pollock.
They caught what they could find. When fishing was really bad, they looked for
shore work for a while—anything to feed their families.[433] I've created separate
sections for the fish species Vinalhaven fishermen targeted most often—as a
way to distinguish the men's experiences as well as the nature of the fish.

Cod

From the 1950s into the 1970s, annual Maine cod catch ran between 2
and 5 million pounds. After the Magnuson Stevens Act (1976) moved US

boundaries 200 nautical miles from the coast, ejected foreign fishing fleets and offered financial aid to New England fishermen to buy better equipment and bigger boats, Maine's cod catch increased gradually to peak in 1991 at 21 million pounds right before the 1995 crash. Since then it has declined steadily; in 2021 it was 47,000 pounds. [434]

Some fishermen say that the cod that made their home close to the island were mostly fished down at the end of the nineteenth century or during the first several decades of the twentieth. Ted Ames interviewed men of his grandfather's era, who recalled big boats out of Portland, Gloucester and Rockland wiping out the spawning beds near Vinalhaven. Ames put together the known science—that cod return to particular sites to spawn—with the fishermen's knowledge of where around Vinalhaven cod actually did spawn. Through this research, he was able to demonstrate that cod populations were local and specific. Once fished out, the grounds did not magically refill with other cod. His own grandfather told of a day when he'd counted over 100 sails of unknown fishing vessels near Saddleback—a fishing ground near Isle au Haut.[435]

In his classic work *New England's Fishing Industry*, published in 1941, Edward Ackerman asserted that the inshore fishing grounds had become so inadequate by then that even with *"an intensive prosecution of the fishery"* fishermen near Vinalhaven could not catch enough fish

> *to make a freezing plant [possibly Fathom Fishery, a part of Bay State Fishing Co.] a profitable enterprise. . . [I]n spite of the fact that Vinal Haven is central to some of the best inshore fishing grounds on the coast, the plant has rarely done more than meet expenses.*[436]

That plant closed in 1940, but Burnham-Morrill opened on Vinalhaven in 1944 and did well enough to expand to 60 employees by 1950. It bought fish locally, as well as in other ports, and employed islanders. During those years they apparently found adequate cod for their purpose: *"Up to 65,000 fish cakes were canned each week using 7 tons of codfish and 20 tons of potatoes."*[437] Those 7 tons of cod—and, Ames notes, cusk, pollack and hake— were probably caught during a few spring and summer months. If Ames' memory of his father's crew taking 10,000 pounds of cod and haddock a day is typical of the other small trawlers, then island boats and those from nearby could have supplied all the catch needed, with some left over.

Ivan Olson and other older fishermen who started in the 1930s and 1940s spoke about catching cod, and about the specific fishing grounds where they were found. His account offers another example of the kind of detailed knowledge fishermen possessed.

[Cod] would come in about the middle of April, we'd start catching them be-
tween here and Matinicus. There was one bunch of fish that came in the South
Bay area every year and they'd run up the river up by Lincolnville and spawn.
They were usually huge . . . about 5 feet long some of them. Some of them
weighed like 50 or 60 pounds apiece.[438]

As a boy fishing with his father in the 1950s, Alfred Osgood (b.1943)
caught lots of big pollock and cod. To find them, they'd motor two or three
miles outside Seal Island. Another younger fisherman, born in the late 1950s,
remembered his father "dragging" for cod—as just a normal part of the fishing
season during that era. *"So you'd do codfish in the spring, haddock in the sum-*
mer, flat fish [flounder] year round with a little bit of by-catch of cusk . . ."[439]
Walt Day recollected that by the 1960s, when he was a teenager, the big
cod were maybe two to two and half feet long and weighed between 18 and
25 pounds. He mentioned an exhilarating day,

I remember one day just to the west of the Hurricane Ledges we had like 900
pounds of cod in the outboard boat. We had so many codfish in the outboard
boat that we would catch one and we'd have to dress it to make more room in
the boat because it was getting pretty well filled up.[440]

Things changed for cod when synthetic gillnets appeared around the island
in the 1960s. Gillnets have been used for thousands of years to catch smaller
fish but were used to catch cod in Maine starting in the late nineteenth and
early twentieth centuries. Charlie York, who fished to the southwest of Vinalhaven from the late 1800s into the 1950s, bought his first cod gillnet in 1918
when he heard they were being used on boats out of Portland.[441]
Originally, when made from linen or cotton, gillnets had been hard to
handle, heavy, visible and susceptible to rotting. The new synthetic nets were
much stronger, lighter, and longer lasting and—crucially—they were invisible in the water. Picture a wall of netting that hangs in the water column
like a curtain. There are different ways to suspend them, and they can stretch
across vast expanses. Unable to see the mesh, fish swim into the net. Their
heads go through an opening in the net, but their gills catch on the line and
trap them. Bigger mesh allows smaller fish to slip through, but mostly early
nets were small mesh, unselective and wasteful. They also caught and killed
sea turtles, dolphins and whales.[442]
Ivan Olson believed that, once fishermen started using the new gillnets in
the 1960s, they quickly finished off the last of the inshore cod: *"Then the guys*
with gillnets got wind of [the South Bay cod] and they filled the bay full of
gillnets and there was no way in hell those fish could get by them. Within 2
or 3 years you couldn't catch 'em." Disgust in his voice, Olson continued, *"If*

you <u>could</u> catch a fish on a hook and line his nose was off" because the cod had been mutilated escaping from a gillnet.

Yeah, I never went gillnetting. I hated them things. The fish is no good either. Once they get into those nets they don't die like they do when you haul them aboard the boat and they're all alive. In the gillnet, they drown. . . . That's like if [you] find a dead hen. You wouldn't take it in and cook it. That's the same way with them damn fish.

Alfred Osgood reflected, looking back, "*Yeah, gill netting is pretty lethal. They caught a lot of fish real quick. But they caught spawners; you know the codfish before they spawned. And that started the end of it right there.*"[443]
George "Burt" Dyer remembered a few island fishermen who gillnetted successfully.

Oh Jimmy Poole (b.1956) and Frankie Thompson (b.1956) they went gillnetting. They did damn good for a while. . . . [They caught] big cod and pollock and hake. . . . They'd get a load of fish with the gillnets. . . . some of them had 20 nets. So that was quite a lot of gillnets. They would fish outside of the Matinicus Rock and outside the Wooden Ball and outside Monhegan Falls they called it—all around, different places they'd set the gillnets.[444]

Burt believed gillnets had a lot to do with the demise of hake as well as cod.

Ronnie Walker explained how fishermen emptied the nets.

[Y]ou'd have a whole bunch of nets tied together and they string out for miles and you just put it in the hauler and it hauled it right in . . . As the fish come in over the boat you have a little hook like and it goes around their head and you just flip the net off the fish's head and it's like picking the fish out of the net.

They caught mostly cod and hake. "*Anywheres from five thousand to twenty five thousand*" pounds in a setting. Even though the nets themselves were non-selective, you could try to place them in areas where you thought you'd find more of the fish you wanted. "*People usually tried to catch codfish because they were a cent or two more than hake was.*"[445]
Gillnets had advantages. Like all net gear, it freed fishermen from having to spend time, effort and money obtaining increasingly expensive bait and baiting hooks. It was "*a quicker way and cheaper way to go. Cause you didn't have to bait the trawls. You could haul your gill nets every day, where the trawl fishing would involve three days of work.*"[446]
But lost gillnets keep catching fish long after fishermen have replaced them, as do the lobster traps, hooks and line and other missing gear littering

the ocean floor. Burt Dyer observed, *"All the nets they lost, they call them ghost nets. They move along the whole coast of Maine and they're always fishing. They're fishing night and day and they catch the fish, and then the lobsters crawl up and eat the fish and some of the lobsters get caught too. . . . God knows how many that there are. I think that's taken a hell of a toll on the fish."*[447]

Though cod was desirable, there was not always a market for it. Cod, too, could go to waste as by-catch. Because ground fishing in the Gulf of Maine is a mixed species fishery, by-catch is an issue. You trawl or drag for one species because that's what the market is buying or, when regulations get tighter, that's what you have a license and adequate quota for. But almost inevitably other species are hauled up, as well as undersize fish and females critical for reproduction. As nets got bigger and vessels pulling them got longer and stronger, ever more fish were maimed or crushed to death by the pressure of fish piling up in the "cod end."

Burt Dyer worked out of Rockland for a while in the 1960s on a trawler fishing off Halifax, Nova Scotia, for redfish. *"Yeah. It's a shame but they always wanted redfish. And the big cod and the pollock—we would pitch them right over the side. We're paying for it now."*[448]

Ivan Olson offered up an example of catching a less desirable species.

We baited on fresh herring, I mean with fresh bait you get a lot of codfish . . . We set the trawl and got it up in shallow water . . . over to Monhegan, and we went back and started hauling the trawl and all of the sudden the whole trawl floated up [filled with cusk]. And we came in and of course they wasn't worth nothing— probably a couple of cents a pound. We had 6000 or 7000 pounds of the damn things. . . . We had an awful struggle to get rid of cusk because there was plenty of haddock around.[449]

So why isn't codfish, once the dominant species in the Gulf of Maine, more a part of living memory on Vinalhaven? The final blow (to date) to the "inshore" fishery occurred in 1984, when the "Hague Line" divided Georges Bank between the United States and Canada. Following the US, Canada adopted its own EEZ (exclusive economic zone) and the two national boundaries overlapped in the Gulf of Maine and Georges Bank. The Hague Line settled the Atlantic nautical boundary between the two countries. American fishing vessels lost access to fisheries off Nova Scotia, Newfoundland and Labrador. Though it gave the United States most of Georges Bank, it closed off a fish-filled corner. Unable to make a profit fishing offshore, the big American offshore vessels moved inshore and cleaned up the remaining Gulf of Maine cod. Small mid-coast fishermen could no longer afford to compete. Within a decade, the cod fishery had crashed across the Northwest Atlantic.[450]

Ronnie Walker observed, "*I stopped fishing for groundfish probably in '85 because there wasn't enough fish to go. You couldn't catch enough to make any money—'85, '86 right in there.*" He addressed the need to scale up operations to compete, adding,

> *Then I stopped herring fishin' probably '90,'92, somewhere in that area. There was herring but there was a situation where you either had to go bigger or get out. Everybody was getting bigger boats and going further and I didn't have the money to invest in getting a bigger boat so I got out of it.*[451]

The bay was changing. Fishermen's questions were straightforward: Can I make ends meet? Are there fish to catch or not? The ocean is huge, opaque, and dangerous. Who knows what's really going on?

Burt's image of ghost fishing is haunting. It comments not just on the real phenomenon, the nets that no longer rotted, but also on the inconceivable demise of a livelihood after generations of families had fished the same waters. Island fishermen knew that, whatever part they had played, the real problem was caused by something bigger, over the horizon and out of view. Had you asked, many could have listed ecological, technological, commercial, and political reasons. But facts, while true and essential, missed the point. The point was that fishermen fished. If they didn't keep at it and earn what living they could, others would come into their water and take what seemed theirs by birthright.

Writing in 2015, Jeffrey Bolster observed, "*The Gulf of Maine cod stocks today are probably only a fraction of 1 percent of what they were during George Washington's presidency.*"[452]

Haddock

Although haddock are in the cod family, they don't salt as well as cod, and tend to spoil more quickly. Until ice and refrigeration changed the market, some were sold, but they lacked the status and desirability of cod. Haddock are also smaller fish, and it took more effort with hook and line to catch an equal weight.

Things changed when gasoline engines appeared, and otter trawling commenced in New England waters. Haddock filled nets. Edward Ackerman noted in the 1940s, "*Because they are abundant fish on the smooth grounds which otter trawlers frequent, haddock have been taken out of the water with alarming rapidity since the start of New England trawling operations in 1905.*" Haddock were the right size for frozen fish processing and fed the burgeoning demand for breaded fish fillets.[453]

Islanders recalled the species abundance well into the twentieth century. Thinking about the Depression, Sadie Dyer observed,

> *Well it wasn't that bad because in the Depression you had the government food . . . But fish was plentiful . . . We had a lot. We ate lobster and clams like it was going out of style because it was poor man's food . . . Haddock, you could always get haddock. We fished off of the wharf, my Dad's wharf . . .*[454]

As a boy, Ted Ames started out baiting tub trawl for haddock. "*I think Carl Nelson's was the first tub I baited. It was a tub with haddock gear. Smaller than a regular hake tub. I stood on a soda box down to Bickford's . . . and baited away.*"[455]

Herb Conway said his father fished for haddock briefly in the late 1930s and early 1940s, before switching over to catch the then more desirable redfish. "*[H]e went dragging for quite a number of years. To begin with it was haddock. Down to the east haddock were running really strong but then . . . they went after redfish.*"[456]

Walt remembered,

> *When I was still in high school [in the 1960s], I had an outboard boat, and a friend of mine and myself would go out hand lining in my outboard boat and we'd just go like down, just outside the harbor . . . You could catch codfish and quite a few haddock there. We'd dig clams because haddock liked clams better than they did herring.*[457]

In 1950, Maine fishermen caught 7.5 million pounds of haddock. In 2021 that number was at 192,092 pounds. Haddock stocks are currently rebounding better than cod and a small quantity are fished according to government quotas—though no longer by islanders.[458]

Redfish or Ocean Perch

Redfish, also called Ocean Perch, is a kind of "rockfish." It became a popular in the 1930s once fish-freezing technology appeared. Clarence Birdseye, a remarkable inventor, studied Inuit techniques and learned from them that super-cold freezing temperatures made all the difference in the post-thawed quality of frozen food. He invented filleting and fish freezing machines, and in 1926 established the General Seafoods Corporation in Gloucester. "The marketing of [Redfish] as frozen fillets in 1935," according to Bigelow and Shroeder, radically increased demand. Fish plants on Vinalhaven and, on a much larger scale in Gloucester, found that Redfish froze well and could both meet and grow that demand.[459]

A note in Sidney Winslow's diary on August 31, 1938 suggests that redfish was being processed in Vinalhaven plants in the 1930s, and that some of the boats catching and delivering it were from away: "*The big Gloucester dragger 'Donald Amirhault' arrived at the local plant of the Bay State Fisheries Co. last week with 130,000 lbs redfish.*" Winslow's diary records varied events. A particular community insight it offers is by conveying the way fishermen shared their catch, and how daily island meals were made out of it. On May 1, 1946, he wrote, "*A fine day. I worked at Brown's 8 hours. Had a mess of redfish given to me today, we had them and some of Dick's smelts for supper . . .*" [460]

Sonny Oakes confirmed that, between the 1940s and their disappearance from the surrounding waters in the 1970s, redfish was an active island fishery. "*I used to go dragging with my father-in-law and a lot of boats would be together. There would be 8 or 9 boats together dragging, you know, some of them bigger than others . . .*" Later he added, "*The whole coast of Maine they'd be dragging. It was a livelihood.*" Fifteen thousand pounds made a good night's catch for them. "*My father-in-law's boat would be about sixty foot, but some were over 100 feet long.*" [461]

Oakes rued how the profitable single species market in the late 1960s could be wasteful. Most noticeable, he believed, were the bigger off-island boats.

Those big boats were primarily after these redfish because that's where the money was. A lot of times the big boats had thirteen or fourteen men aboard. They'd pitch these big codfish, sometimes nearly as big as this table, overboard. They'd drown, of course. They'd be floating on the surface and they'd leave them. That hurt the industry, really. . . . But they didn't want it. They wanted redfish. That was a saleable fish . . .

Big cod didn't fit in the processing plant machinery. [462]

Other times they found ways to sell diverse kinds of fish: "*There were four or five different ground fishes they would save. Haddock and flounder and all that stuff they'd save but they'd put them in a separate bin and sell them separately at market, you know.*" Oakes believed that redfish reproduction couldn't keep up with what the draggers caught.

So many [draggers] got into it they kept catching more and more and a lot of [the redfish] were destroyed with draggers especially . . . When you were dragging [the redfish would] go into what was called a "cod end" and they'd get so much pressure the smaller fish would pop out. You could see them floating on the water. But then sharks would be going around your boat slurping them up.

Then [in the 1970s] the redfish started petering out and you had to go further to get them and the boats were too small to get enough load to make it worthwhile.

As Oakes noted, redfish, unlike cod and haddock, is a very long-lived, slow maturing fish that is not nearly as fertile as cod or haddock. They become overfished more quickly and are slower to recover.[463]

The Maine redfish fishery was at its peak in the 1950s—with 79 million pounds caught and sold in 1950. It stayed active through the late 1960s before dropping slowly. In 2020, 54,500 pounds were harvested and sold—though none by Vinalhaven fishermen.[464]

Hake

White Hake is related to cod and haddock, but doesn't resemble either one closely. It can grow to four feet and weigh up to 40 lbs. Usually the ones caught in the Gulf have averaged around 8 pounds, according to Bigelow and Shroeder.[465] Like haddock, hake doesn't last well unless it's kept cold, so its commercial market developed only in the early twentieth century. In the decades after the Second World War, white hake joined redfish as one of the major commercial species pursued by Vinalhaven fishermen. Island plants sold it fresh, frozen, salted and canned.[466]

A headline from the *Maine Coast Fisherman* in November 1950 announced—"*Island Company Finds Market for Salt Hake.*" Apparently, Eddie Bonacorso, the superintendent of the Vinalhaven Fisheries, experimented successfully with drying hake. The article describes his method and continues, "*The dried fish are boned, stripped, and packed in 40-pound wooden boxes. These are packed for a company called Murphy and Aschon of Baltimore Md. and sold throughout the South.*"[467]

To catch hake, island fishermen described going out to Seal Island, or Wooden Ball, or further out past Matinicus—different fishing grounds at different times.

Men mostly longlined (tub-trawled) for hake. Walt Day started catching it when he was sixteen or seventeen in the late 1960s.

I used to go with Marshall Coombs, Jr. a lot, and you would bait the gear the day before, put it in the cooler, go down about 10:00 that night, put all the gear aboard the boat and steam outside Matinicus Rock . . .

There was probably about 30, 35 or 40 boats out of here that went haking in the spring, and in the summer—longlining—and then there were 7 or 8 [more boats] that used to come up from Swan's Island and a bunch from Stonington. . . . [They were] wooden boats, a lot of them built right here, probably 30, 32, 34 feet—that was a big boat back then. For engines, a lot were from V8 Buicks, Chryslers, because [we] used car engines back then. Gasoline was cheap. . . .

You'd get all your gear baited with the 800 hooks and most people took 7 or 8 tubs—6,400 hooks. You would load the gear and you would go out and get off around midnight or 1:00 and they you'd set all the gear in the dark cause the hake come up off the bottom at night. And you would get set in a straight line and you'd see other boats just almost like a set of stairs falling off.

Once you had set all your trawl, it was time to haul it. Tied together, the line with its 6,400 hooks could stretch two or three miles.

Marshall would steer the boat and the other guy had what you called a heaving stick so that you didn't have to reach into the tubs for the hooks. It was a stick about [4 feet long.] . . . You would set it all out slowly over the rail, until you got it all set out, drop your anchor on the other end and it would take long enough to do that so you would run back to the first you set and immediately start hauling just before daylight or as the sun was starting to come up . . . in the summertime around here it starts getting daylight quarter to 4:00, 4:00 o'clock.

They worked steadily. "*Marshall would be hauling, the other guy would be cutting fish—you cut their throat and split them down the middle, and my job was to just pull guts and all day long . . . and toss them overboard.*"
The fish would be lying in the boat. It would be cool in the early morning. By 12:30 or 1:00 in the afternoon they'd be in port to take them out. They weren't too concerned. "*[Y]ou would try to keep them wet on top so the sun didn't cook them. But a lot of that stuff was used for catfood at the time anyway.*"[468]
They sold the hake either to Burnham & Morrill or to Clyde Bickford, depending on who could handle it that day. From 1951 to 1964 when Sonny Oakes managed Burnham & Morrill, he remembered hake as "*the predominant fish at the time. Those guys would sometimes bring in fourteen to fifteen thousand a day . . . One day we handled—the biggest day I remember while I worked there was 136,000 pounds we bought that one day.*"[469]

I asked Herb Conway about the length of his workday. He said that when he was haking they'd go out anywhere between 9:00 p.m. and midnight, and not return sometimes until five the next afternoon. So it could push twenty hours. But he allowed that it was rare that they'd go day after day without a break. In the days before GPS, the fog often offered them time to rest:

If it was foggy before you left, 9 times out of 10 you didn't go. Because if . . . a shark bit you off, or whatever, the chances were that you wouldn't find the gear until the fog let go. There was a good chance of losing all your trawls. If you was getting good fishing you would go maybe a couple of days in a row.[470]

Some days the haking was almost too good. Sonny chuckled recalling an outing in the 1950s when

Walter Hutchinson (1925–2002) put so many [hake] in his boat he sunk it. . . . Him and the fella that was helping him, they were setting up on the bow of the boat, she was still floating but she was mostly under. . . . Kept taking the fish aboard, and fish aboard, and more fish—he sunk himself.

Making a miniscule gesture with his fingers, he explained how fishermen would generally

come in and the boats would be just about so far out of the water, you'd see them coming and you'd think they were going to sink any minute. There were a lot of fish on them. B&M bought them. There were a lot of boats went out here went haking . . . there were a dozen maybe, something like that or more maybe.

I think they got a cent a pound or half a cent a pound, they didn't get nothing for 'em but back then you could, you know, with a dollar you could buy something.[471]

Fishing in small boats and hauling in large hake was exhausting work, "*So you would have to haul the trawl by hand and you had all them fish on [the trawl line you were hauling] which was a terrible strain of fish and tide. So you really hauled really hard.*" It was worse in the fog. Men usually set the line from northeast to southwest—the way the tide ran. Hauling in fog, Les Dyer Jr. (1921–2003) allowed, "*was a son of a gun.*" They couldn't risk going back to the beginning of their set (the eastern end of the trawl) because they were unlikely to find the buoy. So they pulled against the tide, which was brutal. Finding the buoys was a challenge on many days. According to Dyer, you had to have "*eyes like an owl.*" When Les served in the Navy during World War II in the South Pacific, he spotted an enemy periscope a mile and a half away, a feat so remarkable his captain let slip a "Holy Shit!" Dyer believed it was a skill he'd learned spotting buoys.[472]

Les and Sonny had to stop trawling when their shoulders went bad with chronic bursitis. And bursitis was only one physical risk among many. Ana Balfour, the English physician on the island for two years during the war, described to her children how in spring when island fishermen moved their boats back into the water.

She would be asked to treat the fishermen for toes and fingers crushed under the launching rollers. During the fishing seasons she often had to remove fish hooks stuck in fingers and treat hands septic from pricks of fish fins and lobster claws. The men often strained their backs hauling loaded lobster pots. There was frost bite in the winter and severe sun burn in the summer, adding to the usual problems of a country doctor.[473]

The Maine Hake catch peaked in 1993 with 11,114,488 lbs caught. In 2020, 349,145 pounds of white hake were caught in the state. [474]

SUMMER, AUTUMN, WINTER

Halibut

While halibut was never a big part of post-war island fishing, fishermen caught them in June and July when they could. Ivan Olson (1926–2013) caught many halibut and took pride in his ability. *"I was really interested in that. That was one thing I could do pretty good."*
He described two outstanding days in the 1970s.

I had quite a few hooks on the bottom. Long-lining . . . and I think I got, all together it was 32 or 33 halibut . . . the first day. They were anywheres from 15 to 20 pounds up to 80 or 90 pounds. It was the first time I make $1,000 in one day. It wasn't lobstering, it was with halibut.

Just as he had learned fishing from a neighbor who took him out, he took *"the kid of a friend of mine"* with him at 4:00 a.m. to haul in the trawl he'd baited and set the night before. *"We always went fishing . . . I practically brought him up."*
Halibut usually swam into reach in June or right at the beginning of July. The season ended when spiny dogfish arrived.

Then spiny dogfish would show up—right in the middle of July—and after that there was no sense [in trying.] By the time you put down your trawl, the dog-fish—there was many of them—they cleaned it off. That's all you could catch. You couldn't even get a line to the bottom. You'd look overboard and it would just be like that everywhere. There was so many of them . . . They were terrible and they still are.[475]

The island fishermen despised dogfish. Burt Dyer called them "green-eyed bastards" and claimed to have once been so infuriated by their attacking his lines, that he bit the nose off one—no mean feat against a small, but vicious shark. Dyer mentioned having arthritis in his shoulder, *"from pounding dog-fish."* He would pull up one dogfish after another, hoping for some saleable groundfish; and then be forced to unhook each while it thrashed around. They were nasty to deal with and, in return, bore the brunt of his wrath.

In the words of Bigelow and Schroeder, "*The spiny dogfish (dogfish or dog in common parlance) makes up for the comparative rarity of other sharks in the Gulf of Maine by its obnoxious abundance.*" They can live one hundred years.[476]

10

Herring

Even more than cod, Vinalhaven's signature fish in the nineteenth and twentieth centuries was herring. None are caught around the island now, but for a long time they were abundant.

"Well, when I went as a boy," Alfred Osgood explained, *"we went torching herring. They used a little small net, probably wouldn't reach from here to the end of the room. And they would set it out in a shape kind of like a horseshoe. And then there'd be herring in the cove. You'd see the herring firing in the water, and you would have what looked like a dip net with a wire bottom, and you'd put rags in it, and put gasoline in it, and set a fire, and you'd row with it, and the herring would chase you, and you'd go in with the net and close it up and catch them. It'd hold probably a couple of hundred bushel. Which is a lot. They did it a lot. When I was younger, they'd get their own bait every year."*[477]

During Alfred's lifetime changing technology enabled diverse, and gradually larger-scale, ways of catching herring. There was the torching he describes; there were weirs; there was stop seining and later purse seining; and finally, there were the huge mid-water trawlers.

Through the first decade of the twenty-first century, Atlantic herring was the second largest commercial fishery in Maine—surpassed only by lobsters, and closely linked to that fishery. In 2020, 11,538,719 million pounds of herring were landed in Maine, and while there are no precise figures, most of it went for lobster bait. Currently, the species is "in rapid decline" and "drastic measures" are being taken. The New England population has dropped nearly 90 percent "from the species' peak in 1967."[478]

More concerning still is the absence of juvenile herring. A stark frontpage headline in the "Fisherman's Voice" declares, "Severe herring fishery cuts on tap as young fish remain elusive: Very large quota reductions may be inevitable in 2019–2021." And indeed, they have been forthcoming. In 2019 mid-water trawling was banned indefinitely within 12 nautical miles of shore from Grand Manan to Cape Hatteras as a way to protect inshore spawning herring populations and their ecosystems from the destructive gear. By 2020 herring represented only 1 percent of the total Maine catch value.[479]

For hundreds of years, herring was used for bait in the hook fisheries, and smoked or pickled in brine for human consumption. Though always pursued on the island, the herring fishery took off in the mid-1870s when Maine entrepreneurs started canning them as "sardines." By 1900, 117 canneries dotted the Maine coast. For a while the island hosted its own plant—the Sawyer & Sons Sardine Factory opened in 1917 and operated on and off for about a decade. Since the sardine market declined mid-twentieth century, most of the herring has gone to bait lobster traps.[480]

Today, the herring fishery is losing the last of its island roots. Until lately, Alfred Osgood still owned a part of The Starlight, a kind of mid-water trawler that fishes out of mainland harbors and was recently banned in nearshore waters. This appears to be the only fishery in which an islander has in recent years owned part of a "corporate" fishing vessel. Throughout his life, Alfred was a legendary highliner, always out on the water catching more than anyone else.

The mid-water trawlers tow enormous funnel-shaped nets midway in the water column on places like Georges Banks. Their electronic equipment easily spots schools of herring deep under water. Fish that get scooped up in the net's open mouth get pushed back to the cod end, which is tied shut. The trawls can catch hundreds of thousands of pounds of herring in a haul.

Islanders remember their modest harvest of vanished inshore herring. Roger Young thought back on his father and his family tending a weir in the years after World War II. His memory reminds us again how the fishing business was so often about family and personal connections.

> There was a big demand for herring. My father was a good people person. And he got in with this family, they had the Green Island Packing Company and they said, you can man it. Well my father had all his relatives. So they came over with the barge and drove the stakes for a weir up in Old Harbor. They tended that weir and they also had one down on Green's Island, they call it Sand Cove, and they had a camp there. Right after the war, they caught a lot of herring and did real good for those times.[481]

An ever-shifting array of weirs fringed island coves from spring to fall. Sidney Winslow described a weir being taken down one November in the 1930s.

Alex Davidson and Ira MacDonald are busy taking their weir netting. Nearly every one of the small trees which had been placed along the side of the lead of the weir had attached to them nearly half a bushel of small mussels. The boys say that the weir has paid fairly well this year.

The following April, Winslow noted that the boys were busy readying it for the summer.[482] Numbers of weirs went up and down, and locations changed. There were 9 licensed weirs in 1919, but none in 1921. Sonny Warren counted at least 6 functional weirs during the 1950s.[483]

Through the 1980s, islanders "stop seined": they waited for schools of herring to swim into a cove, then closing off the cove with "twine" nets to trap the fish. Then they would haul them into boats, or later call sardine carriers to come from the mainland and "vacuum" them up.

Crews would go out at dusk looking for herring, checking the coves one after the other. They looked for the small fish schooling in the water, or birds above feeding on them. After dark, their luminescence revealed schools near the surface. Experienced fishermen knew to use a "feeler pole" lowered down into the water; they could judge the density of fish by the way it vibrated. As with lobstering, territories and understandings governed when and where you could tie off a cove.[484]

Ted Ames observed, "Stop seining was very competitive. Irate competitors would 'jump' into a cove not being tended or, having lost access to a cove, would drop an oil filter overboard in the cove, causing herring to avoid the site for the rest of the season."[485]

In the 1960s, Victor Ames (1932–2016), a fisherman on Vinalhaven and Matinicus, got a pilot's licence, and would go up at dusk to spot herring for fishing vessels. The view from the air made it easy to scan many coves in a short time. Sam Perkins, who spent his boyhood summers on Vinalhaven, remembered watching a spotting plane when his neighbor, Arnold Barton, stop-seined for herring.

Herring fishing was the most exciting stuff that we saw as kids. They'd send up spotting planes at twilight and the planes would be up looking for schools of herring, looking to see where they were headed, and the planes would call out to the guys with the nets. It was like this big chase, where they'd race out, they'd set the nets across the cove. Fishermen's Cove where we have the boathouse was actually a really good cove for herring.

So they would set a net, they'd pen them in there and then the next morning they'd start driving them into smaller nets and they'd "pocket" them in a net. The really exciting part was when they'd bring a pumper over . . . Four guys in a dory would be hauling the net into the dory compressing the herring into a smaller and smaller pouch. The pouch would just be boiling with fish and it would get shallower and shallower and shallower and then they'd have this

gigantic pumper which had a vacuum hose. It must have been kind of brutal on
the herring but they'd stick this vacuum hose down in there and start sucking
the herring up into the pumper and in the hold.[486]

While the plane-spotting Sam describes made it easier to find the schools,
it could be dangerous. A July 5, 1955, headline reads "Vinalhaven Crash Kills
Herring Spotter Pilot." The accompanying article tells the story.

Jack Harrison, 41, herring spotter plane pilot, crashed his Taylor craft pontoon
plane at Conway Point on Vinalhaven at 8:45 p.m. Friday, killing himself and
wrecking the light aircraft. . . . Harrison was a veteran herring spotter and had
worked along the Penobscot Bay shores for several years. . . .

Spotters often swooped low so they could let fishermen know where to find
the herring.

[T]he plane dipped down as if the pilot was to shout a message to the boat crew.
Then the pilot opened the motor to full power in an attempt to pull up from what
was apparently a dangerously steep dive. A down draft from the shore after the
exceedingly hot day dropped the plane even more and it crashed about 20 feet
from the seine boat, flipping over and sinking at once. . . .

This plane was not the first one to auger into island waters.
    "The spotting of herring by plane was introduced along the coast shortly
after World War 2 with Hugh Lehtinen of St. George and Jack Dodge of Ash
Point being among the first to enter the field. Lehtinen was injured some
years ago in a similar crash which took place in Vinalhaven harbor. He later
returned to the business . . . To justify the risk," the reporter concluded, *"her-*
ring spotters are paid a percentage of the income from schools of fish they
locate for seiners." [487]
    Humans weren't the only species after herring.

They'd have a guy who was monitoring the stuff that was going into the vacuum
to make sure it was herring. They had to deal first of all with harbor seals who
would be circling around trying to get stuff, but also dogfish because there were
billions of dogfish around at the time.[488]

Any of these interlopers could tear the net, destroying the night's work. *"If*
there was seal in it," Bodine Ames explained, *"the seal would go out through*
the net and 10,000 herring would go behind it. They were a pain in the neck."
Other times, if fishermen trapped too many fish, they could mass together and
break the net. Even without the help of other creatures, nets were always tear-
ing from the sharp rocks that are everywhere around the islands.

The fishermen had to keep the fish alive as the pockets got smaller.

"The secret was not to smother the herring. You know, a number of times it would be that whole pockets full of herring would get smothered. . . I don't know why—maybe because they were just too fierce and the water was running too much, then you'd have 20,000 bushel of herring all floating dead up and the gulls filling themselves." The dead fish weren't all lost, *"[P]eople would come down with buckets and want some to eat."*[489]

Fishermen shared their catches when they'd caught more than they could sell themselves. Joe Upton, who fished and bought and sold herring for bait on Vinalhaven in the 1970s wrote:

There was a tradition with the local boats, and it was this: when someone had a big set and filled his "market," he gave what was left in the net to whomever else was around. That way the fish, often dead by then, weren't wasted, and everyone got a share. Nothing was asked except that the favor be returned if the situation was reversed.

As vessels and nets became bigger and interlopers arrived to fish, sharing vanished.

But a couple of times when the big outside boats, the "Gloucester boys," had been around with their big nets, driving the fish deep so that the local boats couldn't get any, they would have maybe half a million pounds in a set and only be able to load, say, half that into their holds. But instead of offering what was left to the remaining fleet, they'd just open their net, and the dead fish would sink to the bottom, wasted, hundreds of thousands of pounds at a whack.[490]

Selling the herring could offer entertainment as well as cash, Lorraine Walker described how much, as a child in the 1950s, she enjoyed the outings.

A lot of [the sardine carriers] were from Canada, some from Rockland, because we had three or four processing [plants] right in Rockland at the time. . . .

[A] lot of times on Sundays especially, we'd spend the whole day on the sardine carrier and it was great because they separated the scales off the fish. The fish went through some sort of a chute and the scales came off and then there would be baskets of scales. Big woven baskets and they called them scale baskets. I guess that they all went to things like cosmetics, and buttons. All the scales were resalable. It's hard to believe, when I think back on it. I remember that my mother had scale baskets for washing. The clothes baskets were scale baskets. . . .

The scales would come off the fish . . . They were shiny. They were so beautiful. They were like silver. So we'd sit there and watch the baskets of scales fill up and watch the fish come.

She continued, *"We would go with my father in the lobster boat to the cove and he would put my sister and me on the sardine carrier, my mother would go with us too. We would sit on the sardine carriers while they took the fish out of the seine . . . [They] would pump the fish right out of the water."*

"When the boat left for Rockland we'd get back aboard [our] boat . . . and come back to the house. It was just a day trip thing for us. We just loved it because it was so exciting. There were so many fish. You know, it would be a beautiful day . . . The scales, though, I always remembered the scales. I think people forgot about the scales."[491]

Some fishermen arranged to sell all their catch to one plant. In return they'd get to keep a tab—for gas, boat or engine repairs, or other supplies they needed. But they could get trapped in debt or stuck in really bad deals. Joe Upton writes that by the 1970s some canneries would take a whole boat-load of fish, but only pay for the part they eventually canned, and fishermen felt that they had to go along.[492]

Even as Lorraine was watching them, herring were disappearing from the coves. A 1976 article from the *Courier Gazette* in Rockland describe Vinalhaven fishermen returning to stop-seining after a long dry spell, not-ing that it had been between fifteen and twenty-five years since herring had showed up in such big numbers: *"Long neglected nets, dories and other 'stop seining' gear were brought out to 'stop off' the small fish, and gather them in . . ."*[493]

As stop-seining became more difficult, some island fishermen turned to purse seining from small boats, fishing further away from shore in deeper water.

In purse seining, fishermen let out a huge curtain-like net—in the old days by hand, later with a winch—as they circled their boat around a school of herring. A rope or wire ran along the bottom of the net. Once they closed the circle, they pulled the bottom rope tight, "pursing" the seine and catching the fish. As with stop seining, they gradually forced the fish into a smaller and smaller "pocket" and waited until the sardine carriers came.

Victor Ames owned a 30-foot double-ender open boat. Bobby Warren and some other islanders started purse seining with Victor. Victor's relative Lee Osgood started going out with the crew in the late 1950s.

I was 15. When we first started with Victor, Joe Cheney had rigged him up. He was a summer guy that had come here. . . . He made big money . . . They bought an old double ender boat, put a small seine in it. Victor was a Cracker Jack herring catcher . . . we used go out and we used to fish Matinicus, Wooden Ball, Seal Island and sometimes you'd venture down to Matinicus Rock. That was pretty big sailing in those days . . .

Lee remembered seeing radar on an island boat for the first time in the early 1960s. It's also interesting that a summer visitor joined the long island tradition of investing in fishing boats.

Because he was the "rookie," Lee didn't get to sleep on the way out.

I always steered at night, and Victor was standing on the bow and he'd just point his arms right or left which way he wanted me to steer. Those guys would sleep on the seine. They'd been before. They knew when to catch a nap. I thought it was great, it was real cool to steer the boat for my uncle . . .

You always tried to get there just before dark. Nine times out of ten—and I understand even today—they're getting their best sets about dark [when] the sun is setting, because the fish is just coming up off bottom. See they settle during the daylight. . . .

You look for porpoises, gulls. Seagulls is always there—if they was feeding on them you know if the herring are up in the water . . .

If you've never been and seen a school of herring it is a sight to behold . . . it's just like a sheet. They whiten, it's just super. If they're really solid, it's just unreal. Just as far as you can see, just . . . beautiful it really is. On a pretty night it's beautiful. You can smell them.

There is nothing like it. Purse-seining is quite addicting . . . when everything is going good, which lots of nights [it] did. Lots of nights [it] didn't. It's just typical fishing. But it was beautiful. The fish in the water, the guys all working together, having a good time . . . It was just a good time. A real simple good time. Like I said nobody probably had a $10 bill in their wallet but nobody really cared. You didn't think about stuff like that.[494]

Some fishermen seined herring at night and lobstered during the day, getting little sleep all summer. Ronnie Walker fished for herring and sold to bait boats, an alternative to selling to a sardine carrier.

My main thing was catching lobster bait. There was a couple of guys that would just sell lobster bait. They had a big boat and I'd catch the herring for them. So then, I'd stay up all night long. We'd get back in from herring fishing about 5 in the morning I'd have breakfast and then go haul my lobster traps all day until 2pm and I'd come in and lay down for an hour or two in the afternoon and eat supper at 5 and go back out at 6 herring fishing. Done that for ten years—for June, July, August, September, October.

He would sometimes take a half hour nap on the boat, but he was afraid of what might happen while his eyes were closed.

Just about everybody else that went herring fishin', they always had a backup guy. Ya know, somebody that was able enough to take the boat and understand what to do and when to do it. I never had anybody aboard my boat that was trustworthy enough to let him take the boat. Every time I did, they'd frig it up. One night we was comin' back from Mt. Desert and I was just exhausted. I told one of my crew to steer the boat, and I give him the course to steer and where to go. I went down and laid down and half an hour . . . I got up and . . . he was headed back in the same way we was just comin' from.[495]

Like Ronnie, Hal initially worked day and night stop-seining or purse-seining herring, and lobstering. As the herring moved offshore and boats got bigger, a handful of island men, including Hal, started fishing out of Gloucester in the winter. Beginning in the mid-1970s, he fished from New Hampshire in the summer, and Gloucester or further south in winter.

When fishing on Vinalhaven, Hal left port at 4 in the afternoon, slept an hour in the boat on the way to the fishing ground, and another hour on the way back home. They arrived home with daylight, between four or five in the morning, and unloaded the fish. He'd grab breakfast and go out to haul his traps until noon. Only then, after twenty hours of work, would he go home, unwind watching half an hour of his favorite soap opera, then sleep for two hours until 3:00 p.m. Just home from her job, his wife would fix him supper, and his day would start over. Hal kept that pace for almost thirty years.

His wife described the rest of the year: "*[A]round Thanksgiving they would take off and go to Gloucester. From Thanksgiving to April 15th. He would live in a motel and go herring-fishing, I'd stay here [and work] . . . He'd come home on weekends.*"

In Gloucester Hal had three crewmen, all from Vinalhaven.

You're always trying to make a living for your crew. Because if you tie the boat up and don't do anything, you lose your crew because they had to go and do something else. So you're always trying to make a living year round for them.

There is a lot of shoal water in Cape Cod Bay. A lot of time we could fish 24 hours a day, day and night. . . . Back then we were fishing a lot for the Russians . . . They were anchored right outside of Gloucester and we were taking a lot of fish to them. That was a main market.

In the end, faced with the choice between getting an even bigger boat or retiring from herring, Hal shifted to hauling lobster traps.[496]

Ted Ames describes the way fishermen had to keep scaling up to stay in the game, and how it gradually destroyed island–and Maine coastal fisheries:

[T]here were quite a few seining outfits in the earlier years and then, purse-seining came and Victor [Ames] and Alfred [Osgood] and a couple of others entered the fishery and as that declined, boats got larger, seines got deeper and the number of people participating got fewer until, towards the end, I think Alfred was the only one that was going from the Island and last I knew, he used

*a 40 fathom seine compared to the 10 or 20—just in order to maintain good
production.*

He summed up the community impact when bigger vessels moved offshore:

*Again, when you go offshore all the economic activity associated with inshore
fishing disappeared and the bulk of the work was done with larger outfits.
Which meant the fish had to be landed in larger ports and in the wintertime they
[islanders like Alfred Osgood] were fishing down in Massachusetts and down
towards New York, landing there, so that it changed the role of fishing in the
community, except for lobstering. And that's where things are at the length of the
coast basically from Vinalhaven east.*[497]

Even when times were good and fish still came inshore, herring fishing
wasn't without dangers. Bobby Warren told this story about a bad night. He
had been purse-seining down the *"back side of Criehaven,"* an island maybe
20 miles south of Vinalhaven. While he was scrambling to gather in the corks
that kept the net afloat, he caught his heels in the stern of the boat.

*I just went over backwards, rolled over the back of the boat. Overboard. They
didn't know it. I hollered, come up and spit the water out and hollered and hollered but they was makin' so much noise on the winch heads, you know, the rope
was screechin', and they didn't know it.*

*Finally, [the boss] looked around, it was after dark but there was enough light so
that he could see that I was gone. He hollered to the others "Bob is gone." So, then
they rushed back and let go of the seine ropes and looked down and there I was
hangin off [the net.] It seemed like it was 15 minutes but it may not have been quite
that long. They got me aboard the boat. I got my boots off and we kept a goin . . .*

He was luckier than he knew. A bit later, a sardine carrier tied up to them.
As they were starting to pump the herring, he looked and, *"I swear this shark
was eight or ten foot long—This great big shark come up and opened his jaws
and took a bite at the corks tryin' to get the herring."* Bobby caught my eyes,
smiled and added, *"If I'd known he was down there I wouldn't have needed
any help getting in the boat."*[498]

As the various fish stocks depleted, licensing rules also changed. Gradually,
island fishermen were closed out or bought out, and lost their federal permits.
This ended their seasonal ways. "So what happened to all the fishing permits
that used to be owned by islanders?" Walt Day explained:

*They were bought up by the corporations. Say I got permits and I didn't use
mine. Say I had a ground fish permit. And say in '77, '78 and '79, I didn't fish.*

It was more lucrative to go lobstering, so I went lobstering them three years and I never caught a fish. . .

Then the federal government comes out and says, 'In order for you to keep your permit you have to show us your landings for '77, '78 and '79.' Well it was more lucrative to go lobstering and I didn't go ground fishing them three years. So they take your permit.[499]

Once you've lost your permit,

You can never get it back because you have no history. No fishing history for them three years. Anybody that had fishing history in them three years can retain that permit. And the permit I lost, some corporation will buy that, or some guy that his whole business is ground fishing.

As time passed, it became too hard to make a living ground fishing, not just because there were fewer fish, but because federal regulations controlled when you could go to sea and how much you could catch. This system worked against men who lobstered sometimes and fished other times. Their operations were too small, too varied, and too dependent on retaining some autonomy and flexibility.

You might say, they were too organic for a world dominated by large-scale industrial fishing. Their very diversification—small scale, seasonal rhythm, and pursuit of numerous species—so important for a healthy ocean and inter-generational sustainability, was no longer deemed feasible.

Corporations and large fishing operations kept looking for fishermen who were ready to give up and sell their permits. "*They have people looking all the time. In the back of every fishing magazine is a list of permits that's for sale.*" The more permits a big company owned, the more days they could fish, and the more fish they could catch.

After centuries of following the seasons, going about fishing pretty much on their own terms, suddenly island fishermen felt controlled and done in by rules that caught them coming and going. Walt elaborated on the impact:

In order to maintain your hand line license, you had to land 3,500 pounds a year. So it all went well and good, but then the fishery collapsed so the government came out and says we're cutting you from 3,500 to 2,500 because the fishery has collapsed and everybody's got to conserve. All well and good, everybody caught the 2,500 pounds and was down. The next spring when they sent for the license, well you didn't have 3,500 pounds last year, you're ineligible for a permit and every one of them went to one or two big corporations that had the big trawlers for offshore.

So island fishermen who'd tried to comply, *"all lost their permits because they hadn't landed their 3,500 pounds even though under mandate they had been cut back to 2,500."*[500]

Comparing his fishing life forty years ago to now, Walt explained:

All I have [now] is a lobster license. Most of the guys around here that's all they have. A few of them get the commercial halibut license for the two months. But I mean when I first started fishing, we would set in April and [lobster] to the 1st of June, take up all the traps and go herring fishing June, July, August and September; set traps back out in September for the shedder round [lobstering]. Take them up around Christmas time and then you'd put a scallop drag on and you'd scallop from January-February or part of February and the middle of February put a shrimp net on and shrimp for February, March and April and then it would be time to set traps again.

Well we're all locked out of these fisheries now.[501]

Acknowledging fishery collapse as well as the lock-out, Ted Ames summed up, *"So with the loss of each one of these fisheries, the island just became more concentrated on lobsters."*[502]

11

Women and Fishing

Although fishing has long been called men's work, women—often the kin of fishermen and familiar with every detail of the effort involved—are crucial to its success. They are everywhere hard at work. Sometimes even on fishing boats.

Generations of island life have shaped the people who live there according to its imperatives. Vinalhaven women have long found ways to be as sturdy and adaptable as humanly possible—ready to manage challenging domestic tasks, to face uncertain days of fishing, to keep ledgers, and handle crises, looking only to their families and neighbors for assistance. No one who understands the resiliency of the island community would ever doubt their centrality to the labors of fishing.

In an oral history, Sonny Oakes offered a view of the daily demands on women. He described how his grandmother, Bessie Delano Conway (1873–1940), began her day at 3:30 every morning by building a fire in the stove and baking biscuits for everyone's breakfast. She churned butter from the cow her husband milked. Many years later Sonny could still recall the pleasure of the butter, *"Wasn't that some good on fresh biscuits."*

He appreciated his mother's mother, but he did not sentimentalize her or her tasks.

Grammy was quite a strong individual. They had cats that had kittens and she used to put them in an old sugar bag and throw them overboard. We always had chickens, and she'd take a couple of those chickens, throw them on the chopping block, chop their heads off and throw them on the ground and they'd flap around. She was tough.[503]

183

Fishing life is all about community—a place of considerable mutual caring, some mutual torment and violence, and constant sociability. Women have always turned to each other for support, and to accomplish together the physical and emotional work at hand.

The relative isolation of island life has encouraged women to master many skills. Families and family members sorted out the arrangements that suit them. There were decidedly "female" tasks—weaving, knitting, cooking, churning butter, raising poultry for eggs, teaching children. But real island life has always been more varied. Alice Gould wrote about Vinalhaven fishing for the *Maine Coast Fisherman* during the 1950s. Her pseudonym, "Larry Gould," was a sign of the masculine bias of the fishing world, and of its pragmatism. If the only "man" able to write the "male" newspaper's fishing column is a woman, a quick name change will do. So too with other work.

IN FISHERIES

Women On Boats

Thanks to Gould's reporting, we know that, in spite of old superstitions deeming it unlucky, some women worked on fishing boats by the mid-twentieth century. In January 1951, the *Fisherman* published Gould's photo of Etta (1902–1970) and Johnny Morton (1902–1988) in their boat on their way out to handline for ground fish. She described them as *"one of several married couples on the island who are dory mates."* Emphasizing the domestic angle of mutual aid, Gould explained how Johnny had helped Etta when her net business was going strong during World War II; and how, in turn, once netting became unprofitable, Etta started going fishing to assist him. *"Their day's catch was 900 lbs., mostly cod."*[504]

Another island couple, Birger (1894–1970) and Elizabeth Magnuson (1903–1983) camped on Seal Island in the spring of 1950, and lobstered together. They caught Gould's attention:

> the Magnusons have been camping since April on remote Seal Island, twelve miles out to sea from Vinahaven. At first they had the place to themselves in a tent, but later they were joined by others fishing for Rackcliff and Witham, the Rockland lobster buyers who own the island and have built camps there.[505]

Bodine Ames recalled her and her husband's efforts to close off coves to trap herring. Shore work was just part of the day. When she lived on Matinicus, they fished the cove in back of their house.

[I]f there was herring in, you went in [the water] with a pole—and you could feel them on the pole—the herring. You could pretty much gage if it was a night when there were enough [to make the hard work worthwhile]. So I could go in the house and call my husband . . . and he would say, 'Will you start it and I'll come around from the other cove.

She would begin rowing the "twine" across the cove herself.[506]

It was not unusual for island women to set a few lobster traps. A good example is Ruth Young Ames (1917–2015), who started going out as a companion to one of her two young sons. Later she fished her own traps—with both her sons' assistance. At the end of their workdays, the boys would ride her out in the motorboat. In the evenings, she and her daughter would fill bait bags for everyone to use the next day.

For twenty-four summers Ames prepared crab rolls and lobster rolls at the *Sea Breeze*, an island take-out. She also worked many summers filling bait bags on one of the lobster "cars." *"The last summer I filled bait bags I was eighty-three."* And she knit "pot heads"—the funnel-shaped netting through which lobsters enter traps. At ninety-one, when interviewed, she allowed that she had stopped knitting net, except for her grandson's traps.[507]

According to a 1976 newspaper story, another Vinalhaven "mom," Nancy Carlsen, was *"one of a handful of women in Maine licensed to fish for lobster."* Carlsen went out two or three times a week early in the morning in a small, open boat with her twelve-year-old son, Rich. Rich "manned" the outboard engine, and Nancy hand-hauled thirty traps each day, a labor requiring considerable strength.[508]

Today it's common for island women, particularly young ones, to work "sterning" on lobster boats. "About twenty-five" was the estimate offered in 2020. High school students seek this well-paid position as a way to save for college; college students use their earnings to pay their tuition—or the young sternmen use it to live, pay rent, support children, buy cars, boats, clothes. Several lobstermen told me their teenagers asked them, "Why should I go to college when I can earn $60,000 to $100,000 a year sterning?" Such wealth is part of the current boom cycle, but few people make that much, and many believe it will be short-lived.

Women who love being on the water, or who need to earn more than other island jobs pay, may keep sterning for decades. At the moment, their labor is particularly welcome: so many islanders captain their own boats that sternmen can be in short supply. Women also captain their own boats. As of 2020, about 15 percent of Maine's commercial lobster licenses were held by females. That percentage is higher than in the past but still difficult to grow because of the state limits on licenses, and the waiting list to get them. [509]

As of this writing, Yvonne "Beba" Rosen (b. 1965) is one of only four Vinal-haven women licensed to captain. When I interviewed her in 2016, she had just bought a thirty-foot boat and hired her first "sternman" to help her haul her 500 traps. *"[W]e usually haul anywhere from 150 to 170. Depends on the day. You know. We hauled 180 the other day because it was super calm. It just went well."*

Like many islanders, Beba grew up on lobster boats. As a child she some-times went out with her grandfather, John Beckman, other times with her uncles.

> *When we were kids, we didn't play all summer, we worked all summer. If you wanted school clothes and records and magazines, you . . . earned the money for them yourself. So I started working when I was 10 years old . . . cutting grass and filling bait bags on boats . . .*
>
> *My grandfather . . . didn't take all his grandkids lobstering, just a couple of them. It was a kind of an honor to be out there on his boat . . . . [We] just loved it. You'd be out on the water, we were working, but we still got to play with the starfish, you know and see what came up in the traps. . . . You never know what you're gonna pull up. It seems as though there's not going to be anything in there, but . . . There is always something. It's exciting . . .*[510]

Beba moved off-island after high school and worked on the mainland. In 2003 she came back. She thought she'd only stay for a while, but . . . *"I started lobstering as a sternman and just fell in love with it and decided that I would get my captain's license through the apprentice program. So I got my captain's license and my own little boat, which was a 14-foot skiff for the first boat. Then I really fell in love after that."*

The apprentice program, part of a larger package of Maine lobstering regulations passed in 1995, supports continuity for island fishing families by licensing their young people through apprenticeship and letting them skip the waiting lists. Each apprentice chooses a fisherman mentor to teach the rules and good practices. Apprentices have to log 1000 hours fishing and 200 days on the water. *"The hours were easy, the hard part was getting the days which basically takes about 2 years. So then you get that finished up and you get your license to have 800 tags."* Lobstering made the island <u>her</u> home. *"I just liked being on the ocean. I just liked the work . . . [I] just wanted to be here, instead of feeling that [I] had to be here."*[511]

With a long family history of fishermen, Beba was aware of having an unspoken "right" to lobster. But she reiterated what others told me: male or female, joining the fishing community as an outsider is next to impossible. Even an "insider" needs a thick skin. A typical form of harassment is someone cutting the line connecting the trap to the buoy so the trap is irretrievable and the buoy drifts away.

If you are not from Vinalhaven, it can be a hard place to establish yourself lobstering. Someone moves out here from away and they live here for a couple of years and they get their apprentice license and they think they're gonna put traps in the water, they're not going to fare very well. I mean this is our territory. You got to earn your stripes, so to speak. Some guys have done it, they have married a girl out here and they paid their dues and they have lost gear and then stuck it out; and if they stick it out then they made their right to fish here. But they are few and far between.

You're tested. *"If you come from away, you're gonna just have to expect that you are going to lose a lot of gear the first couple of years. We're gonna wedge you out or you're going to stick with it and you're gonna earn your right."*

People lose gear, even when, like Beba, they have every right to fish. The way through for new lobstermen is to confront the people harassing them, and then just persevere. Beba observed that anyone who wanted to make a place had to send a message: *"I am just gonna get more traps and I'm gonna put them back in the same spot. You're wasting time."*

Reflecting on her own situation, Beba observed,

This is my 8th year as a captain . . . This is my 4th boat . . . So I kind of moved up pretty quickly. I don't know if this is going to be my last boat or not, but I don't think I need to go much bigger . . . [I]t all depends, and I still have a lot to learn. Especially about deepwater fishing . . . I'm used to fishing inshore, and now [with a bigger boat] I kind of moved out a little ways. But I still have a lot to learn about that. So I don't know if this will be my last boat or not.

The risk is taking out a loan to purchase a boat bigger than you can support. Especially when the only certainty in fishing is the uncertainty: *"Lobstering is like gambling, you can't bank on it. You just can't. It's never the same. Every year is different."*[512]

Doing an unlikely job for an island woman in the 1950s and 1960s, Madeline MacDonald (1911–2003) ran her own lobster "car" in one of the island coves. Lobster cars are floating docks in harbors where lobstermen buy fuel and bait and sell their lobsters. Women often assisted on them, but men usually managed them. MacDonald would buy lobsters from the fishermen, and Dan Bickford recalled that his father Clyde would buy from her. He also supplied her with the bait and fuel she sold. For a long time, *"she had her own business and she liked her own independence. I think it was in the '60s he bought her out because she was getting older and wanted to retire."*[513]

When I interviewed Lois Day (1951-2–2016) in 2013, she described her job on a lobster car in the 1980s. She would row out in the morning with two men who also worked there. Rain or shine, from April to November, she tended to fishermen all day. Along with pumping diesel, selling bait and weighing and buying lobsters, she'd try to fill 300 bait bags each day. Her companions would set her up with bait. *"I would have crates of bait bags— say on the right side of me—so I'd be able to stand there, grab a bait bag, put my hands in the bait barrel, [fill the bag] and throw them to the left into a crate."* The ten cents she earned for each bag helped her survive, *"I figured if I could [fill bait bags for] three of the lobstermen a day, it was enough to get my daughters through school for the week."*

She loved the laughter she shared with the men. Talking about her boss, she remembered, *"Oh my God, he'd have you in stitches every day. He had a joke every day. But he was just funny."* I have been struck by how often the people I interviewed associated work with laughter, savoring moments of fun as they labored.[514]

Boat Building

In 1990, Lida Ames (1906–2002) wrote about helping her husband build a dragger during World War II. Her description highlights how closely couples often worked together so a fisherman could fish—and the sacrifices required.

According to Ames, fish were plentiful during the war, and the market was good. But Ames' husband lacked a boat suitable for dragging and knew it would cost several thousand dollars to build one. Banks didn't often make loans to fishermen since their earnings were unpredictable, so the couple had to piece together the money to build the new boat on their own. They had to sacrifice: *"We started figuring how the lobster boat could be sold, insurance cashed, our car could be sold, and I could go back to teaching school."*

They set to work in the spring of 1943 using the abandoned (and very cold) "Horse Net" factory as their building site. Able-bodied men had mostly left town to enlist or to work in mainland factories as part of the war effort. Even if you could pay, there was no one to hire.

The family women stepped up. *"When school closed in June, Mary Helen, my teen age niece, and I helped caulking the seams on deck until our hands were raw."* They climbed down to paint the fish hold, but intense fumes quickly sickened them, making them too ill to continue. When the boat out-grew the factory space, family and friends hauled it to the shore. It lacked an engine, which they installed, a pilot-house and a galley cabin—both of which they built outdoors by the water.

In spring 1944 the *"Lida & Dick"* launched—its name testifying to their close cooperation. *"It was a beautiful boat, 56 feet long, beam 14' 6"* and it had *"a 148 horsepower Chrysler engine."* Looking back, Lida felt that their gamble paid off, *"Fish were plentiful. The project had been a success."*[515]

Baiting Hooks

Women baited hooks for tub trawls to assist their kin or friends or when they needed cash. Often it was done on the shore, but it could be done in the boat as you let out the trawl. Bodine baited and set out trawl with her husband. Their bait *"could be poggies [menhaden]. It could be most anything. Could be herring."* In the four or five hours between setting the trawl and hauling it in, the couple would haul lobster traps. When they returned to check the hooks they might have halibut, or dogfish, or a mix of fish to pull in. Bodine and her husband often hauled thousands of feet of line hand over hand— sometimes against wind, tide or current. The weight of the line, heavy with fish, strained their muscles and blistered their gloved hands.[516]

Teaching

Island women informally taught fishing skills to children—how to bait the hooks, how to knit net, to scrape and paint a boat, or to skin and gut a fish. Sonny Oakes remembered his grandmother standing on the rocks and watching him as he practiced rowing her rowboat away from shore and then back. She taught him how to handle the oars.[517]

Female and male "knitters" taught other men and women to make nets. Ivan Olson recounted,

I used to knit my own nets for the lobster traps . . . [T]here was an old lady up the street here used to knit them for the fishermen . . . Lynn Young. And I asked her one day, and she showed me how to knit. And then there was a doctor on the Island, Dr. Earle, he knew how to knit too. . . . One night he was at my house for some reason or another— someone was sick—and I was trying to learn how to knit, and he showed me. I picked it up, it's just like anything else, once you got the hang of it, there's nothing to it.[518]

On Shore

As well as working on the water and on the home front, lending a hand everywhere, women worked in restaurants that prepared fish, in fish factories, and they knit nets to sell.

Restaurants

Women prepped food, cooked, and waited tables in all the town take-out stands and restaurants—*The Sea Breeze, the Dunnette, the Mill Race, The Haven, The Sand Dollar, The Harbor Gawker, Night Owl, Sands Cove,*

Surfside, Greet's Eats—to name a few among many that have come and gone. Some form of seafood—lobsters, crab rolls, steamed clams, fried haddock— graced every menu.

Restaurants opened before dawn to serve the fishermen, offering them a place to eat and talk before they rowed out to their boats to begin the day's work.

Although reluctant at first to take on an early morning shift at *The Mill Race*, "Lizzie" spoke about how much she enjoyed the sociability working there in the 1980s. *"I did breakfast and I think I did it for three, four or five years and loved it. I loved being with the fishermen first thing in the morning."*

She'd start around 4:00 a.m. *"When they first come in I'd be the only one there. So you'd be trying to cook, wait on them and do everything else all at the same time until the . . . waitresses come in."* The fishermen: *"They'd just chit chat, sit there and talk and stuff . . . and you know."* The "you know" pointed vaguely to the flirting, funny innuendoes and teasing that made the mornings fun. Everybody teased. *"There's one guy that used to give us a hard time because we used to put oranges on his plate . . . to make it look nice. [He'd say] 'I don't want that orange,' and he'd throw it at us. Then we'd throw it back at him. I used to have a lot of fun . . ."*

But the job was demanding, *"When you go in at 4:00 in the morning, at 11:15 you're ready to go home."* The place was crowded as soon as it opened.

Oh Lord! . . . Probably 20, 30 people. That's when you made your money. Even nowadays, you make your money first thing in the morning when the fishermen come in because them's the ones spending. They're the ones . . . Always did good when the fishermen were around.[519]

Into the 1980s, local fish were on the *Mill Race* menu.

Yah, he [John Edward Morton (1929–2003), the owner and cook] *used to have haddock dinners . . . and his fish cakes were to die for. . . . Oh yah, you used to fry up the salt pork and add a lot of pepper. Cook your potatoes, cook your fish and then just put it all together. Mash it all up . . . and make little fishcakes like. . . . The onions and salt pork you fry together. . . .*

John sometimes caught the fish. *"[A] lot of times he'd come over and say, 'Here's a cusk. You have to make fishcakes today.' And I'd say,' John don't let me use that cusk. I don't want to use that cusk.'"* Cusk can be wormy, and Lizzie hated worming it. *"Sometimes he'd get haddock or pollock right out of the [salt water] ponds and bring it in and cook it up and that's what we made fishcakes out of."*[520]

Of course, women cooked fish at home. I asked people about their favorite seafood dishes. Fried haddock and fried halibut were often at the top of the list, as well as fresh crab, lobster, and scallops, and home-frozen shrimp when they were still fished. People repeatedly mentioned "corned hake" when I asked them about fish dinners they enjoyed growing up. It is made from hake that's been salted to preserve it.

Corned Hake. Rinse and boil the salted hake, sometimes two or three times if it is really salty. While the hake is boiling, separately boil some potatoes and fry up some pork scraps. Once everything is cooked, mash the potatoes and fish together, and pour on the pork scraps. Some families added "egg gravy"– a white cream sauce with egg chopped up in it. Finally, mix up a dressing of vinegar and chopped red onion to sprinkle on at table.[521]

WOMEN IN THE FISH PLANTS

Vinalhaven fish factories employed many island women. "Dawn" spent several years in the early 1980s at "PenBay," the Penobscot Bay Fish and Cold Storage Company—newly built at the time and one of dozens that came and went between 1847 and the recent past. *"More women worked at the fish plant than men. Men might manage the dock—unloading and stuff—but I don't think most of them [worked inside], unless they were floor managers or something."*

"Dawn" described the fun of working together—the sociability and raunchy humor that made the hours pass.

[T]here was a lot of island women of all ages that worked there and it was really quite productive for a time. . . . Everybody had their own little groups of people and they had a good time while they were working, they really did. And women can be pretty "base" when they want to be—and funny—and it was funny.

There was a lot of laughter and a lot of teasing. *"You know we were a blue collar town, and a lot of our parents weren't educated so we weren't."* One day, needing to testify against legislation they feared might harm the plant, the boss asked one of the women to travel to Augusta (the state capital) with him and testify that *"if they did 'such and such' it would cause irreparable harm. And she could not [learn it]. She was trying to learn the word and we thought it was so funny at the time because she was having such a struggle with 'irreparable damage.'"*[522]

Lizzie, who in the 1980s worked in Vinalhaven Seafood (informally called "Nickerson's," where PenBay had formerly been) corroborated "Dawn's" account of the fun mixed into repetitive work. *"We used to play jokes on each other and we used to laugh, and the boss would come in and tell us, 'You know I'm bringing important people in today so please be ladies.'"* The women would tease,

Ladies! We're not ladies! you know. And we used to go up in the break room and we'd play jokes on each other. . . .

We had some funny instances where someone would come in under the weather, so to speak. One morning . . . this is like 7:00 o'clock in the morning and [the employee—whom Lizzie managed] was still feeling good, and the boss had told me, "You have to go talk to her and tell her she has to go home." You know 'cause we're working around equipment and stuff. I told her I says, "You have been drinking," and she said, "I haven't had a drink since 3:00 o'clock this morning." And I said, "Well it's only 7:00 now."[523]

Lizzie walked me through her work as a fish cutter.

We'd usually go in around quarter of 7:00 and start working around 7:00 o'clock. Sometimes if they had to load a truck early in the morning . . . they'd need some of the women to go in and help do things. . . . But [otherwise] you'd go in, go up to the break room, sit there and chit chat first thing in the morning. . . . And then at 7:00 o'clock we'd all go down and take our stations whatever we was working on.[524] *You'd have on a heavy shirt and then you'd have an apron . . . and of course you had your boots because there was a lot of water and stuff . . . around the fish and where they wash everything down. So you had to be completely waterproof . . .*

When I first started, I started as a fish cutter. You would fillet fish, and I wasn't there too many days, [when] I cut my arm, she pointed, *that's the scar right there; and I was so scared that I just grabbed my arm. . . . And they took me up to the medical center and I can remember them telling me to "Let go! Let go!" . . .*

I was just learning. [The knives were] very sharp. As a matter of fact, my ex-husband's father used to sharpen them for us. . . . He had one of those old wheels. It could be once a week, it could be once or twice a week, depending. . . .

I was nervous at first [going back to work after the accident], because I said "I don't think I'll ever cut fish again." And they said, "Oh you will. A lot of people get cut." A lot of the other women down there said they had been cut, too, and so it made me feel better. I did go back to cutting fish. I love cutting fish. . . .

We worked on cod, haddock, we worked on pollock. Pollock was a good size. Pollock was probably bigger than cod. [W]e used to do the flat fish . . . flounder. Sometimes we did some monk fish. I really can't remember all the fish. I'm not

a fish person. . . . When Nickerson [owned the factory] they'd truck a lot of the hake in. We did a lot of hake. They'd cut the heads off, then you'd have to scrub 'em out and clean 'em and stuff like that . . . Some fish were local, some from Canada, *"But you know when there's a market and they want so many and you can't get it, you get it wherever you could get 'em."*[525]

Lizzie continued describing the processing. *"They're floated in big tubs. . . . Everything is iced down. When you work in a fish factory everything is iced down."* A forklift carried the heavy tubs into the factory and dumped them in a "bin." Water forced the fish along. *"[S]o they'd just shoot down in front of you . . .When you wanted one you'd just pull it up, fillet it, put the fillet somewhere. Throw the trash where it's supposed to be. You know, well, the rats. Then grab another one and keep on doing it until they're all done. . . . I mean, there was like 10 or 15 girls, we'd all be doing it. Because you had certain girls that would cut the fish, then you had the skinning machines where they would skin it. So everyone had their own job to do. [I] just had to fillet it. Take the fillets off and throw the carcass. . . ."* To fillet, *"you'd grab ahold of the head and you'd make a slash down and then you'd go down the back and then you'd work your way up and slice it right down, I'd say underneath the belly like. Then you'd have your fillet . . . and then you'd flip it right over and do the same on the other side. It doesn't take very long—just a few minutes. And the sharper your knife the better it is."*

It looked difficult when you were watching some of the pros that had been there for a long time . . . and you'd think, well you'll never be able to do that. But you can do it. I felt comfortable cutting fish.

Of course you had to wear gloves so you can hang on to the fish . . . because the fish are slippery and they have scales, so you want to make sure your hands don't slide . . . Sometimes your hands get tired . . . [b]ecause some of the fish are big. When you're doing that all day long, it's like anything when you're doing it all day long you get tired . . .

Still, *"It was always a fun thing. Because we were always laughing and singing songs and listening to the music. And doing things like that. It wasn't just a job. . . . Everybody was talking. You might have 2 or 3 people down there talking about something different, 2 or 3 people on the other side talking or sometimes you'd just be quiet and work."*[526]

After the fish were filleted and machine skinned, the people, *"who did codfish would have to worm 'em. Take the worms out and then they're packed in boxes. . . . They say you eat a dozen worms before you die. [They are] just little round worms. Codfish has a few worms in it. . . . They say a fish isn't any good if it doesn't have any worms in it. . . . I just know I don't eat [cod] tongues and cheeks. I see worms in them, and that don't interest me one bit. . . . I wouldn't eat a cusk. Sometimes you get a cusk and there are so many worms you wonder where's the fish."*

Some fish needed to be boned. *"So you'd have the deboning station where you're pulling the bones out of it. Out of the fillets. . . . [We would use] little pliers. Yah, get right ahold of the bone and just yank it right out. . . . And then they'd pack it in, I think it was 5 pound boxes at the time. . . . Everything is always iced up. The minute you got something done it would go into the freezer or the cooler. Nothing stayed out, you know, and sat."*

Processing hake could be challenging. *"We had a lot of work, too, when we did the hake . . . We'd scrub it with brushes. . . . Then some of them we filleted. And skinned 'em. And then they would be packed in the boxes and frozen. And some stuff we'd ship out fresh. You know put them in boxes and ice everything down and it would go on the ferry boat. . . ."*

> *I remember one time we was doing all kinds of fish and it was going to the prisons . . . We never asked any questions, but we asked the boss one time where are these going? And he said, 'Oh they're going to the prisoners.*[527]

When some winters they shelled and processed shrimp, they couldn't have the heat on because the shrimp spoiled so quickly.

> *Well you'd wear 2 or 3 shirts or sweaters and sometimes we even wore coats. . . . That's how cold it was inside. You'd wear heavy boots with heavy socks on . . .*
> *We went through a lot of colds and sicknesses and stuff with people . . . a lot of people have had back troubles because of all the heavy things you did. You were always lifting and tugging and pulling . . . and stuff like that. . . . Probably [lifting] 80 to 100 pounds.*

The heavy totes and fish bins reminded Lizzie of other tricks they'd played:

> *I remember one time we had a maintenance man, Peanut, we used to call him. He's gone now and he was just a little guy. . . . It was so funny 'cause we was always playing jokes on him . . . One time, this other woman and I—she's gone now too—a lot of them are gone now, that's the thing.*
> *And we said, "Let's have a little fun with Peanut." We picked him up and threw him up in the bin. That was a riot. Honest to God that was a riot because he was just a short guy, we just picked him up and plopped him right in the bin [with the herring]. That's what we was doing then. We packed herring in 3-pound boxes I think it was. Yup, they'd dump the herring right into a bin and the chute would come on and you'd just push them in the boxes.*[528]

Net Knitting

Knotted netting, often called "knitting," has always been part of life on Vinalhaven. Made of natural materials (sisal, manila, cotton, or hemp) until synthetic fibers replaced them after World War II, nets ripped constantly as they were dragged over sharp rocks or got caught on bits of junk or wreckage. Sometimes sharks or seals tore through them to get at the herring. Other times they split from their own weight, or from the force of the water in a stormy sea. They could tangle with other fishermen's lines and it would be a mess. Big rips might end a fishing day, but fishermen sewed the frequent small tears while they fished.[529]

Writing about net strength, a twentieth century doryman declared that, "[i]n addition to being short-lived, the strength of the natural fibers when they were new was . . . some five or ten times or more weaker than today's artificial fibers of the same size." Depending on which fish was targeted, a fisherman would use different sized mesh and line: one size for a tiny smelt net, and another for a huge drift net to catch cod.[530] The Vinalhaven Historical Society possesses a wooden recipe box from 1944 containing yellowed cards on which someone recorded stitch patterns. There are instructions for knitting wool socks and fishermen's mittens, but most are for making specialized nets to catch trout, crabs, or eels, including "eel nozzles, heavy eel nozzles, special long eel nozzles, eel scoop nets, eel drop nets, pot heads." The necessary stitches are carefully specified.

With nets always needing repair, many Vinalhaven women were kept busy. Netting became paid women's work as early as 1847, when the American Net and Twine Company hired John Carver as their island manager in charge of making fishnets. Nineteenth century women often worked from home. Between other chores, knitting was one of a handful of ways (another being the sale of extra farm produce) that they could earn their own cash or supplement family income.[531]

Sometime before the Civil War, some Vinalhaven women started knitting for L. C. Chase and Co. of Boston in a small island "factory" making tasseled nets to cover horses (when the horses moved, the tassels shooed away flies). John Carver's daughter, Josephine, ran the business briefly in the 1860s. When the Civil War ended, the netting "girls" were said to have joined the Victory Parade decked out in horse nets. In 1898 L. C. Chase and Company built a new net factory on the hill at the end of Main Street.[532]

Starting around 1889 factories began to produce fish nets as cheaply as those made by hand. As island fishermen acquired motorized vessels, "dragged" more and needed bigger nets, they increasingly bought machine-made nets from Icelandic and other companies. During World War II, foreign-made nets couldn't reach the island, and the women stepped up. Barbara

Morton (1921–2000) remembers many island parlors taken over by otter trawl nets.[533]

The huge Vinalhaven effort supplied fishermen beyond the island. To get around wage-hour laws established in the late 1930s, women got help to organize themselves into two cooperatives of about 100 members each. The cooperatives bought the twine and gave it to their members. Once the nets were completed, they bought back the finished products and shipped them to "commercial companies" that sold them. When cotton twine became unavailable because of the war, the women appealed to Maine's Congresswoman, Margaret Chase Smith, who helped them get it, since fishing in order to feed troops and civilians was a war priority.[534]

A few years into the war, Etta and Herbert "Johnny" Morton started a winter knitting business making large seines for beam trawlers. In an article titled *"$3000 Weekly Seine Industry Ain't Seaweed,"* a reporter described the nets: *"Each complete seine consists of nine parts: the belly and two each of top wings, bottom wings, squares and cord ends,"* which, once assembled, were sewn together.[535]

Sadie Dyer (b. 1931) recalled how the netting work gave her mother money to buy her and her brother each a present.

> *They did the big fish nets and my mother helped. . . . I can remember that Dad made her—in the living room. . . . a big bar that went across. They were heavy. They were real heavy and she would stand up with a big board and she would knit those long nets. Fishnet of some kind. And when they got them done, they'd be fairly good size, and mother made good money. And I remember that . . . after she had knit some nets, she said, "Now I want to buy you and Victor something. What would you like to have the most?" . . . Victor said, "I want a bicycle," so she bought him a bicycle. But do you know what I wanted? We always had rocking chairs, we never had stuffed chairs in the house and I said "Mom, I would like to have a nice stuffed chair," so she bought a recliner.[536]*

Children helped out. As a small boy, Louis "Louie" William Martin (b. 1940) and a friend would carry boxes of twine all over town, "quite a distance," and deliver them to the knitters. The sociability of the women's labor comes through in his account, and in the way the whole community participated.

> *One destination was up on Skin Hill at Beulah [Drew's]. A bunch of ladies gathered there every day to knit nets. . . . Each lady had a net stand and each of those had a spool mounted beneath, shaped like a cone, and once the spool was loaded the knitters fed their needles from the rotating spool and went at it. When they had a pile of nets ready to go Arthur and I would deliver them to*

[George (1887–1959) and Gracie (1898–1958) Lawry's] store which was up in Dogtown.[537]

Eventually, the business became so lucrative that 140 men took over the seine making. The newspaper attributed their interest in knitting to the high wages, and their taking over to their greater ability to tolerate handling the "rough sisal" needed for the bigger nets. "Rough sisal" seems an incomplete explanation—apparently, the women did fine with it until it became so profitable.

When the war ended, factory nets again became available, and the netters gradually ran out of work. The last profitable "knitting" business on Vinalhaven shut down after World War II, but the skill remained in families—whose members continued knitting bait bags and pot heads.[538]

Net Mending

Because of the constant wear and tear when the men fished, net ("twine") mending was crucial and time consuming. Women often did the work onshore, or assisted men with it, laboriously sewing or re-knitting damage too serious to fix quickly while fishing. Dallas Anthony (1938–2022) was proud of his mother's skill and endurance. *"My mother used to mend 'seine' twine and 'shut-off' twine. She'd be out in the fields cutting out the holes and netting them back in, baking in the hot sun, day after day and hour after hour. That was hard work. She had done that since she was a kid."*[539]

GIRLS AND FISH

Island girls born mid-century grew up watching, playing in, working in, and absorbing the world of fish. Lorraine Walker, born in the 1950s to a multigenerational island fishing family, said,

My first memories were of Old Harbor and the weir that was in Old Harbor and I always loved weirs. You don't see them anymore. . . . Men would go out in the evening as the sun was setting and wait for the herring to come into the harbors . . . [I] remember the weirs because in the morning, as a child of 7 or 8 or 9 years old we would row out and hang onto the twine on the weir and look in and see all the fish schooling.

She spoke of the smell of salted bait in fish houses in the spring, and how play with friends included catching eels, flounder, and mackerel.

We would catch eels. Eels, huge eels. We'd have a tub of water and we'd haul in all these eels. One right after another. These great big tubs of eels. We would sit on the end of my grandmother's wharf and we would fish for eels . . . [We] probably just had a cotton line with a hook and we'd use some of that herring from those bait barrels. We'd go in there and throw a few herring overboard to attract them and then we'd bait the fishing lines and throw the old cotton lines down.

Laughing, she added,

My mother didn't want all those eels. My mother didn't want all of those eels.
  My sister and I would catch them and then we would handle them and put them in the tub and watch them. . . . We got tired of it after a while and we'd just dump them overboard. . . . It was just something that we did. The eels were anywhere from two to four feet long. They were big and we were not afraid of them. If I had to take one of them off a hook today, I would never do that. . . . That's what we did at night. Every night when the tide was right in the summertime. If the tide was right and it was a nice night we'd go eeling.

And not just eeling: *"Then you could catch flounders. You know we'd row out just off the end of the wharf and catch flounder. . . . With a hook and line. Old cotton, green line with a hook on it and herring out of the bait barrel . . . It was just easier to catch fish then."* She paused and added, *"Now you'd never catch an eel or flounder."*

Their fishing was for play more than food. *"We ate some of them but we didn't eat many. It was more of a hobby. Just something we did to play. And we'd go out on the lobster car and they'd give us dead lobsters for bait. . . . We'd catch mackerel or flounders."* Between the ages of seven and probably twelve, Lorraine, her sister, and her neighborhood friends *" were great fishermen. We'd fish the summers away."*[540]

Another favorite activity was going up with her father, Victor Ames, in his tiny plane to spot herring.

I used to go a lot and we would spot fish at night. . . . We would go right after we had supper at night like on the edge of dark—or an hour or so before dark, and he flew for some seining outfits . . . We'd fly up and down the shores looking for pods of fish. . . . [I was] probably in 5th or 6th grade . . . We're talking about July through October. It used to be pretty cold at the end of it. It was fall. . . .
  I had the front seat, but he flew from the back. But it was very cold a lot of times because the whole side of the plane opened up. The top door opened up. And the bottom door dropped down. So you were in your seatbelt in your little seat and you'd be up flying at an angle where you were up looking down at the water, and going in a circle a lot of the time. So I was lucky that I wasn't one that got sick because you were just going around and around and around

and the whole side of the plane was open. . . . Oh, I loved it . . . it was just so exciting.[541]

Some children collected lobsters and clams for meals. Henry Ewell (1921–1991) described his mother as a girl gathering lobsters.

Mother used to tell about when she was a girl, she used to go down the Rider's Beach, where great-grandmother and great-grandfather lived . . . Mother said that at low tide, they would go down around the shore and pick lobsters out of the tidal pools. . . .[542]

Bodine told of clamming as a child. In the winter, she clammed and scalloped—the image that began this book for me—with her father and brother, Jimmy, on North Haven, where she lived before moving to Matinicus and then Vinalhaven.

Well we had an old clunky truck and sometimes we'd go in the truck . . . We might have to take a sled and ropes and tie the . . . burlap bags [of clams] and tow them up the bank or [over] the ice to get them in the back to the truck. Or we'd go by rowboat . . .

It would be very cold but he would go into someplace that was [in the] lee . . . We'd go into an actual cove and we'd take a lot of lunch with us because it would be very cold and sometimes or not we'd have a thermos or we'd have an old kettle. The old kettle we'd just throw on the fire to just boil water or to make cocoa or to make whatever we had with us, and before the day was over we might take a few clams and cook them in the kettle . . .

But while we were there when the tide was at its lowest, especially if we were up in Pulpit Harbor or one of those places, we'd go underneath the bridge where the water ran. It never runs out, you know, it is never dry and we'd just pick up scallops . . . At home, my mother would make a chowder. You know there were four kids and two parents and they didn't have a whole lot of money. But scallop chowder, especially with a few clams in it, is a tasty meal.[543]

12

The Island Community

What makes Vinalhaven a fishing community? Certainly, it shares many traits with other small rural towns, especially coastal towns with working harbors and fishermen. But the surround of ocean is defining. Paved or dirt, island roads end at the shore or loop back upon themselves. There's no easy exit. For generations, being close with each other, facing the sea's dangers and reaping its benefits has shaped communal life invisibly, incrementally, as surf sculpts rock. People on Vinalhaven are experts in how to love, hate, care for, cooperate with, work with, laugh with, mourn with, yell at, torment, ignore, and accommodate each other enough to survive on a tiny rocky patch in the midst of the sea.

Passions can run high. Vendettas can fester. Occasionally, alcohol-fueled fists can fly. Yet for every harsh moment, many more are decent and kind, and some are splendidly generous. The give and take, the wrangling and mutual aid bind the community together, and form the heart of fishing life. They allow it to happen. Since fish are the axis for our tale, stories about sharing fish—willingly or not so willingly—show how fish helped sustain the community.

In August 1934, one of the worst years of the Great Depression, Sidney Winslow wrote happily in his diary about a promised gift of mackerel.

For the past few weeks townspeople have been catching mackerel. They are near the mouth of the harbor and also are quite plentiful almost anywhere in the waters around the island and along the whole coast of Maine. They are of good size too. We had some today that will average 10 inches in length, and many have been caught that are a great deal larger. Mr. Bennett, the keeper of Heron Neck Light, promised to give me a bushel of them which I will salt for winter use.[544]

The men working at Grimes fish plant helped hungry families, often by turning a blind eye. Ivan Olson remembered:

During the depression . . . .before I went into the Navy, things was tougher than hell. My mother was always struggling, and my father was . . . trying to make a living in Westerly, Rhode Island. She asked me one time if I could get a haddock some place; she was going to make haddock chowder.

Grimes [Fish Plant] was always open . . . they never locked it. There was a big refrigerator down there, or a big room full of ice where they kept the fish before they shipped them. On the right hand side was where they always kept the haddock in big boxes, so I went down and opened the box and reached and kept feeling the heads on them. I had to get the size I wanted—so I took a box. We had all the haddock and we had haddock chowder. They never cared, those guys down there.[545]

Once when the plant owner (as opposed to the men working there) wouldn't give them fish, Olson and his friends retaliated by helping themselves. Earlier, they had seen Vonny Ames—a fisherman from Matinicus— deliver a boatload of mackerel.

Spider Grimes [Frank Grimes (1877–1966)], *he used to run the place. We asked him, "Do you have any mackerel, Spider?" He said, "You little bastards get out of here." They were putting them in barrels and putting ice in them and cover- ing them up with a burlap thing and a ring round them. Then they rolled [the barrels] out and made a mistake. [They] rolled them out next to the window. Somebody unlocked the window when they wasn't looking and we opened up the window. Kids you know. We got a knife and opened up the barrel and I don't know how many great big mackerel we swiped. We went up to Carvers store . . . and sold them. We sold them to the grocery store.*[546]

Well into the twentieth century, islanders would bundle up against the chill each spring, often in April, and come together in groups at local brooks in search of smelt. Smelt (*Osmerus mordax*) used to be abundant around Vinalhaven. Small "salmons in all essential respects," they are slender anadromous fish, "with large mouths and a long, pointed head . . . and a forked tail." Smelt can grow to about a foot long and weigh up to six ounces. Maine fishing historian William Leavenworth observes, "Smelt were caught by the millions in mainland estuaries and shipped via rail to cities. They were overfished by 1920."[547]

Islanders would sit in the dark waiting for the tide to rise so the smelt could ride it in from the ocean and mate in fresh water. As the fish thrashed past, men, women, boys and girls—old and young—reached into the cold water to catch them bare-handed. At the end of a successful outing, each family would carry at least a bucketful home to fry, and to share.

Several islanders I interviewed who were born before World War II, John Beckman, Jennie Webster, (1917–2010) and Bodine Ames, recalled smelting frequently as children. Jennie captured the excitement,

Well we used to go way up to Murch's Brook. We walked and that was a great thing when we were in high school. We felt that it was a great adventure. My father would sometimes go, too. We'd use either nets or we'd catch them with our hands in the brook. Now they say they don't even run up there like they used to.[548]

Bodine described smelting at Perry Creek before World War II when she was maybe four or five years old. *"It has to be very very dark. So you'd go down through the paths to get there, and you would sit up on the bank. . . . you'd get cold and wet."*
She would sit very still.

It was so exciting because we watched the stars . . . and we could actually see the glimmer of the smelts as they flipped up the brook to go and spawn . . . The tide would be almost high. There would be several groups of people . . . and we'd all be talking quietly. . . And it was fun. There were some people from Vinalhaven and some from North Haven. God knows who might be there. Old people too.

Others were out in the cove, *"in their peapods or tenders. [They] would reach over the sides and fish that way."*
Everyone waited. *"We wouldn't hear anything for a while. And then someone would do something and start right down the brook like that."* She moved her hand fast, to show the rush of activity once the fish were spotted.
"We could use our flashlights then, and when you would just see a flick, a glimmer, you just reach in and you'd get that smelt and he'd be all wiggling in your hand—and it felt enormous to me. Then you put it in a bucket. Everybody had buckets . . . You know if we got a bucket of smelts that was a whole lot of smelts and we could share it with the neighborhood. . . ."
"A lot of times if it wasn't too, too late at night . . . . say it was only 10:30 or 11:00 at night, whoever was there smelting with you, you might say, 'Well this is the first smelts of the season why don't you come home and have some with me?' And we would." After cleaning them, Bodine's family rolled them in cornmeal and fried them in bacon fat or lard. *"They are wonderful."*[549]
Islanders born after 1950 went once or twice when they were little. A younger man who went smelting once or twice offered this perspective: *"It was mostly just time for young people to go drinking."*[550] Smelt seem to have

disappeared during the 1960s, taking the seasonal community tradition with them.

Summer people missed the smelt season, but if they were lucky, they, too, might be given fish, in this case, herring. Elin Elisofon, born mid-century, remembered the pleasure of watching fishing activity all around her family's home:

There were dories everywhere. These beautiful double-ended wooden long boats with the nets piled high with the corks in them. They were everywhere. In every cove. . . I know that there were certain people who always had this cove.

When her father saw the cove "stopped off," he would put his two young daughters into a rowboat and row out. Elin described a family photo from the era that captured the scene:

Jill and I were in a rowboat and we have little red bandanas tied around our necks, we have little blue cardigans on and we each have a little bucket in front of us, and my father is rowing and I know he is taking us out there to get fish. Sort of using us as bait instead of just rowing out himself and saying, "Can I have some herring?"

Their father, Eliot, wanted to pickle it. The fishermen would be between labors, "*waiting for the boat to come in and take the fish out of the net. My father had this all figured out so we would go out there and get the fish and he would be in heaven.*"

Later, with a touch of wistfulness, she added, "*And there are no dories in the coves anymore. It's really sad. There're no weirs. . . . I just remember seeing them and how beautiful they were with their sticks and their nets.*"[551]

The most important moral precept of Vinalhaven fishing and the bedrock of community relationships is the fishermen's code, a kind of "golden rule" of mutual care and safety on the water. I heard variations of it many times from fishermen. Here are two.

Everybody looks out for each other. I mean . . . I'm not saying any names, but there's a couple of guys I'm not fond of. But you still look out for each other. If their boat engine quit or something and I was nearest, I would go put a line on it and bring it in to Hopkins [boat yard]. Another fisherman reiterated, "*Like I told you, I wouldn't leave [even an] enemy. You just can't do that. . . . You can't. Sooner or later it's going to be your turn.*"[552]

The meaning of their words becomes all too clear when someone drowns. As Walt Day observed sadly to me a day after an islander, fishing alone, had tangled in trap rope and been pulled overboard, *"This happens yearly at least to 1 or 2 people probably on the coast of Maine."*[553]

Other island fishermen and the state Marine Patrol searched for and found the man's body, which is not always possible, but a relief when it happens. They hauled in his traps to save the equipment, sell the lobster and give the money to his family. Although no one said this aloud, this collecting of traps likely serves as a community ritual and tribute.

Walt explained the peril of lobstering alone, without a sternman. *"We have several in the harbor that do fish without [sternmen], but it's not a good idea. Like in his case, he didn't have a very big gang of traps . . . I think he only had like 360 out."* So he couldn't yet afford to pay a second person. Walt understood his plight. *"[When I] got back into lobstering for probably 3 years I went alone while I was building my string up."*

For safety, Walt worked out an informal buddy system.

I used to have [a friend] who hauls a lot. Now his wife goes with him a lot, but back then, he hauled alone and we fished pretty much the same area. Like when it got to be 2:00 or so in the afternoon, I'd either call him or he'd call me. He'd say, "How are you doing?" and I'd say, "Well it's getting along, I think I'll do one more then clean up and go home." He'd say, "I'll do the same thing." . . . We'd always kinda come along together home. . . He could visibly see me unless it was foggy, and we were within shouting distance to each other.[554]

On land when there's no emergency, community responses to someone's plight are more varied. How much help a neighbor in trouble receives, one person suggested, depends on how people view them. Have they helped others? Do they contribute and carry their weight? Do they work to get along? Still, my informant allowed, each situation is different. Neighbors try to take a larger view—what they remember about the person's past situation or struggles—before choosing their responses to any one predicament.

But on the water, you rescue first and reflect later.

Island communities are always changing. In 1983 Philip Conkling cofounded *The Island Institute*, an organization dedicated to supporting Maine island communities. When I interviewed him in his home on Vinalhaven in 2012, he had lately retired and turned his attention to writing a book about island communities all over the world. Not surprisingly, they are disappearing. Of the seventy remaining in America, fifteen are in Maine. And Vinalhaven is the most populated.

According to Conkling, nothing changes an island community quicker than a bridge. Vinalhaven has no bridge. But since 1960 it has had a state-run ferry. Trip frequency has gradually increased and altered people's relationship to the mainland. Bigger, more powerful lobster boats can make the run to Rockland or Stonington in half an hour if need be; and, weather permitting, the Owl's Head airport is a ten-minute plane hop.[555]

Generally, even though the psychological distance is different for each islander, mainland "America" grows ever closer. Virtual bridges narrow the gap. Houses have satellite dishes for television, and Internet access is free at the public library for those without home access. On this writing, cell phone service remains spotty but is improving.

"*So the difference between life today and life then,*" Phil Crossman observed looking back from the present to his mid-twentieth century boyhood, "*can pretty much be summed up simply by saying: 'Now we have a boat that carries eighteen cars and makes six trips a day, and as a result people can do for themselves on the mainland what they used to have to do here locally.' Which is really very sad, but perfectly understandable.*"[556]

Emily Lane described the island she found when she moved out in 1971.

> *My neighbor who was in her 70s when I came here hadn't been to the mainland for 25 years. We had a full time doctor here, we had 3 grocery stores, we had a thriving Main Street—hardware store, clothing store . . . Everything that people needed was basically here. As time went on and we got more ferries and the Internet became a part of everybody's life, the close sense of community and the reliance upon the island, totally for all services and needs changed. People started being more mobile . . . The dynamics of business in town started to change . . .*
>
> *People's relationships I think, changed because you were no longer totally reliant upon each other in the community. You could get on a ferry and you could go to the mainland for appointments, services that you couldn't get on the island or you chose not to get on the island. So people became a little more independent. There wasn't quite as much reliance on one another for support, for a total sense of community . . . When I first came here there was one restaurant . . . so we relied on going to one another's homes for entertainment. We would get together on a weekly basis at someone's home for potluck suppers so there was a sense of making your own good time where now I think there's more of a reliance on being entertained.*[557]

One woman allowed that when she returned to the island after years away, her father reminded her how important it would be for her to hang her laundry out very early in the morning. I read accounts of other women hearing the same admonishment. Having others see that you are industrious earns respect.

Looking back to the years when he was growing up, Phil Crossman remembered,

> *Every single parent on the island, bar none, knew every single kid inside and out. Every kid knew every parent by the same token. . . . Everyone knew every-*

thing there was to know about everyone, the good and the bad, and that carried
with it all the pluses and minuses that you could imagine it carried with it.[558]

Emily Lane married an islander and raised her children on the island; she reflected fondly,

Yes, there was always, particularly with older people, quite a networking of
information that occurred on a daily basis. In fact, when I first came here, I was
dating two different men, and the woman that I was living with was on the phone
daily telling most of her friends my social life.[559]

Stories about the role of the telephone operators convey the intimacy of the place: As a child summering on the island in the 1950s, Elin Elisofon suffered bad asthma attacks that left her struggling to breathe. Her parents would search out Dr. Earle for a home visit.

Ralph Earle would come here. My parents would call him. We had the crank-up
phone. You picked the receiver up and the little arm would go up and you'd get
the operator. And my mother would just say, "We need Ralph Earle," and [the
operator would] say, "Well he's down at so and so's for dinner. I'll ring." She
knew where everybody was all the time.[560]

Phil Crossman noted that after the operators connected you, *"they'd often*
partake in the conversation until they felt they were no longer wanted." And their informal surveillance went further: if an operator looked out her office window on Main Street and saw Phil ducking into the alley to sneak a smoke, it was over. *"My mother would be down there before I had a chance to put it*
out, because the operator would call my mother."[561]

Through much of the twentieth century, island families produced a lot of the food and clothing they used. Besides fishing, men sometimes farmed and raised animals for meat, hunted ducks, rabbits and deer, and gathered other wild food. Women knitted, crocheted and sewed clothes, tended vegetable gardens and preserved food for winter.

Lorraine Walker recalled watching her grandmother on Matinicus putting up food.

My grandmother used to jar lobster. She would jar mackerel. . . . They did sea
ducks . . . They'd pick sea ducks and my grandmother would jar them. To get
through the winter. That was all they had to eat in the winter would be the jarred
things. The sea ducks and lobster.

Thinking about her mother's daily labor, she said,

I think it was a very hard life—in my mother's generation. . . . When we grew up in the 50s and 60s, I just had memories of her always working. Everything was a project. We picked berries in the summer, and she made jam. We picked cranberries in the fall, and she canned cranberry sauce.

And to do laundry, we had the wringer washer. And you have three kids you're washing clothes for, and the wringer washer which takes just about the whole day to get that caught up, and then hang them on the line because we had no dryer. I can remember in the winter [my sister] and I would have to take the clothes in when we got off the bus and how cold it would be. Then we had to put them on racks in the house to dry by the stove. And then my mother would iron—so that's just one task—the laundry—so much more involved than what we do today. . . . And no Pampers, you know. So you had all those diapers.

I don't remember anything much bought . . . She cooked everything. And . . . there wasn't much that was too simple to prepare . . . [W]e ate rabbits, and she would have to cook those all day. And then make a rabbit pie or whatever. . . . It was delicious . . . [A]nd we ate seaducks which my father had to pick all those feathers and do all that. Everything was work. Much more than now.

My mother . . . didn't have a lot of idle time. She would read and she embroidered some and she would read to us. But she worked all day—and she picked crabmeat for extra money . . . It just was not, I don't think, an easy life . . . She grew things like green beans, cucumbers, tomatoes. But my mother basically grew flowers . . . That was one of the things that she got pleasure out of through her days.

[I]t was a good life I guess, and it was a simple life in many ways. They'd get a deer in the fall and they'd make mincemeat. . . . You know, grind all that meat, get all those apples, peel all those apples, cook that all that down, jar it, process it. . . . And she was a great donut maker. She would make donuts and the whole neighborhood would stop in and get a donut. . . .[562]

Alton "Sonny" Oakes felt mixed about the wild food.

Mother used to can vegetables, and one year the mackerel struck so my father borrowed a skiff or peapod and my sister and I went with him. We caught a whole washtub full of mackerel. We brought them in and father dressed them and we went out the next day and got another washtub full. My mother put them in jars. I was so sick of mackerel after that.

My father got a lot of gull's eggs from the outer islands. We'd come in and put them in a tub of water; if they sunk they were good, if they floated there was a bird in them. . . . A gull's egg in a cake would make kind of a spongy cake, but they were fishy tasting because that was all gulls ate . . .

[My father] sent away to Sears & Roebuck for this bunch of rabbits, and of course, they multiplied to beat the band . . . I bet at one time we had as many as sixty to seventy rabbits running around the dooryard. Every Sunday we'd have one for dinner; you know they're awful good eating.[563]

"There were three dairy farms out here," Sonny Warren remembered, *"and of course there were farms that people brought vegetables into the town. There was one fella . . . from up towards Mill River . . . He used to come down once a week with this horse and buggy with vegetables and flowers and things. It was a lot of farming and of course a lot of people had cattle, they had their own cows. I used to raise pigs for myself . . . I'd get them in the spring and feed them during the summer, and then in the fall when it started to get cold I'd butcher them and salt the pork down. I've done my own butchering. I had chickens and pigs. And raised my own vegetables and shot deer and ducks and rabbits. It was pretty much living off the land."*

Commenting on the limited work for those who didn't fish once the quarries closed, he added,

> *There were some of them, you know, who were caretakers for summer people . . . and of course there was some that were town workers and things like that, but there was not much of anything going on like there is now . . . Once in a while somebody would get enough money to have a house built . . . Mostly you would build them yourself.*[564]

Until at least the 1960s and 1970s, many homes lacked indoor plumbing. *"Me and my brother,"* Walt Day said, *"used to take baths in one of the old big washtubs. Every Saturday I got second dibs on the washtub."*[565]

"Dawn" chuckled when thinking back on their outhouse.

> *We didn't have a bathroom. We had an outhouse. But my fondest memories are with my sister in the outhouse. We had a two-hole-er and it was in the backyard and we'd peek out. There weren't many cars then, but we'd peek out when the cars went by. And we'd take the Sears Roebuck Catalogue and the rule was that whoever was on which side of the hole, that was their page and this was your page; and we'd fight over who had the best page . . . That's how we played . . . So it was just simple, simple living . . .*[566]

Walt described his family's work ethic: everyone contributed. *"When the parents went to get berries for winter, you just went and picked right along with them, and yours went into the big bowl and you contributed what you could . . ."* He added, *"Sometimes you might have something you don't like, but I never went to bed hungry. I was never cold. I always had clean clothes . . ."* Having a car was less important than having a boat. *"I was probably 8 or 9 years old before Dad ever got a car and I remember we had it in the summer to use, and every winter when money was tight he'd just back it in the yard and he wouldn't use it until he started making money again in the spring."*[567]

There was plenty of time to play. Jennie Webster, a generation older than Walt, Dawn, Hal or Lorraine, described a childhood lived outdoors in the company of other children.

> *When we were small, we played all sorts of games on the street. We played outdoors all the time. Of course, there wasn't any television or anything and we were outdoors playing one thing or another, way into the evening.*
>
> *We'd play ring-a-levio. [S]omebody would be "IT" and the other kids would all go and hide. Then those kids who were hiding would try to come and run through the circle and yell "Ring-a-levio" before they could get caught. And then they would see if they could get them all back in the circle. Of course,"* she added, *Hide and Go Seek was a game that everybody's played. Jump rope and all those things we did too.*[568]

Lorraine and her sisters loved playing board games when they were indoors, but they mostly played outside when they could. *"[W]e were out-doors a lot. Very different than now. We spent our days outside most everyday, outside all day til dark . . ."*[569]

In summer, boys played baseball, often on teams that competed with each other or did themselves proud on the mainland. *"From the time I got up in the morning until the time I got back at nigh*t," Cy Davidson (1939–2011) said, *"I used to play a lot of ball. You had your ball and glove with you all the time . . . all the boys. We'd play right down here*, he said pointing. *"Down at the old dump."*

In winter, everyone went sledding. *"I tell you there wasn't any cars . . . I was thinking about that the other day. In the winter they used to close off Harbor Hill. They'd never plow it. They used to let the kids go sliding. Everybody used to slide. . . . It was good."*[570]

Most children were acquainted with almost everyone on the island. Often members of extended families, they were cousins and double cousins or else friends, and lived in small neighborhoods, called Dogtown, Pequot, Pogus Point, East Boston, City Point, Poole's Hill, Calderwood's Neck, and North Haven Road, with plenty of other children.

From the beginning, church and Sunday School were regular parts of the week. When incorporated as a town in the 1780s, the Fox Islands set aside 200 acres for the "use of the Ministry." By 1797 they had hired their first minister, and five years later a Baptist Church was up and running on what was then called the "north island." Early on, many islanders were Methodists. Mormons appeared briefly in 1837, and Episcopal services commenced in the late 1800s for the "Rusticators." By mid-twentieth century, families and their children often attended the Union Church, built in 1860. Because it had brown shingles, people referred to it as "the brown church."[571]

Lorraine explained,

I went to the "brown church" . . . It was just a Protestant church . . . My grand-mother taught. My aunt taught. . . . [We] had big Christmas pageants. We had Children's Day in June. The church was very active. A lot of people went to church. All the kids . . . Not everybody—but like most of the kids in your class went to Sunday school.[572]

Unlike smaller Maine islands, Vinalhaven has always had its own high school. Being together in the classroom for so many years adds another intimate context. For some young fishermen who felt pressed to help support their families from an early age, school was a luxury. For others, it was simply irrelevant to becoming good fishermen. They went—sometimes through 8th grade, sometimes through high school—and then set about fishing full time.

Life was slower, summer visitors were fewer, and fun was homemade. "Lizzie," who grew up on the Maine coast and moved to Vinalhaven in the early 1960s, remembered when the island was more isolated and self-sufficient,

The island was quiet back then. . . .[M]y son used to go out and play . . . for hours and hours and hours. Him and the little girl that lived next door. And you didn't see much traffic . . .

But you didn't have the busyness like you do now you know. And you didn't mind not working because when you was home you were doing things like knitting and having people in for coffee in the morning . . . Now everything is rush, rush, rush. And there is so much traffic on this island. It's unbelievable. . . . Most people have 2 or 3 [cars and trucks]. . . . I was in my late 20s before I even got a license. I never needed one I suppose. . . . [When the girls] were little I bought one of those strollers with the 2 seats. I'd walked down street two or three times a day. Now, you'd get into a vehicle, you don't walk anywhere.[573]

Islanders made their own fun. They participated in all kinds of groups, clubs, and organizations—from the Masons to the island marching band. Speaking about the 1940s and 1950s, Sonny Warren remembered,

There was a lot going on on Main Street at night. There was a whole bunch of people down there at night bowling and going to the movies and dances. Every Saturday night there was a dance. . . . Oh, they was fun you know. Local bands, fiddlers and banjos and you know. Oh yeah, everybody, everybody turned out Saturday night to the dances. That was in the '40s and '50s and then it kinda faded out. You know the movie theater closed down when the television come along . . .

When I came here . . . this end of the island probably had five cars. . . . We'd go down, us young fellas, 17 or 18 years old. We'd walk downtown . . . and go to the movies and go have a soda at the drug store. . . . We might stop in the bowling alley. But there was no automobile. . . . We had a good time. It was easy living and we all had a good time. . . .[574]

Lorraine's parents loved playing cards.

My father played cards all the time . . . He would have big games that would go into the night. But my mother and he also played cards socially . . . I think when my mother played, they might have played 63 and canasta . . .

They made ice cream a lot in the wintertime. Homemade ice cream . . . And they roller-skated here—the adults did and the kids did. [It] was at the Memorial Hall. . . [My sister] and I would be sitting in these chairs and my mother and father would be roller skating and you never knew when someone was going to crash into you.

And they always went to dances. . . . They had orchestras here—they had local people that played. And they had plays that were there. We would go to those a lot of times. . . . I remember that they always had a cowboy show in the summertime and we'd get to go to that. That was a little strange. . . . You know—it was like yodeling and old-time cowboy music.[575]

Lorraine underscored the centrality of family.

My father and mother had a few outside friends, but it was mostly family. We were at my grandmother's a lot. We were at my grandmother's for Sunday dinner. . . . There were so many of us, cousins, that on Sundays, if she had a big dinner there would be almost rows around the table. She didn't have room for all of us, but everybody had a seat and everybody had a plate. She used to cook a lot of things like lamb . . . she was a fabulous cook. . . . My Aunt had us over a lot. We'd go over there and go swimming in the quarry. My mother would visit with her. Then my [other] aunt lived next door—my mother's sister—so it was just all family oriented. I don't remember too many people outside the family. And I think it's pretty much that way right now. . . . I don't think that's totally changed.[576]

That quieter world started slowly disappearing in the late 1960s and 1970s, about the same time new vacationers joined the few wealthy summer "cottage" owners, whose families had first built on the island around the turn of the century. "Cathy" pinpointed it pretty exactly to when

they started making more ferry runs and it became a vacation place. They always had their vacation homes, but they were mostly cottages . . . they weren't winterized. So we used to spend a lot of time going around exploring the houses, which you don't dare to do at all. Because now they have alarm systems and a lot of [the summer people] started never leaving. . . . I think the number of ferry trips made a big difference—slowly, gradually. . . . and cable TV and computers, I think that changed the social aspect a lot.[577]

"Dawn," born in the 1950s, also dated the changes in the community to the late 1960s on. She pointed to the arrival of more summer people courtesy of the *Outward Bound* program on nearby Hurricane Island.[578] Started in 1964 by Peter Willauer, *Outward Bound* became a cultural phenomenon, a symbol of a growing wish to briefly experience a more physically challenging, yet materially simpler life closer to nature.[579] *Outward Bound's* staff and students were often urban and sometimes international, so when they rowed or motored over to buy supplies on Vinalhaven, *"You noticed different types of people,"* Dawn observed.

And then with the economy . . . middle-income people could start buying houses out here. That's when you saw a lot of interaction, and you saw a lot more different types of people. And then it just slowly grew from that. [In the past, when] you went downtown you knew everybody there and now there's lots of people you don't know. And that is a big difference.[580]

The impact of strangers was magnified in those years because many island families didn't make a lot of trips to the mainland. *"I mean,"* Dawn explained, *"Rockland was a big deal for a lot of us kids back then. And back then you dressed up. You'd put on your pretty dress and your shoes and it was so exciting, and it was just a big event. You got excited about a lot less back then."*[581]

When I asked Hal how often he went to the mainland during those mid-century decades, he answered, *"Once in a blue moon. I never went anywhere."*[582]

Sonny thought that, after moving to the island in the 1950s, he'd initially gone to the mainland maybe

three or four times a year, something like that. . . . You'd go for groceries sometimes. You know it was kind of a luxury to go the mainland to go shopping. . . . when the kids were gonna start school you'd go over there to do school shopping . . . The women would go over Christmas shopping. There were small stores here but there wasn't much to pick from . . . After I got a decent boat, I used to go over more. Once a month I'd take my boat over and go grocery shopping on the mainland . . .[583]

Phil Crossman wryly suggested why, for many, crossings were not so frequent: The boat rocked and rolled a lot in rough water. He claimed, *"[A] vomit bag was routinely passed around the cabin. . . . I don't recall going to the mainland for anything."*[584]

Sonny allowed that at times island life could be tough. However, he made an observation, often repeated, that points at another facet of how the community experienced itself:

Everybody was in the same boat so it didn't seem hard. Nobody was doing much better than the other so it didn't seem hard. You just went along with the rest of the people. You know you worked hard to get a living, but everybody was doing it, so it didn't seem hard.[585]

Similarly, "Dawn" reflected,

We were really quite poor. Fishing wasn't lucrative like it has been in the past good many years. We didn't know we were poor until I grew up and then I was like, "Wow, we were poor!"

You didn't have credit cards so you weren't buying stuff you couldn't afford so you lived within your means. Some people had cars and we thought . . . if people had full baths and a car with an ignition on the column, they had money. Serious money. And we laugh [now] about what we thought was wealthy.[586]

Not everyone saw the changes as a loss, however. Cy, who started out fishing and later, with his wife, ran the island grocery store, allowed that he was just as glad to see the hard times (and poverty) behind him. *"Talk about the good old days. I don't know if they were the good old days or not . . . I kind of like today myself."*[587]

Today, more than 1,200 people still live on Vinalhaven year-round, in close proximity and surrounded by ocean. They are still highly involved in each other's lives and in the many organizations they create and maintain to support island life. Many people pitch in. For someone used to suburban or urban anomy, it feels like walking into a lost national past—almost as it appeared on black and white television.

The Union Church hosts free lunches every Monday and bean suppers in summer. The VFW hosts Beano and breakfasts and events of all stripes. The Lions Club sponsors a summer clambake. Residents and summer people alike volunteer to serve on the Friends of the Library committee, on "PIE" which supports the public school, on the Island Community Medical Services Board, the Historical Society, the Land Trust, or the Fox Island concert series, to name only a few.

People organize yard sales, potluck suppers and fundraisers to benefit local causes and programs: Homestead Assisted Living, the Vinalhaven Fire-fighters Association, veterans' services, school trips, the ambulance service, the Girl Scouts, the Eastern Star, the Pleasant River Chapel, to name a few. The Vinalhaven Chamber of Commerce meets Wednesday mornings. The "Grange Fuel Fund" helps with heating bills. Parades with floats and a local marching band are held on important holidays, particularly July 4, and musicals or shows are put on with community talent.

A paid town manager and a board of selectmen (who earn a small stipend each year) govern the island. All voters can participate in the annual town meeting. Committees like the Planning Board, the Sewer Commission, and the Lane's Island Stewardship function through the generosity of volunteers.

Gradually during the twentieth century, many tiny schools were consolidated. Since 2016–2017, one building has housed the island's 157 children, grades K–12. The school curriculum teaches island children about Vinalhaven's history, including its quarries and its fisheries. Students "*learn to have pride in the island and the unique lifestyle that living here affords them.*" History classes visit the island historical society and science classes study the ocean and its living creatures.[588] Most years a majority of seniors, including those who intend to fish, continue schooling after graduation. A few take gap years to do volunteer work far away.

Informal organizations include regular knitting groups, prayer groups and book discussions. Volunteer groups pick trash up off the beaches, deliver meals to housebound neighbors, place books to read on the ferry, or help keep public trails clipped. People contribute. A week doesn't pass without the newsletter, *The Wind*, containing a thank you—to a fisherman who dropped off a dozen lobsters for the residents of the Homestead, or a nurse practitioner who escorted someone ill to the mainland in the middle of the night, and so on.

A small example of the local ethos comes to mind from a day one August when a summer person threw an afternoon party. Guests were parking along the road near the house. Three young women pulled their car too close to a ditch and slid down, getting stuck in the sloping wet grass. Spinning their tires to gain traction, they dug deep into the mud. A small group of people tried to push them out, to no avail. Finally, a passing lobsterman, likely on his way home and tired from hauling traps, stopped, assessed the problem, grabbed a rope from the back of his pick-up, tied it to both vehicles, and pulled the car free. Barely pausing to accept thanks, he jumped into his pick-up and drove away. His effort is a typical, almost quintessential part of an island day that no one living there would think twice about. But to off-islanders it seemed unexpected and kind.

Conversation still plays a large role in daily life on Vinalhaven. Talk is the filament that weaves communities together. If you read nineteenth and twentieth century novels set in villages—Alessandro Manzoni's *The Betrothed*, Zora Neale Hurston's *Their Eyes Were Watching God*, or George Eliot's *Middlemarch* come to mind, each one taking place in a different country and era—you know that talking about the days' events, about each other, and telling stories is how people passed many of their "sitting" hours together. Besides passing time, the conversations conveyed values, set standards, shamed, instructed, sometimes hurt feelings, but more often made people laugh and kept them connected.

No matter how hard islanders work, it's hardly an exaggeration to say that they make time to talk to one another about everything that happens during the day—the details of a wedding, a death, a birth, a shouting match in the local bar, how a boat hit a ledge. So many activities are shared, so many people known in common, that there's always something and someone to talk about.

You hear the community's conversation in the similar phrases that different people use. Sometimes in interviews, I heard people speak exactly the same sequence of words and thoughts as someone I'd interviewed the week before. This common vocabulary may be the end point of many conversations in which experiences have been chewed over until a certain consensus—or clear difference—is achieved.

Stories told around the kitchen table or in the fishhouses have long been the heart of the place. An ever-changing stew of fact and fantasy, these tales carry forward personal, family and island history, often accompanied by lots of laughter.

People were careful about what they told me directly, but occasionally I glimpsed the wild side of the place, which is certainly present. An interviewer recorded Burt Dyer, in his 80s, telling a tale that made me wince, but that gives a vivid sense of a rougher time. I imagine the incident dates to the late 1940s. Burt had climbed up into a woman's cherry tree to eat cherries. Furious, she burst out of her house and came after him with a horsewhip, lashing him twice before he could flee. He waited for a chance to get even. Some weeks later he grabbed her cat, tied a large firecracker rocket around it, lit the fuse and shot the creature "down the road." He told his friends to keep quiet or his father "would beat the shit out of me." Relating the story decades later he expressed youthful glee; but he also allowed he'd been cruel to the cat—if not to its owner.[589]

Islanders know well how quickly word travels, so they often decide against setting messages in motion. Many spoke to me discreetly. Sometimes when I interviewed people, I felt they were invested in presenting me with a more idealized view of the island—almost as a gift for summer guests who needed to retain a fiction of tranquility. One person signaled me to turn off my tape recorder before she uttered something negative. Occasionally, though, my inevitable departure made me privy to confidences and secrets.

Some of the frankest comments about the contemporary island that I heard "on the record" came from "Ben," a man born in 1958 who died a year or two after we spoke. His father had come to Vinalhaven as a boy and been informally adopted and raised by an islander. Ben expressed much of what other people said in snatches. Perhaps because his family was relatively new to the island, and he still felt like something of an outsider, he felt freer to talk about good and bad experiences.

I didn't always like living on Vinalhaven and sometimes I still don't. Sometimes, although island life seems very simple, it's not always simple. . . . . Island life can be very complex. It has its trials and tribulations. Sometimes, the boat doesn't go. There are always cases of medical emergencies and trying to get off the Island . . . Another issue is that in the wintertime things practically shut down here. After Labor Day things slowly, gradually start shutting down, and so we're limited.

I found growing up here sometimes very difficult. There were times I wished I had been on the mainland . . . But the advantage of living on an island, of course, is . . . the community. Because there's a very large sense of community. . . . and so that's probably one of the things that keeps me here.

One of the things I find about Vinalhaven, you don't find in a lot of places, is the fact that if someone is down financially, or there's a death, or someone's house burns or in times of hardship just in general, I find that's when the island people really rally around each other. You know, they are generous; they bring food . . . they're there for the person who's having the hardship. That's when you really get the sense of the closeness of the community.

The other flip side of that of course, too—I know that this is going to sound funny—but everybody knows everybody else's business an hour before it happens. . . . It's very frustrating . . . [L]iving on an island can sometimes be too close-knit a community. It's sort of living in a fishbowl, and a lot of times I still feel that way. I feel like I'm inside of a fishbowl looking out and everyone is looking in at me. Sometimes it could be good but most times no . . .

So things have a tendency of getting blown out of proportion. Beyond, sometimes well beyond, what they really are. . . . The rumor mill has a way of making its rounds . . .

Sometimes people hold grudges—or people, see a person as something other than what they are. By that I mean, if somebody has done something wrong then people on the island don't wave to them, they don't speak to them in the store, or they pretend that they're not there. Eventually it does wash over. Sometimes the person gains a reputation, depending on the circumstances, that sticks with them for the rest of their lives. While on the mainland it wouldn't be an issue . . . Here we're on an Island . . . So it becomes magnified.[590]

Ben's description of shunning people who have behaved badly suggests that much island justice is still dispensed informally. While there often has been a Knox County Deputy on the island and people are taken to court on the mainland, many problems are still settled via the silent treatment, avoidance, and conversation, or occasionally by fist fights, cutting traps and slashing tires.[566] One fisherman I interviewed, now deceased, believed that a bullying, slightly older relative had been responsible for his brother drowning when they were children. Years later, fueled by alcohol, he beat the now grown man almost to death. My sense was that he felt satisfied he had settled a score.

On tape and off tape, people confided thoughts and stories similar to these. Yet, for most, feeling part of a community carried the day.

Many people noted, like "Ben," that Vinalhaven could be like a fishbowl, where everything anyone did was observed, and where people seemed to know what their neighbors were up to almost before they knew themselves. Like other pervasive impressions, this one was considered good and bad— bad for leaving people feeling without privacy and over-scrutinized, but good for letting them feel accepted and looked out for. Several people told of leaving the island when they were young to get away from the scrutiny, but then missing the sense of community later on, and deciding to return.

I asked Jennie, age ninety when we spoke, what she wanted her great-grandchildren to know about what it was like growing up on the island when she was little. She smiled and went straight to the heart of the matter,

Well, it was a very friendly town. As soon as anyone is off the boat you knew who they were. If there was anything wrong there was always somebody come to help. If they had good gardens or something, they'd bring you things from the garden. If they had hens laying well, they'd bring you eggs. All those things.[591]

Afterword

Imagine it is 1900 or maybe 1910. You are a fisherman on Vinalhaven talking with a friend about the inshore fishery, your shared hopes, and your worries. For one of his 1960's newspaper pieces, Ivan Calderwood did just that. He made up a conversation between "Uncle Dave" and the Vinalhaven Sea Captain Reuben Hopkins. In it, Hopkins anticipates much about the twentieth century story of fishing on Vinalhaven, particularly the dependency of island fishermen on the local spawning grounds, and the accelerated harm that would come to those grounds from relentless "dragging" and overfishing—starting with the arrival of the gasoline engine.

> *"I tell you, Dave, it's a godsend to these fellas after a long hard winter because the fish are there waiting at any season," replied Reuben. "I hope these fish will always be allowed to spawn on these grounds and that man doesn't find a way to harrow and destroy these breeding grounds. Man does queer things and often destroys what God has granted him . . . [especially] now that we are all changing over to motor power. . . . Progress is a wonderful thing, Uncle Dave, but sometimes it upsets nature's plans and in the long run can make a man unhappy even if the profit has increased for a time."*[592]

"Even if the profit has increased for a time" is a laconic way to capture the heart of the twentieth century tale of "progress"—the way new technologies allowed men to catch more fish—without truly reckoning the long-term costs of their efforts. What Uncle Dave describes locally happened and continues to happen worldwide to most places and species. I sometimes wonder if the fate of the earth wasn't decisively inflected when John Calvin (1509–1564), whose lopsided theology arrived in Colonial America with the Puritans, claimed that "it was chiefly for the sake of mankind that the world was made."[593]

Calderwood's imagined conversation offers wise perspective. Gasoline engines _did_ transform fishing and fishing communities; they transformed all communities. Indeed, we _have_ collectively "done queer things," (however splendid and at times beneficent) which _have_ compounded to destroy much of what "God has granted." Across the twentieth century, industrial fishing worldwide, to borrow what Wendell Berry observed about industrial agriculture, increasingly "told nature what it wanted . . . and since it proposed no limit on its wants, exhaustion has been its inevitable and foreseeable result."[594]

When I first visited Vinalhaven almost forty years ago, I saw not only more sea urchins, but also more starfish, periwinkles, sea cucumbers, crabs, gulls, cormorants, young pollock, mackerel and herring than are in and around its waters now. Many generations could say the same. A stream of peoples— from Archaic-era bands 5,000 plus years ago to Europeans in the seventeenth century—settled the Maine Coast because they recognized a natural abundance that would sustain them. Over the past several hundred years, that abundance diminished; first slowly, then more quickly, then very, very fast.

The sorrow, as Calderwood implied, is that the European settlers—and the majority of us since, have lived within a system that inadequately counterbalanced the pursuit of profit with other restraining imperatives. I am certainly complicit and a beneficiary. But at what price? Denying the sentience and worth of humans or creatures whose preservation is inconvenient to that quest has been part of the Maine—and United States—"story" from the colonists' earliest days. What would Penobscot Bay—the continent, and the planet— look like now if our nation had established credible checks on harvesting resources? Had protected the right to thrive of all creatures, human and wild? Would the current population of Maine include many more Wabanaki people? Would there still be better "finfish" fishing in the Penobscot Bay, and cod, haddock, pollock, halibut, mussels, clams, scallops and crabs still flourish? Would island fishing families have a clearer future? Would we all?

Ivan Calderwood did not believe that the earth was created for us to ravage. He saw how the motorized draggers ruined the breeding grounds and the inshore fishery in the bay he loved. Yes, overfishing existed before 1900, but until gas engines, and then radar, synthetic nets, and sonar entered the picture across the twentieth century, Vinalhaven fish harvests remained adequately in balance with their surround.

Today's overused but still meaningful word for that balance would be "sustainable"—if not by intention, then by circumstance. For a long time, islanders harvested, traded, bought, and sold. A few people became wealthy; a handful more, prosperous. Most families mixed farming and fishing and got by pretty well. Some folks—like Andrew Merchant—had to leave repeatedly in search of employment. To manage the work of fishing, the risk, the every-day violence, the departures and returns, families developed habits of mutual support so intertwined and sturdy in their emotional construction that they "sustained" the community members and helped them absorb the hardships and relentless loss. Recall Andrew's upset when Sarah forgot to put a "min-iature" of herself in his fishing trunk before he left, his scolding when her letter writing slowed. Until the late twentieth century, the majority of people on Vinalhaven lived materially thrifty, community-rich lives. As with most places, it suited and served some people better than others.

The lobster monoculture that is now so profitable might be construed as a gift, and, at the same time, as a cosmic joke, ironic and hard to figure. Lobster has become a single wild source of plenty within a depleted bay. The dearth of many other creatures in Penobscot Bay, together with changes in conserva-tion law, climate, and water temperature, has created great abundance—and much opportunity.

For now, this harvest has brought prosperity. It has also surged like a spring tide, flooding over other, older island ways: the rhythms of labor and econo-mies determined by season, the interdependence and shared travail, the lei-surely fishhouse conversations about technique and craft, the feeling so often repeated of solidarity: "we were all in the same boat." Without sentimental-izing past hardship—recall Sarah Merchant's fears of being without any food, or all the Lindsey men who died at sea, or the constant injuries in the quarries, or Cy Davidson's comment that he preferred his more affluent present life to his more impoverished past—we can appreciate the loss of what that tide submerged. Several fishermen alluded to an almost ineffable new emotional hardship wrought by so much opportunity to profit—the increased competi-tiveness, the exhaustion, the guilt about not wanting to fish without rest just to catch every available lobster, and the fear of falling behind as neighbors made more money and bought bigger boats, more gear, new trucks, new homes, and winter vacations in warm places. Their concerns seem emblematic of ones shared by many of us wherever we live.

Since few island families now actively pursue the older subsistence prac-tices—raising pigs, chickens and vegetables, hunting deer, putting up seabirds and mackerel, clamming, or smoking herring—local fishermen are more vulner-able than ever to markets. And since they have only one "product" to sell instead of several, they no longer possess a ready fallback when global consumption falters; or climate change drives the lobsters out of reach toward cooler waters. Indeed, with fishing, boatbuilding and net-knitting mostly on hold for now, lob-stering is the last skilled fishing-related craft the place supports.

Many fear what will happen if the lobster fishery crashes. Will Vinalhaven become one more summer colony or retirement haven? Will all islanders become seasonal employees of people "from away"? No doubt some will become farmers of kelp, oysters, and other once-wild creatures. Yet it would be a terrible loss of birthright for families on the island. It would be existentially worse for the rest of us, whether we live 100 miles away or several thousand.

We all will be impoverished if small-scale fishing for wild ocean fish ends permanently, and fishing families—on Vinalhaven and worldwide—die away. Of course, "everything changes," but the loss of communities set within the coastal "ecotone," where land and water meet, is a disaster of a different order. We cannot bring back the people 4800 years ago who understood how to live well in the ecotone; we cannot undo our violence toward their descendants. Yet all fishing communities are foundational. They have existed for thousands of years. The more urban and "virtual" the world becomes, the more disconnected populations are from wildness, and from food sources and hunting and gathering, the more crucial it is for some among us to continue these earth-anchored practices.

Everyone alive needs the opportunity to witness fishermen haul nets from the sea or heave fish from a boat, and witness with at least a touch of awe our collective past of pursuing and harvesting our food.

In truth, everyone needs time closer to nature than urban and suburban life allow, needs the opportunity to gasp, as I did one June night on the island, watching fireflies illuminating spruce boughs against a star-filled night sky. Perhaps it isn't too late and we might yet collectively re-sanctify the wild. Not for novelty, but for joy, for justness, and for humility: to regain perspective on ourselves within the universe. To remind us that the earth was not created for us; that it is a random miracle to be shared by all living creatures.

In the summer of 1987 when we first moved into our island house, we found, beside the wood stove, a sturdy old, wood-handled implement, maybe 16 inches long, with a round, blackened iron shank that curved into a pointed hook. We often poked fires with it, yet it took a quarter of a century for me to realize its purpose. It is a fishing gaff—a fisherman's tool for wrestling fish from the ocean into a rowboat; I imagine the ninety-year-old Timothy Dyer wrangled his halibut with one like it, and that an island blacksmith hammered mine.

Recognizing a gaff seems a good symbol of the distance I have traveled writing this book. It took me a long while to give up my visitor's fantasy gaze and begin to understand what was before me. When I started my research, I had hoped that someday, retired, I could linger for whole seasons on the island, and that my visits would be enriched by all I had learned. But time moved quickly, and in 2018 we sold the house. I took the gaff with me as a memento . . . a token of the beauty of the place—of the lives lived, of the vitality, toil, violence, loss, joy and sorrow of the fishing island. I took a tool whose wooden handle records days and years of sweat, of salt-water labor—an object I can look at to remind myself how generously the island taught me about its past.

I don't know who used the gaff. But someone did. I imagine it lying on the damp bottom of a peapod along with fishing line, hooks, and cut-up bait. A fisherman climbs in, stows his lunch can under the bow seat, unknots the rope, and pushes away from the dock. Standing, facing forward, he rows steadily into the first sliver of dawn. A slight breeze laps the salt water against the prow, and the oars creak in their oarlocks.

Acknowledgments

I want to begin by thanking the many islanders and long-term summer residents who consented to let me interview them. Most interviews lasted about an hour or a little more; they were wide-ranging and taught me much about the island and about fishing. I began doing them in 2008, and in the interim many people I spoke with died: Bodine Ames, Victor Ames, John Beckman, Lois Day, George Dyer, Alton Oakes, Ivan Olsen, Bill Brown, Marge Conway, Tim Dyer, Phil Dyer, Wyman Philbrook, Jenny Webster, Marion Young, Sonny Warren, Sherry Bunin and Roy Heisler to date. The lost stories and knowledge is daunting; the loss of each life, immeasurable.

I am indebted beyond measure to everyone at the Vinalhaven Historical Society: Bill Chilles, Elizabeth Bunker, Loretta Chilles, Lorraine Bunker, Sue Radley and Roy Heisler (with whose death Vinalhaven lost not just a lovely man, but one with an encyclopedic knowledge of island history). The patience with which these kind people treated me as I asked the same questions over and over and endlessly plied them for documents, photographs, genealogy and on and on—is unrivaled in my research and writing experience. And while they will no doubt breathe a deep collective sigh of relief when this enterprise finally ends, I will miss them all.

I thank Michael Steere, my editor at Down East Books, for letting this effort see the light of day by acquiring and publishing it, and for generously agreeing to include maps, images and illustrations.

Vinalhaven history lives in each islander and summer visitor. I thank Roger Young for sharing his documents and knowledge with me, and Ken Reiss and Cynthia Martin for speaking with me. I thank Lorraine Walker for many different kindnesses, and Ronnie Walker for letting me on his boat and still talking to me after he did. I thank Bruce Bourque, Charles Curtain, Kris Osgood and Del Webster for responding to my email queries.

Off island thanks also go to Stefan Claesson for producing so adeptly the fishing grounds map, and to Richard Dey, a fisherman and fine writer, who generously aided me with a chapter of the book that has since been removed. I thank Olivia Herschensohn, a collections steward in 2014 at the Peabody Museum at Harvard University, who gave generously of her time teaching me about the human remains in their collection; and Michèle Morgan, Ph.D., who read the "Coda: Relics and Skeletons" in an earlier draft and edited it to comply with the museum criteria for publication. I am grateful to Donna Condon and Charlotte Golden for transcribing various recordings.

Without research libraries and their ever-generous librarians, it would be impossible to piece together any bits of the past. I want to acknowledge Meghan Pipp at Harvard's Schlesinger Library, Dan Hinchen at the Massachusetts Historical Society, Melanie Hardy Mohney and Michele L. Brann with Reference Services at the Maine State Library, William Barry and Tiffany Link at the Maine Historical Society, Kevin Johnson, Cipperly Good and Research Volunteer Deborah Nowers at the Penobscot Marine Museum's Stephen Phillips Memorial Library. Special thanks to Cathy Fetterman, Director, Licensing Division of the Maine Department of Marine Resources.

Finally, I thank William Leavenworth for first answering email questions, then meeting with me and introducing me to Karen Alexander. It has been my good fortune that Karen agreed to edit the book so that it would conform to her fish historian's eye. She guided me to fill in missing data, made me cut unproven or sidetracking notions, and she helped me produce an historically documented and coherent text. On that score, William Leavenworth's, Ted Ames's, Robin Alden's, and Natalie Springuel's readings of portions of the manuscript have been invaluable.

I thank Elin Elisofon for helping me get permission for the use of her father, Eliot Elisofon's, photograph.

As always, I thank Miriam Altshuler, my wonderful agent, though wonderful doesn't really do it—generous, extremely competent, knowledgeable, and kind come closer. And, of course, David, Peter, and Sadie Smith, all so beloved, my family with whom I shared the island. I apologize to anyone who I should have named but did not.

Notes

PREFACE

1. Heather Deese and Susie Arnold, "Fathoming: A Tale of three winter fisheries," *The Working Waterfront* (WW), February/March 19; modified, December 4, 2019. http://www.islandinstitute.org/working-waterfront/%E2%80%8B-tale-three-winter -fisheries (Retrieved May 26, 2020).

2. Addie Roberts Diary, Vinalhaven Historical Society (VHHS) collections.

3. One word in 1789, the US Postal Service changed the name of the island's Post Office from South Vinalhaven to Carver's Harbor in 1850, to Vinal Haven (two words) on October 29, 1879, and back to Vinalhaven (one word) again on March 15, 1925. VHHS, personal communication.

INTRODUCTION

4. Phil Crossman introduces the island's geography and character in his blog, *Island Circumambulation: A Walking Tour of the Perimeter of Vinalhaven*, http://islandcircumambulation.blogspot.com/search?updated-min=2009-01-01T00:00:00-08:00&updated-max=2010-01-01T00:00:00-08:00&max-results=1 (Retrieved January 2, 2018).

5. John Gillis, *The Human Shore* (Chicago: University of Chicago Press, 2010), 5, 7.

6. Bruce Bourque, *The Swordfish Hunters: The History and Ecology of an Ancient American Sea People* (Piermont, NH: Bunker Hill Publishers, 2012), 17, 97, 54; Bruce Bourque, *Twelve Thousand Years: American Indians in Maine* (Lincoln: University of Nebraska Press, 2001 [2004]), 49-51. The name "Red Paint People" has become controversial because it initially came with the implication that they had mysteriously appeared and disappeared and were more competent than later native people. See

Rebecca Cole-Will, "Who were the Red Paint People?" Abbe Museum, Bar Harbor, ME, https://static1.squarespace.com/static/56a8c7b05a5668f743c485b2/t/5a6a1fa6 53450a9b35ee4729/1516904359054/Who+Were+the+Red+Paint+People+2002.pdf (Retrieved June 12, 2020).

7. Bourque, *Swordfish Hunters*, xv.

8. Bourque, personal communication.

9. Arthur E. Spiess and Robert A. Lewis. *The Turner Farm Fauna: 5000 years of hunting and fishing in Penobscot Bay, Maine. Occasional Publications in Maine Archaeology* Number 11 (Augusta: Maine State Museum, Maine Historical Preservation Commission, and Maine Archaeological Society, 2001), 86-92; 82, 2.

10. Bourque, *Swordfish Hunters.*

11. Yuval Noah Harari. *Sapiens: a brief history of humankind* (New York: HarperCollins, 2015), 49–51.

12. Plummet, VHHS collections.

13. Bourque, *Swordfish Hunters*, 46.

14. Daniel Pauly, Villy Christensen, Johanne Dalsgaard, Rainer Froese, and Francisco Torres Jr. (1998) "Fishing down marine food webs," *Science* 279 (1998): 860-863.

15. David B. Quinn and Alison M. Quinn, eds., *The English New England Voyages 1602–1608* (London: Hakluyt Society, Second Series, 1983), 216-17.

16. Steve Nicholls. *Paradise Found: Nature in America at the Time of the Discovery* (Chicago: University of Chicago Press, 2009), 24, 25.

17. Lorenzo Sabine. *Report on the Principal fisheries of the American Seas: Prepared for the Treasury Department of the United States by Lorenzo Sabine of Massachusetts; and submitted by the honorable Thomas Corwin, Secretary of the Treasury, as part of the annual report on finances, at the second session of the thirty-second congress.* (Washington: Robert Armstrong, Printer, 1853), 8. For another description of Native American and European populations in Maine following first contact, see *Maine Memory Network*: https://www.mainememory.net/sitebuilder/site/879/page/1290/display?page=2 (Retrieved October 16, 2018).

18. William B. Leavenworth, "The Changing Landscape of Maritime Resources in Seventeenth-Century New England," *International Journal of Maritime History* 20(2008): 33-62.

19. W. Jeffrey Bolster, *The Mortal Sea: Fishing the Atlantic in the Age of Sail,* (Cambridge: Harvard University Press, 2012), 58. Also see John Frederick Martin, *Profits in the Wilderness: Entrepreneurship and the Founding of New England Towns in the Seventeenth Century* (Chapel Hill: University of North Carolina Press and Omohundro Institute, 1991). I assume "per capita" refers to white males.

20. Nicholls, *Paradise Found*, 43.

21. Among them, Marsden Hartley, Margaret Wise Brown and Robert Indiana.

22. Martha's Vineyard Chamber of Commerce, *Complete Guide to Martha's Vineyard: Island Information.* https://www.mvy.com/island-information.html (Retrieved September 17, 2019).

23. Interview with Herb Conway. July 21, 2015, 1.

24. Interview with Ivan Olson. August 21, 2011, 8.

25. Virginia M. Wright, "What can baby lobsters tell us about the future of Maine's $1 billion fishery?" *DownEast Magazine*, October 2018, 46. Penelope Overton, Jenna Russell, "The Lobster Trap." Boston Globe Spotlight and Portland Herald, December 12, 2021. http://apps.bostonglobe.com/metro/2021/12/the-lobster-trap/climate-change-threatens-livelihood-of-maine-lobster-fishermen (Retrieved February 13, 2022). In a conversation in May 2020, Robin Alden further explained the complexity of warming water and the future of Maine's most important fishery.

CHAPTER 1

26. Christopher Paul Magra, *The New England Cod Fishing Industry and Maritime Dimensions of the American Revolution*, PhD Thesis, University of Pittsburgh, 2006, 16.

27. Horace P. Beck, *The American Indian as a sea-fighter in Colonial Times* (Mystic CT: The Marine Historical Association, Inc., and Mystic Seaport Press, 1959), 46.

28. Beck, *The American Indian as a Sea-fighter*, 43.

29. Beck, *The American Indian as a Sea-fighter*, 53.

30. Michael Dekker, *French and Indian Wars in Maine* (Charleston: History Press, 2015).

31. "Indians" remains one agreed upon way of describing native people, and it is the word used in the quoted texts, so I am using it for clarity in sentences trying to distinguish between conflicting groups.

32. *Wikipedia*, "Penobscot," http://en.wikipedia.org/wiki/Penobscot (Retrieved February 20, 2015). The entry further states that "[t]he Maine state government appointed a Tribal Agent to oversee the tribe. The government believed that they were helping the Penobscots, as stated in 1824 by the highest court in Maine that ". . . imbecility on their parts, and the dictates of humanity on ours, have necessarily prescribed to them their subjection to our paternal control."

33. Joseph B. Felt. *History of Ipswich, Essex and Hamilton* (Cambridge: C. Folsom. 1834), 316. https://archive.org/details/historyofipswich00felt (Retrieved December 8, 2020). The Tiltons are included in Ipswich fishing stories. For another boat taken "while other parties made an attempt upon a fishing vessel from Ipswich, lying in one of the eastern harbors. . ." see John Barry, *The History of Massachusetts*, Vol. 2 (Boston: Phillips, Sampson and Company, 1856), 118. https://books.google.com/books?id=3qE6AAAAcAAJ&printsec=frontcover&dq=intitle:The+intitle:History+intitle:of+intitle:Massachusetts+inauthor:John+inauthor:S+inauthor:Barry&hl=en&sa=X&ei=ANuzVLmHKoayggTu5oLgBg&ved=0CB8Q6AEwAA#v=onepage&q&f=false (Retrieved December 8, 2020).

34. Felt, *History of Ipswich*, 316.

35. Felt, *History of Ipswich*, 316.

36. Beck, *The American Indian as a Sea-fighter*, 57.

37. Felt, *History of Ipswich*, 316.

38. Bolster, *The Mortal Sea*, 67.

39. Rev. Samuel Niles, A.M., "A summary historical narrative of the wars in New England with the French and Indians in the several parts of the country," *Collections of the Massachusetts Historical Society*. Fourth Series, Vol. V (Boston: Printed for the Society, 1861), 351. https://books.google.com/books?id=4agyAQAAMAAJ&p g=PA351&dq=The+enemy+not+finding+their+expected+success+on+our+frontier, +resolved+to+obstruct+our+fishery+by+sea&hl=en&sa=X&ei=A6uWVaWmHsm4 -AG4rYLYDQ&ved=0CB4Q6AEwAA#v=onepage&q=The%20enemy%20not%20 finding%20their%20expected%20success%20on%20our%20frontier%2C%20re solved%20to%20obstruct%20our%20fishery%20by%20sea&f=false (Retrieved July 3, 2015).

40. Sidney L. Winslow, *Fish Scales and Stone Chips* (Portland: Machigonne Press, 1952 [1989]), 13. Winslow reports this story as an "oral legend" handed down generationally on Vinalhaven.

41. Beck, *The American Indian as a Sea-fighter*, 63.

42. Beck, *The American Indian as a Sea-fighter,* 77.

43. W. L. McAtee, "Plants collected on Matinicus Island, Maine, in late fall, 1915." *Rhodora* 18 (February 1916): 29-45, quote on page 29. http://www.jstor.org/ stable/23297419?seq=1#page_scan_tab_contents (Retrieved February 17, 2015).

44. Charles B. McLane and Carol Evarts McLane, *Islands of the Mid-Maine Coast*, Vol. 1, *Penobscot Bay*, revised edition (Gardiner ME: Tilbury House Publishers, 1997), 22.

45. McLane and McLane, *Islands of the Mid-Maine Coast*, 9.

46. Letter from Ezekiel Cushing to Lieutenant Governor Spencer Phips, August 15, 1751, *Documentary History of the State of Maine*, Vol. 23, 416. https://archive .org/details/documentaryhisto23main (Retrieved November 28, 2014).

47. Letter from the Chiefs *Cosemes, Modobt, Chebnood, Mugdumbawit* to Lieutenant Governor Spencer Phips, April 25, 1753. The letter went via Captain William Lithgow at Richmond Fort, who wrote to Phips urging him to act to forestall violence. *Documentary History of the State of Maine*, Vol. 23, 448. https://archive.org/details/ documentaryhisto23main (Retrieved November 28, 2014).

48. *Documentary History of the State of Maine*, Vol. 23, 449.

49. Wikipedia, "Governor Phips," http://en.wikipedia.org/wiki/Spencer_Phips (Retrieved Nov. 11, 2014).

50. Nedoba, "Culture Conflict - Ebenezer Hall of Matinicus Island – 1757" http:// www.nedoba.org/ne-do-ba/nhis_hal.html (Retrieved February 17, 2015). This webpage is dedicated to providing accurate information about Abenaki/Wabanaki events and history. It offers several versions of the Hall's story, and sites its sources. In her 1760 account of events, Mary also mentions a man named Benjamin Magrage, thought to have been either a son-in-law, or a fisherman working with Hall (or perhaps both).

51. O.P. Lyons and Albra Josephine Vinal, *A Brief Historical Sketch of the Town of Vinalhaven, from its earliest known settlement. Prepared by order of the Town on the Occasion of its One Hundredth Anniversary* (Rockland: Press of the Star Job Print, 1900 [1981] [1986]), 58.

52. Stephen J. Hornsby and Richard W. Judd (eds), *Historical Atlas of Maine* (Orono, ME: University of Maine Press, 2015), 12.

53. Lyons and Vinal, *Brief Historical Sketch*, 57.

54. Addie Roberts Diary, VHHS collections.

55. Athene R. Anthony, *Vinalhaven Reminiscences* (Vinalhaven: Printed by The "Wind" of the Union Church, 1978), 47.

CHAPTER 2

56. William B. Leavenworth, personal communication.

57. Kenneth Reiss, *From the Beginning: Vinalhaven from 1760 to 1850,* (Vinalhaven: Vinalhaven Historical Society, 2017), 80, 98, 100.

58. "Petitions," Vinalhaven Records, VHHS collections.

59. Lyons and Vinal, *Brief Historical Sketch*, 8-11.

60. Lyons and Vinal, *Brief Historical Sketch*, 15-17.

61. Chuck Gadzick, personal communication.

62. Unsourced newspaper article (probably the Rockland Courier-Gazette) titled "The Tramp" quoting Rueben Carter about his father, Thaddeus, 1885.

63. Charles A. E. Long, *Matinicus Isle: Its Story and People* (Lewiston ME: Lewiston Journal Printshop, 1926; reprinted, Salem MA: Higginson Book Company), 191-192; John Pendleton Farrow, *History of Islesborough Maine* (Bangor: Picton Press, 1892; reprinted by the Islesboro Historical Society, 1965, 1982, and 1991), 263-266; VHHS, personal communication.

64. *The Ancestry of Anna Louise McClean*, xeroxed pages, VHHS collections.

65. Wayne M. O'Leary. *Maine Sea Fisheries: The Rise and Fall of a Native Industry, 1830–1890.* (Boston: Northeastern University Press. 1996), 11, 20; O'Leary quoted from John B. Brebner's *Canada: A Modern History* (Ann Arbor: University of Michigan Press, 1960), 160; Karen Alexander and Bill Leavenworth, personal communications.

66. Reiss, *From the Beginning*, 93.

67. James Roberts' Ledger, 67, VHHS collections.

68. Reiss. *From the Beginning,* 82, 93.

69. Christopher Paul Magra. *The New England Cod Fishing Industry and Maritime Dimensions of the American Revolution* (PHD Thesis, University of Pittsburgh, 2006) http://d-scholarship.pitt.edu/7982/1/Magra_ETD_1_.pdf (Retrieved October 30, 2018).

70. Miss Stinson's purchases in 1776: January 8—1 quart of molasses, barrall, 1 old shirt; May 6—2¾ quarts of molasses; July 13—half a busshel of meal, 1 pare of old shoes, 2 quarts molasses; August 24—2 quarts of molasses, 2 pounds 6 ounces of coffee; September 29—¼ a bushel of meal, 3¼ pounds of porck,1 pound of coffee, 1 quart of molasses plus ½ pint molasses; June 17—5¾ pounds Beef. James Roberts's Ledger, 67, VHHS collections.

71. Lyons and Vinal, *Brief Historical Sketch*, 42. Another other bit of information we have about Thomas Ginn is that he defied the island's healthy norm: he fathered ten children, nine of whom died, and he died himself at 52.

72. Natalie Springuel, William B. Leavenworth, and Karen Alexander, "From Wealth to Poverty: The Rise and Fall of Cod around Mount Desert Island" *Chebacco* 16 (2015): 66-91; quote on page 69. Maine Sea Grant Publications 29. https://digital commons.library.umaine.edu/seagrant_pub/29.

73. Thaddeus also left $68.00 to his grandson named Thaddeus, but only if "he shall serve me or my Wife until he is twenty-one years of age." The teenager apparently looked after his aging grandparents. Since the will was written in 1820, and Thaddeus lived until 1831, his young namesake must have long since reached his majority and received his due.

74. Laurel Thatcher Ulrich. *A Midwife's Tale, the life of Martha Ballard, based on her diary, 1785-1812* (New York: Alfred A Knopf, 1990), 177.

75. Undated letter, written by Mrs. Arthur D. Patterson, in the *Carver Notebook*, VHHS collections.

76. VHHS, personal communication.

77. Lyons and Vinal, *Brief Historical Sketch*, 45. Lyons and Vinal suggest that Isaac paid $30 dollars for a tract of around 700 acres, now called Arey's Cove and Arey's Neck. A "man named Wheeler" seemed to be the seller. This account seems incorrect as a document in the VHHS collections supports the purchase from Carr a year earlier. In addition, 30£ would be the correct currency for the era, since it is more likely than Spanish dollars from the Caribbean. See also Eric W. Nye, *Pounds Sterling to Dollars: Historical Conversion of Currency*, http://www.uwyo.edu/numimage/cur rency.htm (Retrieved November 13, 2018).

78. Lyons and Vinal, *Brief Historical Sketch,* 43-50, 73-74; also, VHHS, personal communication.

79. Isaac Arey and the bear appear in Thomas Waterman's 1821 letter describing Vinalhaven and North Haven, where he tells stories about several early settlers, http://www.mainememory.net/media/pdf/20802.pdf (Retrieved March 3, 10 2015). One is about Mr. Isaac Airy, who I'm guessing was our man, spelled intuitively.

80. Waterman's 1821 letter; Lyons and Vinal, *Brief Historical Sketch*, 43.

81. 1790 US Census, Vinalhaven. http://www.rootsweb.ancestry.com/~megenweb/census/1790/1790.html (Retrieved March 3, 2015); personal communication via email, VHHS, March 3, 2015.

82. Reiss, *From the Beginning,* 110.

83. Isaac Arey's death date is uncertain, but I believe he likely died in his early sixties. In the VHHS genealogy chart, Isaac's death is listed as occurring in 1800. But the Probate judge validated the inventory on December 23, 1807, and the list itself is signed and dated April 28, 1807. It seems unlikely that the inventory would have been taken seven years after Isaac's death. Mary died in 1808.

84. *Wikipedia*, "Isle au Haut, Maine," http://en.wikipedia.org/wiki/Isle_au_Haut,_ Maine (Retrieved February 24, 2015).

85. *Arey Estate Inventory*. Copy from the Belfast, Maine, Probate Court Records in the VHHS collections.

86. Ulrich, *A Midwife's Tale,* 170.

87. *John Carver Account Books*, VHHS collections.

88. Sabine, *Report on the Principal Fisheries of the American Seas;* Sabine's review of the fisheries was in part to advise Congress on the bounty question. O'Leary, *Maine Sea Fisheries*, chapter 2, also, William B. Leavenworth and Karen Alexander, personal communications.

89. L.J. Webster & M.A. Noah, *Letters Home from Sea. The Life and Letters of Solon J. Hanson, Down East Sailor* (Brookline, New Hampshire: Hobblebush Books. 2006), 23-24.

90. Robert B. Applebee, *Sailing Vessels of Vinalhaven Maine*, Typed, unpaginated manuscript ca. 1954 from the Castine WPA records, in the Robert Appleby Collection, Penobscot Marine Museum.

91. Cited in O'Leary, *Maine Sea Fisheries*, 237, this 1833 petition is in the VHHS collections.

CHAPTER 3

92. "Timothy Dyer's Halibut," *Rockland Courier-Gazette*, 19 December 1893: 1. Sidney Winslow has another account of the story from an undated, un-sourced newspaper article, a single copy of which is in the *VHHS Notebooks*. VHHS collections. Winslow states Dyer rowed six or seven miles and gives his age as 91. At the time the article was written, both his siblings, Jane, 86, and Joshua, 82, were still living on the island.

93. O'Leary. *Maine Sea Fisheries*, 7.

94. "Timothy Dyer's Halibut," *Rockland Courier-Gazette*, 19 December 1893: 1.

95. O'Leary. *Maine Sea Fisheries*, 85-87.

96. Harvey Strum, "Smuggling in Maine During the Embargo and The War of 1812." *Colby Quarterly* V 19-2 (1983): 90–97; quote on page 97. http://digitalcommons.colby.edu (Retrieved May 22, 2015).

97. Strum, "Smuggling in Maine During the Embargo", 92.

98. Strum, "Smuggling in Maine During the Embargo", 92.

99. Joshua Dyer, *The Wind*, 2 February 1884: 1-5. Front page letter to the editors, unsigned.

100. Cyrus Eaton, *History of Thomaston, Rockland and South Thomaston, Maine* (Hallowell ME: Masters, Smith & Co. Printers, 1865); https://archive.org/stream/historythomasto03eatogoog#page/n308/mode/2up/search/Fox+Island (Retrieved May 22, 2015), 289. In Waterman's 1821 letter, the same story is told in less detail, and the privateer is called the *LILY.*

101. Eaton, *History of Thomaston*, 289–90.

102. United States Department of Labor, *History of Wages in the United States from Colonial Times to 1928* (supplement added 1929-1933), *Bulletin of the United States Bureau of Labor Statistics* # 604 (Washington: United States Printing Office, 1934; republished in Detroit: Gale Research Co./Book Tower, 1966), 98. https://

babel.hathitrust.org/cgi/pt?id=ucl.32106007458745&view=1up&seq=5 (Retrieved September 5, 2019).

103. Applebee, *Sailing Vessels of Vinalhaven Maine,* unpaginated.

104. O'Leary, *Maine Sea Fisheries*, 43. I found no wills or inventories for the Dyers, which suggests that there wasn't a lot of property to divide. They seem not ever to have had the money to buy a share of a fishing schooner. Still, if some family members had worked seasonally on others' boats, which seems likely, they could have benefited as crewmembers.

105. O'Leary, *Maine Sea Fisheries*, 43-44.

106. This account was submitted in June 30, 1941, by Sidney L. Winslow, and is in the VHHS collections.

107. Benjamin Beverage, *History of Vinalhaven*, 1819, letter in the Maine Historical Society collections. http://www.mainememory.net/media/pdf/20801 (Retrieved May 29, 2015). I added a bit of punctuation to make the text easier to read. Surveying the islands' religious affiliations, Beverage found that there were 125 Baptists and 30 Methodists, and a handful of people (fewer than 5) in several other unnamed denominations. A minister was employed year-to-year, and supported by voluntary subscription. About island schools he noted, "The town is divided into eight School Districts and contains about three hundred scholars from four to sixteen years of age, four hundred dollars is annually raised to support Schools." Starting in 1647, any town in Massachusetts (then including Maine) with more than 100 families had to open a grammar school to educate their children. School districts were mandated in 1789, and the total of 8 (in what area, the State of Maine? Vinalhaven and North Haven?) included those on both islands. See "Public Schooling": http://www.maine .gov/education/150yrs/150part1.htm (Retrieved June 2, 2015).

108. Thomas Waterman, *Letter concerning Vinalhaven History*, written to William D. Williamson, 1821, in the Maine Historical Society collection. https://www.maine-memory.net/artifact/20802 (Retrieved October 5, 2015).

109. George Brown Goode. *The Fisheries and Fishery Industries of the United States*. Section II. *A geographical review of the fisheries industries and fishing Communities for the year 1880.* (Washington: Government Printing Office, 1887), 60. For information on Chebacco boats, see the Essex Shipbuilding Museum: https://www .essexshipbuilding.org/the-lewis-h-story (Retrieved December 10, 2020).

110. Genealogy records contradict the December birthdate given in the *Courier-Gazette*, and suggest that Timothy was born on October 11, 1803, and married on March 27, 1828. So, he was actually 24 when they tied the knot. His wife, Susan Getchell, was born in 1806 in Lisbon Maine, and 21 at the time.

111. J. D. Hacker, "Decennial Life Tables for the White Population of the United States, 1790-1900." *Historical Methods* 43-2(2010): 45-79. doi: 10.1080/ 01615441003720449. PMID: 20563225; PMCID: PMC2885717 (Retrieved May 19, 2015). According to the author, "As discussed in more detail below, recent research indicates that earlier assumptions of long-term mortality decline are in error. Mortality increased significantly in the mid nineteenth-century United States before beginning its long-term decline."

112. Some Dyer genealogy is in the VHHS collections. Also, see the following (retrieved in May, 2015):

Timothy Dyer http://www.wikitree.com/wiki/Dyer-2519.

Susan Getchell http://www.wikitree.com/wiki/Getchell-5.

Meltzer Dyer http://www.wikitree.com/wiki/Dyer-6316; Benefits as war invalid: http://sharing.ancestry.com/6605666?h=fecb16&o_xid=61782&o_lid=61782&o_ sch=Email; Death certificate: http://sharing.ancestry.com/6605675?h=408a52&o_xid =61782&o_lid=61782&o_sch=Email.

Eliza Dyer http://www.wikitree.com/wiki/Dyer-1863. Email from VHHS states that consensus of genealogy dates seems to be a birthdate of 1831;

Daniel Dyer http://www.wikitree.com/wiki/Dyer-4544.

Susannah Dyer http://www.wikitree.com/wiki/Dyer-6398;

Freeman Dyer http://www.wikitree.com/wiki/Dyer-6059.

Hannah Jane Dyer http://www.wikitree.com/wiki/Dyer-6194;

Thomas Dyer http://www.wikitree.com/wiki/Dyer-3372.

113. Henry B. Bigelow and William C. Schroeder *Fishes of the Gulf of Maine. Fishery Bulletin 74. Fishery Bulletin of the Fish and Wildlife Service.* Volume 53. (Washington: United States Government Printing Office. 1953), 250.

114. Bigelow and Schroeder, *Fishes of the Gulf of Maine*, 250-252.

115. James Roberts, *Northeast Multispecies Fishery Management Plan Resource Guide: Atlantic Halibut (Hippoglossus hippoglossus) Bibliography* (NCRL subject guide 2018-13) 11: DOI:10.7289/V5/SG-NCRL-18-13. Maine DMR, Halibut landings: https://www.maine.gov/dmr/commercial-fishing/landings/documents/halibut.table.pdf (Retrieved March 7, 2022)

116. Kohl Kanwit, Trisha De Graaf, and Christopher Bartlett, "Biological sampling, behavior and migration study of Atlantic Halibut (Hippoglossus hippoglossus) and cusk (Brosme brosme) in the Gulf of Maine, Year 2," Final Report for the Northeast Cooperative Research Partners Program (2008), https://www.maine.gov/dmr/science-research/species/documents/08halibutcusk.pdf (Retrieved January 2, 2021).

CHAPTER 4

117. Karen Alexander, personal communication.

118. Hornsby and Judd, *Historical Atlas of Maine*, Plate 33, "Deep sea fisheries," provides "Value of Cod," "Cod Oil," and "Mackerel Landed" in Penobscot Bay and Frenchman Bay in 1850. Taken from the U.S. Department of Commerce and Labor, Bureau of the Census, Schedule 5, "Original Returns of the Assistant Marshal for Maine, Fifth Series, in *Products of Industry, Non-Population Census Records, 1850*, National Archives and Records Administration.

119. Goode, Section II, *A Geographical Review of the Fisheries*, 51–52. ftp:// ftp.library.noaa.gov/docs.lib/htdocs/rescue/oceanheritage/SH221G591884-sec2.pdf (Retrieved May 4, 2018).

120. O'Leary. *Maine Sea Fisheries,* Appendix 17, 361–362.

121. Maine Department of Marine Resources (MDMR), *A Guide to Lobstering in Maine*, produced by the under appropriation 01413A 0029 (30 July 2017), 2; https://www.maine.gov/dmr/commercial-fishing/licenses/documents/GuideToLobstering 2019.pdf (Retrieved December 10, 2020).

122. "In 1841 Capt. E. M. Oakes began to carry lobsters from Cundy's Harbor and Horse Island Harbor, Harpswell, to Mr. Eben Weeks, at East Boston. He was then running a well-smack, named the Swampscott, of 41 tons, old measurement. The season extended from the 1st of March until about the 4th of July, after which time the lobsters were supposed to be unfit for eating; the black lobsters, or shedders, were even considered poisonous." Goode, Section V, *History and Methods of the Fisheries*, Vol. II, 700–701.

123. William B. Leavenworth, personal communication.

124. Maine Bureau of Industrial and Labor Statistics, *Annual report of the Bureau of Industrial and Labor Statistics for 1900* (ARBILS), Maine State Archive, Augusta, ME, 84.

125. Edward A. Ackerman. *New England's Fishing Industry* (Chicago IL: University of Chicago Press, 1941), 95, 99.

126. Goode, Section V, *History and Methods of the Fisheries,* Vol. I, 459–461; also see Goode, Section II, *A Geographical Review of the Fisheries,* 50–51. https://books.google.com/books?id=61A5AQAAIAAJ&printsec=frontcover&dq=bibliogro up:%22The+Fisheries+and+Fishery+Industries+of+the+United+States%22&hl=en& sa=X&ei=0VSRVa6mCYW0-QHAjbaABg&ved=0CDcQ6AEwBA#v=onepage&q& f=false (Retrieved July 14, 2015).

127. Goode, Section V, *History and Methods of the Fisheries,* Vol. I, 459–60; O'Leary, Maine Sea Fisheries, 108–10.

128. Sabine, *Report on the Principal Fisheries*, 193.

129. Sabine, *Report on the Principal Fisheries*, 194; "Offing" definition from *The Compact Edition of the Oxford English Dictionary*, Vol 1, A-O (Oxford UK: Oxford University Press, 1971).

130. Goode, Section II, *A Geographical Review of the Fisheries,* 50–51.

131. David Vinal letter, Letters Notebook, VHHS collections.

132. O'Leary, *Maine Sea Fisheries,* 197–198.

133. O'Leary, *Maine Sea Fisheries,* 202–203; also, William Chilles, personal communication.

134. Mark Kurlansky, *Salt: a world history* (New York: Penguin Books, 2003), 38, 113.

135. Sabine, *Report on the Principal Fisheries,* 74.

136. Richard M. Ames. *Risky Business: A Maine village goes global. Castine souls and ships during the golden age of sail*, (Thomaston, ME: Custom Museum Publishing. 2019), 73.

137. William Vinal letter, Letters notebook. VHHS.

138. Sabine, *Report on the Principal Fisheries*, 74.

139. 1860 U.S. Census, Vinalhaven, VHHS folder. Also, see genealogy lists, VHHS collections.

140. As recently as 2008, Linda Greenlaw, the famous Isle au Haut swordfish captain featured in the book and film, *The Perfect Storm*, had her boat seized and towed into St. Johns, Newfoundland. She was briefly jailed and eventually fined $25,000 for setting a long line near the 200-mile Canadian boundary that somehow drifted – or crept – into Canadian waters. Linda Greenlaw. http://www.boattest.com/view-news/2940_linda-greenlaw-thrown-in-the-slammer-for-fishing (Retrieved April 9, 2018); https://www.npr.org/templates/transcript/transcript.php?storyId=127240614 (Retrieved April 9, 2018).

141. William Hutchinson Rowe, *The Maritime History of Maine* (New York: W.W. Norton & Co., 1948; reprinted by the Bond Wheelwright Company, n.d.), 269.

142. Tonnage of the Magnolia, from Applebee, Sailing Vessels of Vinalhaven, Maine, unpaginated.

143. In "1839 there were some seventy-five sail of fishermen owned in the town of Vinalhaven. They were mostly small craft, from twenty to thirty tons, what was termed the pinky fleet." Laurie Fullerton, *Boatbuilding with Burnham* blog entry, "What is a Pinky Schooner Exactly?" September 12, 2010. http://boatbuilding withburnham.blogspot.com/2010/09/what-is-pinky-schooner-exactly.html (Retrieved August 31, 2015). Rowe (Maritime History of Maine, 271–272) says that "the pinky – a development of the Chebacco boat – came into use along the Maine coast sometime before 1820. Until 1840 it held the field against all others. They were of all sizes from 20 to 80 tons. The hull was very full forward, very sharp aft, deep and of good breadth. Thus, in heavy weather they could scud or work to windward, and in heavy seas they rode easily at anchor. Theirs was a simple schooner rig. The bowsprit was laid very high so that when lying at anchor with a long scope of cable the tremendous seas would not throw the cable over it. The timbers were gathered in at the stern, carried well abaft the sternpost, and brought to a point like those of a whaleboat." William B. Leavenworth, in personal communication, provided additional information.

144. An earlier (1819 or 1820) chase in Nova Scotian territory had a more dramatic outcome. This article about Captain John Lindsey is in the Newspapers Notebook, VHHS collections:

A pinkey owned by two Isle au Haut brothers, Captain James Turner and John Turner, trespassed for a load of bait. Their 34-ton schooner *Eight Sisters*, built on Vinalhaven in 1816, carried a fishing crew from the island. The armed brig *Burlett* surprised them one morning while they were pilfering near-shore. "Among those taken were Capt. Turner in the good pinkey *Eight Sisters*, together with several Vinalhaven fishermen." In order to secure their prize, the provincial authorities took the crew off the boat, and left only Captain Turner on board along with two Canadian sailors and the officer in charge, the "prize-master". Since they were three and he was one, and they were armed and he wasn't, the Captain was allowed free movement as they sailed toward Halifax.

Eventually dark descended. The night was foggy. You couldn't see from the bow of the schooner to the stern. When the prize master went to sleep, "Capt. Turner thought now was his chance, and accordingly closed the slide to the gangway, putting in the after shutter and securing the whole by shoving an oar under the windlass on top the slide, which made all secure and the prize-master was a prisoner below, sound asleep.

"The prize-master, before going below had laid his cutlass and musket down beside the gangway on the cable-tier. Capt. Turner after finding the prize-master all secure, armed himself with what arms he wanted, threw the rest overboard and then walked aft and ordered the man at the helm to keep her off N.W. and stick out the main sheet, which he did rather reluctantly." Turner locked the other crewman in the salt room and sailed into Machias, Maine, where he released his imprisoned imprisoners, then returned home with his cargo of fish. (article from the *Vinalhaven Messenger,* March 20, 1885: 2; information about the *Eight Sisters* from Applebee, Sailing Vessels of Vinalhaven, Maine, unpaginated)

145. John Carver letter to David Vinal, June 24, 1846. Letters folder, VHHS collections. According to Applebee, Sailing Vessels of Vinalhaven, Maine, the *Rival* was owned by Timothy Lane.

146. Cynthia Burns Martin, *Images of America. Vinalhaven Island's Maritime Industries* (Mount Pleasant SC: Arcadia Publishing, 2015), 21; O'Leary, *Maine Sea Fisheries*, 217; William B. Leavenworth, personal communication. The Lindseys were Mayflower descendants of William Brewster. Plymouth roots: http://mv.ances try.com/viewer/b71afeed-897b-4855-91c2-537f2f705038/4729181/-1060274988 (Retrieved October 15, 2015).

147. O'Leary, *Maine Sea Fisheries,* 127.

148. Manuscripts 1 and 2, Letters folder, V*HHS* collections. David Lane Carver was born on Vinalhaven in 1822, but he moved up the Bay to Bucksport as an adult. Between voyages, Bucksport was his home base for several decades. He was married to Jane Calderwood (Ginn) Carver. By 1880 they had returned to live on the island.

149. Hornsby and Judd, *Historical Atlas of Maine*. Part II, Plate 32; Applebee. *Sailing Vessels of Vinalhaven, Maine.*

150. Hornsby and Judd, *Historical Atlas of Maine*. Part II, "Shaping Maine"; O'Leary, *Maine Sea Fisheries*, 36, 37, 131; William B. Leavenworth, personal communication.

151. Letter from Reuben Carver to Capt. J Carver, Feb 29, 1848, "Manuscripts 1 and 2," Letters folder, VHHS collections. Hannah Carver, Reuben's wife, died in 1856 at age 58, apparently thrown from a carriage.

152. William W. Warner, *Distant Water: The Fate of the North Atlantic Fisherman* (New York: Penguin Books, 1977 [1983]), 160.

153. Log of the schooner *Two Brothers* in 1830, Matt Calderwood master; archival collections of the Penobscot Marine Museum, Searsport ME.

154. Karen Alexander and William B. Leavenworth, personal communication.

155. This log – hereafter Log of the *Flying Arrow*, Carver master, 1852 – turned up in a house owned by the Carvers amidst other family papers. No name of a captain or a vessel is written on the pages themselves. From its content, we know that they sailed from Vinalhaven and returned there, which is the critical information for our purposes now. The log was briefly lent to VHHS and copied for the collection. Names of the captain and vessel came from the log of the Beverly schooner *Petrel,* Calvin Foster master, in the National Archives and Records Administration, Waltham MA, RG36 (Log - Box 81: F512a; Fishing agreement - Box 9: F1852 [2]). In their research on

the historical New England cod fishery, Alexander and Leavenworth discovered and copied some of the Beverly logs. Among them, serendipitously, was that of the *Petrel*.

156. W. Jeffrey Bolster, Karen E. Alexander, and William B. Leavenworth, "The historical abundance of cod on the Nova Scotian shelf." in Jeremy B.C. Jackson, Karen E. Alexander, Enric Sala (eds) *Shifting Baselines: The past and the future of ocean fisheries* (Washington: Island Press. 2011), 89.

157. Bill Leavenworth, personal communication.

158. Rowe, *The Maritime History of Maine*, 273.

159. Bolster, Alexander and Leavenworth, "Historical Abundance of cod on the Scotian Shelf", 97, 35.

160. Goode, Section V, *History and Methods of the Fisheries,* Vol. I, 128. "watch on watch" fishing. https://books.google.com/books?id=61A5AQAAIAAJ&printsec=frontcover&dq=bibliogroup:%22The+Fisheries+and+Fishery+Industries+of+the+United+States%22&hl=en&sa=X&ei=0VSRVa6mCYW0-QHAjbaABg&ved=0CDcQ6AEwBA#v=onepage&q&f=false (Retrieved July 14, 2015).

161. Rowe, *The Maritime History of Maine*, 274.

162. L. J. Webster and M.A. Noah. *Letters Home from Sea*, 83.

163. Log of the *Flying Arrow,* Carver master, 1852.

164. Bolster, Alexander and Leavenworth, "Historical Abundance of Cod on the Scotian Shelf", 96, 100. Also, see O'Leary, Maine Sea Fisheries, 161: "The 33,000 cod taken on Quereau Bank off Nova Scotia in 1851 by the Vinalhaven schooner *Mirror* was the largest catch recorded on that ground by a Maine fishing vessel during the deck-fishing era.

165. Log of the *Flying Arrow,* Carver master, 1852.

166. Log of the *Petrel,* Calvin Foster master, 1852.

167. Log of the *Flying Arrow,* Carver master, 1852.

168. Bolster, Alexander and Leavenworth show that, by 1860, fishermen were already trying a new way to fish that put more hooks in the water to catch the same number of fish. Dory fishing was more dangerous. Stories abound of fishermen forced to row for days to save themselves after a fog, sudden storm or other misfortune separated them from their schooner ("Historical Abundance of Cod on the Scotian Shelf", 100).

169. Andrew A. Rosenberg, W, Jeffrey Bolster, Karen E. Alexander, William B. Leavenworth and Matthew G McKenzie, "The History of Ocean Resources: Modeling cod biomass using historical records," *Frontiers in Ecology and the Environment* 3.2 (2005): 78-84.

170. Bolster. *The Mortal Sea*. Caption to the photo, "Fish drying at the Cranberry Isles, Maine" ca. 1900" by Fred Morse, unpaged illustrated section between pages 120 and 121.

171. James Roberts' Ledger, VHHS collections.

172. *The Limerick Gazette*, Rockland ME, 12 March 1846: 2. The article goes on to state that: "More than 1500 barrels of mackerel were taken by these vessels under mackerel papers, after their four months of cod-fishing had expired, and about 1400 barrels were packed here. The value of these amounted to $10,000 and were shipped to New Orleans and other ports in the country. A vast quantity of cod and other fish

are brought in, made, and shipped to other ports and sold. The vessels employed in the fishing business are from 20 to 75 tons, the large vessels being mostly bankers. All vessels employed in the fishing business, and who perform what is required by law are entitled to a bounty of about $4 per ton, payable on the first of January, at the custom house."

173. *Democrat and Free Press*, Rockland ME, 16 November 1859: 2. In 1846, Vinalhaven and North Haven had separated. Nine school districts were spread across the two islands.

174. The 1850 Census counted 13,123 mariners in the state of Maine, of whom a modest 28 lived on Vinalhaven. But of the state's 2,192 fishermen, 198 – about 9% – called Vinalhaven their home. Only two boys in the island's 10–16 cohort were sons of mariners, who tended to have smaller families. Perhaps mariners were at sea even more than fishermen. US Census 1850a-05.pdf, p.11 http://www.agcensus.usda .gov/Publications/Historical_Publications/1850/1850a-05.pdf (Retrieved October 13, 2015).

175. Letters Notebook, VHHS collections. The date of 1874 could be off by a year.

176. Applebee, Sailing Vessels of Vinalhaven, Maine, unpaginated.

177. Karen Alexander and William B Leavenworth, unpublished data.

178. *Democrat and Free Press*, 16 November 1859: 2. The presence of the factory reminds us that although cod was the money-maker, already by mid-century lobsters were beginning to join the ranks of income-producing species on the island, although not until the 1870s did Vinalhaven fisherman fished them in earnest. Gathered by hand along shore, or netted, and delivered to markets in Boston and New York as early as the 1820s, lobster fishing along the Maine coast picked up around 1840. By 1842 there was a cannery at Eastport. Maine was the only state that canned lobster. About half of what they canned was exported to Europe and the rest went to the US south and west. Goode Section V, *History and Methods of the Fisheries,* Vol. II, 687, 700. For canning history, see, "Lobster Fishing in Maine," Penobscot Marine Museum, http://penobscotmarinemuseum.org/pbho-1/fisheries/lobster-fishing-maine (Retrieved Oct. 6, 2015).

179. Letter by Charlotte Ginn Carver (McDonald) to her father, John Carver. Manuscripts Vol. 1 and 2, VHHS colections.

180. Rowe, *Maritime History of Maine*, 227.

181. Vinal, *Brief Historical Sketch*, 44. Also, "The Lane Family" pdf, VHHS collections. To appreciate Timothy's island roots, we need to go back, once again, to Ebenezer Hall Jr, who returned in 1763 to Matinicus, the site of his own father's violent death. You might recall that Ebenezer Jr. and his wife, Susannah Young, had fifteen children. When Timothy's father, Benjamin Lane (1762–1842) and his uncle Issachar Lane (1760–?), settled on Vinalhaven in the 1780s, each married one of Ebenezer's daughters. Their brother, Joseph Lane, arrived soon after. Benjamin Lane and Margaret Hall (1769–1849) gave birth to seven children, including Timothy (1805–1871) and his older brothers, Benjamin jr. (b. 1791) and Joseph (1800–1871).

182. Everyone on Vinalhaven goes by nicknames, and now I begin to understand why! They are crucial to distinguishing multiple family members with the same given name. As the generations became clearer, I was struck by how Benjamin and

Margaret's children intermarried with a few island families. Three of their seven off-spring, Margaret, James and Timothy married three members of the Smith family—Margaret married David Smith. Her brothers married the cousins Lydia and Rebecca Smith, both nieces of David's. In other words, David's two nieces became his sisters-in-law as well. Meanwhile, brothers John and Joseph Lane married two Arey cousins, Rebecca and Abigail, both granddaughters of Isaac and Mary Crosby Arey. To braid matters a bit more, Abigail Arey's mother and Lydia Smith's mother were sisters, so Lydia and Abigail were also double-linked as cousins and sisters-in-law. Elizabeth Bunker, personal communication, October 16, 2015.

183. Emily Lane was married at one time to the last male Lane, Timothy, who lived on the island. She still lives part time on Vinalhaven and works in Portland as a lobster-marketing consultant. During the 1980s she was involved in managing Vinalhaven fish factories. Interview with Emily Lane, August 8, 2012.

184. Vinal, *Brief Historical Sketch*, 44. Also, U.S. Census, Vinalhaven, 1860.

185. *Democrat and Free Press*, 16 November 1859: 2, "The average amount per quintal received for these, has been about $3,50, making them bring $14,000. He has also eighty barrels of oil worth $14,00 per barrel, which will amount to $1120; six hundred and fifty barrels of Mackerel worth $10,00 per barrel, amounting in the aggregate to $6500; and halibut and other pickled fish to the amount of $500."

186. Already in the 1860s, you can begin to see the money being made from granite. Of the second six wealthiest men—there was a tie—two were stone contractors. Luther Calderwood, the island miller, has done well, and a fisherman, Nathaniel Ames, ties for 10th with John Carver, the farmer son of the original settlers Thaddeus Carver and Hannah Hall: 6th Moses Webster, granite contractor, $7825; 7th William Burgess, merchant, $7500; 8th Josep Kitredge, stone contractor, $6700; 9th Luther Calderwood, millman, $5900; 10th (tied) John Carver, farmer, and Nathaniel Ames master fisherman, $5000).

The 1860 Census looks at labor costs by industry and county. In Knox County in 1860, the average fisherman earned about $97 dollars a year. For comparison, a skilled ship builder earned about $600. A shoemaker earned $160. Since the fisherman worked on a share system, it's hard to know how the census calculated the figure – and who was included in the number. For the 2017 worth of real and personal estate value, see *Measuring Worth* https://www.measuringworth.com/index.php (Retrieved May 7, 2018).

Of the six wealthiest fishermen, four were master fishermen who captained vessels. They earned a larger share of the total take and sometimes owned part or all of their vessels: 1st Nathaniel Ames, 59, master fisherman, $5000; 2nd Martin Hopkins, 47, master fisherman, $3000; 3rd Jeremiah H. Buckmaster, 37, master fisherman, $2200; 4th James Carver 50, master fisherman, and Anthony Smith, 51, fisherman, tied with $2000; 5th James Ginn, 65, fisherman, $1800. While I don't have direct evidence, judging from their relationship to early settlers who owned significant land, one hypothesis would be that other two fishermen on this list inherited their basic wealth. U.S. Census 1860c-08 pdf.

187. *Democrat and Free Press*, 16 November 1859" 2.

188. Carver Folder, VHHS collections.

189. Undated note, Carver Folder, VHHS collections.

190. Calvin Arey, "Vinalhaven in the Civil War: the 19th Maine Regiment." *VHHS Annual Newsletter*, 2004: 3, in the VHHS collections.

The Civil War, and the islander's generous service did not change its long tradition of avoiding regulations they didn't like - in this case by illegally collecting the cod bounty and smuggling goods. During the war, Captain John Carver worked as the islands "Accountant of Revenues" a job salaried by the state. In a letter marked "Private" sent on June 20, 1863, the Belfast Custom House agent is trying to prevent fishing vessels from claiming a bounty on fish other than cod, and without proof of their salt expenditures (evidence they must offer to get the bounty). He urges Captain Carver to keep an eye out for fraud and to keep his work secret. (Customs agents and tax collectors were used to being very unpopular.)

"Please ascertain where the vessels get their salt, and how much they take, & the amount they ought to have. Also whether any of them fish for Mackerel or pogie's under Cod Licenses, &c, &c. The vessels belonging to your Island and N. Haven are generally of a good class, & fish well, but if they are they won't suffer by being looked after. Please not make it known what your instructions are, or what you do. Yours truly W. E. Frye"

In 1864, Carver boarded at least one island vessel looking for foreign contraband imported without paying the Customs duty. In July 1865, "Stephen Delano of Old Harbor" went to trial for hiding goods so as to "defraud the Revenue of the United States." It seems that several men were smuggling "goods" and storing them in warehouses on nearby Green Island.

CHAPTER 5

191. Merchant/Marchant Letters, VHHS collections. Andrew mentions in letters that his mother is living on the island, but the census shows no older "Merchants" or "Marchants," Andrew's father, John, was born on Deer Isle. His mother was born on Vinalhaven to Thomas Brown and Mary Hopkins. In 1850, the Garret's son, Sarah's uncle, Thomas, was also living on Vinalhaven, married and working as a fisherman.

192. William Leavenworth explained the fine points of reefing in personal communication.

193. Reiss, *From the Beginning: Vinalhaven from 1760 – 1850,* 101.

194. This would be either Anthony Coombs Sr. and son James (b.1779), or Anthony Coombs Jr (1781 –d. 1846?) and his brother James. Anthony Sr. and his wife had fourteen children.

195. Goode, Section V, *History and Methods of the Fisheries*, Vol. I, 247.

196. Webster and Noah, *Letters Home from Sea,* 45.

197. Goode, Section V, *History and Methods of the Fisheries*, Vol. I, 255.

198. O'Leary, *Maine Sea Fisheries*, 160; Goode, Section V, *History and Methods of the Fisheries*, Vol. I, 250–54. The *Belfast Republican Journal*, in the Penobscot

Marine Museum Library, contains a wealth of information about Penobscot Bay fisheries,

199. Sabine, *Report on the Principal Fisheries*, 183-184.

200. William B. Leavenworth, personal communication.

201. Sabine, *Report on the Principal Fisheries,* 181. Goode, Section V, *History and Methods of the Fisheries*, Vol. I, 267.

202. Sabine, *Report on the Principal Fisheries*, 181-184.

203. Karen Alexander and William B. Leavenworth, unpublished results.

204. Webster and Noah, *Letters Home from Sea,* 25, 26.

205. Webster and Noah, *Letters Home from Sea,* 129.

206. Bolster, *The Mortal Sea*, Chapter 5, 169-222.

207. Andrew Marchant's Civil War registration records. interactive.ancestry.com (Retrieved November 17, 2015).

CHAPTER 6

208. *Rockland Gazette,* 9 November 1876: 2, 31. After the Civil War, additional local newspapers appeared to report on events in southwest Penobscot Bay. Three short-lived weeklies appeared on Vinalhaven in the 1880s. According to Sue Radley and Elizabeth Bunker (*Horse Nets, Holliwoggers, & Littlefield Blue and everything you need to know about Vinalhaven* [Lebanon, NH: R.C. Brayshaw & Co., 2015], 125), *The Wind* started up in 1884, *The Messenger* printed 25 issues before closing in 1885, and *The Vinalhaven Echo* began in 1887 and ran for 14 months. The only extant copies are those that someone on the island thought to save. Still, their tidbits of fishing news offer a feel for the way mostly small catches of fish added up to create a local economy. *The Rockland Gazette* appeared between 1851-1881, followed by *The Courier-Gazette* in 1882.

209. *The Vinalhaven Echo*, 22 December 1887: 3.

210. *Rockland Gazette*, 23 November 1876: 2; *The Vinalhaven Echo*, 26 April 1888.

211. Maine Memory Network, "1870-1920: The End of the Ocean Highway", *Maine History Online* http://www.mainememory.net/sitebuilder/site/905/page/1316/ display (Retrieved October 15, 2020).

212. Sarah Orne Jewett, *Country of the Pointed Firs* (New York: Signet Classics, Penguin Books, Kindle edition, [1896] 2009), 18.

213. O'Leary, *Maine Sea Fisheries*, 141-149.

214. William B. Leavenworth, person communication.

215. O'Leary, *Maine Sea Fisheries*, 150.

216. Overall, in 1880 Maine had 8,110 men directly employed in the fishery and another 2961 people on shore processing and marketing fish products. This was the fourth largest number of people among the 29 fishing states. Goode, Section II, *A Geographical Review of the Fisheries,* 50, vi.

217. For the prices of lobster, see Kenneth B. Martin and Nathan R. Lipfert, *Lobstering and the Maine Coast* (Bath ME: Maine Maritime Museum, 1985), 77. The

increased population, and the quarry work particularly, also sustained island farmers, as Jeannette Lasansky has documented in her book, *Island Saltwater Farms: Farming on Vinalhaven 1820 – 1960* (Vinalhaven, ME: Vinalhaven Historical Society, 2006), 6, 11. "[I]n 1870, 114 heads of Vinalhaven Island households defined themselves as farmers. . . [T]heir land holdings varied widely: from 6–300 acres." Some farmed to feed their families; some raised produce, meat, eggs and milk for market. A number of them, in keeping with the old coastal New England farmer/fishermen template, sometimes fished locally or had been to sea in their youth before settling down to farm. As an example, two grandsons, Martin N. and George, of the early settler Dr. Theophilus Hopkins, "were farmers on Hopkins' Point though both were tied to a trade on water first: fisherman and "shore man" respectively." Their transition from water to land may have related to the post- Civil War changes in the markets for fish.

218. O'Leary, *Maine Sea Fisheries,* 149-157.

219. Goode, Section II, *A Geographical Review of the Fisheries,* 50-51. Goode devoted himself to many projects, each one vast enough to consume a lifetime. He studied fish and wrote papers about them. He also helped found and run two museums, and he organized and managed aspects of several international expositions. He was part of a generation that helped establish a more scientific approach to studying the natural world. See Samuel Pierpont Langley, *Memoir of George Brown Goode, 1851-1896*. Read Before the National Academy, April 21, 1897. https://books.google .com (Retrieved October 19, 2020).

220. Goode, Section II, *A Geographical Review of the Fisheries,* 50-51. Information on Friendship sloops from William Leavenworth, personal communication.

221. Winslow. *Fish Scales,* 21–45.

222. Goode, Section II, *A Geographical Review of the Fisheries,* 51. Despite the trend, some Vinalhaven captains still invested in new vessels: "Mr. Aaron Smith, One of our enterprising young men has arrived from Gloucester with his new vessel, the Cora E. Smith. She is a splendid vessel, about 90 tons . . . Capt. Smith intends to go south on a seining trip," reads a Vinalhaven note in the April 20, 1876, *Rockland Gazette.* The *Cora E. Smith* stands out for size and ambition. There are two Aaron Smiths in that era on the island. The more likely one was born on Vinalhaven around 1845 but was living on North Haven by 1860. In that case, he may just have been in Carver's Harbor for a brief stop to visit family and friends on his way to seine mackerel.

223. *Rockland Gazette,* 24 October 1878: 2.

224. Alphonsus Rukevwe Isara, Vincent Yakubu Adam, Adesuwa Queen Aigbokhaode, et al., "Respiratory symptoms and ventilatory functions among quarry workers in Edo state, Nigeria", *The Pan African Medical Journal* 23 (2016): 212; doi: 10.11604/pamj.2016.23.212.7640

225. *Rockland Gazette,* 9 November 1876: 2.

226. Associated Press, "St. John Divine columns got their start in Maine" 20 December 2001, updated 16 December 2010. https://www.seacoastonline.com/ article/20011220/NEWS/312209982 (Retrieved January 2, 2020).

227. *ARBILS* for 1892: 198.

228. *Maine Memory Network*, "Extracting Wealth," https://www.mainememory
.net/sitebuilder/site/823/slideshow/439/display?use_mmn=&format=list&slide_
num=1 (Retrieved October 19, 2020).

229. "One vessel, the Black Swan, made two trips to George's in the winter of
1861-'62, after which the business was abandoned on account of the danger attending
the work." Goode, Section II, *A Geographical Review of the Fisheries,* 50-51.

230. Letter in the *The Vinalhaven Messenger,* 3 April 1885.

231. Lane-Libby installed a cold storage building in the first decade of the 20th
century. But occasionally, as in this February 1876 notice, frigid weather happily did
the preserving: The Vinalhaven fishermen, "Capt. James Beggs arrived from a trip to
Grand Manan, with a load of frozen fish." *Rockland Gazette*, 17 February 1876: 3.
Also see *ARBILS* for 1910: 23.

232. *Rockland Gazette*, 22 November 1877: 2. (The fish plant was initially
referred to in 1878 as Lane & Libby, then, in 1895 was incorporated as Vinalhaven
Fish Company in in 1908 became Lane-Libby Fisheries. Co.)

233. *The Wind.* "Our Industries." Undated, likely 1884-5.

234. *The Vinalhaven Echo.* 9 August 1888: 1.

235. Goode, Section II, A Geographical Review of the Fisheries, 52.

236. *The Wind.* "Our Industries"; Warner, *Distant Water*, 39.

237. O'Leary, *Maine Sea Fisheries*, 193; *ARBILS* for 1910: 23; *The Wind*, 26
January 1894.

238. Letters folder, VHHS collections.

239. Undated newspaper clipping in the VHHS Archive, probably from the *Rockland Gazette,* reprinting a piece from the *Gloucester Daily Times*, ca. 1895.

Fish Factories on Vinalhaven – a partial chronology courtesy of research by Sydney Winslow, Karen Roberts Jackson, "Larry Gould" and others all found in the archives of the
Vinalhaven Historical Society.

1847 – First lobster canning Johnson and Hamlin of Boston. After a few years succeeded
by Rice and Carker of Boston, and then by Wells and Prevost of New York.

1866 (or thereabouts) – Schenck and Romaine of NY erected a large factory on the Reach.
They were succeeded by U.H. Dudley of New York and later by J.W. Jones of Portland
(Maine). The building was razed in 1887.

1873 – Canned lobsters – J.W. Jones & Co.

1878 – Thomas G. Libby and his father-in-law, Edwin Lane, establish – Lane & Libby, in
1872 - first as a general store, and then expanding it in 1878 to include the Vinalhaven Fish
Co. The Fish Company would become the biggest fish processing plant in New England
and one of the biggest in the country.

1879 – F.M.Brown on Sand Cove buying and curing fish – extensive business for several
years.

1881 – H.V. Lane, J.H. Sanborn and F.S. Walls formed a partnership and started curing fish on Lane's Island. 6 to 8 thousand quintals each year until 1885 when they stopped.

1884 – Johnson and Young constructed large lobster pound in the Basin.
   vol. 1. #14 April 5, 1884, The Wind.

p. 1 Fish Canning. The indications now point to a lively season in the canning business. The old lobster factory at the Reach will soon be in running order, and it is expected that a considerable increase of business over last year will be done. Lyford & Ginn have a crew of men at work on the foundation for their new factory. They expect to be ready for business about the 1st of July. This will be a very extensive establishment and when completed will add greatly to the business and wealth of Vinalhaven.

R.T. Carver, who has been operating somewhat in fish for several years past, has been fitting up quite extensively for the canning of lobsters and mackerel and is now ready for business. Mr. C. has on hand 10,000 cans and has also engaged competent help, and we have no doubt will conduct a very successful business. The above firm will be styled the Carver Canning Co., and as we are bound to encourage home industry, we express our good wishes by hoping that our fishermen will be liberal in their supply, rather than to sell to out-of-town parties. "

Late 1880s "During the latter part of the 1880's J.H. Sanborn and R.T. Carver were numbered among the local lobster dealers buying large quantities which they shipped to Boston.

1889 - Jos. Knight canned lobsters.

1903 - "The Vinalhaven Fish Co." (Lane & Libby) had the largest amount of business of any year – handling between seven and eight million pounds of fish. (Employed about 100 people in the factory and about 200 more fishing)
   Vinalhaven Glue Company – organized in 1903 by Lane & Libby – Short-lived because no one on the island could stand the smell!

1910 – Lane - Libby build a cold storage plant on Vinalhaven. It is capable of making 5 tons of ice a day, freezing herring, and bait.

1917 – H.F. Sawyer & Son built a building and opened a sardine factory. Small-time, but operated on and off for 10 years.

1921 – C.F. Grimes started operating a fish plant dealing in fresh and salt fish.

1925 – Vinalhaven Fish Company starts freezing fish filets.

1927 – What had been Vinalhaven Fish Company closed and in 1929 became "Libby-Burchell Co.", but after a short period it also closed.
   After LB closed, Bay State Fisheries bought the property, and General Sea Foods opened. It discontinued business in 1940 and buildings were mostly torn down.

1943 – Ralph Barter of Stonington leased part of the wharf formerly occupied by Sawyer Sardine and built a building for a fish cannery. 1944 it was sold to Burnham & Morrill

Co. (Burnham & Morrill produced fish flakes from cod and hake. Employed 36 people, half of whom were women.)

Mid-1940s – R.J. Bickford & Son and Arthur B. Arey are the lobster dealing concerns of Vinalhaven under local management.

1948 – Vinalhaven Fisheries, Inc. – Article by "Larry Gould" in November 1950 names Eddie Bonacorso as superintendent of the plant. Article says that he has been successfully experimenting with producing dried salt hake. "The dried fish are boned, stripped and packed in 40 pound wooden boxes. These are packed for Murphy and Aschon of Baltimore, Md., and sold throughout the South.

1952 – Burnham & Morrill leased the plant of Vinalhaven Fisheries, Inc.

"Larry" Gould : Inshore Draggers Keep Vinalhaven Plant Busy
April 1952

Four boats were unloading at the wharf one day recently, and two had just preceded them, and two more were due. The four were Norland, Portland, Skipper Robert Dow; Myrt II, Owls Head, Skipper Erwin Grover; Onward II, Portland, Skipper Lewis Alexander; and the Li-Lo, Rockland, skippered by Veli Holstrom, a local man. Other boats that had just unloaded or were due were the Marie H., Port Clyde, Levi Hupper Kipper; the Little Growler, Owls Head: the Elin B., Stonington. Jack Billings, skipper; and the two Vinalhaven draggers; the Dorothy M. owned and skippered by Clarence Bennett, and the Dora and Peter, with Skipper Ira Tupper.

Landings and prices around the first of March were running something like this: an average of 2,000 pounds for inshore fishing by boats like the Dorothy M., docking daily; around 15,000 for boats like the Dora and Peter, landing once a week; 15,000 redfish, 12,000 groundfish for larger boats like the Rhode Island; or 20,000 redfish and 5,000 groundfish for the Elin B. Prices averaged: haddock, 10 to 14 cents; black backs, 12 – 16 cents; redfish, 4½ cents; Pollock, six cents; hake six cents; gray soles, nine cents; dabs, seven cents; cod, eight cents.

1963-4 – Burnham & Morrill shut down the fish processing plant. "Lack of fish and shortage of workers." Unsourced and undated article, "Vinalhaven has little industry beyond lobstering. The town has another canning factory, a bait freezing plant and boat repair and building facilities. During the busy part of the season the B&M plant employs 50 to 55 people. The season runs from five to six months." Another unsourced article says that the plant closed in October, and that the cause was a shortage of hake. Even with fishermen from Stonington adding to the supply, there were not enough.

1955 – New Fish Plant
    Vinalhaven Fisheries expects to have 40 year –'round employees and up to 100 at the season's height. Purchases should be around a million pounds of fish a day giving local fishermen a daily market whereas now they can sell locally only certain days of the week.

1976 - Thursday September 9, 1976 – [newspaper unknown]
    Finfish Era Passes at Vinalhaven

Citing a variety of reasons, the manager of Vinalhaven's largest seafood company has stopped buying, processing, and shipping finned fish. A native and lifetime resident of the island, Clyde Bickford built up the business over a long period of time, eventually selling out to Bay State Lobster Co. of Boston, but retaining management of the Vinalhaven operation

Bickford has always dealt primarily on lobsters, but in 1951 started buying finned fish "more or less to fill in during seasons when lobstering was slow." This allowed fishermen to expand their operations and add to their incomes by going after a variety of species, herring, hake, haddock, cod and others for example. Some were shipped fresh, and some were salted in barrels and later dried in the sun.

Now Bickford says, "The market has outpriced itself. The price on the other end hasn't changed in years but expenses have doubled."

Conflicting governmental regulations contributed to Bickford's decision too. Since fishermen more often than not deliver their catches outside of what rules and laws consider "normal" working hours, much of the processing is done late at night and on weekends and holidays. State labor officials ruled that regular wages rather than overtime could be paid, but on a federal level this decision was reversed. The result was the Bickford had to pay thousands of dollars in back overtime to his employees, as well as continue at the higher rate.

Other costs have skyrocketed, the price of equipment, shipping rates (particularly from the island) etc. The result was that Bickford was unable to pay the same prices to fishermen that they could get from mainland buyers, so a steady supply of fish was not delivered. Bickford is philosophical about this, saying he would do the same thing if he were a fisherman, but as a businessman he could not increase what he paid.

"I won't say I won't ever buy fish again, but right now it doesn't look good," Bickford says. He continues with lobsters, clams and scallops where the market remains profitable, but after the last fish now salted in barrels at the fish plant is dried in the sun, crated and shipped, there will be no more.

Rockland Maine newspaper Tuesday April 28, 1981
First Landing reported at Island co-op

Vinalhaven - Almost two years after a committee was formed to re-establish the fishing industry on Vinalhaven, the first large load of groundfish was sold Thursday to the island's cooperative fish plant.

Many islanders gathered along the docks to watch as four local fishermen, William Wadleigh, James Poole, Spencer Fuller, and Frank Thompson, brought in a total 15,000 lbs of Pollock, cusk and haddock to Vinalhaven Seafoods Inc. to be resold to the Boston market. Seven local men are employed by the plant at the docks to unload, weigh, salt and repack in ice the fish for the trip to Boston.

The four boats arrived at the Vinalhaven dock Thursday after spending all night dragging for the groundfish.

Some fishermen had tried to sell their fish earlier last week but learned that the Vinalhaven plant can only accept gilled fish, those whose gills have been removed. The plant does not have its gill-removing equipment in place yet, so fishermen must do the processing on board before selling the fish. Plant manager Walter Lippincott explained that the gills retain blood which would enter the body of the fish during the trip to Boston, making the fish less valuable at market.

The fishermen are optimistic about the possibility of selling their fish at home in Vinalhaven instead of making the trip to Rockland and back after a long night of fishing. Wadleigh said Thursday that it will be good to not have to go all the way to Rockland before returning home after a fishing trip.

Lippincott, who was hired earlier this year to be manager of the plant said that within the next few weeks the entire plant will be in business, with the fish being processed, frozen and packed in Vinalhaven. Some of the machinery is in the plant, but, according to Lippincott, cannot be set up until the construction crew finishes its work on changes to the building.

Lippincott said the construction should be completed by the end of next week and clean up work can begin to ready the building for processing fish.

It all began in mid-1979 when Vinalhaven selectman established a Harbor Development Panel to discuss bringing back a fishing industry. With the help of several agencies, the Maine Bond Bank, the Economic Development Administration, Producer's co-op f Vinalhaven, Penosbcot Bay Fish and cold Storage Co. which leased the plant to the Nickerson Co., the Farmer's Home Administration and Governor Joseph Brennan's office, an outlet has been established for local fishermen.

Before construction was complete the H.B. Nickerson Col, of North Sydney, Nova Scotia, leased the local plant, giving Vinalhaven fishermen a world wide market for their catches.

Undated – probably 1983 – Fish co-op: island success
By Jeff Nims – coastal bureau

Vinalhaven – These are hard economic times in most communities but the Vinalhaven economy has experienced steady improvement in the past two years due to growth of its fishing industry.

At one time, dozens of boats supplied fish to the old B&M fish plant, but when that operation shut down two decades ago, many thought it was the end of the fishing industry here. Boats which were groundfishing switched to lobstering. The few boats which continued fishing for herring or groundfish sold their catch in Rockland for lack of a local market.

Today a million-dollar, town-owned fish plant employs 91 people when running at full capacity. The fish plant was so busy last summer it sent a recruiter to the high school to find students who could work the second shift.

The Penobscot Bay Fish and cold Storage Co., a local cooperative lease the facility from the town in an arrangement established prior to construction. The co-op got off to a rocky start when a joint arrangement with the H.G. Nickerson Co. of Nova Scotia failed after the first summer of operation. Nickerson announced that it was withdrawing from the arrangement because of the lack of fish, but members of the local co-op voted to operate the plant alone and to continue operations through the winter. Although the operation was scaled down during the winter months, the co-op succeeded and now has been operating for 19 months.

General Manager Spencer Fuller has been a strong advocate of diversification. The fish plant began processing crabmeat in addition to groundfish and herring. This winter, the plant has been buying scallops and some shrimp. Up to 20 people have been employed a few days out of each week.

Local boats travel farther during the winter to keep the fish plant supplied. Two boats have been catching herring off Sandwich, Mass., this winter and shipping the product back to the fish plant by truck. Another boat is heading to the boothbay area to do the same.

Products from the fish plant have been shipped as far as Japan. Last fall, the fish plant supplied 300,000 pounds of herring in a joint venture with the Boothbay fishermen's cooperative.

The Penobscot Bay Fish and Cold Storage Co. is succeeding where others have failed and that success may be partly due to a willingness to diversify. At one time there was skepticism on this island about the fish plant. That skepticism has been transformed to enthusiasm as the local economy enjoys the benefits of a prosperous fishing industry and increased employment.

1980 – 1989 – Penobscot ("Pen") Bay Fish and Cold Storage – employed between 30 and 50 island residents. –"Emily Lane, president of the cooperative, took over management of the fish plant in July after former manager Spencer Fuller left to concentrate his efforts on his own company Resource Trading Co. Fuller has an agreement with the cooperative to process shrimp, herring, and squid, which he markets nationally and internationally." Lane's effort was one to save local jobs - - 30 to 50 people. Plant owed hundreds of thousands of dollars to investors. "During 1988, the plant was paid 8 ½ cents per pound for herring, which was frozen whole and prepared as feed for zoos through the country; 8 ½ to 11 cents for squid; 75 cents for shrimp; and 15 cents for scallops." "Penobscot Bay Fish and cold Storage struggles for survival"-byline – Ted Sylvester – Midcoast Bureau. Bangor Daily News, Friday December 2, 1988. P. 10, 11.

1990 F.I.S.H. (Fox Islands Seafood Handlers)— reopened Pen Bay, got a block grant, and tried to make a go of it marketing groundfish, dogfish, mussels, crabs, herring and sea urchins." (Didn't have enough operating capital, so by 1992 were leasing from Claw Island – as a subsidy.)

1992 – Claw Island Foods, Inc. of Raleigh North Caroline – whole cooked frozen lobster.
    Karen Roberts Jackson, "Vinalhaven Fish Plant Welcomes new Tenant. 1992. (Unsourced.)
    Sydney Winslow. History of Vinalhaven. Installments in *The Courier Gazette*. Rockland, Maine. Circa 1944-45.

240. *The Vinalhaven Echo*, 24 May 1888: 2.

241. Randall R Reeves, Tim D. Smith, Robert L. Webb, Jooke Robbins, and Phillio J. Clapham, "Humpback and Fin Whaling in the Gulf of Maine from 1800 to 1918", *Marine Fisheries Review* 64-1 (2002): https://spo.nmfs.noaa.gov/content/humpback-and-fin-whaling-gulf-maine-1800-1918 (Retrieved September 16, 2019).

242. *Vinalhaven Messenger* (undated) 1885. Another dated story, possibly referring back to this story, suggests it may be from late April early May. "The whale recently brought to the try works on Green's Island yielded about twelve hundred gallons of oil. Work has been suspended at the Island until another whale is captured. The carcass now lies upon the beach, the owners not having decided what disposal to make of it, but it will probably be utilized in some way. *Vinalhaven Messenger* 22 May 1885.

243. Goode, Section IV, *The Fishermen of the United States*, 10.

244. Goode, Section III, *The Fishing Grounds of North America*, 26.

245. On mackerel boats, see George Brown Goode, Joseph Williams Collins, Robert Edward Earll, Alonzo Howard Clark, *Materials for a History of the Mackerel Fishery* (Washington: Government Printing Office, 1883), 420–427.
Vinalhaven boats were:
Reserve – 5.6 tons – handline – coast of Maine – 2 crew
Luther 19.73 tons – handline – coast of Maine – 3 crew
Island Queen 11.13 tons handline coast of Maine – 4 crew
Crown 6.08 tons handline Coast of Maine – 3 crew
Carroll 9.68 tons handline Coast of Maine – 4 crew

246. *The Wind* 10 May 1884: 4; also *The Wind* 4 July 1884: 4. In addition, see *The Vinalhaven Echo* 1 March 1 1888: 1; and *The Vinalhaven Echo* 19 April 1888: 1.

247. Radley and Bunker, *Horse Nets, Holliwoggers*, 186. Also see *ARBILS* for 1900, 78-87.

248. *The Wind* 4 July 4 1884: 4. According to *The Vinalhaven Echo* (12 January 1888: 3), January 1888 must have been mild: "Chas. Dyer of Crockett's river, has caught and shipped over five thousand pounds of smelts in the past several weeks. He has also shipped some twenty barrels of flounders during the time." *The Rockland Gazette* (27 July 1876: 2) noted that "The porgy [menhaden] fishermen are plenty in the bay and it would astonish the unthinking or the uninitiated to know that there have been taken as many as 7000 barrels of the oily fishes in one day in this vicinity." See also, Radley and Bunker, *Horse Nets, Holliwoggers*, 172; and Winslow, *Fish Scales*, 73-74.

249. *The Wind* 11 July 1884: 1 (barrels to pounds conversions, http://www.gma .org/fogm/Scomber_scombrus.htm [Retrieved, September 11, 2017]). For modern comparison, see Maine Department of Marine Resources, "Commercial Fish Landings": https://www.maine.gov/dmr/commercial-fishing/landings/index.html (Retrieved January, 2020.)

250. Goode, Section IV, *The Fishermen of the United States*, 10–11. Goode tagged the fishermen as lacking ambition: "When at home the fisherman of this class passes most of his time in lounging about with his companions, relating personal adventures and talking superficially over the outlook. Not possessing a "business head," he does not carry these speculations further than to "hope for better luck." The same time spent in hunting for bait, scarce as it is, might better serve to realize his hopes. He may, despite his failings, be considered as honest, good-hearted, and content with his lot, or perhaps we may better express it, resigned to fate." His appraisal seems to reveal more about the superficiality of his knowledge of their lives, community participation and their awareness of their real circumstances then about the men themselves. On relative earnings, see *History of wages in the United States from Colonial times to 1928* (Washington: Government Printing Office, 1934), 523. https:// babel.hathitrust.org/cgi/pt?id=uc1.32106007458745;view=1up;seq=271 (Retrieved, October 17, 2017.

251. Goode, Section III, *The Fishing Grounds of North America*, 26; also Goode. Section V, *History and Methods of the Fisheries*, Vol II, 660-661. The lobstering section was written by Richard Rathbun.

252. According to Goode. Section V, *History and Methods of the Fisheries*, Vol II, 700, 701: "In 1841 Capt. E. M. Oakes began to carry lobsters from Cundy's Harbor and Horse Island Harbor, Harpswell, to Mr. Eben Weeks, at East Boston. He was then running a well-smack, named the Swampscott, of 41 tons, old measurement. The season extended from the 1st of March until about the 4th of July, after which time the lobsters were supposed to be unfit for eating; the black lobsters, or shedders, were even considered poisonous."

253. Goode, Section V, *History and Methods of the Fisheries*, Vol II, 667-7.

254. From Goode, Section V, *History and Methods of the Fisheries*, Vol II, 671: "Both ends are exactly alike; the sides are rounded and the bottom is flat, being, however, only 4 or 5 inches wide in the center, and tapering toward each end, at the same time bending slightly upwards, so as to make the boat shallower at the ends than in the middle." See also, Martin and Lipfert, *Lobstering and the Maine Coast,* 23.

255. Obituary dated October 10, 1936, likely from the *Rockland Courier-Gazette*, VHHS collections. Also see Radley and Bunker, *Horse Nets, Holliwoggers,* 23-24. Claes Boman must have had a winning personality, because he quickly moved to the center of island life. He was a Mason and an Odd Fellow, an active member of the Union church, a town selectman, and twice elected a representative to the state legislature. Many community events – meeting, dances, theatrical productions, all used "Boman's Hall." When tricycle riding became a craze, around the turn of the century, an indoor tricycle rental business briefly prospered on the building's first floor.

256. Boman's Sail Loft receipt, VHHS collections.

257. George S. Wasson. *Sailing Days on the Penobscot* (New York: W.W. Norton, [1932] 1949), 115.

258. Richard Rathbun, "Notes on the Decrease of Lobsters," *Bulletin of the United States Fish Commission for 1884* (Washington: Government Printing Office, 1884), 424. https://books.google.com/books?id=mVc9AAAAYAAJ&printsec=frontcover&dq=Bulletin+of+the+United+States+Fish+Commission+vol.+4+1884&hl=en&sa=X&ved=0ahUKEwiLv6arjdLWAhUF5CYKHe47Cf8Q6AEITjAI#v=onepage&q=Bulletin%20of%20the%20United%20States%20Fish%20Commission%20vol.%204%201884&f=false (Retrieved October 21, 2020)

259. Martin and Lipfert, *Lobstering and the Maine Coast,* 45; and Colin Woodard, *The Lobster Coast* (New York and London: Penguin Books, 2004), 188. Also see Ackerman, *New England's Fishing Industry*, 5.

260. *The Vinalhaven Echo*, October 11, 1888, 3.

261. Goode, Section II, *A geographical review of the fisheries industries,* 50. Dan Bickford touched on this subject in Interview #48 (August 21, 2012).

262. *Report of the Commissioner of Sea and Shore Fisheries of the State of Maine 1889 – 90* (Augusta ME: Burleigh & Flynt, Printers to the State, 1891), 44.

263. Goode, Section V, *History and Methods of the Fisheries*, Vol II, 679-680.

264. *The Vinalhaven Echo*, 12 January 1888: 2. "Lobsters are in demand. They are selling at 12 cents each. Elisha Oakes, the manager of Johnson & Young's lobster pound here, has commenced shipping this week." Also see, *The Vinalhaven Echo* 8 March 1888: 3.

265. *The Vinalhaven Messenger* 17 April 1885: 2.

266. Diary of Maria Webster, VHHS Collections.

267. *Rockland Gazette 21* February 1878: 3; *The Vinalhaven Echo* 22 December 1887: 3.

268. *The Vinalhaven Echo* 23 August 23, 1888: 3.

269. Maine activists started pushing for women's suffrage before the Civil War but made inadequate local progress until the 19th amendment was ratified in August 1920. Almost forty years after Campbell's visit, in 1917, islander Addie L Roberts wrote in her diary: "*Suffragette speaker here and spoke in C.S. Hall; spoke on the street in the evening.*" *Rockland Gazette* 24 October 1878: 2. Addie L. Roberts Diary, June 2-3, 1917. *Maine Memory Network* "Suffrage in Maine," (https://www.maine-memory.net/bin/Features?fn=13&fmt=list&n=1&supst=Exhibits&mr=all (Retrieved, August 10, 2017).

270. *Rockland Gazette* 24 October 1878: 2; Kelley Bouchard, "When Maine Went Dry", *Portland Press Herald*, October 2, 2011, http://www.pressherald.com/2011/10/02/when-maine-went-dry_2011-10-02/ (Retrieved October 21 2020); *Maine: An Encyclopedia*, "Alcohol" http://maineanencyclopedia.com/alcohol/?hilite =alcohol (Retrieved, September 15, 2017).

The sponsoring island group was called The Ironclads. According, Michelle L. Brann, Reference Services, Maine State Library, "I'm not sure who the "Ironclads" were as I can't find any mention of them as a group, anywhere. I've checked reference books on prohibition and temperance and our clipping file on temperance with no result. The only relationship I can find between the temperance movement and the term "ironclad" I found in Google Books and is as follows: 'In defiance of "Ironclad" statutes, federal regulations concerning interstate shipments, the limitation of quantities that may be imported for private use, the fidelity in policing, and so forth. . .' From *Alcohol and Society* by John Koren (New York: Henry Holt, 1916, 82). Perhaps these 'Ironclad statutes' are where the name of the group originated. Unfortunately, I can't find anything about such a group, and can't tell you whether they were local, regional or nationwide."

271. "Temperance," *The Vinalhaven Echo* 29 December 1887: 1; Radley and Bunker, *Horse Nets, Holliwoggers*, 24; Kellianne Dolan, "Maine's Prohibition: 82 Years in the Making", *Maine Memory Network* https://www.mainememory.net/sitebuilder/site/2619/page/4223/display?use_mmn=1 (Retrieved, August 10, 2017).

272. *Rockland Gazette* 14 January 1875, 2; Winslow, *Fish Scales*,122.

273. Rosanna Coombs Arey's story from the VHHS collections, written and signed by Marion L. Chandler. Temperance has often been portrayed as a movement by women who suffered from having too many of their husbands' or father's paychecks burned up at taverns. But a tiny, faded pamphlet in the Historical Society shows that the island had at least one men's group intent on collectively resisting "the evil effects of intoxicating drinks" and open to, "[a]ll male persons of the age of sixteen years and upwards, who have been in the habit of using intoxicating liquor to a greater or less extent. . . ." *Constitution and By-Laws of the Vinalhaven Reform Club – Organized March 27, 1876*, VHHS collections.

274. Arianna MacNeill, "How Hatchet-Wielding women ended liquor sales in Rockport for 163 years," *Boston.com*, January 28, 2019, https://www.boston

.com/news/history/2019/01/28/hannah-jumper-hatchet-gang-rockport-alcohol?fbclid
=IwAR3smuRFsnE8vvmnsbBEtfEVk2HjXLBYymreqMjdlxgCe0Xi1Lr_wVx3Phc
(Retrieved January 29, 2019).

275. *Rockland Gazette 2* March 1876: 2. Even the scant newspaper record suggests that many islanders were in the game. One Wednesday in late July 1876, Con-
stable Brackett "and three or four assistants" first visited the "Cascade House" and
"seized 7 barrels of liquors of different kinds, besides two or three smaller lots." From
there, Officer French "went up to Timothy Lane's house and informed him a company
awaited his presence at his saloon. Timothy reluctantly responded." Unwarned, Lane
lacked time to conceal the "one barrel and two halves of the contraband article" in his
own saloon. *Rockland Gazette 3* August 1876: 2.

There is still in Carver's Cemetery a late 19th century gravestone with a hollow
center especially fashioned to hold liquor bottles. In the dark of night, or perhaps the
fog of day, the seller would deposit several, and the buyer would retrieve them whenever he believed the coast to be clear.

276. Wasson, *Sailing Days*, 137.

277. August 1906, Letter from Cap of BK "Salvatori" G. Trapani, VHHS
collections.

278. Winslow, *Fish Scales*, 221-2; Roger G. Reed. *Summering on the Thoroughfare: The architecture of North Haven, 1885–1945* (Portland, ME: Maine Citizens for
Historic Preservation, 1993), 18-19.

279. *ARBILS* for 1909, 187.

280. *The Vinalhaven Echo,* Advance issue, 7 October 1887: 2–3.

281. Reprinted in *The Vinalhaven Echo 27* December 1888: 2.

282. *ARBILS* for 1887, 111.

283. *ARBILS* for 1887, 112.

284. *ARBILS* for 1887, 113.

285. *ARBILS* for 1892, 157.

CHAPTER 7

286. VHHS collections.

287. Diary of Evelyn W. Arey (Hall), VHHS collections.

288. Memoir of Alice Paine, transcribed by Valerie Morton,7/18/ 2005; VHHS
archives.

289. Evelyn W. Arey Diary (Hall).

290. Anthony, *Vinalhaven Reminiscences,*15.

291. Addie L. Roberts Diary, VHHS collections.

292. Radley and Bunker, *Horse Nets, Holliwoggers,* 102, 199–200.

293. Addie L. Roberts Diary, VHHS collections.

294. Winslow, *Fish Scales, 69;* apparently Winslow also published longer versions
of his chapter on fishing in the *Rockland Courier-Gazette.* VHHS is in possession of
undated text apparently from 1945-46.

295. "Tragedies" notebook, VHHS archives; also see VHHS Winslow pieces, *Rockland Courier-Gazette,* 1945-6.

296. All newspaper notices are from the "Tragedies" notebook, VHHS archives. This newspaper article in the VHHS "fish" file, is entitled "Locked in death's embrace," is unsigned, but dates April, 16.1915. Sent by VHHS on November 20, 2017.

297. Board of Underwriters, *The Tariff of Rates for the Knox County* (Rockland ME. 1908). The 1908 publication date belies the insertion of later corrections and suggests a slight ambiguity about the exact year of several of these stores. But if there is a bit of deviance, it's irrelevant to the larger point of how rich the offerings were.

298. Board of Underwriters, *Tariff of Rates.* Lane-Libby Fisheries Co. was also incorporated in 1908, combining the Lane & Libby, the Vinalhaven Fish Co. and the Vinalhaven Glue Co. in one company. ARBILS for 1910, 18–23.

299. ARBILS for 1910, 18–23.

300. James Donahue, Commissioner, *30th Report, Commissioner of Sea and Shore Fisheries, State of Maine, 1907-1908* (Augusta ME: Maine Farmer Publishing Company, undated), 22; Maine Department of Sea and Shore Fisheries, *Harvesters of the Sea: the story of Maine's Commercial Fisheries* (n.p.: Maine Department of Sea and Shore Fisheries, published with the cooperation of the U.S. Department of Commerce, NOAA, National Marine Fisheries Service, 1971), 25.

301. Addie L. Roberts Diary. Roberts kept a diary from 1908 to 1914. But there is an earlier entry in another hand from 1906 – apparently, someone had used the same diary briefly before her. The 1910 census listed 148 lobstermen, and 60 fishermen on the island – including five men running fish weirs and one running a herring weir. Two other men called themselves "trawlers" and three said they were "seiners," distinguishing themselves from hook fishermen.

302. Anthony, *Vinalhaven Reminiscences,* 134.

303. "Lobstermen Organizing. First Union of the Kind in this country formed at Vinalhaven . . .", untitled, unsourced newspaper article, May 1905, VHHS collections. Quotation from an untitled article in the *Portland Express* 13 May 13 1905, reprinted, in part, in *The Wind,* 22-28 April 2010.

304. Charles A. Scontras. "Maine Lobstermen and the Labor Movement." *Labor's Heritage: Quarterly of the George Meany Memorial Archives* 2-1 (January 1990): 50–63, quote on 52.

305. Scontras, "Maine Lobstermen and the Labor Movement," 53.

306. The Editors, "Samuel Gompers", *Britannica,* https://www.britannica.com/biography/Samuel-Gompers (Retrieved February 11, 2019): also, "Samuel Gompers", *AFL-CIO, America's Unions,* https://aflcio.org/about/history/labor-history-people/samuel-gompers (Retrieved February 11, 2019).

307. Scontras, "Maine Lobstermen", 57.

308. Scontras, Maine Lobstermen", 59.

309. Scontras, Maine Lobstermen", 60.

310. Pay sheet copy, courtesy of Roger Young. The average weekly wages for a laborer in the Iron and Steel industry was $11.18 a week (United States Bureau of Labor Statistics, "Wages and Hours of Labor in the Iron and Steel Industry in the

United States, 1907 to 1912" *Bulletin of the United States Bureau of Labor Statistics, No. 151*, 44). https://fraser.stlouisfed.org/scribd/?item_id=497571&filepath=/files/docs/publications/bls/bls_0151_1914.pdf (Retrieved, November 14, 2017). Average earnings for all employees in 1910 was $517.00 a year. (United States Bureau of the Census, "Series D 722-727 – Average Annual Earnings of Employees: 1900 to 1970," *Historical Statistics of the United States, Colonial Times to 1970*, Bicentennial ed. [Washington: U.S. Dept. of Commerce, Bureau of the Census, 1975]); https://babel.hathitrust.org/cgi/pt?id=uiug.30112104053548;view=1up;seq=182 (Retrieved, November 14, 2017).

311. U.S. Custom House, *Record of Licenses of Vessels Under 20 Tons* (U.S. Department of Commerce and Labor Government Bindry 12-21-08-40), 25 fn 1286. VHHS collection.

312. Two of the workers are listed ambiguously in the census as working for the "fish factory" - plus three more worked for the glue factory, although its main processing plant had moved off island.

313. *ARBILS* for 1910, 22.

314. *ARBILS* for 1910, 23.

315. *ARBILS* for 1910, 22–23.

316. Winslow, *Rockland Courier* articles written in 1945 and 1946, 43; VHHS archives. Also, see Lane-Libby Ledgers, VHHS archives.

317. *ARBILS* for 1910, 23.

318. Winslow, *Fish Scales,* 70.

319. *ARBILS* for 1910, 23. "They pay out for labor at their factory from $35,000 to $50,000 a year, besides paying to the fishermen at Vinalhaven and along the coast from $75,000 to $125,000 a year for their catch." However glowing the report, the company had ups and downs, their profit margin was often small, and their bookkeeping may not have reflected realities. In 1915, this note appears in their ledger: "Mr. Mildram reported that since taking up his duties as Treasurer of the company he had made an investigation of the accounting methods and financial conditions of the company; that it appeared that the methods used in the past had been insufficient and inadequate; that the method of keeping account of the stock of the company had been inaccurate, and that the amount of merchandise called for by the books of the company had proved to be largely in excess of the amount actually on hand; and he had had an inventory . . . and stated that it seemed advisable to pen new books as of the first of July upon the basis of appraisals and to install and use new and better accounting methods." Lane-Libby Ledgers, VHHS archives.

"Isinglass, a gelatin-like substance made from the air-bladders or sounds of fish like the sturgeon, is added to cask beers like Guinness to help any remaining yeast and solid particles settle out of the final product." K. Annabelle Smith, "Hey Vegans, there may be fish bladder in your Guinness," *Smithsonian* March 13, 2013: http://www.smithsonianmag.com/arts-culture/hey-vegans-there-may-be-fish-bladder-in-your-guinness- (Retrieved, June 20, 2016). Information about napes, from Ted Ames, personal communication.

320. Anthony, *Vinalhaven Reminiscences*, 111.

321. Anthony, *Vinalhaven Reminiscences*, 20-21.

322. Anthony, *Vinalhaven Reminiscences*, 69.

323. Fish and herring weirs were common on the island during the early decades of the 20th century. Here's a sampling of years and weir licenses granted from Annual Reports of the Municipal Officers of the Town of Vinalhaven:

1909	1918	1925
E. W. Ames	C.E. Mills and R.G. Gillis	James Barton
James Gregory	Sanborn and Arey	Russ Whitmore
J.F. Austin	Frank A. Kimball	Frank Kimball
Watson Barton	N. Cook Sholes	W.L. Clayter
Chas. E. Young	Frank O. Crockett	
E.W. Ames		
James Gregory		
Ira McDonald		
E.E. Brown and J.H. Tabbutt		

Here's my count of fishermen and fish related workers in 1920 census – OA means worked for Own Account, W means worked for Wage:

Fishermen small boat OA – 84; Fishermen small boat W – 13; Fishermen weir OA – 8; Fishermen weir W – 2; Fishermen Schooner W – 3; Coastwise Mariner – 5; Lobster Pound OA – 2; Captain Schooner W – 1; Captain Oceangoing W – 1; Lobster Smack W – 2; Sardine Factory OA – 1; Sardine Factory W – 7; Glue Factory W – 2 Fish Factory W – 21 (including 1 who called job "glue maker"); Boat Carpenter W – 1; Fishyard W – 1; Mariner, Oceangoing W – 11; Seller of Marine Insurance – 1; Fish Commissioner office worker – 1; Fisherman cook – 1; Boat Builder OA – 1; Lobster dealer wholesale OA – 1; Sailmaker OA – 1, W – 1; Fishermen Sloop W – 3; Fisherman Sloop OA – 1; Fisherman schooner OA – 2; Schooner Captain W – 1; Laborer marine fireman – 1.

Islanders serving in WWI: VHHS. PC, February 22, 2022.

324. Alton Oakes. Interview #31, August 2008: 20.

325. Radley and Bunker, *Horse Nets, Holliwoggers,* 107–109.

326. Mary E. Arnold. "Lobster Fishermen on the Coast of Maine", Report #7, 1941. Mary E. Arnold documents, A-122 2v 7v and A122 5v, 8v., Schlesinger Library Archives, Harvard University.

327. "Observer" in *The Wind* 21-27 January 2004.

328. "A Salute to the Men and Women of WWII," *Vinalhaven Historical Society Annual Newsletter*, 201

329. "Journal of Dr. Ana Balfour," transcribed by Jessica Martin, August 2005. VHHS collections. Also, Dorris A. Westall, "English Physician Practices her profession at Vinalhaven." Undated newspaper clipping, VHHS collections.

Coda: Relics and Skeletons: Vinalhaven, 1939

330. The naturalist Henry David Thoreau had searched for and found Maine relics long before the practice became more popular. Thoreau writes in *The Maine Woods*, "After dinner, we strolled down to the "Point," formed by the junction of two rivers, which is said to be the scene of an ancient battle between the Eastern Indians and the Mohawks, and searched their carefully for relics, though the men at the barroom had never heard of such things; but we found only some flakes of arrow-head stone, some points of arrow-heads, one small leaden bullet, and some colored beads, the last to be referred, perhaps, to early fur-trader days. Henry David Thoreau, *The Maine Woods: a fully annotated edition*. Edited by Jeffrey S. Cramer. Yale University Press. 2009. p. 9.

Artifacts at Centennial Exhibition: For mention of the role of the exposition, see http://www.justice.gov/usao/briefing_room/ic/artifacts.html Retrieved October 10, 2014.

Louis Krasniewicz "All the World in One Place." *Penn Museum*. V.57 No.1 2015. https://www.penn.museum/sites/expedition/all-the-world-in-one-place/ Retrieved May 22, 2018

331. Thomas C. Patterson. *Toward a Social History of Archaeology in the United States*. Case Studies in Archaeology. Jeffrey Quilter series editor. Harcourt, Brace & Co. 1995. p. 54.

332. Ulmer Smith entry in Sue Radley and Elizabeth Bunker. *Horse Nets, Holliwoggers, and everything you need to know about Vinalhaven*. The Vinalhaven Historical Society. R.C. Brayshaw & Co. Lebanon, New Hampshire. 2015. p.204.

Sarah Orne Jewett. *Country of the Pointed Firs and other stories*. Signet Classics. 1896/ Kindle Edition. p.63. Location 1019.

333. Sidney Winslow Diary. Unpublished CD Rom. VHHS. (May 27, 1939)

334. *Ibid.* Winslow diary (August 19,1935)

335. www.wikipedia.org/wiki/Whaleback_Shell_Midden. Retrieved October 10, 2014.

Catherine Schmidt. "More than a pile of Shells" 2018. https://www.islandjournal.com/nature/more-than-a-pile-of-shells/ retrieved May 23, 2022

336. Warren K. Moorehead. *The Archaeology of Maine: Being a narrative of explorations in that state 1912-1920 together with work at Lake Champlain 1917*. Andover, MA: The Andover Press. 1922. p. 177.

337. *Ibid.* Warren K. Moorehead. p.130.

338. Episode 18. The Myth of Maine's Red Paint People. July 22, 2018) (http://historiumunearthia.com/episodes/episode-18-the-myth-of-maines-red-paint-people/) Retrieved February 17, 2020)

339. "Falls dead into grave of Indians." A.P. article. May 22 1939. Without byline. Likely written by Sidney Winslow. (VHHS)

340. Sidney Winslow. *Vinalhaven Neighbor # 27*. May 24, 1939.

341. Op.Cit. A.P. article May 22, 1939. Op.cit. Winslow Diary. May 21, 1939. Also, Winslow (1952) *Fish Scales and Stone Chips*. p.254

342. "Dies in Indian Grave: Gust Carlson a victim while delving among skeleton remains," Courier-Gazette, May 23, 1939, v. 94 # 61 p.1 no byline. https://digital maine.com/cgi/viewcontent.cgi?article=6627&context=courier_gazette Retrieved May 23, 2022

343. Ibid. Courier-Gazette, May 23, 1939.

344. Op. Cit. A.P. Article May 22, 1939.
Vinalhaven Neighbor # 28. May 31, 1939

345. Phil and Sadie Dyer. Interview #46. August 12, 2012.

346. "The Native American Graves Protection and Repatriation Act is a Federal law passed in 1990. NAGPRA provides a process for museums and Federal agencies to return certain Native American cultural items—human remains, funerary objects, sacred objects, or objects of cultural patrimony—to lineal descendants, and culturally affiliated Indian tribes and Native Hawaiian organizations. NAGPRA includes provisions for unclaimed and culturally unidentifiable Native American cultural items, intentional and inadvertent discovery of Native American cultural items on Federal and tribal lands, and penalties for noncompliance and illegal trafficking." http://www.nps.gov/nagpra/FAQ/INDEX.HTM#What_is_NAGPRA? Retrieved Nov. 21, 2014.

347. Kevin Baker "'1491': Vanished Americans." Book review of Charles C. Mann's *1491* in *The New York Times*. October 5, 2005. https://www.nytimes.com/2005/10/09/books/review/1491-vanished-americans.html Retrieved July 7, 2022.

348. Ibid. Baker quoting Mann.

349. When you visit with human remains in the Peabody Museum, you agree to have anything that you write, or any photographs you take, reviewed by the Department. In accordance with that requirement, this chapter was reviewed in February 2019 by Michèle Morgan, Ph.D., Museum Curator of Osteology and Paleoanthropology Peabody Museum of Archaeology and Ethnology, Harvard University. She requested 10 changes, nine of which were implemented and one of which was negotiated so that more material could remain. I am grateful for the visit and for the permission to publish.

350. Just as I finish working on this Coda, a "Steering Committee on human remains in Harvard Museums" at Harvard University has been working on a report, leaked on June 1, 2022 and reported ahead of publication, that urges a more expedited return to descendants of the "19 individuals who were likely enslaved," and of the more than 7000 Native American skeletons in the Peabody collection. It includes these two paragraphs about the skeletons:

"They were obtained under the violent and inhumane regimes of slavery and colonialism; they represent the University's engagement and complicity in these categorically immoral systems," the *Crimson* quotes from the draft report.
"Moreover, we know that skeletal remains were utilized to promote spurious and racist ideas of difference to confirm existing social hierarchies and structures."

Cara J. Chang, "Harvard Holds Human Remains of 19 Likely Enslaved Individuals, Thousands of Native Americans, Draft Report Says," https://www.thecrimson.com/article/2022/6/1/draft-human-remains-report/ Retrieved June 16, 2022

CHAPTER 8

351. I visited Island Lobster Supply on August 31, 2017. On that he day, the company had three employees. In winter, when there are more employees (fewer islanders are fishing), the workers can make up to fifty traps a day. Trap dimensions and parts were learned in conversation with Bill Chilles, August 25, 2017. Trap price in 2023. Email from Bill Chilles. (1/30/23) Also see the YouTube video, "How to Build a Lobster Trap: https://www.youtube.com/watch?v=kBQKFMwsPAs (Retrieved January 4, 2018).

352. Robin Alden, personal communication.

353. Woodard, *Lobster Coast*, 260.

354. Maine Department of Marine Resources, LOBSTER ZONE LICENSE AND TRAP TAG ANNUAL SUMMARY : https://www.maine.gov/dmr/science -research/species/lobster/documents/2008-Current%20Licenses%20and%20Tags.pdf (Retrieved February 23, 2022.) Maine Department of Marine resources, A Guide to Lobstering in Maine, 2017: https://www.maine.gov/dmr/commercial-fishing/licenses/ documents/GuideToLobstering2019.pdf (Retrieved February 23, 2022.)

355. Value of 2021 Maine lobster catch https://www.maine.gov/dmr/news-details .html?id=6779320 (Retrieved February 23, 2022.) Penelope Overton, Portland Press Herald, and Jenna Russell, Globe Staff, "The Lobster Trap," *The Boston Globe* and *Portland Herald Press*. https://apps.bostonglobe.com/metro/2021/12/the-lobster-trap/ climate-change-threatens-livelihood-of-maine-lobster-fishermen Published December 12, 2021. (Retrieved February 23, 2022.) Op. Cit. Acheson and Acheson, 85.

356. Beth Quimby, "Some dislike proposal to ease long waits for Maine lobstering licenses" *Portland Press Herald* 24 January 2016. http://www.pressherald .com/2016/01/24/some-lobstermen-cool-to-proposed-licensing-changes/ (Retrieved May 5, 2016).

357. Kevin Miller, "*Lobstermen tired of Conflict support law to allow GPS tracking of boats*" *Portland Press Herald* 24 April 2016. http://www.pressherald .com/2017/04/24/lobstermen-tired-of-conflicts-support-bill-to-allow-gps-tracking -of-boats/?mc_cid=60b9e71281&mc_eid=e02f8d5aa6 (Retrieved, April 27, 2017).

358. On the number of licenses, Walt Day, 2014: 9. Cathy Fetterman, Director of the Licensing Division, Maine Department of Marine Resources, spoke on the number of traps in conversation on April 25, 2017. Acheson, James, and Ann Acheson. "What Does the Future Hold for Maine's Lobster Industry?." Maine Policy Review 29.2 (2020) : 83 -90, https://digitalcommons.library.umaine.edu/mpr/vol29/iss2/11 (Retrieved February 28, 2022) Total commercial licenses for 2021, Personal Communication, Cathy Fetterman, March 3, 2022.

359. Phil Crossman, *Observations: A Maine Island, a century of newsletters and the stories found between the lines* (Vinalhaven ME: Talking Crow Press, 2015), 324. Patrice McCarron and Heather Tetreault, *Lobster Gear Report*, Maine Lobstermen, http://www.mainelobstermen.org/pdf/Lobster_Gear_Report.pdf ;

Heather Deese and Rob Snyder, *Waypoints: Community Indicators for Maine's Coast & Islands* (Rockland ME: Island Institute, 2017), 6-7. Maine Department of Marine Resources, "Commercial fishing landings" https://www.maine.gov/dmr/

commercial-fishing/landings/index.html https://www.maine.gov/dmr/commercial-fishing/landings/index.html
(Retrieved February 28, 2022)

360. Robin Alden, personal communication, also see the Wahle Lab's *American Lobster Settlement Index,* https://umaine.edu/wahlelab/american-lobster-settlement-index-alsi/ (Retrieved November 1, 2020).

361. "Lobster Catch 121 Million pounds, 500 million – state scientists predict landings downturn over next five years." *The Working Waterfront* March 2016: 1; and "Lobster worries: Record harvests, but fewer juveniles. Settlement numbers at lowest levels in 15-plus years." *The Working Waterfront,* July 2017: 5. Also see Deese and Snyder, *Waypoints,* 22. In May 2020, Robin Alden spoke with me about lobster settlement, climate change and changes in the fishery:

"For many years, lobsters have shifted offshore in the winter in order to be in WARMER water. The shallow, nearshore areas get very cold in the winter so the deep offshore areas are warmer in comparison. So, larger boats, new technology of various sorts have made It possible for fishermen to fish offshore in the winter, chasing those lobsters that move into deeper waters. What Is different now, is that we think that, as the Gulf warms, juvenile lobsters are being able to settle and survive in some areas offshore—in other words this abundance may be because the range of lobster productivity has expanded into waters further offshore, which didn't used to have warm enough waters for reproduction. Some of those Vinalhaven lobstermen are being able to fish offshore year round now."

362. Richard Nelson "'Red Sky in Morning, Fisherman's Warning': Climate change in the Gulf of Maine." Address to the Maine Climate March in Augusta, 2017. Web exclusive of *The American Scholar,* April 20, 2018. https://theamericanscholar.org/red-sky-in-morning-fishermans-warning/?utm_source=email#.WvRO5xiZPUo (Retrieved, May 11, 2018).

363. Jon Birger. "Looking for a bargain dinner? Try lobster. At a wholesale price of $2.25, the once costly crustacean is a treat for consumers but a crisis for Maine lobstermen." *Fortune,* Last Updated, July 18, 2009. http://archive.fortune.com/2009/07/17/news/economy/cheap_lobster_bargain.fortune/index.htm (Retrieved January 4, 2018).

364. Overton and Russell, *Boston Globe,* December 12, 2021.

365. "Hank," August 9, 2015: 37-38.

366. Gulf of Maine Research Institute, "An Independent Evaluation of the Maine Limited Entry Licensing System for Lobster and Crab, Prepared for the Maine Department of Marine Resources, November 30, 2012. https://nanopdf.com/download/an-independent-evaluation-of-the-maine-limited-entry_pdf# (Retrieved November 1, 2018. 2019 Maine Median Family income, U.S. Census: https://www.census.gov/quickfacts/fact/table/ME/BZA110219#BZA110219 (retrieved February 24, 2022)

367. "Hank": August 9, 2015: 12–13.

368. Susan Dyer Radley, collector and editor, *Remember When: A collection of oral histories* (Vinalhaven ME, Vinalhaven Historical Society, 2010), interview with Sadie Dyer on page 91.

369. Lois Day, August 21, 2013: 12.

370. "Gary's" son, August 8, 2015: 28–30.

371. Yvonne "Beba" Rosen, August 21, 2016: 2–3.

372. Ronnie Warren, August 21, 2008: 1.

373. Lee Osgood August 2, 2015: 2–3.

374. Jerry Doughty, August 8, 2015: 13–15.

375. "Hank," August 9, 2015: 16.

376. Tim Dyer, August 6, 2015: 5–6, 8–9.

377. Ivan E. Calderwood, *Days of Uncle Dave's fish house* (Rockland ME: Courier-Gazette, 1969), 69-71.

378. Video interview of Ed Dyer by Nate Michaud, 2001. VHHS collections.

379. Roy Ames interview in Anthony, *Vinalhaven Reminiscences,* 2.

380. Tina Rosenberg. "Swan's Island's 'water girls'", *The Working Waterfront*, June 2016: 12.

381. Walter Day, August 23, 2010: 31–32.

382. John Beckman, August 6, 2008: 12.

383. Video interview of John Morton by Nate Michaud, 2001. VHHS collections.

384. Alex Wilkinson, "Profiles: The Lobsterman: How Ted Ames turned Oral History into Science" *The New Yorker Magazine*, July 31, 2006. http://www.newyorker.com/archive/2006/07/31/060731fa_fact_wilkinson

About Ted fishing with his grandfather, see http://video.nhptv.org/video/2365760136/ (Viewed June 3, 2016).

385. Ted Ames, August 10, 2012: 8–9.

386. "Hal", August 18, 2009: 10.

387. Sonny Warren, August 22, 2009: 27–28.

388. George "Burt" Dyer, August 12, 2008: 5–7.

389. Ivan Olson, August 21, 2011: 1–3.

390. Sonny Warren, August 22, 2009: 16.

391. Lee Osgood: 2–3.

392. Ivan Olson: 10, 4.

393. Herb Conway, July 31, 2015: 13.

394. Lee Osgood: 43.

395. Charles Eliot, *John Gilley of Baker's Island, Maine* (Carlisle MA: Applewood Books, 2005 [1899]).

396. Ronnie Walker, 2008: 14–15.

397. Walter Day: 42.

CHAPTER 9

398. Ted Ames: 1–3

399. Warner, *Distant Water,* 58–59, 55.

400. Robin Alden, personal communication.

401. Paul Molyneaux. *The Doryman's Reflection* (New York: Avalon, 2005), 54.

402. DMR screen shots. Email, March 1, 2022. Cathy Fetterman, Director, Licensing Division,Dept. of Marine Resources. Also DMR. https://www.maine.gov/

dmr/science-research/species/halibut/documents/DMRHalibutComplianceGuide%20 2021.pdf (Retrieved March 3, 2022) Also DMR, License numbers; personal communication, email Cathy Fetterman, Director of Licensing Division., 3/3/22 and 3/30/22.

403. Ted Ames : 1-3.

404. George "Burt" Dyer, August 12, 2008, 4; Sonny Warren, August 2, 2009, 9.

405. Herb Conway. Notes from a conversation with Herb Conway and Bill Chilles, August 29, 2018.

406. Diary of Maria Dolloff Webster. 1892. VHHS collections.

407. Walter Day 2010: 4.

408. Roger Young, August 2014: 5–7.

409. Steve Rosen 2011: 1–2.

410. Sonny Warren, 2009: 29–30. As with every species, markets came and went. Sometimes the scallopers sold to buyers in Rockland, other times, Portland. Sunny Oakes remembered times in the 1950s when the Burnham-Morrill plant on the island was freezing packs of 10 scallops – obviating the need for quick markets. Alton Oakes, 2008: 6.

411. Maine DMR, "Scallop Table", http://www.maine.gov/dmr/commercial -fishing/landings/documents/scallop.table.pdf (Retrieved, March 3, 2022). Rotational management – personal communication Natalie Springuel, 6, 4, 2021.

412. Alice "Larry" Gould. "Scalloper has adaptable rig," *Maine Coast Fisherman*, March 1956.

413. Tim Dyer, 2015: 19–24.

414. Bodine Ames, 2009: 23.

415. Ivan Olson, 2011: 24.

416. Tim Dyer, 2015: 22–23.

417. Bobby Warren, 2008, 14–15.

418. Maine DMR, "Shrimp Table" http://www.maine.gov/dmr/commercial -fishing/landings/documents/shrimp.table.pdf (Retrieved, February 25, 2018); Heather Deese and Susie Arnold, "Fathoming: Warmer waters pushing shrimp out of Gulf of Maine." *Working Waterfront*, May 2017: 21.

419. Sonny Warren, 2009: 16.

420. "John", 2010: 10–11.

421. "John", 2010: 11- 12.

422. Bobby Warren, 2008: 13–14.

423. Walter Day 2014: 29–31.

424. Bobby Warren, 2008: 13–14.

425. Walter Day2014: 29–31.

426. "Hank", 2015, 17–19.

427. Walter Day, 2014: 4.

428. Sonny Warren, 2009: 12–13.

429. "Hal", 2009: 15–16.

430. John Beckman,: 8.

431. Alton "Sonny" Oakes, 2008: 26.

432. Maine DMR. https://www.maine.gov/dmr/commercial-fishing/landings/doc uments/softshellclam.table.pdf (Retrieved March 4, 2022). "Green Crabs, Nitrogen

Identified as top threats to Maine's soft-shell clams," *Bangor Daily News*. December 3, 2013. https://bangordailynews.com/2013/03/12/business/green-crabs-nitrogen-ide ntified-as-top-threats-to-maines-softshell-clams/ (Retrieved March 4, 2022). "Marine Shellfish Populations Estimated to be at Risk from Ocean Acidification. " January 23, 2020. https://coastalscience.noaa.gov/news/marine-shellfish-populations-estimated -to-be-at-risk-from-ocean-acidification/ (Retrieved March 4, 2020).

433. To put it in the words of fish economists describing a later era, "Because fixed investments in boats and gear were small, the inshore fleet readily shed or added capital in response to economic change. This flexibility kept incomes more stable in the inshore industry than in the offshore sector." Peter B. Doeringer, Philip I. Moss, David G. Terkla, *The New England Fishing Economy: Jobs, Income, and Kinship.* (Amherst MA: The University of Massachusetts Press, 1986), 32.

434. Maine Atlantic Cod landings. https://www.maine.gov/dmr/commercial -fishing/landings/documents/cod.table.pdf (Retrieved, March 4, 2022).

435. Wilkinson, "Profiles: The Lobsterman."

436. Ackerman, *New England's Fishing Industry*, 229.

437. Winslow, *Fish Scales*, 71; also Radley and Bunker, *Horse Nets, Holliwog-gers*, 108.

438. Ivan Olson, 2011: 15.

439. "Sam," 2011: 2.

440. Walter Day, 2010: 15.

441. Harold B. Clifford, *Charlie York: Maine Coast Fisherman* (Camden ME: International Marine Publishing Company, 1974), 87.

442. LA Times Editorial Board, "Editorial: Dead, dolphins, sea turtles and whales are not acceptable collateral damage for swordfishing" *LA Times* 23 July 2018: https://www.latimes.com/opinion/editorials/la-ed-swordfish-gillnet-bill-20180723 -story.html (Retrieved, January 1, 2021).

443. Ivan Olson, 2011: 5–6; Alfred Osgood, August 11, 2010: 6.

444. George "Burt" Dyer, 2008: 6-7. According to Herb Conway, Dick Walker also fished with a gillnet, but it doesn't seem like there were a lot of local men using them.

445. Ronnie Walker, 2008:6; also George "Burt" Dyer, 2008.

446. Ronnie Walker, 2008:6. Only gradually have I understood how important bait is to fishing. And fresh bait particularly. You can preserve bait by freezing it or salting it. Fish tend to prefer it fresh or frozen rather than salted. And while there are plenty of creatures, like mussels and clams, that you can dangle off a hook, some attract fish better than others. Fish have preferences, and in the days before dragging, purse sein-ing, or gill netting – anytime you fished with baited hooks – you spent days or weeks frantic for bait but unable to get what you wanted.

447. George Dyer, 2008:16.

448. George Dyer, 2008: 12–13, 3. Nets have gradually been modified so that it's possible to target a species with more precision. While deployed in other countries, they are only lately being tried in Maine waters.

449. Ivan Olson, 2011:18.

450. Michael J. Fogarty and Steven A. Murawski. "Large-scale disturbance and the structure of marine systems: fishery impacts on Georges Bank." *Ecological Applications* 8, no. sp1 (1998): S6-S22.

451. Ronnie Walker, 2008: 6.

452. W. Jeffrey Bolster, "Where have All the Cod Gone", *New York Times*, January 2, 2015, http://www.nytimes.com/2015/01/02/opinion/where-have-all-the-cod-gone .html?hp&action=click&pgtype=Homepage&module=c-column-top-span-region &region=c-column-top-span-region&WT.nav=c-column-top-span-region&_r=0 (Retrieved October 10, 2016).

453. Ackerman. *New England's Fishing Industry*, 16.

454. Sadie Dyer, 2012:4.

455. Ted Ames, 2012:6.

456. Herb Conway, 2015: 3.

457. Walter Day, 2010: 17.

458. Maine DMR, "Haddock Table", https://www.maine.gov/dmr/commercial -fishing/landings/documents/haddock.table.pdf (Retrieved, March 4, 2022); Tom Bell, "New restrictions to essentially prevent cod fishing in Gulf of Maine," *Kennebec Journal and Morning Sentinel*, 10 November 2014, http://www.centralmaine .com/2014/11/10/regulators-to-place-strict-limits-on-cod-catch-in-gulf-of-maine-2/ (Retrieved, November 14, 2016).

459. Marie Arana, "Review of Mark Kurlansky's *Birdseye: The Adventures of a Curious Man,*" *Washington Post* 8 June 2012: https://www.washingtonpost.com/ opinions/book-review-birdseye-the-adventures-of-a-curious-man-by-mark-kurlan sky/2012/06/08/gJQAbf3DOV_story.html (Retrieved, June 4, 2020); Bigelow and Schroeder, *Fishes of the Gulf of Maine*, 436.

460. Sidney Winslow Diaries, VHHS collections.

461. Alton "Sonny" Oakes, August 2008: 2–3, 10.

462. Alton "Sonny" Oakes, August 2008: 2–3, 10; for the remands of the frozen food industry, see also Matthew G. McKenzie, *Breaking the Banks: Representations and Realities in New England Fisheries* (Amherst MA: University of Massachusetts Press, 2017).

463. Alton "Sonny" Oakes, August 2008: 2–3, 10.

464. Maine DMR, "Redfish Table" https://www.maine.gov/dmr/commercial -fishing/landings/documents/redfish.table.pdf (Retrieved, March 4, 2020).

465. Bigelow and Schroeder, *Fishes of the Gulf of Maine*, 21–23.

466. Maine DMR, "White Hake Table" https://www.maine.gov/dmr/commercial -fishing/landings/documents/whitehake.table.pdf (Retrieved, November 1, 2020).

467. Alice "Larry" Gould, "Island Company Finds Market for Salt Hake," *Maine Coast Fisherman*, undated (ca. Oct. 1950).

468. Walter Day, August 2014: 25–29.

469. Alton "Sonny" Oakes, August 2008: 13–17.

470. Herb Conway, August 2015: 22–23.

471. Sonny Warren, August 2009: 14.

472. Video interview, Les Dyer with Nate Michaud, July 27, 2001. VHHS collections.

473. Balfour Journal, unpaged. VHHS collections.

474. Maine DMR" Whiting Table"
https://www.maine.gov/dmr/commercial-fishing/landings/documents/whiting
.table.pdf and (Retrieved, December 2018). Also called Silver Hake, Whiting is not
a "true" hake, but a close relative of cod that was fished extensively in the Gulf of
Maine in the 20th century, although its numbers radically diminished from mid-
century on. According to Ted Ames, one Vinalhaven fisherman fished for Silver Hake
for a while and sold it in Boothbay. In 1964, 25 million pounds of silver hake were
caught in Maine; in 2016, 46,000 pounds.

475. Ivan Olson, 2011: 5–6.

476. Bigelow and Schroeder, *Fishes of the Gulf of Maine,* 49. Also see video
interviews of George "Burt" Dyer by Doug Hall, 2002 and 2006. VHHS collections.

CHAPTER 10

477. Alfred Osgood, August 2010: 6–8.

478. New England Fisheries Management Council, "Herring" http://archive.nefmc
.org/herring/ (Retrieved November 2, 2020). Maine DMR. https://www.maine.gov/
dmr/commercial-fishing/landings/documents/herring.table.pdf (Retrieved March 7,
2022.

479. Laurie Schreiber, "Severe herring fishery cuts. . ." *Fishermen's Voice,*
July 2018, http://www.fishermensvoice.com/archives/201807Index.html (Retrieved,
November 2 2020); David Abel, "Drastic Measures to Arrest Drastic Plunge in
Herring Population", *The Boston Globe,* September 24, 2018, https://www.bos-
tonglobe.com/metro/2018/09/24/drastic-measures-considered-arrest-plunge-herring
-population/bpDnWMXomlBBkxRzwubNpK/story.html (Retrieved November 2
2020); Karen Alexander, personal communication. Maine DMR. Herring value
percent 2020. https://www.maine.gov/dmr/commercial-fishing/landings/documents/
ValueBySpecies.Pie.Graph.pdf (Retrieved March 7, 2022.)

480. ARBILS for 1901: 162, 75; Radley and Bunker, *Horse Nets, Holliwoggers*,
108. 76. By the mid-1970s, the factories were beginning to disappear from the coast,
and in 2010 in Prospect Harbor, the last plant in Maine (and in the United States) shut
down – a casualty of changing tastes and diminished numbers of fish. See, Katha-
rine Q. Seelye, "In Maine, Last Sardine Cannery in the U.S. Is Clattering Out", *New
York Times* 3 April 2010, http://www.nytimes.com/2010/04/04/us/04cannery.html
(Retrieved December 1, 2016).

481. Roger Young, August 2014: 12.

482. Sidney Winslow, *The Neighbors* vol. 1-1, November 24, 1937, and *The
Neighbors* vol 1-23, April 27, 1938. Later, Winslow notes in his diary on November
19, 1947, that as part of his job, (he had many jobs) he made a trip to Old Harbor to
grant permits for several wharves and weirs. Sidney Winslow Diary: 39, 122, VHHS
collections.

483. Sonny Warren, August 2009: 20.

484. Sonny Warren, August 2009: 7.

485. Ted Ames, manuscript note, 2020.

486. Sam Perkins, September 2009: 2–3.

487. Unattributed newspaper article in the Tragedies Folder, VHHS collections.

488. Sam Perkins, September 2009: 2–3.

489. Bodine Ames, October 2009: 29.

490. Joe Upton, *Amaretto* (Camden ME: International Marine Publishing Company, 1986), 115.

491. Lorraine Walker. August 2008: 6–8.

492. Upton, *Amaretto,* 154.

493. William "Mac" McKinley, *Rockland Courier-Gazette* 19 April 19, 1976, and 12 September 1976. Clippings collected in the Herring Notebook, VHHS collections. Victor Ames, Mike Mesko, Walter Day, Harold Alley, and Robert Warren are mentioned by name. The buyer was the herring carrier *"Bernadine"* out of Saint Andrew, New Brunswick.

494. Lee Osgood, August 2015: 8–12.

495. Ronnie Walker, August 2008: 3.

496. "Hal", August 2009: 29–32.

497. Ted Ames, August 10, 2012: 1–3.

498. Bobby Warren, August 21, 2008, 10.

499. Walter Day, August 23, 2010: 23–25.

500. Walter Day, August 23, 2010: 23–25.

501. Walter Day, August 23, 2010: 22.

502. Ted Ames, August 10, 2012: 1–3. For a chronology of changes in fishing, see Glen Libby and Antonia Small, *Caught: time. place. fish.* (Port Clyde ME: Wrack Line Books, 2016), 85–87.

CHAPTER 11

593. Alton "Sonny" Oakes in Radley, *Remember When,* 135.

504. Alice "Larry" Gould, "Husband and Wife Handlining," with photo, *Maine Coast Fisherman,* January 1951.

505. Alice "Larry" Gould, "Mrs. Magnuson finishes first year fishing with husband," *Maine Coast Fisherman,* October 1950.

506. Bodine Ames, October 2009: 30.

507. Ruth Young Ames, quoted in Radley, *Remember When,* 7–8.

508. Undated, unpaginated story by William McKinley, *Rockland Courier-Gazette,* 1976. VHHS collections.

509. Jennifer Van Allen, "Maine Women Welcome a Sea of Opportunities, *Portland Press Herald,* October 5, 2014, http://www.pressherald.com/2014/10/05/maine-women-welcome-a-sea-of-opportunities/ (Retrieved, January 26, 2017). "The growing number of women" Maine Lobstering now. https://www.mainelobsternow.com/blog/women-in-lobster-fishing (Retrieved March 8, 2022)

510. Yvonne "Beba" Rosen, August 21, 2016: 1–2, 4.

511. Yvonne "Beba" Rosen, August 21, 2016: 1, 17,

512. Yvonne "Beba" Rosen, August 21, 2016: 6, 17, 18, 6.

513. Dan Bickford, August 21, 2012. Apart from fishing, island women today manage businesses that contribute to the island and to their household economies. They serve as selectmen, town managers, and committee heads. Women work loading and off-loading cars on the ferry. They teach in the school. They run nail and hair salons, a fitness center, an art gallery, a fishermen's supply store, as well as assorted cafes, bed and breakfasts, and gift shops. They "caretake" for summer people, "hay" fields, farm, co-manage the lumberyard, and sell real estate. Keeping the island in food, especially in summer, is a huge project for the single grocery store, and women order from the mainland, unload, stock and keep track of all the groceries people seek out each day.

514. Lois Day, August 21, 2013: 7.

515. Handwritten letter from Mrs. Leroy Ames, in the Fishing Vessels Notebook; and undated article, "The Net Factory Turns Boatshop", in VHHS collections.

516. Bodine Ames, October 2009: 16–17.

517. Alton "Sonny" Oakes, August 2008 (Untaped. Note made after meeting.)

518. Ivan Olson, August 21, 2011: 28.

519. "Lizzie", October 2010: 26, 34–35.

520. "Lizzie", October 2010: 31.

521. "Cathy" August 18, 2009: 38. I got so curious about corned hake I decided I would try to make it. Fortunately, one spring day my husband spotted it as a lunch special at the *Harbor Gawker*. I ordered it and when it arrived in a big white Styrofoam box with sides of coleslaw and a biscuit, I dug right in. Hot, salty, fat and vinegar drenched fish and potatoes, who could resist? I was an immediate convert. In spite of my serious effort to down it all, I couldn't keep up with island portions meant for people who do hours of hard physical work, so half went home for supper.

522. "Dawn", August 9, 2010: 28–31.

523. "Lizzie", October 2010: 1.

524. "Lizzie", October 2010: 2–3.

525. "Lizzie", October 2010: 4–6.

526. "Lizzie", October 2010: 6–8.

527. "Lizzie", October 2010: 9–11.

528. "Lizzie", October 2010: 12–14.

529. A 1972 photo on page 11 of the *Rockland Courier-Gazette*, July 29, 1972, shows three Vinahaven fishermen sitting by their boat and repairing a sardine net – a daily event.

530. Captain R. Barry Fisher. *A Doryman's Day* (Gardiner ME: Tilbury House Publishers, 2001), 57. For a definition of "ganging", see the Penobscot Marine Museum, Fishing Gear and Boats, http://penobscotmarinemuseum.org/pbho-1/fisher ies/fishing-gear-and-boats (Retrieved, Oct. 6, 2015).

531. Nancy Payne Alexander, "'Taking up the Slack': Penobscot Bay Women and the Netting Industry," *Maine History* 45, 3 (December 2010): 259–280.

532. Barbara M. Morton, *Down East Netting* (Camden ME: Down East Books for Pea Soup Publishing, 1988), 3–4; Jacqueline Davidson, "The Net-Making Tradition

of Vinalhaven," *Piecework* July/August (1996): 41–42. Also see Winslow, *Fish Scales,* 115.

533. Morton, *Down East Netting,* 4–5.

534. "Where they Knit: How the Women of Vinalhaven Find Chance to Turn a Pretty Dollar" *Christian Science Monitor*, 1940s, undated and unpaged. VHHS archives.

535. Undated and unattributed article. "$3000 Weekly Seine Industry 'Aint Seaweed'", VHHS archives. According to VHHS genealogy, Herbert Edward Morton, called John (1902-1988), married Etta Lunt (1902-1970) and their son John Edward Morton (1929-2003), married Barbara Murphy (1921-2000). John Edward and Barbara Morton ran the Mill Race, while Herbert "John" and Etta Morton made the nets.

536. Sadie and Phil Dyer, August 12, 2012: 36.

537. "Louie Lived here?" *The Wind* 21–27 January 2016: 4. The article also names island women Effie Dickey, Florence Estes, Lottie Polk and Bertha Baggs.

538. Morton, *Down East Netting.* So much net-making skill remained on Vinalhaven that in the 1980s, Barbara M. Morton, a woman who'd married onto the island, wrote a book about the details of the craft.

539. Radley, *Remember When*, 19.

540. Lorraine Walker, October 20, 2008: 1.

541. Lorraine Walker, August 2017: 4.

542. "Lou" August 19, 2010. p. 41.

543. Bodine Ames, October 18, 2008. 4–5.

CHAPTER 12

544. Winslow Diaries, August 4, 1933. VHHS archives.

545. Ivan Olson, 2011: 19.

546. Ivan Olson, 2011: 19–20.

547. John Beckman, 2008: 12. For description of the fish, see Bigelow and Schroeder *Fishes of the Gulf of Maine,* 135–137. On June 4, 2020, William Leavenworth added the following information: "When [C.G.] Atkins was surveying the anadromous fisheries he found Maine Central Railroad records showing that Thomaston had shipped out over 40 tons of smelt in one winter. According to the *Maine Mining and Industrial Journal* (1 January 1892: 8). 'Millions of smelts are caught every year along the Kennebec and Penobscot and their tributaries, and as they are the finest, largest and plumpest of their species they always lead the market. Frost fish are also caught with hook and line, but a majority of them are netted and not holding a high rank among food fish, are generally sold by the barrel or bushel to parties who ship them to New York, or to farmers who feed them to their hens. Along the rivers there are many colonies of people who every winter catch and ship many tons of these fish, which thus furnish both pleasure and profit in the dull season.'"

548. Jennie Webster, 2008: 11–12.

549. Bodine Ames, 2009: 8–10.

550. "Hank", 2015: 8.

551. Elin Elisofon, 2010: 1–2,13.
552. Walter Day, August 18, 2014: 4–5; Lee Osgood, 2015: 42.
553. Walter Day, August 18, 2014: 2, 3.
554. Walter Day, August 18, 2014: 2, 3.
555. Philip Conkling, 2012: 1.
556. Phil Crossman, 2013: 2.
557. Emily Lane, 2012: 2.
558. Phil Crossman, 2013: 5.
559. Emily Lane, Interviewee #26, August 2012: 5.
560. Elin Elisofon, 2010: 6.
561. Phil Crossman, 2013: 4.
562. Lorraine Walker, 2008: 15, 22–23; Also, Lorraine Walker, 2017: 1–2.
563. Radley, *Remember When,* 138.
564. Sonny Warren, 2009: 23–24.
565. Walter Day, 2010: 32.
566. "Dawn", 2010: 2–3.
567. Walter Day, 2010: 40–41.
568. Jennie Webster, 2008: 5.
569. Lorraine Walker, 2017: 4.
570. Lawrence "Cy" Davidson, 2009: 26.
571. Lyons and Vinal, *Brief Historical Sketch,* 11; Radley and Bunker, *Horse Nets, Holliwoggers,* 41–43.
572. Lorraine Walker, August 2017: 23–24.
573. "Lizzie", October 2010: 22–23.
574. Sonny Warren, 2009: 23.
575. Lorraine Walker August 2017: 2, 5.
576. Lorraine Walker, August 2017: 6.
577. "Cathy", August 18, 2009: 46.
578. "Dawn", August 9, 2010: 15–16.
579. Philip Conkling, "Hurricane Island Outward Bound School", *Maine, the Magazine,* April 2014. http://themainemag.com/travel/2465-hurricane-island-outward-bound-school/ (Retrieved, January 24, 2017).
580. "Dawn", August 9, 2010:15–16.
581. Jeannette Lasansky, "Swedes, Norwegians, and Finns Work and Settle on Vinalhaven, 1850-1940." *Vinalhaven Historical Society Annual Newsletter,* 2018: 1–2; "Dawn", Interviewee #21, 2010: 8, 9.
582. "Hal", August 18, 2009: 46.
583. Sonny Warren, August 22, 2009: 21.
584. Phil Crossman, August 2013: 2.
585. Sonny Warren, August 22, 2009: 23.
586. "Dawn", August 9, 2010: 9.
587. Lawrence "Cy" Davidson, August 2009: 4.
588. Kris Osgood, personal communication.
589. George "Burt" Dyer interviews by Doug Hall, 2002 and 2006. VHHS archives.

590. "Ben", August 2012: 1-3.
591. Jennie Webster, 2008, 5.

Afterword

592. Calderwood, *Days of Uncle Dave's fish house,* 94.
593. John Calvin, *The Institutes of the Christian Religion*, Book 1, Chapter 16, translated by Henry Beveridge (Woodstock, Ontario: Devoted Publishing, 1916), 91; quoted in Alan Lightman, *Searching for Stars on a Maine Island* (New York: Vintage Books, 2018), 81.
594. Wendell Berry, "Nature as Measure," in *Bringing it to the Table: On farming and food* (Berkeley CA: Counterpoint Books, [1989]2009), Kindle location, 250.

References

Acheson, James M. *The lobster gangs of Maine*. Hanover and London: University Press of New England, 1988.

Ackerman, Diane. *The Human Age: The world shaped by us*. NY and London: W. W. Norton. 2014.

Ackerman, Edward A. *New England's Fishing Industry*. Chicago, Illinois: The University of Chicago Press, 1941.

Alden, Robin. "Building a Sustainable Seafood System for Maine." *Maine Policy Review*. July 2011. https://coastalfisheries.org/wp-content/uploads/2017/03/Maine -PolicyReview-Food-Issue-Building-a-Sustainable-Seafood-System-for-Maine .pdf (Retrieved May 16, 2019).

Alexander, Nancy Payne. "'Taking up the Slack': Penobscot Bay Women and the Netting Industry," *Maine History*. Published by the Maine Historical Society. Vol. 45. N.3. Dec. 2010. pp. 259–280.

American Friends Service Committee. The Wabanakis of Maine and the Maritimes: A resource book about Penobscot, Passamaquoddy, Maliseet, Micmac and Abenaki Indians with lesson plans for grades 4 through 8. Prepared for and published by the Maine Indian Program of the New England Regional Office of the American Friends Service Committee. 1989.

Ames, Richard M. *Risky Business: A Maine village goes global. Castine souls and ships during the golden age of sail*. Thomaston, Maine: Custom Museum Publishing. 2019.

Ames, Ted. " Multispecies Coastal Shelf Recovery Plan "Marine and Coastal Fisheries: Dynamics, Management, and Ecosystem Science 2:217–231, 2010.

Annual and biannual Reports of the Municipal Officers of the town of Vinalhaven. 1906–1925.

Anthony, Athene R. *Vinalhaven Reminiscences. Vinalhaven, Maine:* Printed by The "Wind" of the Union Church, 1978.

Apollonio, Spencer and Jacob J. Dykstra. *"An Enormous, immensely complicated Intervention": Groundfish, The New England Fishery Management Council, and the world fisheries crisis.* Montgomery Alabama: Ebook time. LLC, 2008.

Applebee, Robert B. *Sailing Vessels of Vinalhaven Maine*, Typed manuscript from Castine WPA records from the Robert Appleby Collection at the Penobscot Marine Museum, Searsport, Maine. 1954.

Arnold, Jeanne E., Anthony P. Graesch, Enzo Ragazzini, and Elinor Oches. *Life at home in the Twenty-first Century: 32 families open their doors.* UCLA: The Cotsen Institute of Archaeology Press. 2012.

Bailyn, Bernard. *The New England Merchants in the Seventeenth Century.* Harper

Baker, Emerson W., Edwin A. Churchill, Richard S. D'Abate, Kristine L. Jones, Victor A.Konrad, and Haral E. L. Prins, editors. *American Beginnings: Exploration, Culture, and Cartography in the Land of Norumbega.*Lincoln and London: University of Nebraska Press. 1994.

Beacom, Seward E. *Pulpit Harbor Two Hundred Years: A history of Pulpit Harbor North Haven, Maine 1784–1984.* North Haven Historical Society. 1985.

Bunin, Sherry. *Becoming Hallie.* Rockland, ME: Maine Authors Publishing. 2013.

Beck, Horace P. *The American Indian as a Sea-fighter in Colonial Times.* Mystic, Connecticut: The Marine Historical Association, Inc. No. 35. May 1959.

Berger, John. *Pig Earth.* Vintage International. 1979/1992.

Berry, Wendell. *Bringing it to the Table: on farming and food.* Counterpoint. 2009.

Bishop, W.H. *Fish and Men in the Maine Islands.* Reprinted from Harper's New Monthly Magazine. Camden, Maine: L. Berliawsky. Books, 1880.

Bigelow, Henry B. and William C. Schroeder. *Fishes of the Gulf of Maine.* Fishery Bulletin 74. Fishery Bulletin of the Fish and Wildlife Service. Volume 53. First Revision. United States Government Printing Office. Washington. 1953.

Bolster, W. Jeffrey. *The Mortal Sea: Fishing the Atlantic in the age of sail.* Belknap: Harvard. 2012.

Bourque, Bruce J. "Evidence for Prehistoric Exchange on the Maritime Peninsula," in *Prehistoric Exchange Systems in North America.* Timothy G Baugh and Jonathon E. Ericson, editors. New York and London: Plenum Press. 1994. pp. 23–46.

Bourque, Bruce. *The Swordfish Hunters: the history and Ecology of the Ancient American Sea People.* Bunker Hill Publishing. 2012.

Bourque, Bruce J. *Twelve Thousand Years: American Indians in Maine.* Lincoln and London: University of Nebraska Press. 2001/2004.

Brown, Lester R. *World on the Edge: how to Prevent Environmental and Economic Collapse.* New York and London: WW Norton and Co. 2011.

Bulletin of the United States Fish Commission. 1881–1998. https://library.noaa.gov/ Collections/Digital-Documents/Bull-of-US-Fish-Comm. (Retrieved May 16, 2019)

Bunker, Nick. *Making Haste from Babylon: The Mayflower pilgrims and their world; a new history.* New York: Alfred A. Knopf, 2010.

Byer, Douglas S. and The Nevin Shellheap Burials and Observations. R.S. Peabody Foundation for Archaeology. V.9. Trustees of Phillips Academy. 1979. https:// archive.org/stream/nevinshellheapbu09doug#page/32/mode/2up

Calderwood, Ivan E. *Days of Uncle Dave's fish house*. Rockland Maine: Courier Gazette.1969.

Caldwell, Bill. *Islands of Maine*. Portland Me: Guy Gannett Publishing Co. 1981.

Callahan, P.D. *Door in Dark Water*. Nightwood Press. 2014.

Carter, Robert. *Coast of New England*. Somersworth: New Hampshire Publishing Company. 1969.

Chase, Mary Ellen. *The fishing fleets of New England*. Cambridge, MA: The Riverside Press. Boston: Houghton Mifflin. 1961.

Clark, Edie. "Ted Ames and the recovery of Maine Fisheries" *Yankee Magazine*. November 2006. http://www.yankeemagazine.com/issues/2006-11/features/fishermen/1.

Clifford, Harold B. *Charlie York: Maine Coast Fisherman*. International Marine Publishing Company. 1974.

Commerce, NOAA, National Marine Fisheries Service. *Harvesters of the Sea: the story of Maine's Commercial Fisheries*. Undated.

Commercial Fisheries: State of the Gulf of Maine Report. Gulf of Maine Council on the Marine Environment. 2013. http://www.gulfofmaine.org/2/wpcontent/uploads/2014/03/commercial-fisheries-theme-paper-webversion.pdf Retrieved October 24, 2016.

Connecticut: The Marine Historical Association, Inc. No. 35. May 1959.

Conkling, Philip W. *Islands in Time: A natural and cultural history of the islands of the Gulf of Maine*. Island Institute/Down East Books. (1999)

Conkling, Philip W. and David D. Platt, editors ; Peter Ralston, Island journal art director ;Paige Garland Parker, design. *Holding ground : the best of Island journal, 1984–2004*. Rockland, ME : Island Institute, 2004.

Conkling, Philip W. "On Islanders and Islandness," Geographical Review. vol. 97 no. 2. April 2007. pp. 191–201.

Cramer, Deborah. *Great Waters: An Atlantic Passage*. New York: WW Norton and Co, 2001.

Cramer, Deborah. *The Narrow Edge*. New Haven: Yale University Press. 2015.

Croker, Michael. *Sharing the Ocean: Stories of Science, Politics and Ownership from America's oldest industry*. Gardiner, Maine: Tilbury House, Publishers. N Windham, Maine: Northwest Atlantic Marine Alliance, 2008.

Crossman, Phil. *Away Happens*. University of New England Press, 2005.

Crossman, Phil. *Observations: A Maine Island, a century of newsletters and the stories found between the lines*. Talking Crow: Vinalhaven. 2015.

Cummings, Abbott Lowell, editor. *Rural Household Inventories: Establishing the Names, Uses and Furnishings of Rooms in the Colonial New England Home 1675-1775*. The Society for the Preservation of New England Antiquities. Boston, Massachusetts. 1964.

Davis, Wade. *The Wayfinders: Why ancient wisdom matters in the modern world*. Anansi. 2009.

Davison, Peter. "Off the Maine Coast." *The Atlantic Monthly*; May 1997; 279,5; ProQuest Business Collection. pg. 48.

Diamond, Jared. *The World Until Yesterday*. Penguin Books. 2012.

Documentary History of the State of Maine. Vol. 3. *The Trelawny Papers.* James Phinney Baxter, Ed. Published by the Maine Historical Society. Portland: Hoyt, Fogg and Dunham., 1884. https://books.google.com (Retrieved May 16, 2019).

Doeringer, Peter B., Philip I. Moss, and David G. Terkla. *The New England Fishing Economy.* Amherst, The University of Massachusetts Press, 1986.

Dryer, Susan Radley, editor. *Remember When.* Vol.2. Published by Vinalhaven Historical Society. 2019.

Dwelley, Hugh L. *Pioneer Settlers of Cranberry Islands: the Gilleys of Baker Island and Islesford, Maine.* Occasional Paper # 10. Ilseford Historical Society. 1998.

Dyer, Susan Radley, editor. *Remember When: a collection of oral histories.* Published by Vinalhaven Historical Society. 2010.

Eliot, Charles W. *John Gilley of Baker's Island.* Bedford, MA: Applewood Books. Edition undated. Original edition 1904. (Century Magazine 1899).

Farrow, Capt. John Pendleton. *The Romantic Story of David Robertson.* Belfast Maine: Press of Belfast Age Publishing Company, 1898.

Fisher, Capt. R. Barry. *A Doryman's Day.* Gardiner Maine: Tilbury House Publishers. 2001.

The Fisherman's Voice (2008–2019)

Ford, Daniel *Carter's Coast of New England: a new edition of "A Summer Cruise on the Coast of New England by Robert Carter.* Somersworth: New Hampshire Publishing Company. 1969.

Gilbert, Elizabeth. *Stern Men.* Boston and New York: Houghton Mifflin, 2000.

Gillis, John R. *Islands of the Mind.* How the Human Imagination Created the Atlantic World. Palgrave MacMillan. Uncorrected proofs. 2004.

Gillis, John R. *The Human Shore.* Chicago: The University of Chicago Press, 2012.

Goode, George Brown. *The fisheries and fishery industries of the United States.* Washington, Govt. Print. Off.,1884–1887 Vol. 1–7.

Goode, George Brown, Joseph Williams Collins, Robert Edward Earll, and Alonzo Howard Clark. *Materials for a History of the Mackerel Fishery.* United States Bureau of Fisheries. Washington. Government Printing office.1883.

Graff, Nancy Price. *The Call of the Running Tide: A portrait of an Island Family.* New York: Little Brown, 1992.

Greenberg, Paul. *Four Fish.* Penguin, 2010.

Greenberg, Paul and et. al. "The fish on my plate." http://www.pbs.org/wgbh/front line/film/the-fish-on-my-plate/Viewed April 30, 2017.

Greenblatt, Stephen. *Marvelous Possessions: The Wonder of the New World.* University of Chicago Press. 1991.

Greenlaw, Linda. *The Hungry Ocean: A Swordfish Captain's Journey.* New York: Hyperion, 1999.

Hamlin, Cyrus and John R. Ordway. *The Commercial Fisheries of Maine.* Maine Sea Grant Bulletin 5. NOAA Ocean Research Corporation, Kennebunk Maine 04043. Undated.

Harari, Yuval Noah. *Sapiens: a brief history of humankind.* Harper Imprint. Harper Collins. 2015.

Hefner, Nora. *GIS analysis of historical cod fisheries in the Gulf of Maine.* Marine Lab Student Papers and Projects. Bowdoin College. Bowdoin Digital Commons. 8-2014.

Hood, Margaret Page. *The Murders on Fox Island* (Original Title: *In the Dark Night*). 1957. Dell 1960.

Hornsby, Stephen J. and Richard W. Judd, editors. *Historical Atlas of Maine.* Orono, Maine: The University of Maine Press. 2015.

The Island Journal 1984–2019.

Jackson, Jeremy B.C., Karen E. Alexander, and Enric Sala, editors. *Shifting Baselines: The past and the future of ocean fisheries.* Island Press. 2011.

Jansson, Tove. *The Summer Book.* NYRB reprint on Kindle. Pub. 1972.

Jewett, Sarah Orne. *The Country of the Pointed Firs and other stories.* With an introduction by Anita Shreve and a new afterword by Peter Balaam. Signet Classics. Penguin Books. Kindle edition. 1896/2009.

Johnson, Teresa J., K. Athearn, S. Randall, M. Garland, K. Ross, K. Cline, C. Peterson, R.Alden, and C. Guenther. 2015. *Profiles of sixteen eastern Maine Fishing communities.* Maine Agricultural and Forest Experiment Station Miscellaneous Report 446. (Vinalhaven pp. 13–20.) https://coastalfisheries.org/wp content/uploads/2017/03/Johnson-et-al-2015-Profiles.pdf (Retrieved May 16, 2019).

Kellogg, Elijah. *The Fisher Boys of Pleasant Cove.* Originally published Boston: Lee and Shepard and Dillingham. 1874. Republished on demand. www.Forgotten Books.Com (2017).

Kurlansky, Mark. *Cod: A biography of the fish that changed the world.* New York: Penguin, 1997.

Kurlansky, Mark. *Salt: a world history.* Penguin. 2002/2003.

Kurlansky, Mark. *The last fish tale.* Ballantine Books, 2008.

Langley, Samuel Pierpoint. *Memoir of George Brown Goode 1851–1896.* Read before the National Academy, April 2, 1897. Vinalhaven, ME: Vinalhaven Historical Society, 2006.

Lasansky, Jeannette. *Island Saltwater Farms: Farming on Vinalhaven 1820–1860.*

Le Huenen, Joseph. "The Role of the Basque, Breton and Norman Fishermen in the discovery of North America," *Arctic.* vol. 37, no. 4 (December 1984) pp. 520–527. http://pubs.aina.ucalgary.ca/arctic/Arctic37-4-520.pdf Accessed May 11, 2015.

Libby, Glen and Antonia Small. *Caught: time .place fish.* Wrack Line Books. 2016.

Lightman, Alan. *Searching for Stars on an Island in Maine.* Vintage Books. 2018/2019.

Lyons, O. P. and Albra Josephine Vinal. *A Brief Historical Sketch of the Town of Vinalhaven, from its earliest known settlement. Prepared by order of the Town on the Occasion of its One Hundredth Anniversary.* Rockland ME: Press of the Star Job Print. 1900. (Reprinted by Vinalhaven Historical Society 1981, 1986).

MacLeod, Alistair. *Island: The Complete Stories.* Vintage Paperback, 2000.

Macfarlane, Robert. *The Old Ways.* Penguin.2012.

Magra, Christopher Paul. *The New England Cod Fishing Industry And Maritime Dimensions Of The American Revolution.* PHD Thesis University of Pittsburth.

2006. http://d-scholarship.pitt.edu/7982/1/Magra_ETD_1_.pdf Retrieved October 30, 2018.

Maine Bureau of Industrial and Labor Statistics. *Annual report of the Bureau of Industrial and Labor Statistics.* Augusta.1887–1918. (ARBILS).

Maine Memory Network: Maine's Statewide Digital Museum. Maine History Online. https://www.mainememory.net/mho/ (Retrieved May 16, 2019).

Mann, Charles C. *1491: New Revelations of the Americas before Columbus*. Vintage, 2006.

Martin, Cynthia Burns. "The Bodwell Granite company Store and the Community of Vinalhaven, Maine, 1859–1919." *Maine History* 46:2 June 2012. pp. 149–168.

Martin, Cynthia Burns. *Vinalhaven Island's Maritime Industries*. Arcadia Publishing. 2015

Martin, John Frederick. *Profits in the Wilderness: entrepreneurship and the founding of New England towns in the Seventeenth century*. Chapel Hill and London: Published by the Institute of Early American History and Culture, Williamsburg, Virginia, by the University of North Carolina Press. 1991.

Martin, Kenneth B. and Nathan R. Lipfert. *Lobstering and the Maine Coast*. Bath Maine: Maine Maritime Museum. 1985.

Molyneaux, Paul. *The Doryman's Reflection*. New York: Avalon. 2005.

Molyneaux, Paul. *Swimming in Circles: aquaculture and the end of wild oceans*. New York: Thunder's Mouth Press. 2007.

Moorehead, Warren K. *The Archaeology of Maine: Being a narrative of explorations in that state 1912-1920 together with work at Lake Champlain 1917*. Andover, MA: The Andover Press. 1922. http://books.google.com/books Accessed. Nov. 21, 2014.

Moorehead, Warren K. "The Red-Paint People of Maine." *American Anthropologist*. Jan.–March. 1913. pp. 33–47. http://library.umaine.edu/wabanaki/the_red -paint_people.pdf.

Nichols, Jim. *Hull Creek*. DownEast, 2011.

O'Leary, Wayne M. *Maine Sea Fisheries: the rise and fall of a native industry, 1830–1890*. Boston, MA: Northeastern University Press, 1996.

Paine, Lincoln P. *Down East: A maritime history of Maine*. Tilbury House. Gardner Maine. Op-sail Maine. 2000.

Patterson, Thomas C. *Toward a Social History of Archaeology in the United States*. Case Studies in Archaeology. Jeffrey Quilter series editor. Harcourt, Brace & Co. 1995.

Pauly, D., V. Christensen, J. Dalsgaard, R. Froese, and F. Torres Jr. (1998) *Fishing down marine food webs Science* 279: 860-863.

Pauly, Daniel and Jay Maclean. *In a Perfect Ocean: the state of fisheries and ecosystems in the North Atlantic Ocean*. Washington, Covelo, London: Island Press. 2003.

Philbrick, Nathaniel. *Mayflower*. New York: Viking, 2006.

Pierce, Olive. *Up river: the story of a Maine fishing community*. Hanover & London: University Press of New England, 1996.

Putz, George. *The Maine Coast*. Chartwell Books, Inc. 1985.

Radley, Sue and Elizabeth Bunker. *Horse Nets, Holliwoggers, & Littlefield Blue and everything you need to know about Vinalhaven*. The Vinalhaven Historical Society. R.C. Brayshaw & Co. Lebanon, New Hampshire. 2015.

Rathbun, Richard. "Notes on the Decrease of Lobsters." *Bulletin of the United States Fish Commission*. V. 4. 1884. pp. 421–426. https://books.google.com/books

Reeves, Randall R., Tim D. Smith, Robert L. Webb, Jooke Robbins, and Phillip J. Clapham. "Humpback and Fin Whaling in the Gulf of Maine from 1800 to 1918." *Marine Fisheries Review*. 64(1) 2002. 12 pages. https://spo.nmfs.noaa.gov/content/humpback-and-fin-whaling-gulf-maine-1800-1918 Retrieved September 16, 2019.

Reiss, Kenneth. *The Bodwell & Webster Papers: Big Business on a Small Island: The Birth of the Granite Boom*. Vinalhaven: The Vinalhaven Historical Society. 2013.

Reiss, Kenneth. *From the Beginning: Vinalhaven from 1760–1850*. VHHS. 2017.

Reports of the Commissioners of fisheries of the State of Maine 1867–1884, 1886, 1888.

Report of the Commissioners of Fisheries and Game of the State of Maine. "Report of the Commissioner of Sea and Shore Fisheries of the State of Maine." 1989–1990, 1893–1894.

Report of the Commissioners of Inland Fisheries and Game for the State of Maine. 1895, 1896.

Report of the Commissioner of Sea and shore Fisheries of the State of Maine, 1898, 1900, 1902, 1903–1904, 1905–1906, 1907–1908, 1909–1910, 1911–1912, 1913–1914, 1920 (called "Second Biennial"), 1924, 1926, 1932, 1934, 1944, 1947.

The Rockland Courier-Gazette (This newspaper had several names. It began as the Lime Rock Gazette. From 1846 to 1882 it is known as the Rockland Gazette. Then Courier-Gazette from 1882 to 1920.) (Per the Maine State library website.)

Reed, Roger G. *Summering on the Thoroughfare: The architecture of North Haven, 1885–1945*. Maine Citizens for HIstoric Preservation. 1993.

Sabine, Lorenzo. Report on the Principal fisheries of the American Seas: Prepared for the Treasury Department of the United States by Lorenzo Sabine of Massachusetts; and submitted by the honorable Thomas Corwin, Secretary of the Treasury, as part of the annual report on finances, at the second session of the thirty-second congress. Washington: Robert Armstrong, Printer. 1853.

Schmitt, Catherine. "Adrift in a Sea of information about sustainable seafood: the consumer perspective." *Maine Policy Review*, July 2011. http://mcspolicycenter.umaine.edu

Scontras, Charles A. *Maine Lobstermen and the Labor Movement: The Lobster Fishermen's International Protective Association*, 1907. *Labor's Heritage*. vol. 2. quarterly of the George Meany Memorial Archives. no. 1. January 1990. pp. 50– 63.

Simpson, Dorothy. "Penobscot Bay" in *The Maine Islands in story and legend*. Blackberry. 1987.

Simpson, Dorothy. *The Island's True Child: a memoir of growing up on Criehaven*. Down East Books, 2003.

Spies, Arthur E. and Robert A. Lewis. *The Turner Farm Fauna: 5000 Years of Hunting and Fishing in Penobscot Bay, Maine*. Occasional publications in Maine Archaeology. Number Eleven. The Maine State Museum, The Maine Historical

Preservation Commission and the Maine Archaeological Society. Augusta, Maine. 2001.

Springuel, Natalie, Bill Leavenworth, and Alexander, Karen, "From Wealth to Poverty: The Rise and Fall of Cod around Mount Desert Island" (2015). *Maine Sea Grant Publications*. 29. https://digitalcommons.library.umaine.edu/seagrant_pub/29

Starr, Markham. *End of the Line: Closing the last sardine cannery in America*. Wesleyan University Press. 2013.

State of Maine Biennial Reports Department of Sea and Shore Fisheries. 1946–1948, 1948–1950, 1950–1952, 1952–1954, 1954–1956, 1962–1964, 1964–1966.

State of Maine Department of Marine Resources. Commercial Fishery. https://www.maine.gov/dmr/commercial-fishing/index.html (Retrieved May 16, 2019)

The Tariff of Rates for the Knox County Maine Board of Underwriters. Boston: Frank Wood. 1906?

Thompson, E. P. "Time, work-discipline, and Industrial capitalism," *Past and Present*. no. 38. December 1967. pp 56–97. 2005.

Thorndike, Virginia L. *Islanders: Real Life on the Maine Islands*. Down East Books.

Ulrich, Laurel Thatcher. *A Midwife's Tale. The life of Martha Ballard, based on her diary, 1785–1812*. Vintage Books. 1990.

United States Commission of Fish and Fisheries. Part I. Report on the Condition of the Sea Fisheries of the South Coast of New England in1871 and 1872 by Spencer F. Baird, Commissioner. Washington: Government Printing Office, 1873.

United States Commission of Fish and Fisheries, The Fisheries and Fishery Industries of the United States, ed. George Brown Goode. 7 vol. Washington: Government Printing Office, 1884–1887.

Upton, Joe. *Amaretto*. Camden, Maine: International Marine Publishing Company, 1986.

Vickers, Daniel. *Farmers & Fishermen.: Two centuries of work in Essex County, Massachusetts, 1630-1850*. Chapel Hill: University of North Carolina Press. 1994.

Video: *Saving New England Fisheries*. http://video.nhptv.org/video/2365760136/ Accessed June 3, 2016.

Video: Peg Dice. *Fence in the Water*. 1980. Viewed August 2017. Penobscot Marine Museum. Searsport Maine.

The Vinalhaven Echo 1887–for 14 months - VHHS

Vinalhaven Historical Society (VHHS)

The Vinalhaven Messenger 1885–25 issues printed - VHHS

The Vinalhaven Neighbor–Sidney Winslow 1938–1939-VHHS

Vinal, Harold. (1936) *Hurricane: a Maine Coast Chronicle*. Brattleboro: Stephen Daye Press.

Walls, Laura Dassow. *Henry David Thoreau: A Life*. The University of Chicago Press. 2017.

Warner, William W. *Beautiful Swimmers*. Atlantic, Little Brown. 1976.

Warner, William W. *Distant Water: The Fate of the North Atlantic Fisherman*. New York: Penguin, 1977–1983.

Warner, William W. *Into the Porcupine Cave and other Odysseys*. Washington D.C.: National Geographic, 1999.

Warren, Rusty. *Days in the Life of A Fisherman's Wife*. Published by the Information Department of the Island Institute, 2000.

Wasson, George S. Sailing Days on the Penobscot. New York. W.W. Norton. 1932 also 1949. (used both.)

Webster, L. J. and M. A. Noah. *Letters Home from Sea. The Life and Letters of Solon J. Hanson, Down East Sailor*. Brookline, New Hampshire: Hobblebush Books. 2006.

Weisman, Alan. *The World without us*. Picador, 2007.

Wilkinson, Alex. "Profiles: The Lobsterman: how Ted Ames turned Oral History into Science" *The New Yorker Magazine*. July 31, 2006. http://www.newyorker.com/archive/2006/07/31/060731fa_fact_wilkinson

Wilson, Deborah B. Indiantown Island Archaeological Report. Boothbay Region Land Trust, Inc. 1998. Chapters 2 and 3. http://www.mpbn.net/homestom/clues.html.

The Wind – 1884–1888? 1974–Present. - VHHS

Winslow, Sidney L. Diaries – VHHS.

Winslow, Sidney L. *Fish Scales and Stone Chips*. Reprinted for Vinalhaven Historical Society. 1989. (Portland Maine: Machigonne Press, 1952).

Winslow, Sidney L. Diaries. 1921–1954. Unpublished. Vinalhaven Historical Society. CD Rom.

Wood, William. *New England's Prospect*. Edited with an introduction by Alden T. Vaughan. Amherst: University of Massachusetts Press. 1977. First paperback edition 1993.

Woodard, Colin. *The Lobster Coast*. Penguin Books. 2004.

The Working Waterfront (2008–2019) Commercial Fisheries News. http://fish-news.com/cfn/#sthash.uwmKzLYV.07KY59Rc.dpbs.

Wright, Louis B. editor. *The Elizabethans' America: A collection of Early Reports by Englishmen in the New World*. Harvard University Press. 1966

Index

Note: The photo insert images are indexed as p1, p2, p3, etc